CliffsNotes

AP

European History

CRAM PLAN™

CliffsNotes®

AP®

European History

CRAM PLAN™

Malcolm Mafi, M.A.

Contributor: *Joy Mondragon-Gilmore, Ph.D.*

Houghton Mifflin Harcourt
Boston • New York

About the Author

Malcolm Mafi has a master's degree in Modern European History and is a history professor and consultant who teaches European history at multiple colleges in the San Francisco Bay Area. He has written curriculum for the AP history exams, the SAT, and the ACT, and has published numerous journal articles in historical research and historiographical reviews.

Editorial

Executive Editor: Greg Tubach
Senior Editor: Christina Stambaugh
Copy Editor: Lynn Northrup
Technical Editor: Kyle Knoll
Proofreader: Susan Moritz

Acknowledgments

I would like to thank Mark David for his love and encouragement during the writing of this book and my parents Eugene and Gabriela, my sister Angelina, and my brother Gabriel for their love and support. I am grateful to my colleagues at ThinkTank Learning, especially Polly Pan and Daisy Deng, as well as the excellent faculty at San Francisco State University, especially Professors Sarah Curtis, Anthony D'Agostino, and Jessica Elkind. I thank Joy Gilmore for her excellent contributions and Christina Stambaugh for her sage edits.

CliffsNotes® AP® European History Cram Plan™

Library of Congress Control Number: 2017945057
ISBN: 978-0-544-92612-7 (pbk)

Printed in the United States of America
DOC 10 9 8 7 6 5 4 3 2 1

For information about permission to reproduce selections from this book, write to trade.permissions@hmhco.com or to Permissions, Houghton Mifflin Harcourt Publishing Company, 3 Park Avenue, 19th Floor, New York, New York 10016.

www.hmhco.com

Table of Contents

5. Historical Period Two: Enlightenment and Expansion (c. 1648 to c. 1815) 107

Preface

Congratulations! You've made the decision to take charge of the AP European History course. Whether you are looking for a quick reference guide, an in-depth reference, or an occasional refresher of one or more topics of European history, it is contained in this book. This guide is a supplement to your textbook and your teacher's lectures. Too often, students find themselves lost in the massive accumulation of historical facts and wish they had a copy of the teacher's lecture notes. The review chapters are very much like lecture notes. Each chapter contains the essential information necessary for understanding AP EURO.

CliffsNotes AP European History Cram Plan is an easy-to-follow cram plan study guide that provides the maximum benefit in a reasonable amount of time. Although this study guide is not meant to substitute for a formal high school AP history class, it provides you with important learning tools to refresh your understanding of the general and specific topics outlined in the AP course curriculum and key concept framework. The skills and concepts defined in this study guide will not only help you pass the AP EURO exam, but will provide you with exam-oriented approaches and practice material to help you evaluate your strengths and areas of improvement. If you follow the lessons and strategies in this book, and study regularly, you will deepen your understanding of European history, which will strengthen your performance on the exam.

Navigating This Book

CliffsNotes AP European History Cram Plan is organized as follows:

- **Introduction to the AP EURO Exam** — A general description of the AP EURO exam, exam format, chronological periods, content, themes, AP history reasoning skills, question types, scoring, frequently asked questions, and general strategies.
- **Chapter 1: Two-Month Cram Plan** — A study calendar that provides a detailed suggested plan of action to prepare for the AP EURO two months before your exam.
- **Chapter 2: One-Month Cram Plan** — A study calendar that provides a detailed suggested plan of action to prepare for the AP EURO one month before your exam.
- **Chapter 3: Diagnostic Test** — A shortened version of the AP EURO practice exam. The Diagnostic Test introduces you to the AP EURO question types, evaluates your areas of strength and weakness to help you focus your study, and provides you with a baseline starting point.
- **Chapter 4: Historical Period One: The Renaissance and Reformation (c. 1450 to c. 1648)**
- **Chapter 5: Historical Period Two: Enlightenment and Expansion (c. 1648 to c. 1815)**
- **Chapter 6: Historical Period Three: The Age of Nationalism (c. 1815 to c. 1914)**
- **Chapter 7: Historical Period Four: Global Wars to Globalization (1914 to present)**
- **Chapter 8: Full-Length Practice Exam** — Includes answers and in-depth explanations for multiple-choice questions, and sample responses and scoring guidelines for the short-answer, document-based, and long-essay questions.

How to Use This Book

You're in charge here. You get to decide how to use this book. You can read it cover to cover, or just look for the information that you want and then put the book back on the shelf for later use. Most people find it useful to first start by learning *general* AP history reasoning skills, themes, and historical periods to develop a broad understanding of European history from c. 1450 to the present before memorizing *specific* facts, concepts, and evidence.

Here are some of the recommended ways to use this book.

- Create a customized study "action plan" with attainable goals. Be time-wise, because your study plan depends on the total amount of time until the exam date. Preview the cram plan calendars in chapters 1 and 2 to organize your study time.

- Read (and then reread) the Introduction to become familiar with the exam format, time periods, reasoning skills, themes, questions types, and test-taking strategies.

- Take the Diagnostic Test (Chapter 3) to assess your strengths and weaknesses.

- Get a glimpse of what you'll gain from a chapter by reading through the headings referenced at the beginning of each chapter.

- Follow the recommended sequence of time periods (chapters 4–7). Within each chapter, take detailed notes on the pages of this book to highlight important facts and concepts related to the AP EURO curriculum framework.

- Pay attention to the intermingled callout features in chapters 4–7 that focus on what you need to study to pass the AP EURO exam.
    - **Key Facts** — Lists the significant facts of a topic for a quick study reference.
    - **Did you know?** — Covers interesting information about people, places, and events to aid in your overall understanding of a point in history.
    - **Heads Up: What You Need to Know** — Summarizes details about specific content that may be on the actual AP EURO exam.
    - **Test Tip** — Offers quick strategies and tips for approaching exam questions.
    - **Historiography** — Offers different scholarly viewpoints so that you can "think like a historian" to reconstruct, debate, or critically think about topics that shape our history over time. For example, the causes and consequences, comparisons and contrasts, and similarities and differences of historical events.

- Use the "Chapter Review Practice Questions" to gauge your grasp of questions and strengthen your critical thinking skills. Although it is tempting to look ahead at the answer explanations, try to simulate testing conditions by answering the questions and writing your DBQ responses before reviewing the explanations. Initially, it may be difficult, but this strategy will reinforce your learning, particularly when writing DBQ responses.

- Test your knowledge more completely by taking the Full-Length Practice Exam in Chapter 8.

Finally, the lessons and strategies you are learning in this book will help you throughout your high school and college learning experiences. If you make the commitment to follow the lessons and practice regularly, you will not only statistically increase your odds for passing the AP EURO exam, but you will also learn skills that will help you manage future college coursework!

Introduction to the AP EURO Exam

Teachers and students alike will find *CliffsNotes AP European History Cram Plan* to be a valuable course supplement. This compact book is packed with information about what to expect on the exam, how to approach the questions, how to plan your study time, and how to study the four major time periods. To enhance your learning, a diagnostic test and a full-length practice exam provide practice questions with complete answer explanations.

The AP EURO exam tests your knowledge of the big ideas, themes, and significant events in European history. You will need to show your understanding of the political, social, economic, cultural, and religious trends of each time period from c. 1450 to the present day. You will not be asked to memorize every date, battle, and event in European history. Rather, you will be asked to know about the important changes, continuities, and comparisons and contrasts within each region and time period. This "big picture" approach makes the exam both manageable and thought-provoking. It focuses on your ability to think historically about a variety of concepts, developments, and events that transpired in a period known as Early Modern to Modern European history. For example, on the AP EURO exam you may be asked how the social climate in the Renaissance period was different from the social climate of the Enlightenment period. *CliffsNotes AP European History Cram Plan* takes the guesswork out of how to approach this type of question, among others. So take a deep breath, and know that you can do this.

Before we explore the content and topics, there are a few things about the exam structure that you should know: the exam format, scoring, question types, historical periods, themes, and history disciplinary practices and reasoning skills.

Exam Format

There are a total of 55 multiple-choice questions on the AP EURO exam, plus five free-response essay questions. The entire exam is 3 hours and 15 minutes. The chart below summarizes the format of the exam. Multiple-choice questions are combined with free-response questions for a combined scaled score of 1–5.

Note: Format and scoring are subject to change. Visit the College Board website for updates: http://apcentral.collegeboard.com.

Section	Question Type	Time	Number of Questions	Percent of Total Grade
Section I: Part A	Multiple-Choice Questions	55 minutes	55 questions	40% (Note: Multiple-choice questions are graded on a curve.)

Continued

Section	Question Type	Time	Number of Questions	Percent of Total Grade
Section I: Part B	Short-Answer Questions	40 minutes	3 questions (Note: Answer the first two questions and then choose one question from two choices.)	20%
Section II: Part A	Document-Based Question	60 minutes (includes a 15-minute reading period)	1 question	25%
Section II: Part B	Long-Essay Question	40 minutes (Note: DBQ and LEQ questions appear in the same section. Use the 15-minute mandatory reading period to read and plan BOTH essays.)	1 question (Note: You choose one question from three choices.)	15%
TOTALS:		**3 hours, 15 minutes**	**55 multiple choice** **5 essays**	**100%**

Scoring

Scores on your AP EURO exam will be based on the number of questions you answer correctly for two separate sections.

> Section I: Multiple-choice and short-answer questions are 60% of your overall score.
>
> Section II: Document-based and long-essay questions are 40% of your overall score.

Based on the combination of the two sections, the scores are converted into a grading scale of 1 to 5. A score of 5 is the best possible score. Most colleges consider a score of 3 or better a passing score. If you receive a passing score, the AP EURO exam can be applied as a college course equivalent—two semester units will apply toward your college bachelor's degree as a European history course.

As a reference, in 2017, almost 60% of students who took the AP EURO exam scored a 3 or higher.

AP Score	Score Translation
5	Extremely well qualified
4	Well qualified
3	Qualified
2	Possibly qualified
1	No recommendation

The AP EURO exam is graded on a curve, particularly the multiple-choice questions. Oftentimes, students panic when they get back their first practice exam. "A 65% on the multiple choice? I'm failing!" In reality, a 65% on the multiple-choice questions can be good enough for a 4 or even a 5 on the entire exam, depending on your score on the other sections. Note: For multiple-choice questions, no points are deducted for incorrect answers. If you don't know the answer, take an educated guess because there is no penalty for guessing.

Question Types

The AP EURO question types are multiple-choice, short-answer, document-based, and long-essay. Questions measure your knowledge of the main concepts within the content of the four chronological periods, your ability to analyze primary and secondary documents, your ability to understand the broader historical context, and your ability to apply AP history reasoning skills to one or more of the themes. As you approach each of the four question types, consider the following points to receive your best possible score.

- What are the main points within the context of a particular chronological period?
- What is the broader historical context (what happened before, during, and after)?
- What supporting evidence will strengthen your analysis?
- What are the AP history reasoning skills?
- What are the relevant significant themes?

Multiple-Choice Questions

Multiple-choice questions include a relevant primary or secondary source that college history students might use in their research. The questions assess your ability to draw reasonable conclusions from the source material and your ability to apply your knowledge of European history to select the corresponding answer choice. Each question draws from the key concept outlines and your knowledge of European history.

Key points about multiple-choice questions:

- Multiple-choice questions comprise 40% of your overall score.
- The exam contains 55 multiple-choice questions.
- The questions are grouped into sets. Each set contains one sourced-based prompt (text or graphic image) and two to five questions.
- Questions ask you to analyze, interpret, or find evidence from a primary or secondary source (historical text, quotation, graph, chart, map, cartoon, art, or image).
- Select one answer from among four choices in each question.
- No points are deducted for incorrect answers; therefore, there is no penalty for guessing.

Short-Answer Questions (SAQs)

The SAQs are similar to multiple-choice questions, but consist of short written responses. Questions are taken from a primary source, a secondary source, or no source. Short-answer questions give students a chance to demonstrate what they know by describing examples of historical evidence in a concise response that answers the question. If you answer all parts of the question and apply reasoning skills, the SAQs can be an opportunity for you to increase your overall score.

Key points about short-answer questions:

- Short-answer questions comprise 20% of your overall score.
- The exam contains four short-answer questions, but you are required to answer only three short-answer questions. You must answer Questions 1 and 2, and then you will choose either Question 3 or Question 4 for your third short-answer question.
- Question 1 is a secondary source (1600–2001); Question 2 is a primary source (1600–2001); Question 3 has no source (1450–1815); and Question 4 has no source (1815–present). Select the period you know more about—it's your choice!
- No thesis statement is required in your written response
- If the question contains a primary or secondary source, you must identify, describe, explain, or provide evidence from the document found in a graph, text, map, or image source.
- Use at least one reasoning skill in your written response if prompted in the question: *continuity/change* (look for long-term patterns) or *causation* (look for causes and effects).
- Each short-answer question contains *three* tasks. You must respond to all three tasks to receive full credit.

Scoring rubric for each short-answer question:

SAQ Score (per question)	Scoring Criteria
3 points	The written response accomplishes all **three** tasks in the question.
2 points	The written response accomplishes **two** tasks in the question.
1 point	The written response accomplishes **one** task in the question.
No points	The written response accomplishes **none** of the tasks in the question, or is completely blank.

Document-Based Question (DBQ)

DBQs require that you write an essay with *specific* historical evidence in support of your argument. Don't worry about second-guessing the AP Readers regarding what evidence they expect to be included in your written response. AP Readers take into account that AP teachers have a variety of approaches to selecting and prioritizing evidence that they present to students in class. The only expectation from the AP Readers is that the evidence is *valid* and *relevant* to the prompt and is a specific point that you are trying to defend.

Key points about the document-based question:

- The document-based question comprises 25% of your overall score.
- The exam contains one document-based question.
- The document-based question contains six or seven documents from historical sources in text (speeches, reports, laws, declarations), graphs, charts, maps, artifacts, political cartoons, art, or images.
- Write an essay response to identify, describe, explain, or provide evidence from the documents.
- Write a response that considers the relationship among the topic question, your thesis argument, and the documents.
- Write a response that addresses all points in the scoring criteria as described by the College Board below.

Scoring rubric for the document-based question:

Task	Scoring Criteria	Possible Points
Thesis and Claim	Presents a historically defensible thesis that establishes a line of reasoning **(1 point)**. (Note: The thesis must make a claim that responds to *all* parts of the question and must *not* just restate the question. The thesis must consist of *at least* one sentence, either in the introduction or the conclusion.)	1 point
Contextualization	Explains the broader historical context of events, developments, or processes that occurred before, during, or after the time frame of the question **(1 point)**. (Note: Must be more than a phrase or reference.)	1 point
Evidence	**Evidence from the Documents:** Uses at least *six* documents to support the argument in response to the prompt **(2 points)**. OR Uses the content of at least *three* documents to address the topic prompt **(1 point)**. (Note: Examples must describe, rather than simply quote, the content of the documents.) **Evidence Beyond the Documents:** Uses at least one additional piece of specific historical evidence beyond those found in the documents that is relevant to the argument **(1 point)**. (Note: Evidence must be different from the evidence used in contextualization.)	3 points
Analysis and Reasoning	Uses at least *three* documents to explain how each document's point of view, purpose, historical situation, and/or audience is relevant to the argument **(1 point)**. (Note: References must explain how or why, rather than simply identifying.) Uses historical reasoning and development that focuses on the question while using evidence to corroborate, qualify, or modify the argument **(1 point)**. (Examples: Explain the nuance of an issue by analyzing multiple variables; explain what is similar and different; explain the cause and effect; explain multiple causes; explain both continuity and change; explain connections across periods of time; corroborate multiple perspectives across themes; qualify or modify the argument by considering alternative views or evidence.)	2 points
Total Possible Points		**7 points**
Note: Each point is earned independently by task. You must respond to **all** tasks to receive full credit.		

Long-Essay Question (LEQ)

The final part of the exam is writing one long essay based on the same theme from three different period options (period 1, periods 2–3, or periods 3–4). Just like the DBQ, the long-essay question requires that you write an essay with *specific* historical evidence in support of your argument. LEQs focus on reasoning skills and often require a great deal of contextualization about broad trends in history—the big picture. You need to consider not only overall trends, but also historiographical arguments, long-term developments, and overall characterizations.

Key points about the long-essay question:

- The long-essay question comprises 15% of your overall score.
- The exam contains three long-essay questions, but you will choose only one question to write your essay response.
- Long-essay questions are drawn from broad topics on the key concept outlines.
- Each point is earned independently. For example, you can earn a point for a strong thesis, but fail to earn a point for not providing historical reasoning to explain specific evidence.
- Write a response that addresses all points in the scoring criteria as described by the College Board below.

Scoring rubric for the long-essay question:

Task	Scoring Criteria	Score
Thesis and Claim	Presents a historically defensible thesis that establishes a line of reasoning **(1 point)**. (Note: The thesis must make a claim that responds to *all* parts of the question and must *not* just restate the question. The thesis must consist of *at least* one sentence, either in the introduction or the conclusion.)	1 point
Contextualization	Describes the broader historical context of events, developments, or processes that occurred before, during, or after the time frame of the question **(1 point)**. (Note: Must be more than a phrase or reference.)	1 point
Evidence	Supports the argument in response to the prompt using specific and relevant examples of evidence **(2 points)**. OR Provides specific examples of evidence relevant to the topic of the question **(1 point)**. (Note: To earn 2 points, the evidence must *support* your argument.)	2 points
Analysis and Reasoning	Demonstrates a complex understanding of the historical development that addresses the question and uses evidence to corroborate, qualify, or modify the argument **(2 points)**. (Examples: Explain the nuance of an issue by analyzing multiple variables; explain what is similar and different; explain the cause and effect; explain multiple causes; explain both continuity and change; explain connections across periods of time; corroborate multiple perspectives across themes; qualify or modify the argument by considering alternative views or evidence.) OR Uses historical reasoning (comparison, causation, or continuity and change over time) to frame and develop the argument while focusing on the question **(1 point)**. (Note: Must be more than a phrase or reference.)	2 points
Total Possible Points		6 points
Note: Each point is earned independently by task. You must respond to all tasks to receive full credit.		

Historical Periods

The content of the exam is connected to four major time periods. Look at the time frames for the historical periods and their topics below. Students who are successful on the AP EURO exam can easily connect themes and topics within the chronological context of the period (era, century, or art movement).

As you review the time periods, it is also helpful to keep in mind that the document-based question and two of the short-answer questions focus on 1600–2001. Your review and study for the exam should reflect the importance of this time period.

Overview of Historical Periods					
Era	Period	Percent of Exam	Century	Topics	Art Movement
Early Modern Europe (first half)	**Period 1:** c. 1450 to c. 1648	25%	mid-15th century 16th century to mid-17th century	Renaissance, exploration, reformation, counterreformation, new monarchies, and religious wars	**Late Gothic:** The quintessential medieval style that was still in vogue in Northern Europe. **Renaissance:** Emphasized secular themes, depicted real people, used perspective, used chiaroscuro, emotion. Art was commissioned by the Church and aristocrats.
Early Modern Europe (second half)	**Period 2:** c. 1648 to c. 1815	25%	17th century 18th century 19th century	Scientific Revolution; Enlightenment; philosophies; political, economic, and social changes; French Revolution; Napoleonic era; and the Congress of Vienna	**Baroque:** A style that focused on the most ornate and complex art and architecture for the great glory of God. Most common in Southern Europe (Catholic). **Rococo:** A mid-18th-century style that focused on domestic life, including children, food, music, and the home (classical French). **Neoclassic:** Hearkened back to the Roman and Greek greats in art.
Modern Europe	**Period 3:** c. 1815 to c. 1914	25%	19th century to 20th century	Post-Napoleonic Europe, romanticism, Age of Metternich, Revolutions of 1848, Industrial Revolution, unification of nations, nationalism, the new imperialism, and Belle Epoque	**Romanticism:** Advocated for a return to the mystical and unknown, and the noble for artistic subjects. Rejected science and modernity. **Realism:** Realistic, almost photographic likenesses of real life. **Impressionism, neoimpressionism:** Emotional impressions that were realistically portrayed. **Cubism:** Meant to display human life through showing subjects from multiple perspectives.

Continued

Era	Period	Percent of Exam	Century	Topics	Art Movement
Modern Europe	**Period 4:** c. 1914 to the present	25%	20th century to the present	World War I, the Russian Revolution, interwar years, the Great Depression, World War II, and the Cold War	**Futurism:** Advocating the glory and harsh beauty of modern technology, warfare, and science. **Surrealism:** Rejecting realism for portrayal of the absurd, magical, and bizarre. **Dada:** Pure absurdism in rejection of traditional artistic norms. **Abstract expressionism:** Moving from the real world to abstract expression of the intellectual world of the artist.

Themes

History is not just about memorizing facts and dates; it's about understanding the themes that people had in common from different time periods. All of the topics covered on the AP EURO exam refer to conceptual themes. Most colleges and universities expect students to master these themes to remember *why* particular developments occurred in the context of a larger historical "big picture" of social, political, religious, ideological, technological, and economic motives. These themes will guide your studying and help you group documents for your DBQ essay response.

The College Board has identified six themes that give us the framework for understanding the big picture and why certain developments transpired, or why they were repeated in history.

Theme	Subject Matter	Description
Interaction of Europe and the World	Interactions	The exploration of European nations around the world not only changed Europe, but also changed the world by establishing trade routes to drive a global economy. Europeans were motivated by economic benefits from trade, and were also motivated by imposing religious, political, and social values on indigenous cultures.
Poverty and Prosperity	Economics	The modern period of history featured the two Industrial Revolutions, which not only created an unprecedented amount of wealth (building a middle class and a relatively prosperous working class along the way), but also exacerbated the gap between the wealthy "haves" and the "have-nots" of the world. The change from agricultural production to industrial production introduced new labor systems and gave rise to capitalism and socialism movements.
Objective Knowledge and Subjective Visions	Religion, Philosophy, and Science	Knowledge gradually moved away from the belief in absolute truths to subjective interpretations of reality gained through science, philosophy, religion, and art. Historians came to realize that historical record is subjective in varying degrees of differing worldviews.

States and Other Institutions of Power	Politics and Government	No institution is more important to the past 500 years of history than the state and civil institutions of nations, empires, and kingdoms across transregional structures. In 1400, the state was still weak and rudimentary, a blunt axe applied to individual problems. Over the course of the past five centuries, however, it became honed and hardened as the dominant power in political, social, economic, and intellectual progress in the world as revolutions and political ideologies changed the structures of governance and the balance of power.
Individual and Society	Society and Culture	This period in history was shaped by individualistic cultures in Europe (such as Britain, France, Spain, and Holland) as well as more collectivistic ones (Germany, Sweden, and Russia). In both cases, the relationship of the individual to the society and the state was key in family roles, occupational roles, gender roles, racial and ethnic identities, and social classes.
National and European Identity	Culture and Ideology	Nationalism has emerged as one of the most persuasive forces to shape European identities appealing to common cultures, languages, and governments. While tribal groups and religious unity has existed for millennia, nationalism emerged in the early modern period and quickly spread throughout the world. Nationalism was unleashed by the French Revolution, the 1848 Revolutions, and the rise of mass politics merging with national interests. Nationalism could unite people (such as during the German and Italian unification), but it could also divide them (as in the two World Wars). Other competing forces of unity have emerged, such as international communism and cosmopolitan globalism, but none of them have proved as enduring or as potent as nationalism. Nationalism continues to help shape what it means to be a European, and based on popular understandings, new European identities continue to form and dissolve over time.

AP History Reasoning Skills

To be successful on the exam, you must make sure that you are clear on AP history reasoning skills (called *reasoning skills*). These skills are the core of every question on the exam. The AP EURO exam will present one or more reasoning skills in multiple-choice questions and free-response questions. If you become familiar with these skills, you can focus, predict, and respond to all of the questions just like historians. Historians use these reasoning skills to make mental connections to historical events. By using these reasoning skills, you are exercising your brain's memory muscles to be able to see the big picture of European history.

The four important reasoning skills identified by the College Board are listed in the table below.

AP History Reasoning Skills	
Causation	Causation uses the skill of cause and effect. It involves the reasons for the causes of complex issues that resulted in unexpected developments and consequences (called *turning points* in history). To simplify this skill, think about the logical short- and long-term sequence of events—what happened *before* the event and what happened *after* the event? In free-response questions, it is important to distinguish between something that *correlates* (is associated with by relationship) and something that *causes* (prompts an effect on) an event. A correlation does not cause something to result. For example, before World War I, Germany had a correlation to a powerful military. Germany's military was ready for war, but the military did not cause the war.

Continued

Continuity and Change	Patterns of continuity and change over time are similar to causation. These are patterns in European history that tend to stay the same (or change) over time and are consistent across the big picture of history. You are expected to recognize, evaluate, and analyze the established patterns (and changes in patterns) of historical developments. For example, you may be asked to identify what is the same and what is different in a society, and then compare these findings to the same society 200 years later.
Comparison	Comparison involves comparing and contrasting multiple perspectives of a historical event to draw your own conclusions about that event. For example, you may be asked to explain the similarities and differences of empires in two different regions, or you may be asked to make a parallel comparison between your essay topic and another related theme from a different era, region, or similar topic.
Contextualization	Historical context plays a key role on the AP EURO exam. If you understand this skill, you will be far ahead of other students. Contextualization involves thinking about historical events within the specific circumstances of time and place. Context thinking can include regional, national, or global circumstances in which events or developments took place. What was happening at the time of the circumstances? For example, you may be asked to explain how the context of women living in Europe during the 19th century impacted their legal rights.

Frequently Asked Questions about the AP EURO Exam

Q: **Who administers the AP European History exam?**

A: The College Board prepares and scores the AP EURO exam. For further information regarding exam administration, contact *Advanced Placement Program (AP),* P.O. Box 6671, Princeton, NJ, 08541-6671, (888) 225-5427 or (212) 632-1780, e-mail: apstudents@info.collegeboard.org, http://apcentral. collegeboard.com.

Q: **Are there prerequisites to taking the AP EURO exam?**

A: No. However, you should be able to read college-level textbooks and write grammatically correct and complete sentences.

Q: **How do I register for the AP EURO exam?**

A: If your school offers the AP EURO course, contact your AP teacher or coordinator to register. Otherwise, contact the College Board to register www.collegeboard.org/register.

Q: **Can I take the AP EURO exam more than once?**

A: Yes, but you may not retake the exam within the same year. If you take the exam a second time, both scores will be reported unless you cancel one score.

Q: **What do I bring to the exam?**

A: Bring several no. 2 pencils with erasers for the multiple-choice questions, and bring several pens with black or dark-blue ink for the free-response questions. Bring your 6-digit school code. Bring a watch that does not have Internet access, does not beep, and does not have an alarm. If you do not attend the school where you are taking the exam, bring identification (school-issued photo ID or government-issued ID).

Q: **What items am I not allowed to bring to the exam?**

A: You cannot bring electronic equipment (cell phone, smartphone, listening devices, cameras, or any other electronic devices). You cannot bring books, highlighters, notes, food, or drinks.

Q: **Can I bring scratch paper?**

A: No; however, the exam booklets will not be graded, so you can take notes, organize your essays, and write down key words in the margins of your exam booklet.

Q: **When is the AP EURO exam?**

A: The AP EURO exam is given in May.

Q: **Can I cancel, withhold, or change my report recipient score?**

A: Yes, you can request to cancel your scores at any time before the deadline. Contact AP Services for deadlines and policies.

Q: **How long does it take to receive my score?**

A: Once you sign up for a College Board account at www.collegeboard.org/register, you can receive your scores online sometime in July. You will receive an e-mail reminding you how to access your scores. You will be asked to enter your AP number (the 8-digit number on the labels inside your AP Student Pack), or your student identifier to access your scores.

Q: **Should I guess on the AP EURO exam?**

A: Yes. There is no penalty for wrong answers. Your score is based on the number of questions you answer correctly. If possible, use the elimination strategy (see pp. 12–13) for multiple-choice questions to increase your chances of guessing the correct answer. Don't leave any questions unanswered.

Test-Taking Strategies

This section was developed as a guide to introduce *general* and *specific* test-taking guidelines, approaches, and strategies that will be useful on the AP EURO exam.

General Test-Taking Strategies

Consider the following guidelines as a road map to taking the AP EURO exam.

- **Stick with the College Board guidelines and key concepts.** Take the guesswork out of what to expect on the exam and understand that the College Board guidelines and key concepts are the well from which *all* questions are drawn (see the AP European History Course and Exam Description available at http://apcentral.collegeboard.com). The AP EURO course content can seem overwhelming at first, with so many dates, events, people, movements, clashes, and alliances, along with a variety of geographic changes to follow. Take your first deep breath and understand that the College Board has provided a guide that helps you focus on what is testable. It is true that you must acquire knowledge of significant historical events, individuals, and trends, but as you prepare to take the AP EURO exam, the key to your success begins with understanding the College Board guidelines and key concepts.

- **Know the chronological periods.** Students who are successful on the exam can identify what preceded and what followed particular events. Use the College Board time frames as bookends. While history occurs on a continuum of cause and effect, it can be viewed in smaller chunks; each period of time is set apart from others by *turning points* (events that clearly distinguish the beginning and end of each chronological period). Refer to the "Overview of Historical Periods" on pp. 7–8 to make sure you recognize periods, eras, centuries, art movements, and their topics. To help you focus on topics within chronological periods, pay attention to the "Key Facts" headings in chapters 4–7.

- **Know the important rulers (or important figures) of each time period.** As you go through the period review chapters (chapters 4–7), focus on the rulers (dynasties) for each time period. What were the rulers' political ideologies? Were the rulers absolute monarchists, nationalistic, totalitarian, communist, etc.? What wars arose during their reigns? Knowing the rulers and their political views will give you clues to draw meaningful comparisons between each time period.

- **Know the significant themes.** Students must have a general understanding of how to link historical developments from key periods to principal themes, patterns, and broad trends in European history.

- **Know the causes, outcomes, and consequences.** An overview of the College Board periods and themes will tell you up front that although certainly wars are part of the European story, emphasis is on the causes, outcomes, and consequences for each nation, NOT on battles, strategies, or tactics. In other words, time spent memorizing all of the details of battles is time and effort wasted. If you pay careful attention to the road map the College Board has provided and familiarize yourself with the format for exam questions, it will alleviate much of your worry.

- **Think historically.** Students who are successful on the AP EURO exam are those who can think historically using higher order thinking skills. Students must possess and utilize the ability to link historical events and changes across different periods of European history. Refer to pp. 9–10 for a complete description of AP history reasoning skills.

Specific Test-Taking Strategies

When attacking the questions on the AP EURO exam, it's important to consider the types of questions you are being asked and the best strategies to tackle these questions. This section discusses specific test-taking strategies for multiple-choice questions and free-response questions.

Multiple-Choice Questions

Instructions for multiple-choice questions will appear in your exam booklet. Here are specific strategies to help you work through the multiple-choice questions quickly, accurately, and efficiently.

- **Budget your time wisely.** Spend about 1 minute per question because you have 55 minutes to answer 55 multiple-choice questions. Some questions may take more time, while others may take less time, and remember that this does not inculde the time it takes to read a passage or analyze an image. Students who spend too much time dwelling on a single question don't get the score they deserve because they leave insufficient time to answer other questions they could get right. With sufficient practice, you will almost automatically know when a question is taking too much time and when to take an educated guess and move on to the next question.

- **Remember, there is no penalty for guessing.** Never leave an answer blank. If you don't know the answer to a multiple-choice question, make an educated guess, mark the question in your exam booklet, and proceed to the next question. If possible, try to eliminate some of the answer choices to increase your chances of choosing the right answer. You have nothing to lose and, quite possibly, something to gain.

- **Use the elimination strategy.** Take advantage of being allowed to mark in your exam booklet. Eliminate one or more answer choices to narrow down your choices. Remember that, statistically, your chances improve if you can eliminate at least one answer choice. Keep this marking system very simple and mark the answers in your exam booklet (no need to erase the markings because you are allowed to write in your exam booklet). Remember to practice this strategy as you take practice exams.

In your exam booklet, use a question mark (?) to signify that the choice is a possible answer, use a diagonal line (/) to cross out an answer choice that is incorrect, and leave the choice blank if you are uncertain. This strategy will help you avoid reconsidering those choices you've already eliminated.

? A.

B̶.

C.

D̶.

As a reminder, students who skip questions might make the mistake of continuing to mark their answers in sequence and forget to leave a blank space for an unanswered question. To avoid this mistake, mark your answers (and any other notes) in the exam booklet before you fill in the answer sheet.

- **Read each question carefully.** Read and mark the question by circling or underlining key points. It is important that you understand what the question is asking. Do not make a hasty assumption that you know the correct answer without reading the whole question and all of the possible answer choices. The hurried test-taker commonly selects an incorrect answer when jumping to a conclusion after reading only one or two of the answer choices in the easy questions. Don't let the easy questions mislead you. You must look at the entire list of answer choices in order to select the *best* answer.

- **Be on alert for the "attractive distractor" answer choice.** Watch out for answer choices that look good but are not the *best* answer choice, called *attractive distractors*. Just because an answer choice is a true statement does not mean that it is the best choice. Attractive distractors are usually the most common wrong answers. The facts and concepts presented on the exam are often presented in subtle variations of selected answer choices that make it difficult for test-takers to narrow down the correct answer. Common attractive distractors are choices that are not related to the correct time period, choices that do not use the correct reasoning skill, and choices that are not specific to the question.

- **Be on alert for questions with "EXCEPT" or "NOT."** Another common mistake is misreading a question that includes the words *except* or *not.* A negative question reverses the meaning of the question and asks for the opposite to be true in order to select the correct answer. Negative questions can initially be confusing and challenge your thinking. It is helpful to write down brief notes to avoid misreading a question (and therefore answering it incorrectly). Simply write down what you must answer in the question. To help answer a negative question, treat the answer choices as true or false statements, searching for the one that is false.

- **Practice, practice, practice.** The College Board recommends consistent practice to attain a higher score. This is why we have included practice questions throughout this study guide: Chapter 3 (diagnostic test), Chapters 4–7 (content review chapters), and Chapter 8 (full-length practice exam). These model practice questions include answers and thorough explanations. Be sure to practice in the exam format as often as possible. To benefit from further practice, purchase previously administered AP European History exams at https://store.collegeboard.org. Please keep in mind that some exams prior to 2016 may not reflect the most recent format of AP European History.

Free-Response Questions

Unlike old-school history that is just about memorizing facts, dates, and names, for free-response questions students must do what historians do—write an analysis and interpretation of historical evidence while reasoning historically. To write effective essays, stay focused on the AP scoring rubrics, follow the essay-writing strategies in the table below, and practice writing essays as often as possible.

This section gives you strategies for the three types of free-response questions:

- Short-Answer Questions (3 questions, 20% of your score)
- Document-Based Question (1 question, 25% of your score)
- Long-Essay Question (1 question, 15% of your score)

Checklist for Answering Free-Response Questions			
General Strategies	Short-Answer Questions (SAQs)	Document-Based Question (DBQ)	Long-Essay Question (LEQ)
1. Stay focused on the question.	✓	✓	✓
2. Prewrite to organize your essay.	✓	✓	✓
3. Link AP history reasoning skill(s).	✓	✓	✓
4. Link the broader historical context (key periods and principal themes) to the topic.	✓	✓	✓
5. Link documents to your essay to cite evidence/ examples, provide the document's point of view, and corroborate, qualify, or modify your argument.	✓	✓	
6. Write a strong thesis statement.		✓	✓
7. Write a clear line of reasoning using the standard essay writing format: introduction, body, and conclusion.		✓	✓

Note: Sample essays are available at the end of each review chapter and on the College Board website found on the AP European History Course Homepage.

Now, let's discuss each of these examples in more detail.

Stay Focused on the Question

One of the most important strategies is that your essay must stay focused on the question and address *all parts* of the question prompt. To help you stay focused, underline or circle key words in the question prompt before you start writing. For example, if the question reads, "Explain the political and social consequences of 20th century capitalism," you must respond to *both* parts of the question—political and social consequences. Too often students lose points because they don't respond to all parts of the question.

Prewrite to Organize Your Essay

Think before you write by brainstorming, planning, and prewriting to organize your thoughts. The technique of brainstorming means that you should write down all ideas and examples that come to your mind. After you brainstorm, organize those ideas in a logical sequence of events. These ideas should emphasize important points, offer historical evidence, and provide the broad historical context related to the question prompt. (Note: For the DBQ and LEQ, the exam allows 15 minutes to read documents, take notes, and plan both essays.)

If you're stuck and can't think of ideas, read the question a few times and think about a history reasoning skill. For example, consider the causes and consequences of the historical turning points, or the common similarities and differences in themes during the time period and another time period. Remember that free-response questions are generally designed so that you can receive at least partial credit if you have some knowledge of the subject. Partial responses will get partial credit. Even a response that receives 1 point will be added to your total points. One point may not seem like much now, but earning 1 point is better than zero.

Link AP History Reasoning Skills

Every essay must include targeted reasoning skills. For example, causation (what was the cause/effect of an event), patterns of change or continuity over time (what changed or stayed the same in the big picture), comparison (what were the similarities and differences of an event), or contextualization (what was the historical context of the event). Refer to pp. 9–10 for complete descriptions of reasoning skills.

Link the Broader Historical Context

Remember to keep an eye on the big picture. identify and connect the question topic to the time period and principal themes of European history. What preceded and what followed the events? Study the historical time periods on pp. 7–8 and the themes on pp. 8–9 to help you focus on the big picture of chronological events and the themes.

Link Documents to Your Essay

The AP EURO contains many different historical documents that accompany various multiple-choice and free-response questions. To receive full credit for your DBQ and SAQ essay responses, you must be able to connect evidence from documents to your essay's argument. Although this section primarily addresses strategies for document-based questions, the rules about working with documents can be applied to documents in other sections of the exam.

Primary and Secondary Sources. Before you can decode a document, it's important to be familiar with the differences between primary and secondary document sources. A *primary source* is an original passage, speech, or image that was composed, spoken, or illustrated during a specific time period. A *secondary source* is a "secondhand" account told by a third party who interpreted or wrote about the primary source. For example, secondary sources are often published by historians in historiographies.

Working with documents means that you will have to quickly read passages or graphic images, organize the information from the documents, and make an interpretation. Although these types of questions may be challenging, they may also provide you with an opportunity to excel on the exam because *all* of the documents are related to the question prompt. According to the College Board, "there are no irrelevant or deliberately misleading documents." The real issue is how to decode the documents so that you can connect them to the questions. The good news is that the documents are giving you the information that you need to answer the questions. Follow these five steps to interpret documents.

1. **Preview the documents** by circling or underlining key points. This will help you match information from the documents to your essay question. As you look through the documents, think about how each document might fit with your tentative thesis. Write notes from the documents in the margins of your exam booklet, but remember to keep your notes brief. Don't worry about neatness because you will not be graded on your notes.

2. **Read the documents.** You will not need to read every detail, statistic, date, or emperor in the document. Rather, look for the overall "gist" of the document. Read quickly to gather context, audience, and other pertinent facts.

   Remember to think like a historian when you read each document. Historians don't just look at what a document says, they look for the *context* of the document. Historians find the context by asking *when* and by *whom* the document was written found in the bibliographic reference. If you know the European history time periods, you should have a general sense of events that took place when the document was written, and you should be able to make an educated guess of the major events, ideas, themes, and issues that surrounded the time when the document was written. It also helps to determine what came before and what came after this period (continuity and change over time). By gathering this information, you should be able to guess if the author is male or female, the author's national origins, social status, or ethnicity.

   Use the information from the context to try to determine the author's intended audience. Who is the author addressing and who benefited from the document? And why is the author addressing this particular audience during this particular time period?

3. **Cite evidence from the documents (and at least one piece of evidence not found in the documents).** To receive the highest score possible, you need to be able to explain the fundamental issues related to the question with supporting evidence. DBQs require that you reference at least three to six documents to support your main thesis and at least one additional piece of historical evidence not found in the documents. When given historical documents, data, or images, you must be able to provide evidence while constructing a clear argument to support your claims and add synthesized historical knowledge. (Note: Be sure to use quotation marks around direct quotes when citing information from the documents.) To receive full credit, the evidence must be valid and relevant to the question prompt, identify specific points that you are trying to defend, and reference at least six documents and one outside piece of historical evidence to corroborate, qualify, or modify your argument.

   Remember to add the document number when referencing evidence in your essay. For example, "The Spanish used brutal force and the most depraved forms of violence to establish their new empire. The image depicts a vivid description of brutal methods that were used by the Spanish in their conquest and rule of the Caribbean islands (Document 3)."

4. **Cite the document's point of view**. When reading the documents, try to determine the document's purpose, historical situation, and/or audience. Keep in mind that you must discuss the document's point of view from at least three DBQ documents. A surprising number of students neglect this step and lose points on their DBQ essays. It is not enough to cite the title of a document; you must explain the document's perspective (what influenced the author to create the document?). As you read and take notes in the margins of the document, think about *why* the author produced the document. For example, "Document 5 demonstrates the author's point of view in the political cartoon, 'Big Brother is Watching You.' The context of this unifying theory of totalitarian governance was characterized during Joseph Stalin's reign in the 20th century."

5. **Group the documents into thematic categories**. As you analyze each document and take notes, determine the relationship between the document and the theme(s) related to your thesis statement. Ask yourself two questions: "What is the main point of the document?" and "How does the document relate to the question prompt?" This information will help you group the documents into general or specific thematic groups.

   AP Readers want to see that your essays have specific groupings that logically support your thesis. For example, a generalized grouping might be, "The social roles during the 18th century." A specific grouping on this topic might be, "Documents 1, 3, and 5 characterize European women's roles during 18th-century industrialization and the impact on the labor industry."

Write a Strong Thesis Statement

The introduction of your response should include a strong thesis statement that tells the Reader the main points of your essay within a historical context of European history and the documents. To earn your best possible score, carefully read the question prompt, use key points from the question prompt in your thesis statement, and follow a line of reasoning. Do not just restate the question in the thesis statement. The Readers are looking for your own original thinking. After you read the question prompt, what thoughts jump out at you? Write down these ideas as you brainstorm to prewrite a tentative thesis. Underline or circle what you will need to locate in the document(s) and use this information to formulate your thesis statement. Remember, the brainstorming stage is tentative; you can always adjust the thesis statement once you have gathered all of the information from the documents. A strong opening paragraph tells the Reader what to expect in the body of your essay. Try to avoid a long introduction and aim to keep it about the same length as your conclusion.

Use the Standard Essay Writing Format

Write a clear and legible essay using a general essay writing format:

- Introduction with a strong thesis statement that focuses on the question.
- Body with examples and evidence that are historically defensible.
- Conclusion.

Paragraph one: The introduction of your essay should (a) present a strong main thesis within a historical context that follows a line of reasoning, (b) list supporting point #1, (c) list supporting point #2, (d) list supporting point #3, etc.

Paragraphs two, three, and four: Divide the body of your essay into separate supporting points. The body must develop historical evidence by showing *proof, examples, analysis,* or *interpretations* of the points in your introduction. This includes evidence that corroborates, qualifies, or modifies the argument. Remember to think about the broader historical context of major developments and events to support your argument, and think about the key turning points that caused a shift in developments. It is sometimes helpful to use "who, what, where, why, and when" to support your points. And remember to show a connection between each paragraph and your thesis statement.

Paragraph Two – Develop point #1
Paragraph Three – Develop point #2
Paragraph Four – Develop point #3

Note: Continue this process if you have more than three supporting points.

Paragraph Five: Finish with your conclusion. A lengthy conclusion is not necessary, but your conclusion should summarize your main points from the introduction and expand points from your thesis.

The following strategic plan of attack summarizes the strategies for all three free-response question types:

A Strategic Plan of Attack

Read the question TWICE and note the directions, prompts, and document sources.

PREWRITE. Gather information from the question, sources, or documents by marking and taking notes about key points. Organize your ideas by prewriting an outline (or list) to prioritize important points and evidence from sources and documents.

WRITING YOUR SHORT-ANSWER RESPONSES

No thesis statement.

Answer all three points in each question to receive full credit.

Answer three questions— the first two questions and then choose ONE of the last two questions (the period you know more about).

Keep your answers brief and address historical evidence from the primary or secondary sources (if included).

Use interpretation to historically explain the *content knowledge* related to the question.

Use reasoning skills to address similarities and differences, causes and effects, or changes and continuities over time.

WRITING YOUR DOCUMENT-BASED RESPONSE

Develop a thesis statement that is a historically defensible claim, establishes a line of reasoning, and responds to *all* parts of the question.

Support your argument by showing relationships among the question, thesis, and evidence.

Describe the broader historical context of events, developments, and processes. (What happened before, during, or after that time frame?)

Group the documents and make connections among the documents to corroborate, qualify, or modify the argument.

For the highest possible score, identify, interpret, and cite specific examples from six documents to support your argument.

Provide examples of the author's point of view, historical situation, purpose, or audience from at least three documents.

Use targeted reasoning skills (comparison, causation, or continuity and change over time).

Support your argument using at least one piece of outside historical evidence not mentioned in the documents.

WRITING YOUR LONG-ESSAY RESPONSE

Choose ONE of the three question options (the period you know more about).

Develop a thesis argument that is a historically defensible claim and establishes a line of reasoning.

Explain how historical context influenced the topic.

For the highest possible score, support your argument with specific facts and examples that corroborate, qualify, or modify your argument.

Relate the topic to broader historical events, developments, or processes (before, during, or after the time frame of the question).

Incorporate a targeted reasoning skill (comparison, causation, or continuity/change).

PROOFREAD AND EDIT. Leave yourself a few minutes to correct errors and make minor revisions.

Chapter 1

Two-Month Cram Plan

The calendar below details a two-month action plan for the AP EURO exam. The first step is to determine how much time you have to prepare and then pick the plan that fits your schedule: two-month plan or one-month plan (see pp. 23–24 for a one-month plan). Ask yourself, "How many hours a week can I realistically devote to preparing for the exam?" Be specific. For example, you may be able to study on Tuesdays, Thursdays, and Fridays from 4:00 to 6:00 p.m., or you may only have time on Saturdays and Sundays from 8:00 a.m. to 12 p.m. It doesn't matter what plan you pick; what matters is that you stick to the schedule to get your best possible results.

Two-Month Cram Plan	
8 weeks before the exam	**Study Time:** 3 hours ❑ Take the Diagnostic Test (Chapter 3) and compare your answers with the answer explanations. ❑ Compare your essay responses to the free-response essay scoring guideline rubrics. ❑ Browse the AP EURO official website: http://apcentral.collegeboard.com/apeurohistory. ❑ Read the Introduction. ❑ Study the AP EURO exam format (pp. 1–2).
7 weeks before the exam	**Study Time:** 2 hours ❑ Take notes as you read, study, and memorize the AP EURO history reasoning skills (pp. 9–10). ❑ Take notes as you read, study, and memorize the AP EURO historical periods (pp. 7–8). ❑ Take notes as you read, study, and memorize the AP EURO themes (pp. 8–9). **Study Time:** 2–3 hours at least two times a week (or as often as your schedule permits) ❑ Chapter 4 (first half): Read, study, and take notes in this book for the Renaissance through the Age of Exploration (pp. 47–72). ❑ Use additional resources to read more about general and specific topics discussed in the first half of Chapter 4.
6 weeks before the exam	**Study Time:** 2–3 hours at least two times a week (or as often as your schedule permits) ❑ Chapter 4 (second half): Read, study, and take notes in this book for the Reformation through the Thirty Years' War (pp. 72–93). ❑ Use additional resources to read more about general and specific topics discussed in the second half of Chapter 4. ❑ Reread the "AP European History Key Concepts" for Period One on pp. 48–49. ❑ Answer the chapter review multiple-choice practice questions after you have read the entire chapter. ❑ Answer the chapter review DBQ practice question after you have read the entire chapter. Compare your response to the scoring guidelines and sample response.
5 weeks before the exam	**Study Time:** 3 hours at least three times a week (or as often as your schedule permits) ❑ Chapter 5: Read, study, and take notes on Historical Period Two, "Enlightenment and Expansion." ❑ Use additional resources to read more about general and specific topics discussed in Chapter 5. ❑ Reread the "AP European Key Concepts" for Period Two on p. 108. ❑ Answer the chapter review multiple-choice practice questions after you have read the entire chapter. ❑ Answer the chapter review DBQ practice question after you have read the entire chapter. Compare your response to the scoring guidelines and sample response.

Continued

4 weeks before the exam	**Study Time:** 3 hours at least three times a week (or as often as your schedule permits) ❏ Chapter 6: Read, study, and take notes on Historical Period Three, "The Age of Nationalism." ❏ Use additional resources to read more about general and specific topics discussed in Chapter 6. ❏ Reread the "AP European History Key Concepts" for Period Three on pp. 156–157. ❏ Answer the chapter review multiple-choice practice questions after you have read the entire chapter. ❏ Answer the chapter review DBQ practice question after you have read the entire chapter. Compare your response to the scoring guidelines and sample response.
3 weeks before the exam	**Study Time:** 3 hours at least three times a week (or as often as your schedule permits) ❏ Chapter 7: Read, study, and take notes on Historical Period Four, "Global Wars to Globalization." ❏ Use additional resources to read more about general and specific topics discussed in Chapter 7. ❏ Reread the "AP European History Key Concepts" for Period Four on pp. 200–201. ❏ Answer the chapter review multiple-choice practice questions after you have read the entire chapter. ❏ Answer the chapter review DBQ practice question after you have read the entire chapter. Compare your response to the scoring guidelines and sample response.
2 weeks before the exam	**Study Time:** 5 hours ❏ Chapter 8: Take the full-length practice exam and review your answers, the explanations, and sample responses. ❏ Based on your performance, identify topics and their corresponding chapters that require further review. ❏ Use additional resources to read about general and specific topics discussed in the practice exam.
7 days before the exam	**Study Time:** 3 hours ❏ Based on your review, target general and specific topics. ❏ Review strategies for writing a response to a document-based question (pp. 13–18). ❏ Practice writing a response to one document-based question or one long-essay question using the scoring guidelines on pp. 4–6 to score your essay. Note: Previous free-response question topics can be found online at https://apstudent.collegeboard.org/apcourse/ap-european-history/exam-practice (click on "Student responses").
6 days before the exam	**Study Time:** 2 hours ❏ Based on your review, target general and specific topics. ❏ Practice writing responses to two short-answer questions. Note: Previous free-response question topics can be found online at: https://apstudent.collegeboard.org/apcourse/ap-european-history/exam-practice.
5 days before the exam	**Study Time:** 1–2 hours ❏ Review the AP EURO Key Concepts for Period One (pp. 48–49). ❏ Study and target specific topics as needed.
4 days before the exam	**Study Time:** 1–2 hours ❏ Review the AP EURO Key Concepts for Period Two (p. 108). ❏ Study and target specific topics as needed.
3 days before the exam	**Study Time:** 1–2 hours ❏ Review the AP EURO Key Concepts for Period Three (pp. 156–157). ❏ Study and target specific topics as needed.
2 days before the exam	**Study Time**: 1–2 hours ❏ Review the AP EURO Key Concepts for Period Four (pp. 200–201). ❏ Study and target specific topics as needed. ❏ Reread any material you feel is necessary.

1 day before the exam	Relax. You are well-prepared to score well on the exam. ❑ Get plenty of sleep the night before the exam.
Morning of the exam	Eat a balanced, nutritious breakfast with protein. ❑ Keep your usual habits. Don't try something new today. ❑ Bring your photo ID, ticket for admission (if received), watch (that does not have Internet and does not beep), your 6-digit school code, several sharpened no. 2 pencils with erasers, and a few pens with black or dark-blue ink. Note: Cell phones, scratch paper, books, smartwatches, and food/drinks are not allowed at the testing center.

Chapter 2

One-Month Cram Plan

The calendar below details a one-month action plan for the AP EURO exam. The first step is to determine how much time you have to p repare and then pick the plan that fits your schedule: two-month plan or one-month plan (see pp. 19–21 for a two-month plan). Ask yourself, "How many hours a week can I realistically devote to preparing for the exam?" Be specific. For example, you may be able to study on Tuesdays, Thursdays, and Fridays from 4:00 to 6:00 p.m., or you may only have time on Saturdays and Sundays from 8:00 a.m. to 12 p.m. It doesn't matter what plan you pick; what matters is that you stick to the schedule to get your best possible results.

One-Month Cram Plan	
4 weeks before the exam	**Study Time:** 3–4 hours ❑ Take the Diagnostic Test (Chapter 3) and compare your answers with the answer explanations. ❑ Compare your essay responses to the free-response essay scoring guideline rubrics. ❑ Browse the AP EURO official website: http://apcentral.collegeboard.com/apeurohistory. ❑ Read the Introduction. ❑ Study the AP EURO exam format (pp. 1–2). ❑ Take notes as you read, study, and memorize the AP EURO history reasoning skills (pp. 9–10). ❑ Take notes as you read, study, and memorize the AP EURO historical time periods (pp. 7–8). ❑ Take notes as you read, study, and memorize the AP EURO themes (pp. 8–9). **Study Time:** 3 hours at least two times a week (or as often as your schedule permits) ❑ Chapter 4: Read, study, and take notes on Historical Period One, "The Renaissance and Reformation." ❑ Reread the "AP European History Key Concepts" for Period One on pp. 48–49. ❑ Answer the chapter review multiple-choice practice questions after you have read the entire chapter. ❑ Answer the chapter review DBQ practice question after you have read the entire chapter. Compare your response to the scoring guidelines and sample response.
3 weeks before the exam	**Study Time:** 3 hours at least two times a week (or as often as your schedule permits) ❑ Chapter 5: Read, study, and take notes on Historical Period Two, "Enlightenment and Expansion." ❑ Reread the "AP European History Key Concepts" for Period Two on p. 108. ❑ Answer the chapter review multiple-choice practice questions after you have read the entire chapter. ❑ Answer the chapter review DBQ practice question after you have read the entire chapter. Compare your response to the scoring guidelines and sample response.
2 weeks before the exam	**Study Time:** 3 hours at least two times a week (or as often as your schedule permits) ❑ Chapter 6: Read, study, and take notes on Historical Period Three, "The Age of Nationalism." ❑ Reread the "AP European History Key Concepts" for Period Three on pp. 156–157. ❑ Answer the chapter review multiple-choice practice questions after you have read the entire chapter. ❑ Answer the chapter review DBQ practice question after you have read the entire chapter. Compare your response to the scoring guidelines and sample response.

Continued

One-Month Cram Plan

	Study Time: 3 hours at least two times a week (or as often as your schedule permits) ❑ Chapter 7: Read, study, and take notes on Historical Period Four, "Global Wars to Globalization." ❑ Reread the "AP European History Key Concepts" for Period Four on pp. 200–201. ❑ Answer the chapter review multiple-choice practice questions after you have read the entire chapter. ❑ Answer the chapter review DBQ practice question after you have read the entire chapter. Compare your response to the scoring guidelines and sample response.
7 days before the exam	**Study Time:** 5 hours ❑ Chapter 8: Take the full-length practice exam and review your answers, the explanations, and sample responses. ❑ Based on your performance, identify topics and their corresponding chapters that require further review. ❑ Use additional resources to read about general and specific topics discussed in the practice exam.
6 days before the exam	**Study Time:** 3 hours ❑ Based on your review, target general and specific topics. ❑ Review strategies for writing a response to a document-based question (pp. 13–18). ❑ Practice writing a response to one document-based question or one long-essay question using the scoring guidelines on pp. 4–6 to score your essay. Note: Previous free-response question topics can be found online at https://apstudent.collegeboard.org/apcourse/ap-european-history/exam-practice (click on "Student responses").
5 days before the exam	**Study Time:** 2 hours ❑ Review the AP EURO Key Concepts for Period One (pp. 48–49). ❑ Study and target specific topics as needed.
4 days before the exam	**Study Time:** 2 hours ❑ Review the AP EURO Key Concepts for Period Two (p. 108). ❑ Study and target specific topics as needed.
3 days before the exam	**Study Time:** 2 hours ❑ Review the AP EURO Key Concepts for Period Three (pp. 156–157). ❑ Study and target specific topics as needed.
2 days before the exam	**Study Time:** 1–2 hours ❑ Review the AP EURO Key Concepts for Period Four (pp. 200–201). ❑ Study and target specific topics as needed. ❑ Reread any material you feel is necessary.
1 day before the exam	❑ Relax. You have covered all of the material necessary to score well on the exam. ❑ Get plenty of sleep the night before the exam.
Morning of the exam	❑ Eat a balanced, nutritious breakfast with protein. ❑ Keep your usual habits. Don't try something new today. ❑ Bring your photo ID, ticket for admission (if received), watch (that does not have Internet and does not beep), your 6-digit school code, several sharpened no. 2 pencils with erasers, and a few pens with black or dark-blue ink. Note: Cell phones, scratch paper, books, smartwatches, and food/drinks are not allowed at the testing center.

Chapter 3

Diagnostic Test

This chapter contains a diagnostic test that will give you valuable insight into the types of questions that may appear on the AP EURO exam. It is for assessment purposes only and is NOT a full-length practice exam. Additional practice questions are included at the end of each period review chapter (chapters 4–7), and a full-length practice exam is included in Chapter 8.

As you take this diagnostic test, try to simulate testing conditions and time limits as you begin each of the following sections:

Section	Diagnostic Test	Actual Exam
Section I: Part A—Multiple-Choice Questions	25 questions, 25 minutes	55 questions, 55 minutes
Section I: Part B—Short-Answer Questions	1 question, 13 minutes	3 questions, 40 minutes
Section II: Part A—Document-Based Question	1 question, 60 minutes	1 question, 60 minutes
Section II: Part B—Long-Essay Question	1 question, 40 minutes	1 question, 40 minutes

Answer Sheet for Multiple-Choice Questions

1 Ⓐ Ⓑ Ⓒ Ⓓ
2 Ⓐ Ⓑ Ⓒ Ⓓ
3 Ⓐ Ⓑ Ⓒ Ⓓ
4 Ⓐ Ⓑ Ⓒ Ⓓ
5 Ⓐ Ⓑ Ⓒ Ⓓ

6 Ⓐ Ⓑ Ⓒ Ⓓ
7 Ⓐ Ⓑ Ⓒ Ⓓ
8 Ⓐ Ⓑ Ⓒ Ⓓ
9 Ⓐ Ⓑ Ⓒ Ⓓ
10 Ⓐ Ⓑ Ⓒ Ⓓ

11 Ⓐ Ⓑ Ⓒ Ⓓ
12 Ⓐ Ⓑ Ⓒ Ⓓ
13 Ⓐ Ⓑ Ⓒ Ⓓ
14 Ⓐ Ⓑ Ⓒ Ⓓ
15 Ⓐ Ⓑ Ⓒ Ⓓ

16 Ⓐ Ⓑ Ⓒ Ⓓ
17 Ⓐ Ⓑ Ⓒ Ⓓ
18 Ⓐ Ⓑ Ⓒ Ⓓ
19 Ⓐ Ⓑ Ⓒ Ⓓ
20 Ⓐ Ⓑ Ⓒ Ⓓ

21 Ⓐ Ⓑ Ⓒ Ⓓ
22 Ⓐ Ⓑ Ⓒ Ⓓ
23 Ⓐ Ⓑ Ⓒ Ⓓ
24 Ⓐ Ⓑ Ⓒ Ⓓ
25 Ⓐ Ⓑ Ⓒ Ⓓ

Section I

Part A—Multiple-Choice Questions

Multiple-choice questions are grouped into sets. Each set contains one source-based prompt (document or image) and two to five questions.

25 minutes

25 questions

Questions 1–4 refer to the following passage.

> Did the Soviet leadership believe in their own communist faith? There is a temptation to dismiss communist ideology as a disloyal cover for state interests. Yet we should not let the cynicism of our postmodern age compel us to preclude the possibility that human beings (even statesmen) sometimes believe what they say and that ideological pronouncements (even on the forked tongue of a communist) can sometimes have historical value. It is inevitable that this discrepancy should be greatest in societies based upon utopian ideals, such as the Soviet Union. How then can we square the circle of the contradiction between imperialist and revolutionary tendencies?
>
> Here we should consult Vladislav Zubok, whose recent book *Failed Empire* gives us an excellent conceptual tool for understanding the Soviet Union. From the creation of the Soviet state under Lenin, revolutionary ardor and imperialist motivation were intertwined, as the Bolsheviks combined their intense idealism about the future of the international working class with a supremely cynical view of the balance of power politics of capitalist Europe. Indeed, the Soviet leaders wanted to beat the West at its own game, and Stalin continued this tradition of extreme *realpolitik* with a Machiavellianism unknown to history. But as the Soviet Union expanded its empire into eastern Europe and began to take on revolutionary client states throughout the world, the post-Stalin leadership in the Kremlin was forced once again to reconcile state imperialism with Bolshevik revolutionism. This led to the paradigm that Zubok calls the "revolutionary-imperialist" ideology that defined Soviet foreign policy.

> — Source: Malcolm Mafi, "The Ruins of the Evil Empire," 2014. Historiographical commentary about the Soviet Union's imperialistic motivations to achieve revolutionary goals.

1. Based on the passage and your knowledge of the Soviet leadership, which one of the following Soviet leaders would NOT have been described as a supporter of the intellectual movement?

    A. Mikhail Gorbachev
    B. Joseph Stalin
    C. Yuri Andropov
    D. Vladimir Lenin

2. Which of the following actions would be most similar to the logic described in this passage?

    A. The United States helping to overthrow the democratically elected President Allende of Chile
    B. Britain refusing to concede Indian independence until after the Second World War
    C. Italy demanding territorial gains in the Treaty of Versailles settlement
    D. Germany turning to Nazi rule after the collapse of the Weimar Republic

3. Which of the following is an example of Zubok's "revolutionary-imperialist" ideology as defined in this passage?

   A. The Cuban Missile Crisis
   B. Soviet support for the Chinese communists
   C. Soviet intervention in the Congolese war of independence
   D. The Sino-Soviet split

4. Which one of the following schools of historical thought is most similar to the passage?

   A. Diplomatic history
   B. Economic history
   C. Social history
   D. Intellectual history

Questions 5–8 refer to the following table.

Percentage Distribution of the World's Manufacturing Production, 1870 and 1913 (*percentage of world total*)		
Nation	1870	1913
United States	23.3	35.8
Germany	13.2	19.7
United Kingdom	31.8	14.0
France	10.3	6.4
Russia	3.7	5.5
Italy	2.4	2.7

— Source: League of Nations: "Industrialization and World Trade," 1945

5. Which of the following does NOT accurately explain the relationship in the manufacturing trends in 1870 and 1913?

   A. The United States became the largest manufacturer in the world.
   B. Germany came to seriously rival Britain's industrial might.
   C. Russia began to invest heavily in France's burgeoning industrialization.
   D. Britain remained committed to free-trade economic policies.

6. Which of the following most likely helped to accelerate the military manufacturing trends during this time period?

   A. The rise of Italy to the ranking of a Great Power
   B. The role of the United States at the Versailles Peace Conference
   C. The decline of Russian military prowess
   D. The founding of the Triple Alliance

7. Which of the following best describes how the data might be interpreted if the year was 1820?

    A.   Russia's percentage would be close to zero.

    B.   Spain and Portugal would have higher percentages than Italy.

    C.   France would have the second highest percentage.

    D.   Britain would be the leading manufacturer.

8. All of the following events are linked to the trends in the table EXCEPT

    A.   Britain's conflict with the United States over Venezuela

    B.   Russia's defeat in the Russo-Japanese War

    C.   Italy's humiliation at Adwa

    D.   Prussia's victory in the Franco-Prussian War

Questions 9–13 refer to the following excerpt from a poem.

> Half a league, half a league,
> Half a league onward,
> All in the valley of Death
> Rode the six hundred.
> "Forward, the Light Brigade!
> Charge for the guns!" he said.
> Into the valley of Death
> Rode the six hundred.
>
> "Forward, the Light Brigade!"
> Was there a man dismayed?
> Not though the soldier knew
> Someone had blundered.
> Theirs not to make reply,
> Theirs not to reason why,
> Theirs but to do and die.
> Into the valley of Death
> Rode the six hundred.
>
> Cannon to right of them,
> Cannon to left of them,
> Cannon in front of them
> Volleyed and thundered;
> Stormed at with shot and shell,
> Boldly they rode and well,
> Into the jaws of Death,
> Into the mouth of hell
> Rode the six hundred. [. . .]

When can their glory fade?
O the wild charge they made!
All the world wondered.
Honour the charge they made!
Honour the Light Brigade,
Noble six hundred!

— Source: "The Charge of the Light Brigade," Lord Alfred Tennyson, 1854

9. Which of the following 19th-century British military conflicts is Tennyson most directly referring to in his poem?

   A.   The British-French conflict at the "Battle of Waterloo"
   B.   The British-American conflict at the "Siege of Yorktown" during the American Revolution
   C.   The British-Russian conflict at the "Battle of Balaclava" during the Crimean War
   D.   The British-German conflict at the "Battle of the Somme" during World War I

10. The incidents described in Tennyson's poem prompted which of the following historical events?

   A.   Florence Nightingale's development of a professional nursing school
   B.   Abraham Lincoln's writing of the Gettysburg Address
   C.   Napoleon III's decision to attack Prussia
   D.   Charles Darwin's discovery of the theory of evolution

11. Which of the following later military phenomena is most analogous to the sentiment aroused by "The Charge of the Light Brigade"?

   A.   German soldiers were viewed as the most fearsome in the world.
   B.   Italian soldiers were viewed as mercurial and unreliable in the extreme.
   C.   Russian soldiers were viewed as "slow and dolorous."
   D.   British soldiers were viewed as "lions led by donkeys."

12. Which of the following sayings about war clearly expresses the spirit of this poem?

   A.   "A bad peace is even worse than a war."
   B.   "Sweet and fitting it is to die for one's country."
   C.   "Never was there a good war, or a bad peace."
   D.   "Laws are silent in times of war."

13. Which of the following developments did NOT result from the war during which this poem was written?

   A.   The slow rebuilding of Russian military power
   B.   The emancipation of the Russian serfs
   C.   Antagonism between Russia and Austria
   D.   The Anglo-Russian Alliance

Questions 14–17 refer to the following passage.

[. . .]

3. Therefore, resting upon the authority of Him whose pleasure it was to place us (though unequal to such a burden) upon this supreme justice-seat, we do out of the fullness of our apostolic power declare the aforesaid Elizabeth to be a heretic and favourer of heretics, and her adherents in the matters aforesaid to have incurred the sentence of excommunication and to be cut off from the unity of the body of Christ.

4. And moreover (we declare) her to be deprived of her pretended title to the aforesaid crown and of all lordship, dignity and privilege whatsoever.

5. And also (declare) the nobles, subjects and people of the said realm and all others who have in any way sworn oaths to her, to be forever absolved from such an oath and from any duty arising from lordship. fealty and obedience; and we do, by authority of these presents, so absolve them and so deprive the same Elizabeth of her pretended title to the crown and all other the above said matters. We charge and command all and singular the nobles, subjects, peoples and others afore said that they do not dare obey her orders, mandates and laws. Those who shall act to the contrary we include in the like sentence of excommunication.

— Source: Pope Pius V, *Bull of Excommunication against Elizabeth I of England,* 1570

14. Which of the following events in the Catholic Church's timeline is most closely linked to Pope Pius' discussion?

   A. The declaration of Papal Infallibility
   B. The publishing of *Rerum Novarum*
   C. The Council of Nicea
   D. The Second Vatican Council

15. A historian could best use Pope Pius V's discussion as evidence for which of the following?

   A. The nascent split between Catholic and Protestant Europe
   B. The short-term causes of the Thirty Years' War
   C. The importance of the Council of Trent
   D. The development of democracy in England

16. Based on your knowledge of European history, which of the following is most closely related to Pope Pius V's passage?

   A. The Jacobite Rebellion
   B. The English Civil War
   C. The War of the Roses
   D. The Rising of the Northern Nobles

17. Pope Pius V's discussion would have most likely pleased which of the following European rulers?

   A. Elizabeth herself
   B. Henry IV of France
   C. Ivan IV of Russia
   D. Philip II of Spain

Questions 18–21 refer to the following cartoon.

RENDEZVOUS

— Source: David Low, "Rendezvous," 1939

18. The political sentiment expressed in Low's cartoon represents which of the following?

   A.   The Nazi-Soviet Non-Aggression Pact
   B.   The Munich Agreement Crisis
   C.   The Remilitarization of the Rhineland
   D.   The Anschluss Osterreichs Union

19. Which of the following is **NOT** related to the event depicted in Low's cartoon?

   A.   The Treaty of Locarno
   B.   The joint partition of Poland
   C.   The Soviet invasion of Bessarabia
   D.   The Winter War

20. The creator of this cartoon is most likely criticizing which of the following?

    A. The danger of international communism
    B. The foolishness of Western appeasement
    C. The hypocrisy of Stalin and Hitler's rapprochement
    D. The danger of Stalin and Hitler cooperating against the West

21. The attitude expressed by the cartoon would likely have been shared with which of the following statesmen?

    A. Neville Chamberlain
    B. Benito Mussolini
    C. Francisco Franco
    D. Winston Churchill

Questions 22–25 refer to the following passage.

> RISE, Magyar! is the country's call!
> The time has come, say one and all:
> Shall we be slaves, shall we be free?
> This is the question, now agree!
> For by the Magyar's God above
> We truly swear,
> We truly swear the tyrant's yoke
> No more to bear!
>
> Alas! till now we were but slaves;
> Our fathers resting in their graves
> Sleep not in freedom's soil. In vain
> They fought and died free homes to gain.
> But by the Magyar's God above
> We truly swear,
> We truly swear the tyrant's yoke
> No more to bear!
>
> The sword is brighter than the chain,
> Men cannot nobler gems attain;
> And yet the chain we wore, oh, shame!
> Unsheath the sword of ancient fame!
> For by the Magyar's God above
> We truly swear,
> We truly swear the tyrant's yoke
> No more to bear!

And where our graves in verdure rise,
Our children's children to the skies
Shall speak the grateful joy they feel,
And bless our names the while they kneel.
For by the Magyar's God above
We truly swear,
We truly swear the tyrant's yoke
No more to bear!

— Source: Alexander Petofi: "The National Song of Hungary," 1848

22. Based on your knowledge of European history, which of the following was the result of the Hungarian Revolution of 1848?

    A. The Turks reconquered Hungary.
    B. The Russians put down the revolution per the Holy Alliance.
    C. A communist dictatorship was established in Hungary under Bela Kun.
    D. A republic was established that eventually led to a military dictatorship.

23. Which of the following social groups would have been most enthusiastic about the sentiment expressed in Petofi's song?

    A. Urban proletariats
    B. Peasant farmers recruited into the army
    C. Wealthy Austrian landlords
    D. Middle-class urban liberals

24. Which of the following styles of art best reflects the views shared by Petofi's lyrics?

    A. Realism
    B. Romanticism
    C. Impressionism
    D. Baroque

25. A historian might use the language from Alexander Petofi's song as evidence for which of the following?

    A. The rise of nationalism in the Habsburg Empire in the 19th century
    B. The causes of the Second World War
    C. The xenophobia of Hungarians
    D. The nationalist hatred between Hungary and Italy

IF YOU FINISH BEFORE TIME IS CALLED, CHECK YOUR WORK ON THIS SECTION ONLY. DO NOT WORK ON ANY OTHER SECTION IN THE TEST.

Part B—Short-Answer Question

Reading Time: 3 minutes (brainstorm your thoughts and organize your response)
Writing Time: 10 minutes

Directions: The short-answer question will not require that you develop and support a thesis statement. On the actual exam, some short-answer questions include texts, images, graphs, or maps. Use complete sentences—bullet points or an outline are unacceptable. Answer **all** parts of the question to receive full credit.

Use the passage below to answer all parts of the question that follows.

Source: F. T. Marinetti, "The Futurist Manifesto," 1909. An outline of modernization, industry, speed, and violence.

1. We intend to sing the love of danger, the habit of energy and fearlessness.
2. Courage, audacity, and revolt will be essential elements of our poetry.
3. Up to now literature has exalted a pensive immobility, ecstasy, and sleep. We intend to exalt aggressive action, a feverish insomnia, the racer's stride, the mortal leap, the punch and the slap.
4. We affirm that the world's magnificence has been enriched by a new beauty: the beauty of speed. A racing car whose hood is adorned with great pipes, like serpents of explosive breath—a roaring car that seems to ride on grapeshot is more beautiful than the Victory of Samothrace.

[. . .]

7. Poetry must be conceived as a violent attack on unknown forces, to reduce and prostrate them before man.

[. . .]

9. We will glorify war—the world's only hygiene—militarism, patriotism, the destructive gesture of freedom-bringers, beautiful ideas worth dying for, and scorn for woman.
10. We will destroy the museums, libraries, academies of every kind, will fight moralism, feminism, every opportunistic or utilitarian cowardice.
11. We will sing of great crowds excited by work, by pleasure, and by riot; we will sing of the multicolored, polyphonic tides of revolution in the modern capitals . . .

Question 1: Historians have argued that the futurist art movement was both a culmination of 19th-century European anxieties and a foreshadowing of 20th-century fascism.

(a) Describe one change in Europe during the 19th century that led to Marinetti's ideas in the passage.

(b) Describe one way in which Marinetti's passage reflects continuity in the 19th-century artistic or philosophical trends.

(c) Explain one way in which futurism led to changes in Europe from 1914 to 1945.

IF YOU FINISH BEFORE TIME IS CALLED, CHECK YOUR WORK ON THIS SECTION ONLY. DO NOT WORK ON ANY OTHER SECTION IN THE TEST.

Section II

Part A—Document-Based Question

Reading Time: 15 minutes (brainstorm your thoughts and organize your response)
Writing Time: 45 minutes

Directions: The document-based question is based on the seven accompanying documents. The documents are for instructional purposes only. Some of the documents have been edited for the purpose of this practice exercise. Write your response on lined paper and include the following:

- **Thesis**. Present a thesis that supports a historically defensible claim, establishes a line of reasoning, and responds to all parts of the question. The thesis must consist of one or more sentences located in one place—either the introduction or the conclusion.
- **Contextualization.** Situate the argument by explaining the broader historical events, developments, or processes that occurred before, during, or after the time frame of the question.
- **Evidence from the documents.** Use the content of at least three to six of the documents to develop and support a cohesive argument that responds to the topic question.
- **Evidence beyond the documents.** Support or qualify your argument by explaining at least one additional piece of specific historical evidence not found in the documents. (Note: The example must be different from the evidence used to earn the point for contextualization.)
- **Analysis.** Use at least three documents to explain the documents' point of view, purpose, historical situation, and/or audience relevant to the topic question.
- **Historical reasoning.** Use historical reasoning to show relationships among the documents, the topic question, and the thesis argument. Use evidence to corroborate, qualify, or modify the argument.

Based on the documents that follow, answer the question below.

Question 1: Using the documents and your knowledge of European history, evaluate the 18th-century European shifts in intellectual culture.

Document 1

> **Source: Immanuel Kant, *What is the Enlightenment?*, 1784. The German philosopher's essay describing what is required for people to flourish.**
>
> Enlightenment is man's release from his self-incurred tutelage. Tutelage is man's inability to make use of his understanding without direction from another. Self-incurred is this tutelage when its cause lies not in lack of reason but in lack of resolution and courage to use it without direction from another. Sapere aude! [Dare to think!] "Have courage to use your own reason!"—that is the motto of enlightenment. Laziness and cowardice are the reasons why so great a portion of mankind, after nature has long since discharged them from external direction (*naturaliter maiorennes*), nevertheless remains under lifelong tutelage, and why it is so easy for others to set themselves up as their guardians.
>
> [. . .]
>
> For this enlightenment, however, nothing is required but freedom, and indeed the most harmless among all the things to which this term can properly be applied. It is the freedom to make public use of one's reason at every point.

Document 2

Source: Jacques-Louis David, *The Death of Socrates*, 1786.

Document 3

Source: Voltaire, *A Treatise on Toleration*, Chapter 22: On Universal Tolerance, 1763. Written after the murder of a Protestant merchant, Voltaire targeted religious fanaticism and called for tolerance and acceptance.

It does not require great art, or magnificently trained eloquence, to prove that Christians should tolerate each other. I, however, am going further: I say that we should regard all men as our brothers. What? The Turk my brother? The Chinaman my brother? The Jew? The Siam? Yes, without doubt; are we not all children of the same father and creatures of the same God?

But these people despise us; they treat us as idolaters! Very well! I will tell them that they are grievously wrong. It seems to me that I would at least astonish the proud, dogmatic Islam imam or Buddhist priest, if I spoke to them as follows:

"This little globe, which is but a point, rolls through space, as do many other globes; we are lost in the immensity of the universe. Man, only five feet high, is assuredly only a small thing in creation. One of these imperceptible beings says to another one of his neighbors, in Arabia or South Africa: 'Listen to me, because God of all these worlds has enlightened me: there are nine hundred million little ants like us on the earth, but my ant-hole is the only one dear to God; all the other are cast off by Him for eternity; mine alone will be happy, and all the others will be eternally damned.'" [. . .]

Document 4

> **Source: David Hume, *Idea of a Perfect Commonwealth*, 1754.**
>
> An established government has an infinite advantage, by that very circumstance of its being established; the bulk of mankind being governed by authority, not reason, and never attributing authority to any thing that has not the recommendation of antiquity. To tamper, therefore, in this affair, or try experiments merely upon the credit of supposed argument and philosophy, can never be the part of a wise magistrate. . . .
>
> No large state, such as France or Great Britain, could ever be modelled into a commonwealth, but that such a form of government can only take place in a city or small territory. The contrary seems probable. Though it is more difficult to form a republican government in an extensive country than in a city. . . . It is not easy, for the distant parts of a large state to combine in any plan of free government; but they easily conspire in the esteem and reverence for a single person, who, by means of this popular favour, may seize the power, and forcing the more obstinate to submit, may establish a monarchical government. On the other hand, a city readily concurs in the same notions of government, the natural equality of property favours liberty, and the nearness of habitation enables the citizens mutually to assist each other. Even under absolute princes, the subordinate government of cities is commonly republican; while that of counties and provinces is monarchical. But these same circumstances, which facilitate the erection of commonwealths in cities, render their constitution more frail and uncertain. Democracies are turbulent.

Document 5

> **Source: Jean-Jacques Rousseau, *The Social Contract*, 1763. Argued against monarchs who felt divinely empowered and theorized about the best way to establish a political community.**
>
> Man was born free, but everywhere he is in chains. This man believes that he is the master of others, and still he is more of a slave than they are. How did that transformation take place? [. . .]
>
> The very scope of the action dictates the terms of this contract and renders the least modification of them inadmissible, something making them null and void. Thus, although perhaps they have never been stated in so many words, they are the same everywhere and tacitly conceded and recognized everywhere. And so it follows that each individual immediately recovers his primitive rights and natural liberties whenever any violation of the social contract occurs and thereby loses the contractual freedom for which he renounced them.
>
> The social contract's terms, when they are well understood, can be reduced to a single stipulation: the individual member alienates himself totally to the whole community together with all his rights. This is first because conditions will be the same for everyone when each individual gives himself totally, and secondly, because no one will be tempted to make that condition of shared equality worse for other men. . . .

Document 6

Source: Jacques-Louis David, *Oath of the Horatii,* 1784. Painting of the Horati brothers receiving swords from their father to defend the Roman Empire.

Document 7

Source: Montesquieu, *The Spirit of the Laws,* 1777. A treatise written by a French political philosopher about the proper role of the government.

In every government there are three sorts of power; the legislative; the executive, in respect to things dependent on the law of nations; and the executive, in regard to things that depend on the civil law.

By virtue of the first, the prince or magistrate enacts temporary or perpetual laws, and amends or abrogates those that have been already enacted. By the second, he makes peace or war, sends or receives embassies; establishes the public security, and provides against invasions. By the third, he punishes criminals, or determines the disputes that arise between individuals. The latter we shall call the judiciary power, and the other simply the executive power of the state.

When the legislative and executive powers are united in the same person, or in the same body of magistrates, there can be no liberty; because apprehensions may arise, lest the same monarch or senate should enact tyrannical laws, to execute them in a tyrannical manner.

Again, there is no liberty, if the power of judging be not separated from the legislative and executive powers. Were it joined with the legislative, the life and liberty of the subject would be exposed to arbitrary control, for the judge would then be the legislator. Were it joined to the executive power, the judge might behave with all the violence of an oppressor. [. . .]

IF YOU FINISH BEFORE TIME IS CALLED, CHECK YOUR WORK ON THIS SECTION ONLY. DO NOT WORK ON ANY OTHER SECTION IN THE TEST.

Answer Key for Multiple-Choice Questions

1. A	6. B	11. D	16. D	21. D
2. A	7. A	12. B	17. D	22. B
3. C	8. C	13. D	18. A	23. D
4. D	9. C	14. A	19. A	24. B
5. C	10. A	15. A	20. C	25. A

Answer Explanations

Section I

Part A—Multiple-Choice Questions

1. **A.** The revolutionary-imperial paradigm described in the passage begins with Lenin (choice D), and subsequently Stalin (choice B). It covers Stalinist leaders of the Soviet Union such as Yuri Andropov (choice C), so the best selection is Mikhail Gorbachev, choice A. Gorbachev repudiated the imperialist aspect of the paradigm (and one might even say that he rejected the revolutionary aspect as well).

2. **A.** Since this passage describes the paradigm of a nation diverging between its ideals and its actual foreign policy actions, choice A is the best choice. The United States ostensibly supported democracy at home and abroad, but subverted democracy in Chile in 1973.

3. **C.** The best selection here is choice C since the Soviets intervened in the Congo to help shift the balance of power in Africa during the Cold War. The Soviets also caused the proliferation of revolutionary politics throughout Africa at the same time.

4. **D.** You can eliminate choices B and C since this passage clearly does not deal with economic or social history. The other two answer choices are closer. Diplomatic history (choice A) may seem to be an attractive choice because the passage does deal with foreign policy decisions made by Soviet leaders. Intellectual history (choice D), however, is the best overall choice because foreign policy is only examined as a result of a series of historical Soviet events examined by Zubok.

5. **C.** Choice A is true and is clearly evidenced by data in the table. Choice B is also true, as Germany became a serious rival to Britain during this time period. Choice D is implicit in the table, as free-trade policies are normally followed by nations that are economically strong (while protectionism is normally the refuge of the weaker economies). Choice C, however, is backward. Industrial France began to invest in Russia's sluggish industrialization in the late-19th century to strengthen the Romanov Dynasty as an alliance partner. Therefore, the correct answer is choice C.

6. **B.** Italy scarcely made any positive change in the period; therefore, choice A is incorrect. Choice C is incorrect because economic factors had no role in Russian military decline (it was due to defeat by Japan). Choice D is incorrect because the Triple Alliance had nothing to do with this trend (Austria-Hungary is not even featured in the table). Choice B is the only possible answer. The massive industrialization of the United States allowed the U.S. to enter World War I late, assist in a victory, and provide powerful leverage at the Versailles settlement.

7. **A.** European economies looked very different in the 1820s. Spain and Portugal are not even included in the table, so you can eliminate choice B. France (choice C) had recently started to industrialize, as had Britain (choice D). Remember, France and Britain were probably the only two countries in the entire world that had any industrial footing by 1820. Choice A is correct because in 1820 Russia had virtually none of the markers of industrialization.

8. **C.** Choice A is incorrect because Britain opted to settle its conflicts with the United States, which had become economically and militarily powerful by this point. Therefore, Britain chose to have a friend in America rather than a perpetual enemy. Choice B is incorrect because Russia's lack of industrialization seriously undermined its war effort against Japan (the completion of the Trans-Siberian Railroad would have been a great boon to the Russians). Choice D is incorrect because the Prussians already had better railroads in 1870 than the French, which helped bring about their great surprise victory. Choice C is the best choice among the answers listed.

9. **C.** The date of the poem should lead you to the correct answer. Tennyson's poem is one of the greatest war poems of European history about the Battle of Balaclava during the Crimean War. Although the Battle of Waterloo in 1815 (choice A) was historically important because the British Duke of Wellington gave Napoleon his final defeat, the early time period should tell you that this answer choice is incorrect. The American Revolution was in the 18th century and World War I was in the 20th century, making choices B and D incorrect.

10. **A.** The Crimean War became a sort of laboratory for Florence Nightingale, who perfected the art of nursing and medicine in the field tents of the bloody Crimean War.

11. **D.** The Crimean War did not feature German soldiers so choice A is incorrect. Choice B is incorrect because Italian troops (of Sardinia-Piedmont, as Italy did not exist as a unified state in 1854) played a minor role in the combat. Choice C might be broadly true, at least according to national stereotypes, but choice D is the closest analogy. Just like the men of the Light Brigade were senselessly slaughtered because of their officers' incompetence, the British soldiers of World War I were called "lions led by donkeys," whose bravery was wasted by the foolishness of their officers.

12. **B.** The saying that best matches Tennyson's poem, which glorifies war and lionizes the young men who die for their country on the battlefields regardless of their wisdom of battlefield action is choice B. "Sweet and fitting it is to die for one's country" was written by the English poet Wilfred Owen. This saying became a battle cry during World War I for men enlisting and fighting for their country.

13. **D.** The Crimean War of 1853–1856 led to Russia's rebuilding of its shattered military (choice A) and the emancipation of the serfs (choice B), which was somewhat tangentially linked to the war. Essentially, the defeat of Russia's massive but sluggish army, which was made up of serfs who were forced into 25-year terms of service, convinced Tsar Alexander II that serfdom had weakened the military, among its other drawbacks. Choice C can also be eliminated because Austria refused to support its alleged ally, Russia, when Russia faced a coalition of European enemies. This led to Russia harboring a longtime grudge against Austria. That leaves choice D, the Anglo-Russian Alliance, as the correct answer.

14. **A.** The correct answer is the declaration of Papal Infallibility (choice A); the Bull of Excommunication was an attempt by the pope to use religious authority to intercede in political, secular affairs. The same was true of the announcement of Papal Infallibility in 1870, which was a papal response to the secular government of Italy's conquest of the city of Rome and the other papal lands.

15. **A.** The Bull of Excommunication shows the divide between Catholics and Protestants in Europe (choice A), which had already existed for half a century before this document was written. They were on the brink of an irreconcilable conflict. The viability of Catholic or Protestant unity in Europe was soon to be out of the purview of any possibility.

16. **D.** You can eliminate choice B because the English Civil War featured Anglicanism arrayed against Puritanism, with Catholic versus Protestant feuds long past. You can also eliminate choice C because the War of the Roses was several centuries removed from 1570. Both the Jacobite Rebellion (choice A) and the Rising of the Northern Nobles (choice D) had to do with anti-monarchy insurgencies, but the former is a century removed from 1570 and referred to a different English dynasty. Therefore, choice D is correct, as the Northern Nobles of England rose against Elizabeth to restore tolerance for Roman Catholics in the country.

17. **D.** A call for overthrow of Elizabeth from the throne of England was not welcomed by Elizabeth or her allies in France, so you can eliminate choices A and B. Elizabeth did entertain romantic proposals from Ivan IV (choice C) from afar, but he had little interest in sectarian squabbles between Catholics and Protestants, both of whom were viewed as schismatics by the Russians. Philip II of Spain (choice D), however, was greatly pleased by this document on both religious and political grounds, as he sought to both cleanse England of heresy and to gain a political foothold in the English lands where he had once been king consort.

18. **A.** This image shows Hitler and Stalin symbolically meeting and holding court. It represents the Nazi-Soviet Non-Aggression Pact of 1939 (choice A). This is also known as the Ribbentrop-Molotov Pact, which produced an uneasy truce between the previously antagonistic German Third Reich and communist Soviet Union.

19. **A.** The Ribbentrop-Molotov Pact had secret protocols that allowed for the joint Nazi-Soviet partition of Poland (choice B). It freed up the Soviets to invade Bessarabia and Finland (choices C and D), while the Nazis and Western capitalist powers locked horns. However, the Treaty of Locarno (choice A) preceded the Nazi-Soviet Pact by over a decade and had the least to do with it. Therefore, choice A is correct.

20. **C.** The textual bubbles of both caricatures show an explicit criticism of how hypocritical and craven both Hitler and Stalin were for joining together, even after their polemics against one another. Thus, choice C is correct. Choice D is the next best choice, as it at least narrows the focus to Hitler and Stalin, but it is not as close to the message portrayed in the cartoon.

21. **D.** Mussolini and Franco were delighted by the Nazi-Soviet Pact, so choices B and C can be eliminated. Choice A can be eliminated because Chamberlain was the British leader who failed to prevent the pact and did nothing to alleviate its consequences. Churchill (choice D), however, had trouble deciding whether he despised Nazism or communism more, and would have agreed wholeheartedly with the sentiment in this image; choice D is correct.

22. **B.** The Hungarian Revolution was unsuccessful, not because of the strength of Austrian forces (they were actually in disarray), but because the armies of the Russian tsar marched into Budapest and stopped the rebellion, handing the power back to their allied Habsburgs. Choice B is correct; choices A, C, and D are all chronologically incorrect to 1848.

23. **D.** The liberal revolutions of 1848 were most popular with well-educated, middle-class liberals in big cities (choice D). Choices A and B can be eliminated because working-class urbanites had little time or inclination to be involved in politics and rural soldiers had little interest in nationalism or liberalism. Choice C is incorrect, as few groups could have opposed the revolution more than Austrian landowners.

24. **B.** The nationalism, liberalism, and idealism of this song of national liberation most clearly matches the Romantic style (choice B). The Romantics were highly interested in ethnic minorities, underdogs, unknown cultures, and liberalism. Also, many Romantics joined such revolutions, such as Lord Byron going to Greece during that nation's rebellion against the Ottoman Empire.

25. **A.** This song clearly shows the rise of dangerous nationalism in Hungary, a nation with ancient and medieval predecessors; Hungary enjoyed a surge of nationalism in the 19th century as these age-old people rediscovered themselves (choice A). An argument could be made for choice B, as extreme nationalism was a cause of World War II, but choice A is the best answer.

Part B—Short-Answer Question

Question 1 Sample Response

Historical reasoning skill: *continuity and change over time*

This question is asking you to read a primary source from the Italian poet and founder of Futurism, Filippo Tommaso Marinetti. Marinetti wanted a new world order. He was frustrated by Italy's decline and presented an inflammatory political outline of danger, machinery, and speed, which provoked readers to glorify modernity and war. He later became a fascist and supporter of Mussolini. In this question, you have to interpret what Marinetti is telling you about futurism and describe the cultural, political, and social changes and continuities that resulted from futurism.

(a) Item 3 of Marinetti's document points to a change that took place in Europe in the 19th century when some people revolted against enlightened ideals in "literature" and other forms of artistic expression. The futuristic art movement was a social and political revolt against the status quo, as illustrated in Marinetti's fiery tone. Some Europeans expressed fear and anxiety in the late 19th century that Western culture and comfort had made them soft and physically weak. Instead, the futurists called for an expressive and emotionally powered social and political stance.

(b) Not all of the passage was fresh and new when the manifesto was published. Courage, fearlessness, and modernization (items 1 and 2) were not new viewpoints in Europe as described in Marinetti's manifesto. For example, Peter the Great's modern reform projects to modernize Russia in the late 17th century, and French revolutionaries' fearlessness during the French Revolution in the late 18th century. Marinetti's writing also brings to mind the philosophical thinking of Nietzsche, who in the late 19th century, criticized traditional European morality to promote a cultural renewal. Nietzsche suggested that resentment and "negative mortality" were creative forces for future ideas.

(c) The ideas in this passage, while coming from a futurist movement poet, gave a preview of what would come after World War I in the form of the ideological views of fascism. Point 9 is a clear example of one of the most fundamental aspects of fascism: the glorification of war as an instrument of foreign policy, and as a cathartic action in which the greatness in the men of the nation is shown. The futuristic movement set the stage for the rise of the fascists, who denounced traditional morality and feminism (which they viewed as enabling the inferior gender). In addition, fascists rejected traditional ideas of culture as symbols of Western capitalistic excess.

Section II

Part A—Document-Based Question

DBQ Scoring Guide

To achieve the maximum score of 7, your response must address the scoring criteria components in the table below:

Scoring Criteria for a Good Essay	
Question 1: Using the documents and your knowledge of European history, evaluate the 18th-century European shifts in intellectual culture.	
Scoring Criteria	**Examples**
A. THESIS/CLAIM	
(1 point) Presents a historically defensible thesis that establishes a line of reasoning. (Note: The thesis must make a claim that responds to *all* parts of the question and must *not* just restate the question. The thesis must consist of *at least* one sentence, either in the introduction or the conclusion.)	An effective essay should present a historically accurate thesis that shows the major change in European culture, politics, society, science, and government—the Enlightenment movement. The sample response provides a thesis that launches a line of reasoning about the key aspects of 18th-century Enlightenment, including reason, knowledge, and science, which gave rise to new ideals and modern thinking.
B. CONTEXTUALIZATION	
(1 point) Explains the broader historical context of events, developments, or processes that occurred before, during, or after the time frame of the question. (Note: Must be more than a phrase or reference.)	In addition to the evidence established in these documents, an effective essay should also consider the wider historical context in which the Enlightenment took place, including the beliefs and actions of philosophers of the time who were not included in the seven documents. For example, enlightened ideas were influenced by humanism of the Renaissance and the new ideas of the Scientific Revolution. Enlightened philosophers believed that knowledge and reason could change the world, and they were no longer blindly accepting the Church's abuse of power espoused prior to the 18th century.
C. EVIDENCE	
Evidence from the Documents **(2 points)** Uses at least *six* documents to support the argument in response to the prompt. OR **(1 point)** Uses the content of at least *three* documents to address the topic prompt (Note: Examples must describe, rather than simply quote, the content of the documents.)	To earn the highest point value, at least six of these documents must be used to support your thesis. In this set of documents, it is clear that the Enlightenment emphasized freedom and democracy. Documents 1, 3, 5, and 7 show the basic tenets of the Enlightenment, supporting reason, tolerance, and freedoms. Documents 5 and 7 illustrate the importance of citizens' legal rights in a free and democratic society. Documents 2 and 4 show the representative government's fears of transformation and change, even to the degree of killing Socrates in the artist's depiction of *The Death of Socrates* in Document 2.

Scoring Criteria	Examples
Evidence Beyond the Documents **(1 point)** Uses at least one additional piece of specific historical evidence beyond those found in the documents that is relevant to the argument. (Note: Evidence must be different from the evidence used in contextualization.)	Since several of the documents directly relate to the establishment of governments as a result of the Enlightenment—for example, the American Revolutionary Government (1775–1787) and the French Revolutionary Government (1789–1799)—it might behoove you to think about such relevant examples to speak to the broader importance of this period in history. For example, the U.S. Constitution was based on ideas from enlightened philosophers.
D. ANALYSIS AND REASONING	
(1 point) Uses at least *three* documents to explain how each document's point of view, purpose, historical situation, and/or audience is relevant to the argument. (Note: References must explain how or why, rather than simply identifying.)	The essay response draws from at least three documents to support the documents' point of view, purpose, or historical situation. For example, Document 1 explains why the Enlightenment became popular. Kant challenges others to dare to think for themselves. Document 5 argues for a "social contract" to establish a democratic society. The author of Document 7 argues for the separation of church and state to prevent the abuse of government power.
(1 point) Uses historical reasoning and development that focuses on the question while using evidence to corroborate, qualify, or modify the argument. (Examples: Explain what is similar and different; explain the cause and effect; explain multiple causes; explain connections within and across periods of time; corroborate multiple perspectives across themes; or consider alternative views.)	A good thesis on these documents might draw from the *continuities and changes* that summarize the growing emphasis on rationality, public discourse, and freedoms to create a free and independent society. This would form the core of a strong argument on this topic while providing evidence to corroborate and qualify the main points.

Sample Response

The Enlightenment is one of history's more self-explanatory movements, even if its more obscure aspects are not as well understood. At its heart, the historical context of the Enlightenment was centered on elite philosophers, scientists, and political intellectuals such as the writings of Voltaire, Hume, Rousseau, and Montesquieu (Documents 3, 4, 5, and 7). These philosophers hoped to use their wisdom and an empirical approach to the world to educate ordinary people of societies. Enlightenment intellectuals did so by drawing on the wisdom of the ancient Greeks and Romans (Documents 2 and 6), as well as on the modern science, reason, and knowledge of their own time. By so doing, they focused on an ideal future society in which freedom of religion, speech, and thought could triumph. According to many enlightened thinkers, as humans and as citizens who were part of a greater society, people deserved certain inalienable rights (Documents 1, 3, 5, and 7).

By the 18th century, people were no longer blindly accepting unquestionable authority, and the Enlightenment gave rise to many more scientific discoveries. However, the rise of revolutionary ideas espoused by enlightened thinkers also continued to threaten powerful rulers of state and religion as exemplified in Hume's criticisms in Document 4. The historical continuity of abuse of power and corruption of the 16th and 17th centuries continued in the 18th century. The historical changes caused by the Enlightenment influenced the social, political, economic, scientific, and cultural climate of the people in Europe, and rulers feared losing their grip on absolute power. Documents 2 and 6 are paintings that represent the regrettable opposition of new ideals of the Enlightenment. Document 2 depicts Socrates, the founder of Western philosophy who sought a practical and ethical social system for the greater good of mankind and society. The painting, "Death of Socrates" in Document 2 shows Socrates being forced to drink poison and kill himself by order of the state. What could be a more fitting testament to the fight for the progress of freedoms espoused by the Enlightenment? Socrates represented everything Enlightenment philosophers wanted to be: questioning, probing, discovering, and teaching. His tragic death at the hands of the overbearing state could be the fate of many a thinker condemned to death for the crime of free thought and individualism. In Document 6, we see another classical allusion, in this case to the old Roman legend of the Horatii. This painting and the story behind it emphasized Enlightenment values as these three brothers put their community and their society above themselves and their family.

Document 1 shows the key tenets of the Enlightenment as espoused by Immanuel Kant, "Dare to have courage to use your own reason." Kant emphasized the need to freely use reason in the public sphere, without regard for the prejudices or ignorance of others. This complements David's painting because Socrates suffered for a similar outlook on life. Document 3 represents the open mindedness and rationality of "universal tolerance," that Enlightenment thinkers expressed through reason and wisdom.

Documents 5 and 7 elaborate on the political and social rights of citizens. Document 5 cites declarations and terms for a social contract by Rousseau to end limits among free citizens. The social contract has some Enlightenment ideas from British philosophers that originated in the 17th century about "men being born free." Rousseau's argument in the social contract expands on Enlightenment ideas that a free society should have legal rights and freedoms of speech, press, and assembly. In Document 7, Baron Montesquieu argues for the separation of powers and the checks and balances between the three branches of government: the legislative, judicial, and executive. Only through this separation and balancing act can a government act transparently and fairly in a way accountable to the people. These were the same rights created in the U.S. Constitution and the Bill of Rights in 1787–1791.

Clearly, the philosophers and scientists of the Enlightenment wove webs of theories that foretold the creation of a better society and a better government for all people worldwide. After the horrors of the 20th century, it is easy to look back on the hopes and aspirations of Enlightenment philosophers as naïve. But the fact remains that Enlightenment philosophers greatly impacted the political, economic, cultural, and social life of Europe and continue to influence the world today. The modern world, for better or for worse, owes much to its ideas to Enlightenment philosophers, scientists, and political intellectuals.

Chapter 4
Historical Period One: The Renaissance and Reformation (c. 1450 to c. 1648)

Period One explores the era of early modern European history.

- The Renaissance: Italian and Northern (c. 1400 to c. 1550)
- The Age of Exploration (c. 1492 to 1600)
- The Reformation (c. 1515 to c. 1650)
- The Rise of New Monarchies: Spain, England, France (c. 1450 to c. 1550)
- The Thirty Years' War (1618 to 1648)

Overview of AP European History Period One

The 15th to the mid-17th centuries in Europe were periods of extraordinary transformation that ushered in early modern history. Chapter 4 starts by reviewing events in medieval Europe leading up to early modern Europe. The 14th century medieval European crises caused by the Black Death, the war between France and England, and the division in the Church led to changes in European worldview attitudes, values, and beliefs. These events set the stage for religious reformation, shifts in European power, world exploration, and the emergence of scholarly and scientific inquiry.

The AP European History curriculum framework and key concepts explain the reasoning behind particular beliefs and developments that emerged in Europe during this time period. The historical examples of significant themes, trends, events, and people support the recommended study topics that are specific to the AP EURO exam. As you study key concepts, use the chart on the next page as a checklist to guide you through what is covered on the exam.

Visit http://apcentral.collegeboard.com for the complete updated AP EURO course curriculum and key concept descriptions.

AP European History Key Concepts (c. 1450 to 1648)	
KEY CONCEPT 1.1: REVIVAL OF FINE ARTS AND INTELLECTUALISM **The rediscovery of works from ancient Greece and Rome and the observation of the natural world changed many Europeans' view of their world.**	A revival of classical texts led to new methods of scholarship and new values in both society and religion. The invention of the printing press led to dissemination of new ideas (Protestant reformers). The visual arts incorporated the new ideas of the Renaissance and were used to promote personal, political, and religious goals. New ideas in science based on observation, experimentation, and mathematics challenged the classical view of the cosmos, nature, and the human body, although existing traditions of knowledge and the universe continued.
KEY CONCEPT 1.2: RELIGIOUS PLURALISM AND CONFLICTS **Religious pluralism challenged the concept of a unified Europe.**	The Protestant and Catholic reformations changed theology, religious institutions, European culture, and attitudes toward wealth and prosperity. Religious reform increased state control of religious institutions and provided justifications for challenging state authority. Conflicts among religious groups overlapped with political and economic competition within and among states.
KEY CONCEPT 1.3: EUROPEAN EXPLORATION OVERSEAS **Europeans explored and settled overseas territories, encountering and interacting with indigenous populations.**	European nations were driven by commercial and religious motives to explore overseas territories and establish colonies. For example, Spanish in the New World, Portuguese in Indian Ocean world, and Dutch in East Indies/Asia. Rise of mercantilist ideas (Jean Baptiste Colbert). Shift toward European dominance. Advances in navigation (compass) and the military (guns and horses) allowed European nations driven by commercial and religious motives to explore overseas. New plants, animals, goods, and diseases (the Columbian Exchange) created economic opportunities. Europeans established overseas empires and trade networks through coercion and negotiation. The competition for trade led to conflicts and rivalries among European powers. The Portuguese established trade along the African coast, South and East Asia, and South America. The Spanish established colonies across the Americas, the Caribbean, and the Pacific, making Spain dominant in Europe. The Atlantic nations of France, England, and the Netherlands established colonies to compete. Europe's colonial expansion led to a global exchange of goods, flora, fauna, cultural practices, and diseases (the Columbian Exchange), resulting in the destruction of some indigenous civilizations, a shift toward European dominance, and the expansion of slave trade.

| KEY CONCEPT 1.4: ECONOMIC GROWTH

European society and the experiences of everyday life were increasingly shaped by commercial and agricultural capitalism, notwithstanding the persistence of medieval social and economic structures. | Economic change produced new social patterns, but traditions and hierarchy persisted.

European livelihood from agriculture (seasons) benefited large landowners and nobles with large estates, although economic changes began to alter rural production and power.

Population shifts and growing commerce led to the expansion of cities, which often placed stress on their traditional political and social structures.

The family remained the primary social and economic institution of early modern Europe and took several forms, including the nuclear family.

Popular culture, leisure activities, and rituals reflecting the continued popularity of folk ideas reinforced and sometimes challenged communal ties and norms. Local and church authorities enforced public humiliation (public whipping and branding). |
| KEY CONCEPT 1.5: MOVEMENT TO UNIFY CITY-STATES

The struggle for sovereignty within and among states resulted in varying degrees of political centralization.

A movement from 1) separate states to a unified political power; 2) the political elite to notoriety based on education, wealth, and skills; and 3) religious authority to judicial laws. | The new concept of the sovereign state and secular systems of law played a central role in the creation of new political institutions. New monarchies established monopolies on tax collection, military force, and the dispensing of justice, and gaining the right to determine the religion of their subjects.

The competitive state system led to new patterns of diplomacy and new forms of warfare.

The Peace of Westphalia (1648) marked the end of the medieval idea of universal Christendom and accelerated the decline of the Holy Roman Empire by granting princes, bishops, and other local leaders control over religion.

The competition for power between monarchs and corporate and minority language groups produced different distributions of governmental authority in European states. |

Significant Themes

Now that we've discussed the key concepts, let's discuss the significant themes related to the AP EURO exam. These conceptual themes and trends should help you to think about *why* particular events and developments occurred in the context of a larger historical "big picture." The study questions give you important insights related to specific questions that will help you make mental connections between each given topic and the social, political, economic, and religious significance.

Glance through the study questions before you start the review section. Take notes, mark questions, and write down page number references to reinforce your learning. Refer to this list as often as necessary until you are confident with your answers.

Study Questions Related to Significant Themes in Period One

Theme 1: Interaction of Europe and the World

1. Why did Europeans want to explore and colonize in other parts of the world? (Hint: Christian religious motivations and commercial competition for trade.)

2. How did European cultural beliefs justify European conquests overseas? (Hint: Christianity.)

3. How did Europeans establish and administer overseas commercial and territorial empires? (Hint: Commercial trade routes and technological inventions.)

4. How did networks between Europe and the world shape Europe? (Hint: Think about the Columbian Exchange and how it changed culture, politics, economics, and society through commercial and trading global exchanges of goods, plants, animals, and microbes. It caused a shift of economic power of mercantilism to the Atlantic states, and introduced agriculture and manufacturing, but it also introduced slave trade, disease, and conflict.)

5. How did contact with non-European people change European social and cultural diversity? (Hint: The expansion of trans-Atlantic slave trade and attitudes toward race.)

6. What was the impact on Europe's economy, society, and culture from the Columbian Exchange? (Hint: Global exchange of goods, plants, and animals contributing to the agricultural, industrial, and consumer revolutions in Europe.)

Theme 2: Poverty and Prosperity

1. How did the new wealth generated by new trading and manufacturing impact Europe's consumer economy? (Hint: Rise of mercantilism and the commercialization of agriculture; early capitalism.)

2. How did new wealth create a commercial society? (Hint: New economic ideas with free trade and a free market.)

Theme 3: Objective Knowledge and Subjective Visions

1. How did religious reform in the 16th and 17th centuries challenge the control of the church? (Hint: New values, new inventions such as the printing press, wars, balance of power challenges.)

2. How did the development of Renaissance humanism contribute to new theories of knowledge? (Hint: New methods of scholarship, individual inquiry, and critical thinking; people started to emphasize individualism and question the Church's authority.)

3. How did religion shift from public concern to private belief? (Hint: Humanist secular models, Martin Luther introduced new interpretations of Christian doctrine and practice, start of religious pluralism.)

Theme 4: States and Other Institutions of Power

1. Explain how monarchies were able to centralize power in their states. (Hint: New monarchs, the rise of nation-states, absolutism, religious toleration, control over religion, and reformation.)

2. How did religious reform in the 16th and 17th centuries challenge the control of the Church? (Hint: Religious tolerance of Christian minorities and Jews, emergence of civic venues such as salons and coffeehouses, expansion of printing to disseminate knowledge.)

3. How did the printing press help to develop a civil society? (Hint: The new technology helped to improve literacy and enhance the role of public opinion.)

4. How did religious and secular institutions attempt to limit monarchical power? (Hint: English Civil War, Thirty Years' War, religious minorities, religious pluralism.)

5. What was the impact of war and overseas exploration on European diplomacy? (Hint: Created the Peace of Westphalia and established nation-states—rather than churches—as the center of international politics, including colonial empires that lasted until the end of the 20th century; changed the balance of power.)

Theme 5: Individual and Society

1. What were the characteristics, practices, and beliefs of people in preindustrial Europe and how were they challenged by religion? (Hint: Subsistence on agriculture; urban expansion; people believed in a hierarchy, defined family, and gender roles; and the Church was the authority.)

2. How did identities (race and class) define the individual in relationship to society? (Hint: Think about hierarchies, religion, religious minorities, slaves, and the new economic elites from mercantilism.)

3. How did Europeans marginalize certain populations defined as "other"? (Hint: Slave trade, religious minorities, colonial conquests, urban migrants, witchcraft persecutions, and the regulation of morals.)

Theme 6: National and European Identity

1. How and why did national identities develop and spread? (Hint: Growing state control of religious institutions; nations were built on common language, religion, and cultural identity; competition between states for territories; invention of printing helped to spread new cultural ideas.)

2. How did political, economic, and religious developments challenge or reinforce the idea of a unified Europe from 1450 to the present? (Hint: Religious pluralism and religious divisions; the state control of religious institutions; economic motives for overseas expansion; trade networks; and overseas expansion.)

3. How did overseas expansion, warfare, and international diplomacy affect Europeans' identification of themselves? (Hint: Wars on religion, the rise of mercantilism, colonial competition, exposure to overseas people and goods, and the struggle for a balance of power all helped to shape new or merge old European identities.)

Important Events, Terms, and Concepts

The list that follows shows important events, terms, and concepts that you should be familiar with on the AP EURO exam. Please don't memorize each concept now. Place a check mark next to each topic as it is studied and refer to this list as often as necessary.

Events, Terms, and Concepts You Should Know					
Event	**Year/Brief Description**	**Study Page**	**Event**	**Year/Brief Description**	**Study Page**
The First Crusade	1096–1099. In response to Pope Urban II's request to free the city of Jerusalem, armies of Christians waged war against Muslim forces in the Holy Land. The First Crusade heightened conflict between the Christian and Muslim worlds.	p. 56	The Council of Trent	1543–1565. The Council of Trent was organized by the Catholic Church in response to the Protestant Reformation. The Council played an important role in revitalizing the Catholic Church in Europe.	p. 77
The Black Death	1347–1354. The Black Death reigned in Europe, decimating Europe's population, and undermining feudalism and the Church in the process.	pp. 56–57	Peace of Augsburg	1555. Also called the "Augsburg Settlement." The Holy Roman Empire (Germany) was divided by religion in order to maintain the peace. The Peace of Augsburg was the first legal basis for the coexistence of the Lutheran and Catholic religions in the region.	pp. 81–82
Gutenberg invents the printing press	1439. The printing press represented a quantum leap forward in human history. Education, religion, and politics were fundamentally changed by this technology.	p. 62	Charles V splits his empire between Spain and Austria	1556. This allowed the Habsburgs to encircle France, which would later have dangerous consequences for all of Europe.	pp. 80–81
The fall of the Byzantine Empire	1453. The end of Byzantine rule ended Rome's legacy and strengthened the Islamic threat.	pp. 83–84	The Eighty Years' War	1568–1648. Among all of Spain's disastrous wars, this one against the Dutch drained more of Spain's money, manpower, and morale than any other.	p. 85

Event	Year/Brief Description	Study Page	Event	Year/Brief Description	Study Page
Columbus sails to the West	1492. Columbus set out on an expedition looking for a trade route to China and India for gold, pearls, and spices, but discovered much more as he traveled westward. He found a new shipping route to carry goods to the New World colonies.	pp. 63–64	The Spanish Armada is destroyed	1588. The defeat of the Armada meant that England was safe from Spanish invasion and Protestantism was confirmed in England.	p. 86
Martin Luther publishes "The 95 Theses"	1517. Martin Luther published "The 95 Theses," attacking the Catholic Church's corrupt practices. The document had two main beliefs: The Bible was the only authority, and salvation could only be achieved by "faith," not "deeds." The publishing of his theses set off the Protestant Reformation.	pp. 73–75	The Thirty Years' War	1618–1648. This was the last large war fought in Europe over religious differences, and its end ushered in a new system of international balance.	pp. 88–90
The Society of Jesus is founded	1540. Known as Jesuits and founded by Ignatius of Loyola, this society was the key to the movement of the Counter-Reformation formed by the Catholic Church in Europe.	p. 77	The Peace of Westphalia	1648. A series of peace treaties that ended the Thirty Years' War and formally recognized European nation-states' balance of power.	pp. 92–93

HISTORIOGRAPHY. *After reviewing the chronological periods for the AP EURO exam, you may have wondered why the material for the test starts around the 15th century. Why doesn't the exam material start back in 476 C.E., when the Roman Empire collapsed and the medieval period began? Why is there little focus on the thousand years between the 5th century and the 15th century?*

The focus on roughly c. 1450 C.E. to the present is based on the era of Western Civilization in which Europe became the dominant force in the world. Today, as we live in the United States, our lives are shaped by centuries of European history, as seen in the proliferation of Western language, clothes, ideas, religion, food, and norms. It is easy to make the mistake of thinking that what is true today has always been true. It is easy to forget that in c. 1400, Christian Europe was backward, poor, and weak compared to the mighty empires of the Ottomans, the Ming Chinese, the Timurids, and African kingdoms.

Europe's quantum leap forward began in the late-15th and early-16th centuries, accelerating rapidly into the 17th, 18th, and 19th centuries. That is why we study this period in European history. The period from roughly c. 1450 to c. 1815 is called early modern European history, while c. 1815 to the present is simply modern European history.

Chapter Review

European history is divided into five time periods: 1) Prehistory, 2) Classical antiquity, 3) Middle Ages, 4) Early modern Europe, and 5) Modern Europe.

The AP EURO exam starts with early modern Europe from c. 1450 to c. 1648. As you examine the timeline that follows, it is important to realize that many of the historical events happened gradually over time during this period. The timeline should help you visually and conceptually identify what preceded and what followed particular events.

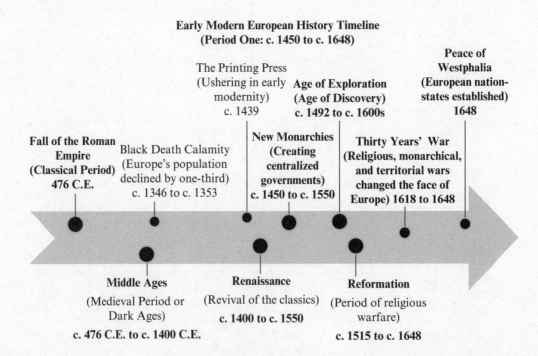

**Early Modern European History Timeline
(Period One: c. 1450 to c. 1648)**

The Printing Press (Ushering in early modernity) c. 1439

Age of Exploration (Age of Discovery) c. 1492 to c. 1600s

Peace of Westphalia (European nation-states established) 1648

Fall of the Roman Empire (Classical Period) 476 C.E.

Black Death Calamity (Europe's population declined by one-third) c. 1346 to c. 1353

New Monarchies (Creating centralized governments) c. 1450 to c. 1550

Thirty Years' War (Religious, monarchical, and territorial wars changed the face of Europe) 1618 to 1648

Middle Ages (Medieval Period or Dark Ages) c. 476 C.E. to c. 1400 C.E.

Renaissance (Revival of the classics) c. 1400 to c. 1550

Reformation (Period of religious warfare) c. 1515 to c. 1648

The Renaissance (c. 1400 to c. 1550)

While most historians agree that it is a matter of interpretation when the Renaissance actually started and ended, the Renaissance marked the arrival of early modern Europe roughly between the 15th and 17th centuries. The Renaissance began in Italy and then eventually spread westward into northern Europe. Known as a "rebirth" or "flowering" of the European civilization, the Renaissance is viewed by historians as a turning point for cultural, religious, and social European attitudes. It was during this period that Europeans showed a renewed interest in the cultural and intellectual achievements of Greek and Roman classical antiquities: art, literature, philosophy, and science.

Did you know? We often think of the Renaissance of classical culture in the West as a European phenomenon. What you might not know is that the Muslim world contributed to the chain of events that led to Europeans having a renewed interest in the classics of the Greeks and Romans. This was the missing link between the fall of the Roman Empire and the Renaissance 1,000 years later. While Europe languished in the Dark Ages, Muslim scholars studied, added to, and modified the classical works that eventually provided the foundation to the Renaissance. Europeans from the Euphrates to the Seine have many cultural groups of people from around the world to thank for the Renaissance.

AP EURO topics covered in this section:

- Pre-Renaissance Europe
- The Italian Renaissance
- Renaissance Humanism
- The Northern Renaissance

Pre-Renaissance Europe

Heads Up: What You Need to Know

The AP EURO exam may require that you identify some of the significant events preceding the Renaissance: 1) decline of religious authority; 2) fall of Constantinople; 3) renewed interest in the arts, literature, philosophy, and science; and 4) increased commerce and competition between the West and East.

Key Facts about Pre-Renaissance Europe

To understand the importance of how and why the Renaissance took place, we must backtrack a bit chronologically. After the fall of the Western Roman Empire in 476 C.E., Europe plunged into a period called the Middle Ages (also known as the medieval period or Dark Ages) roughly from the 5th to the 15th centuries. The Renaissance emerged after a long century of plague and famine setbacks from the Middle Ages.

Medieval thinking. While historians agree that the medieval period was not a time of universal ignorance, intellectuals (i.e., philosophers, artists, and scholars) derived some of their work from the Greek and Roman cultural remnants of the past. In medieval Europe, the Greek and Roman thinkers were only useful if their wisdom was placed in the context of great Christian intellectuals like St. Augustine or the Apostles. Intellectuals emphasized the tradition, dogma, and authority of the Church. All great thinkers, like St. Thomas Aquinas, viewed the theology of the Catholic Church as the source of *all* superior intellectual knowledge. Hence, individual inquiry and critical thinking (humanism) were largely ignored until the advent of the Renaissance, when people started to question the Church's authority.

Muslim influence. In one of the many ironies of history, the **Crusades** (the violent clash of the Christian and Muslim worlds that took place from the 11th to the 14th centuries) actually contributed to the cultural exchange between these rival civilizations. While these wars cost thousands of lives and exacerbated tensions between West and East, contact of any sort always advanced an exchange of goods, language, and ideas. European scholars discovered renewed interest in the arts, literature, philosophy, and science of the Greeks and Romans from their Muslim counterparts. While it took time, the reinvigorated interest in classical works was eventually ushered into the Renaissance.

Catholicism was central to everyday life. The Middle Ages marked the power of the Catholic Church over all of Christendom, religious control of culture, and a Catholic economy that emphasized honorable work rather than *usury* (the charging of interest), banking, or speculation.

Feudalism. The political and social foundation that dominated the Middle Ages was based on political decentralization, or feudalism. The basic structure of a feudal society was based on mutual obligation. In feudalism, people were granted a parcel of agricultural land by landowners (called "lord vassals") in exchange for services to protect the landowners in the event of war.

Social upheaval. Until the Late Middle Ages (14th century), the medieval period was a time of chaos and turmoil. After the destruction of the Roman Empire (the bedrock of Western Civilization), Europe was often in a state of fear and uncertainty. There were ravages of barbarian tribes; invaders from Scandinavia, Central Asia, and the Far East; and religious and social upheaval. Finally, in the Late Middle Ages, a time of relative stability followed.

Ultimately, the shift from the medieval period to the Renaissance was a move in the direction of modernity and planted the seeds for the modern age of Western Europe.

> TEST TIP: On the AP EURO exam, always remember to examine the positive and negative attitudes, sentiments, and experiences of people living in a particular time period. The mindset of people is always shaped by the conditions of the time in which they lived. People are always influenced by a larger cultural context of their social environment. For example, the mindset of people who lived through the tumultuous events of the medieval period was profoundly different from the mindset of people who lived during the revitalization of the Renaissance.

The 14th-century calamity: Black Death (c. 1346 to c. 1353). When historian Barbara Tuchman wrote about the 20th-century world wars, genocide, pandemics, and unprecedented brutality, she argued that the 14th century was like a mirror of the 20th century. Why? Because the 1300s were a time of violence, fear, strife, disease, and ignorance. After centuries of progress in improving the material, emotional, and spiritual lives of ordinary Europeans at a glacial pace, the 1300s embodied a dramatic drop in the health and well-being of Europe and its people. As depicted in the illustration below, a major part of this cataclysmic century was the **Black Death,** also known as the *bubonic plague.*

Source: *The Dance of Death* (1493) by Michael Wolgemut, from the *Liber chronicarum* by Hartmann Schedel.

The Black Death came to Europe in 1347 from Sicilian sailors who had been fighting against the Mongols in the Crimea, a landmass in the Black Sea. Unknowingly, these sailors brought this horrific disease with them as they returned home from the fighting. The plague struck Italy, France, and the Holy Roman Empire. Eventually, the Mediterranean and Atlantic began closing their ports to trade ships, but it was too late. Europe was in the grip of the Black Death, a pandemic that killed one-third of Europe's population.

Key Facts about the Impact of the Black Death

- Population decline. The Black Death killed approximately 75–100 million people.
- Animals died (sheep, goats, pigs, chickens, and cows), which caused a shortage of food and clothing (made of sheep's wool).
- Villages were devastated. Shopkeepers closed stores, causing a shortage of goods and services.
- Doctors refused to see patients, and church clerics refused to administer last rites. (Note: The Church was considered the ultimate authority. People believed the last rite sacrament was their path to heaven.)
- People abandoned their loved ones to escape to distant cities or countrysides to save their own lives.

TEST TIP: The Black Death is an important historical turning point that is frequently referenced on the AP EURO exam. Because Church officials blamed the disease on man's sinfulness and God's punishment, many ordinary Christians began to question the Catholic Church and other sources of authority. This set the stage for the religious crisis during the Renaissance, and later for the Protestant Reformation and the Scientific Revolution.

The Italian Renaissance

It should come as no surprise that a renewal of interest in the classics started in Italy. Several reasons why Italy became the focal point of this rebirth will follow.

Key Facts about the Causes of the Italian Renaissance

The rise of independent city-states. First, keep in mind that Italy was not always the unified nation-state that it has been since 1871. Historians use the term "Italy" (contemporaries also used this term in the 15th century), but there was no such official country as Italy until the 19th century. In the 1400s, Italy was divided into over a dozen independent city-states, with the French and Spanish vying to make imperial inroads from the north and south. The major city-states were Florence, Milan, Venice, Rome, and Naples. Florence is where the Italian Renaissance first began.

The competition between political powers drove innovation. The pope personally controlled a large **demesne** (land held by the pope) around Rome, which was called the *Papal Estates*. The division of the Italian peninsula is important because, as many historians and social scientists argue, competition between political powers often drives innovation. Historians argue that this type of division is what drove ancient Greece to its civilizational position of brilliance. Some historians even argue that Europe entered its Golden Age from the 16th to 20th centuries because it was so divided, rather than united, as were East Asia and the Muslim world.

The center of a trade-enriched economy. The city-state system had other perks. The Italian city-states were centers of mercantile alliances. The city-states had ingenious forms of economic businesses, from textile production and glassmaking to banking and overseas trading. City-states flourished with tremendous economic growth and prosperity because they were no longer ruled by powerful monarchical kings demanding taxation and feudal obligations. This prosperity laid the foundation for the cultural golden age of the Italian Renaissance.

The wealthy patrons became supporters of the arts. Due to the flourishing economy, as well as input from a Catholic Church that was increasingly interested in culture, a large base of wealthy *patrons* (supporters of the arts) requested great works of art in libraries, museums, and books. Artists did not earn a regular salary at this time, so even the greatest sculptors, painters, and writers were forced to create their works of art by sponsorship or patronage from the Church, Italian lords and ladies, or wealthy investors. Among the most wealthy art patrons was the Medici family of Florence who supported Leonardo da Vinci and Michelangelo.

The growth in population. Italian city-states saw great population growth from the 13th century on. Cities like Florence and Venice were more urban than much of Western Europe. This urbanity led to a type of sophistication of taste and cultivation of artistic education and talent.

Did you know? Art is often classified by historical periods because of its political, cultural, and social influences. Against the backdrop of growing economic prosperity, the Renaissance style of art became more realistic than the style of art composed during the medieval era—when artists purposely tried not to re-create reality. For example, during the Middle Ages when artists painted a castle siege, the leading generals were often depicted twice as tall as the walls of the castle. Another famous example of Middle Ages art is the image of the Madonna (St. Mary) with her son, Jesus Christ. Modern observers are often surprised to see that the baby Jesus is disproportionately large compared to his adult mother.

In contrast, during the Renaissance, artists rediscovered the style of painting and sculpting to portray human anatomy, emotion, and perspective in a realistic way, almost like a photograph. This artistic rebirth not only sought to capture the human experience of the beauty of the natural world, but it was also the rebirth of the Greco-Roman classical forms of art. Art was expressed like the reality it was meant to portray—from size, proportion, and scale to color and perspective.

Leonardo da Vinci

When we think of the cultural flourish of the Italian Renaissance, we often think of great artists such as Leonardo da Vinci, Michelangelo, and Raphael and their famous works of art. Leonardo da Vinci, known as the "Renaissance man," painted the *Mona Lisa, The Last Supper, The Creation of Man,* and the *Vitruvian Man;* he was also the source of myriad inventions, philosophical adages, and excellent quotes. He was considered the universal genius of western history because he was not only one of the greatest artists of European history, but also an extremely gifted scientist, inventor, and mathematician.

Source: *Mona Lisa* (c. 1503–1506) by Leonardo da Vinci.

TEST TIP: On the AP EURO free-response questions, Leonardo da Vinci is an excellent reference for the Renaissance culture. His work captures the characteristics of the Renaissance—one's eternal search for beauty, knowledge, and wisdom.

Renaissance Humanism

Humanism was a key movement of new philosophical and literary ideas during the Renaissance. The birth of humanism can be traced to the Renaissance scholars' rediscovery of studying the Greek and Roman ancient works in the field of humanities: philosophy, art, literature, and politics.

Heads Up: What You Need to Know

The concept of **humanism** is a common question on the AP EURO exam. It is the cornerstone of the Renaissance and is one of the most important distinctions between the Middle Ages and the Renaissance.

What is humanism? Humanism was not antireligious, but a *movement* toward learning. People who lived in the Middle Ages blindly followed religious orthodoxy, but during the Renaissance people started to follow intellectual wisdom and knowledge—characteristics of humanism.

At the most basic level, humanism placed the focus of knowledge and learning on human beings and their ability to critically think, reason, and investigate. This may seem pretty obvious—who else would be the focus, aliens? Actually, this was an unusual perspective because it overturned a millenium of people focusing on God (and seeking salvation after death to get to heaven) to focusing on humans. Instead of an afterlife salvation, or damnation, being the guiding principle of human life, humanism spotlighted the value of the earthly lives of people. Humanism was a new form of modern individualism.

Key Facts about Renaissance Humanism

Art. Humanism was most evident in the form of art and education. Many of the most famous forms of art from this period, including the *Mona Lisa,* were portraits. Portraits were not new in the Renaissance, but became far more commonplace when successful merchants and bankers would pay artists to create lifelike portraits and sculptures. The focus of these portraits was the portrayal of individual humanism, not religious and political figures and events. During the Renaissance, artists also turned to the Classical Period to depict mythological themes and characters. The classical standards of beauty became popular, from the *Venus de Milo* to Michelangelo's *David*.

Education. In contrast to the medieval form of education, which was dominant for centuries and focused on religious education, theology, and understanding truth as illustrated in the Bible, the humanist approach to education focused on the Greek and Roman classics. These classics were studied in order to learn more practical facts and theories about science, math, art, and philosophy. Scholarship in history, rhetoric, and philosophy focused less on the Catholic doctrine and more on the scientific natural world.

Did you know? The term *Renaissance man* is used today to reference someone who is adeptly well-rounded in many disciplines (a *polymath*). The Renaissance man has become an archetype to show that a person's value and worth were not solely based on his relationship to the Church and to God, but on the skills, knowledge, and talents epitomized by the Renaissance.

Early humanists. The early humanistic views were primarily those of well-educated Italian upper classes. Francesco Petrarch (1304–1374) was a scholar, writer, and poet, and considered the father of humanism because he rediscovered the literary classics like Plato and the letters of Cicero. Another famous early humanist was Niccoló Machiavelli.

Niccoló Machiavelli's *The Prince*

Niccoló Machiavelli (1469–1527) was a high-ranking Italian diplomat and political philosopher in the Republic of Florence who posthumously published a famous political treatise called *The Prince.*

Heads Up: What You Need to Know

On the AP EURO exam, be prepared to answer questions related to the key ideas of Machiavelli's *The Prince.* Make sure you are not only familiar with what he argued in *The Prince,* but also how his famous sayings continued to be used to explain the political actions of other historical figures later on in European history, such as French leader Cardinal Richelieu, German Chancellor Otto von Bismarck, or Soviet dictator Joseph Stalin.

Key Facts about Machiavelli's *The Prince*

Depicted a ruler's ruthless conduct. *The Prince* comprises essay outlines written by Machiavelli to advise a ruler (the prince) on the ruthless conduct necessary for securing and maintaining political power. *The Prince* has great historical significance because Machiavelli's proposed advice has been successfully applied throughout history by many statesmen. Machiavelli's philosophy represented a dramatic shift from Europe's honorable diplomacy to new principles of realistic, but less principled, methods to secure power.

Depicted examples from personal observations. By the time Machiavelli wrote *The Prince*, he had become deeply cynical about human nature. Machiavelli was a brilliant and astute thinker who witnessed the constant warfare and destruction of Italy by France and Spain for decades. He believed that Italy was a great civilization of genius and the rightful heir to the great Roman and Byzantine empires. Machiavelli also believed that the French and Spaniards were inferior barbarians who had military power over the Italians, but did not have cultural supremacy.

Separated moral and ethical rules from politics. According to Machiavelli, a prince should not make his decisions based on the medieval code of honor and chivalry, nor should he worry too much about the morality of the Church and the Bible. These codes of morality might guide lesser men, but a man with the reins of state in his hands must look to more ruthless ends. The prince must do what other men would not do in order to succeed over his enemies to usher in stability and prosperity.

Believed that the prince should be merciless to secure power. Machiavelli believed that the character of human nature was deceitful, corrupt, and manipulative and that the world was filled with liars, traitors, and cons. For a prince to achieve his goals, he must be "as strong as a lion and wise as a fox." Most of all, the prince should know that the ends justify the means. If the goal is good, any method (even if it is brutal, vicious, or reprehensible) is acceptable as the price to pay for the desired outcome.

Did you know? The term *Machiavellian* has become synonymous with describing a ruthless ruler who is immoral and deceitful. To describe someone as Machiavellian is not a compliment. On the other hand, despite the abuse of the term, for centuries many statesmen and politicians have acted based on Machiavelli's realism, without the toxic label. As so often happens with great minds, Machiavelli's ideas have become somewhat oversimplified and perverted over time.

The Northern Renaissance

When we think of the Renaissance, we often think first and foremost of Italy. But don't forget about the crucial trajectory of the Renaissance in thought and culture that took place in Northern Europe at the time. In the 1400s, it started with the spread of Christian humanism as a philosophy. Because of the famous universities in the Italian city-states, such as Bologna and Padua, many Dutch, German, French, and English intellectual elites learned from the humanist traditions in the Italian peninsula and brought these ideas back north and west.

Christian humanism. The major difference between Italian and Northern humanism was the important role that Christianity played in the Northern Renaissance. Northern Christian humanists believed that combining Christian and Classical ideas would lead to increased religious spirituality. One of the founders of Christian humanism was **Desiderius Erasmus,** a great scholar of Catholic Europe who in many ways straddled the two periods of the Renaissance and the Reformation. He was well-read in theology and debated about many topics, often criticizing the Catholic Church for its inertia and its corruption, though he never went so far as to leave the Church (unlike other reformers) and was never excommunicated by the papacy. Erasmus sought to reform, rather than destroy, the Catholic Church by giving it a more human face and adapting it to the changing times. Other humanist philosophers, such as England's **Thomas More,** sought to reconcile the ancient dogma and practice of Catholicism with the new ideology of humanism and the rediscovered tenets of classicism.

Northern Renaissance artists. Northern artists had their own Renaissance, just as important as their philosophical and literary counterparts. Specializing in oil paintings, these Northern artists used the advances of the Italian Renaissance to craft their own unique style, utilizing geometry, realism, and perspectives. Like their Italian counterparts, Northern Renaissance artists often painted portraits of the "new rich" merchants and diplomats. In contrast to the Italians, the Northern artists often painted natural scenes, focusing on a rambling river, a freezing mountainside, or a placid field. Thus, the Northern Renaissance demonstrated not only humanism, but also a renewed focus on nature. Jan van Eyck is one of the most well-known artists of this period. He had a number of famous works, including *Ghent Altarpiece*. He and other Northern Renaissance painters not only trail-blazed a new path in art, but they also set the stage for future generations of famous artists from France, the Low Countries, and Germany.

Heads Up: What You Need to Know

The **printing press** was one of the most significant inventions known to mankind. On the AP EURO exam, it is important to explain why the printing press was significant during this time period (see below).

Key Facts about the Printing Press

Johannes Gutenberg, a German printer and *polymath* (a person who is an expert in several subjects), invented the printing press with movable type in 1439 during the Northern Renaissance. It took several decades before the printing press was widely used across the majority of the European continent, but the invention of the printing press represented a quantum shift in the history of humanity.

During the medieval period prior to the Renaissance, writers, monks, or scholars would spend several months handwriting and illustrating a book manually. With the advent of the printing press, that same book might be published in a matter of days, or even hours, depending on its length. Literature became a part of the lives of more people than ever before, not just the wealthy elite. Short pamphlets and news bulletins (which proved to be incredibly important to the outbreak of the Protestant Reformation, and later the advent of the Scientific Revolution and the Enlightenment) could be published even more rapidly.

It is mind-blowing to consider the shift from handwritten books to printed books. For example, in the entire 15th century, only about 100,000 printed copies of books were published in all of Europe. In the 16th century, that number grew to more than 200 million printed books! The printing press allowed the exponentially more rapid proliferation of ideas, arguments, and news across the face of the continent and spurred the growth of literacy and the consolidation of new ideas among Europeans.

Heads Up: What You Need to Know

On the AP EURO exam, make sure you have a broad understanding of the similarities and differences between the Italian and Northern renaissances. When comparing the two, don't just focus on art—consider geography, religion, philosophy, and education.

Compare and Contrast the Italian Renaissance and the Northern Renaissance	
Italian Renaissance	**Northern Renaissance**
The Italian Renaissance started c. 1400 in the Republic of Florence (today's Florence, Italy). The Holy Roman Empire lost power in Italy, and independent city-states emerged in Florence, Milan, Venice, Rome, and Naples.	The Northern Renaissance started c. 1450 in the Netherlands (today's Central Europe—in Belgium, Holland, Switzerland, and Germany).
Art and architecture was inspired by classical mythology, ornate scenes, and realistic anatomy. Wealthy patrons supported the arts, and for the first time artists became rich. Fresco, tempera, and oil were the predominant mediums. Artist examples: Michelangelo and Leonardo da Vinci.	Art and architecture was inspired by a distinctive artistic style that focused on natural landscape, daily life portraits, and religious scenes. Oil paint was the predominant medium. Artist example: Jan van Eyck.
The Italian Renaissance city-states were the center for economic wealth, trade, and commerce.	Northerners had fewer centers of economic commerce. However, one of the most important technological advancements happened during the Northern Renaissance—the invention of the printing press.
Italians believed in Catholicism, but focused on religious-based humanism.	Northerners were Catholic, but sought to reform religion. They focused on secular humanism (how humanism might transform the Catholic religion). These beliefs were closely linked to the Protestant Reformation that followed in the 16th century.
Italian humanists were inspired by secular intellectual wisdom and knowledge from the Greek and Roman classics of philosophy, art, literature, and education.	Northern Christian humanists believed that combining Christian and Classical ideas would lead to increased religious spirituality.

The Age of Exploration (c. 1492 to c. 1600)

Christopher Columbus

Key Facts about the Voyages of Christopher Columbus

"In 1492, Columbus sailed the Ocean Blue." Students have used this rhyme for decades to remember the year in which **Christopher Columbus** set out on his momentous voyage across the Atlantic Ocean. We all know the story of how Columbus believed, against the opinion of many Europeans, that the world was round and could be circumnavigated (sailed around). Most of us learned that Columbus meant to find India, and he thought he did, which is why some historians say that Native Americans were called "Indians." History shows that Columbus sailed for King Ferdinand and Queen Isabella of Spain and made it possible for Spain to acquire much wealth.

With well-known historical events, such as the voyage of Columbus, we should backtrack for a moment to separate truth from myth, and history from legend.

Columbus was not the first to discover the Americas. First, we need to reconsider the importance of Columbus' explorations. Columbus was not the first European to set sight upon the shores of the Americas, but he was the first to "settle" in the Americas. Most historians believe that c. 1000, the Vikings were the first to set their sights on the Americas. Other groups may have made similar journeys. For example, some historians believe that the Chinese sent ships to the Pacific side of North America in the 15th century.

Columbus' importance, historically, is that his explorations were the first that led to the permanent settlement of the New World by people from the Old World. His ships entered the Caribbean and stumbled upon an island that the Spaniards labeled Hispaniola (today, the island is split between Haiti and the Dominican Republic).

Columbus was not the first to prove the earth was round. Second, Columbus was not the first to prove that the earth was round, in contradiction of the universally held myth that it was flat. In fact, knowledge that the earth was a sphere went back over 2,000 years before Columbus. The Greek philosopher Pythagoras is considered one of the first to have made this argument. However, it is true that most Europeans in the 15th century had little to no education, could not read or write, and knew little about science compared to the educated elites.

HISTORIOGRAPHY. *Is Columbus the hero who Americans have studied in school? Or is he the villain that some have described over the past few decades? The answer is complicated (as with many historical figures). On the one hand, Columbus did things that we would consider immoral today, such as enslaving and killing native Indian men, women, and children in the Caribbean islands. Columbus certainly had no qualms about using brute force to accomplish his goals. On the other hand, and without resorting to abject moral relativism, we can acknowledge the fact that people acted very differently 500 years ago. Ruthlessness was not atypical of people of his time and culture. It would be unfair to judge Columbus so harshly by the standards of our own time and to not do so to everyone else who lived in the late-15th century.*

Exploring New Trade Routes

TEST TIP: Use the following key facts to answer questions on the AP EURO exam about why Europeans wanted to find a new trade route to China and India.

Key Facts about the Reasons for Exploring a New Trade Route

Europeans needed valuable goods to correct the trade imbalance with China. Ever since the days of the Roman Empire, Europeans had suffered from a trade imbalance with the Chinese on the Eurasian trade route called the *Silk Road*. Simply put, the Chinese had the luxury of many valuable trade goods, from silk and porcelain to spices and dyes. The only goods that the Europeans had that could make up for this imbalance were silver and gold, which were not common. Europeans hoped to find new sources of these precious metals, and perhaps other goods, to trade with China.

Europeans needed a new trade route. Recall that animosity between the West and the Muslim world had been cemented by the experience of the Crusades and other intercultural conflicts over religion. Keep in mind that around 1492, Muslim powers encircled almost all of Christian Europe, from the Mongols in Russia and the Safavids in Persia to the Ottomans in the Near East and the Mamluks in North Africa. Faced with paying fees to trade and possible hostile Muslim powers, Europeans had two main choices of trade routes. In conjunction with the spread of plague, the high cost of trade and the hostility of these Muslim powers effectively ended the old Silk Road. Europeans could travel south, around the Cape of Good Hope at the bottom of the African continent, or they could try to forge a path west, directly to China and India. It is in search of this westward route around the globe that Columbus and other explorers got their start.

European missionaries sought converts. Missionary zeal was kindled in both Catholic and Protestant churches by the Reformation. New religious orders like the Jesuits brought faith to newly discovered lands, while older orders sought out new converts amongst the native Indians to replace the lost Catholic populations of Northern Europe.

Europeans who were persecuted wanted to form new societies. Persecuted religious groups went to the New World to form new societies, either theocratic havens or ones of openness and tolerance. Rather than living in a society with religious persecution—for example, the Dutch dissidents, English Puritans, French Huguenots (French Protestants), and Spanish Conversos (Jews who adopted Christianity)—they fled to build communities based on their faiths.

Heads Up: What You Need to Know

The AP EURO exam commonly asks you to differentiate between the two eras of European imperialism overseas.

Historians currently recognize the **First Wave of Imperialism** between c. 1450 to c. 1800. It was principally centered in North and South America and the Caribbean (with small inroads into Africa, India, and East Asia). The **Second Wave of Imperialism** took place from c. 1850 to c. 1950 and was focused in Africa, South Asia, East Asia, and the Middle East. In Period Three and Period Four, we will see very different political justifications, cultural manifestations, and economic aspects of the Second Wave as opposed to the First Wave.

Spain's Colonization in the New World

In 1450, Spain seemed an unlikely country to become the dominant power in Europe. Its culture was considered pitiful, its military was respectable but hardly legendary, and its customs were considered backward and superstitious. And yet, 50 years later, Spain had dramatically risen to become the dominant power in the world, a place it would hold for nearly a century.

Key Facts about Spain's Colonization

Spain's colonization. Spain began its process of discovery, conquests, and colonization in the islands of the Caribbean from Hispaniola to Cuba, Puerto Rico, and smaller islands. Some islands that were later conquered by the British or Dutch, such as Jamaica and Trinidad, were first settled by Spaniards. In the 1490s, the first generation of explorers speculated that the islands of Cuba might be several times larger than Spain. Only two decades later, however, the world of the Caribbean had become all too small for some enterprising men; it would be these men who made inroads into the great landmasses of North and South America in the years that followed.

TEST TIP: For the AP EURO exam, remember Spain's two main conquests: 1) the conquest of today's Mexico, and 2) the conquest of today's Peru.

Spain's conquest of the Aztec Empire in Mexico. During the 1510s and the early colonization of Cuba, Hernan Cortes arrived. This son of military pedigree decided to make an expedition to the continent of North America against the wishes of his governor, Diego Velazquez. In 1519, Cortes and about 500 men landed in the Yucatan Peninsula and marched into the Aztec Empire, picking up Native Indian allies along the way, which led to a much larger force. Cortes promised to help liberate the people from the *tribute system* (the subordinate role of conquered people). With the help of a native woman who served as a translator, named La Malinche, Cortes was able to negotiate with the Aztec emperor, Montezuma, who initially tried to appease Cortes. Blinded with greed, the Spaniards held Montezuma hostage and eventually killed him and demolished the Aztec Empire. With the leader of the empire destroyed and huge numbers of Aztecs dying from smallpox and other diseases, the Spaniards acquired the land and enforced a new empire. To avoid the wrath of Governor Velasquez, Cortes made his conquests directly for the King of Spain, Charles V. For his part, the king was all too pleased to have gained this empire without any effort from him, and he duly granted feudal *encomiendas* (land and labor grants), to Cortes and many of his men. Thanks to the memoirs of one of Cortes' soldiers, Bernal Diaz del Castillo, the story of these great *conquistadors* (conquerors) has made its place in history.

Spain's conquest of the Inca Empire in Peru. Only a few years later, a man of lower birth status and fewer talents than Cortes (his distant relative), Francisco Pizarro, made his own expedition to South America. After many years of failed attempts, Pizarro made his way into the heart of the Inca Empire in the Andes mountain region in 1532. He encountered Atahualpa, the Inca emperor. Atahualpa had over 100,000 men and had been fighting a civil war, making them weakened and divided; Pizarro had fewer than 200. At the Battle of Cajamarca, the Spaniards used disease, gunpowder, and their horses to crush an exponentially larger Inca army. The Spaniards disease captured Atahualpa, who promised to fill three rooms with silver and gold as a ransom for his life. After receiving the ransom in precious metals, Pizarro brutally murdered Atahualpa and other hostages, an act that even Charles V condemned as an atrocity. A few months later, the Spaniards completed the dismantling of the Inca imperial structure by marching into Cuzco, the capital. Another empire had been conquered, seemingly overnight, by an intrepid band of Spanish conquistadors.

Spain's conquest of Central America. While Mexico (the New Spain) and Peru were the largest and most famous conquests, simultaneously there were small, less glorious expeditions of Spaniards that slowly made inroads into and eventually colonized Central America, the north and south of South America, and today's Florida, Texas, and western United States. By the end of the 16th century, Spain had the largest overseas empire in world history, with massive territories stretching from the Rio Grande to Cape Horn.

Did you know? When stories of Spain's conquests by Cortes and Pizarro made their way to Europe, people were awed by these conquistadors. How did small bands of men bring down two massive empires? While we should not dismiss the bravery, fortitude, and genius of these conquerors, the Spaniards had several advantages. 1) The natives had inferior weapons. Conquistadors used steel weapons, armor, gunpowder, war dogs, and horses. The natives used stone arrows and spears and were terrified of horses because they had never seen them before. 2) The natives did not have resistance to European diseases. The conquistadors had built up immunities to European diseases, but the native population died from smallpox, measles, and other illnesses. 3) The natives misunderstood who the conquistadors were when they arrived. The natives believed in a prophecy that the Aztec god Quetzalcoatl, who was known for the creation of humans, was set to return to Earth in or around that year. When the Spaniards entered Aztec territory, the Aztecs thought Cortes could be Quetzalcoatl, so the Spaniards were greeted with great honor. The Spaniards may have exaggerated this, however, and it is hard to gauge the impact of this prophecy among ordinary Aztecs. Ultimately, we can assert that the Spaniards had many built-in advantages without taking away from the greatness of their achievements in conquering the New World.

HISTORIOGRAPHY. *One of the most powerful and lasting historiographical trends was what is now called the* **Black Legend of Spain.** *In 1542, a Dominican friar named Bartolomeo de las Casas wrote an account of the pillages committed against the Native American Indians by the Spanish colonists, which he had witnessed firsthand. Based upon these lurid accounts, the enemies of Catholic Spain—primarily England and Holland— spread propaganda characterizing the Spaniards as brutal murderers. This characterization was useful when Spain was a great power, treading over smaller powers, but it did not go away as Spain declined. As late as the 19th century, the trope of the Spaniard was uniquely brutal, part Catholic fanatic and part vicious murderer. In the 20th century, Spanish historians labeled this La Leyenda Negra: the Black Legend. The Spaniards were unquestionably brutal in their treatment of the indigenous populations, but no more so than the English, Dutch, or Portuguese. Even the French, often considered the most benevolent colonists of the Americas, were known to display inhuman cruelty when the opportunity presented itself.*

Portugal's Colonization

Portugal started overseas imperialism even earlier than Spain. However, their empire was initially in the Eastern, not Western, Hemisphere.

Key Facts about Portugal's Colonization

Portugal explored the coast of Africa. A century before Columbus set sail, the Portuguese had been exploring and mapping the coast of Africa. They discovered a pathway around the Cape of Good Hope en route to India. Encountering natives on the coasts of West and southern East Africa, they built up trading networks to gain gold, silver, and other precious metals. The Portuguese also began buying up slaves from local dealers. Many slaves were Africans who had been captured as prisoners of war during perennial internal conflicts, although sometimes the Portuguese captured slaves of their own.

Portugal colonized off the coast of the Indian Ocean. By the end of the 15th century, Portugal pushed forward from the African coastline farther east. In 1498, **Vasco da Gama,** an explorer and navigator in the service of the king of Portugal, entered the Indian Ocean. He made his way to several Indian port cities, from Mombasa to Calicut. The Portuguese fleets set up trade networks from China to Africa, establishing a massive trade route that profited the Portuguese kings and their trading partners for centuries. The Portuguese made a few small permanent settlements in the Indian subcontinent, including Goa, which they conquered in 1510; it remained a colony for over 450 years, until 1961! It was one of the longest-lasting European settlements of all time.

Portugal colonized in Brazil. Portugal established an empire in the New World, just as did Spain. Their explorers traveled far and wide and made discoveries that may surprise you. For example, in the first decade of the 1500s, Portuguese explorers discovered today's Canada and Newfoundland. They set up a few small settlements and established ties with local natives, but permanent settlements were not forthcoming. However, in 1500, the ships of Portugal came across Brazil. There were no grand conquests to match Spain's, as Brazil was not the center of great empires like the Aztecs or Incas. For five decades, the kings of Portugal sent men, resources, and slaves to carve out a massive colony in Brazil. With an excess of land available, Portugal set up large sugar plantations that were valuable as a trade commodity in Europe.

Spain and Portugal established dominance. In 1494, the papacy weighed in on the imperial projects of Spain and Portugal, the two Iberian kingdoms. Pope Alexander VI, who was born in Spain and who allied himself with the Spanish monarchs, passed a *papal bull* (or declaration) that eventually became the *Treaty of Tordesillas.* This treaty split the New World between Spain and Portugal, which the Church considered to be its two most faithful children. Although very little was known about the size of the Americas in 1494, the demarcation line gave Portugal the Azores and Cape Verde islands, and much of what is Brazil today. Everything to the west of Brazil was granted to Spain. Armed with the legitimacy of this official papal declaration, Spain and Portugal honored the Treaty of Tordesillas for centuries, with conscientious attempts to observe it as late as the 1770s. France, England, Holland, and other European powers were completely left out of the treaty, so they ignored it as they set up their own empires. Nevertheless, the treaty established a lion's share of Spanish and Portuguese dominance in the New World in the 16th century.

France, England, and Holland's Colonization

While the French, English, and Dutch were late in the game of American imperialism compared to the Spanish and Portuguese, they more than made up for lost time.

Key Facts about France, England, and Holland's Colonization in the Americas

France colonized in Canada. France had been exploring the New World shortly after Spain and Portugal, but took much longer to lay down substantial roots in the Americas. In the 1530s, Jacques Cartier was sent to map out Canada's St. Lawrence River by the French monarchy. France also explored the Rio de Espiritu Santo, or what we now call the Mississippi. Many decades later in 1608, the French established a colony in Quebec, which would eventually become the center of the colony of New France. From the early-17th century until the loss of this North American empire in 1763, New France was characterized as sparsely populated. The colony grew to be massive in size on the map, but few colonists could be spared by France, and fewer still brought wives or families with them. The colonists who did travel to the Americas were mostly fur trappers or traders who dealt with the local native Indian tribes throughout the Canadian and Louisiana territories. Because there were few colonists, they depended heavily on the native Indians. The French were known for having the most amiable relations with local native Indians out of all of the European imperial powers in the New World.

Britain colonized in North America and the Caribbean. The British laid the most important foundation of Western Civilization in North America. British colonists established settlements in three American regions: Southern colonies, New England colonies, and Middle colonies.

British Colonial Settlements in North America		
Settlement	**States**	**Description**
Southern Colonies	Virginia, Maryland, North Carolina, South Carolina, and Georgia	In 1607, King James I of England sent colonists to establish the Jamestown colony (Virginia), the first permanent British settlement after decades of failed colonial projects such as Roanoke Island (North Carolina). The Jamestown expedition was funded by investors from the London Company, a joint-stock company that was later taken over by the British crown. The Jamestown colony focused less on religious sectarian conflicts and more on building economic prosperity and commerce while cultivating cash crops such as tobacco, and later cotton. In this colony, the power of aristocratic transplants from England competed with the rise of self-made merchant classes.
New England Colonies	Massachusetts, New Hampshire, Rhode Island, and Connecticut	Unlike the stockholders of the London Company who funded the Jamestown colony, the founders of the New England colonies were driven to the Americas by their religious beliefs. In 1620, a group of Calvinist dissidents who wanted to reform the Church of England, known as Pilgrims (a coalition of separatist Puritans), fled the persecution and chaos in England to establish the Plymouth Rock colony (Massachusetts). With the assistance and kindness of local Powhatan Indians, the colonists survived long decades of hardship and eventually built up a thriving subsistence agriculture economy that strengthened their sense of community around their faith. In time, these New Englanders began an early protocapitalist economy built around investments and mercantile trading in large port cities like Boston.

Settlement	States	Description
Middle Colonies	New York, Pennsylvania, Delaware, and New Jersey	In 1609, the Dutch began their explorations with Henry Hudson's voyage of what is now called the Hudson River. In the next two decades, the Dutch began to expand farther south into different islands in the Caribbean, and in 1624 New Netherland was established in what is today New York State. Based on the leadership of the Dutch West India Company, the colony of New Netherland grew and prospered while also remaining under constant threat from larger, more powerful European nations. Even the Swedes were able to make inroads into Dutch territory, establishing New Sweden in today's Delaware and lasting for two decades until the Dutch finally put an end to it in 1655. In 1667, without much military support from the homeland, the Dutch colonists surrendered their North American colony to the British. Although the British royal governors in charge of the colony gave its people no legislative representation, Dutch settlers continued to influence architecture, culture, and trade. Fur and farms generated incomes. Wheat and grains often provided food for neighboring regions and the thriving port of New York soon became central to the area's commercial interests.

During that time, the Dutch compensated for these losses by building extremely profitable colonies in the Caribbean, centered on sugar production. The Dutch also carved out parts of Portugal's Brazilian colony during Holland's perennial wars with Spain (which controlled Portugal from 1580 to 1640). The main legacy of the Dutch in the Americas, outside of a few scattered remnants of Dutch and Walloons (Belgium) culture in New England, has been that of intrepid merchants and planters exploiting tiny Caribbean colonies.

The British also began to explore and map out the Caribbean, but their largest conquests in this area, such as Jamaica, did not come until the next historical period of the AP EURO exam (Period Two).

TEST TIP: On the AP EURO exam, you will be asked to examine the similarities and differences, or strengths and weaknesses, of separate nations. For example, the large European empires of Spain, Portugal, England, France, and Holland all had common practices of strength, ideology, and statecraft. Compare and contrast these empires.

An important commonality between all of these major empires was that each European mother country had experience in "practicing" colonization before they conquered lands during their explorations. For example, the Spanish had been involved in colonizing the Canary Islands, just south of the Iberian Peninsula and off the coast of North Africa, for almost a century before Columbus sailed to the west. The Spanish had defeated and subjugated the natives and sent Castilians into the islands. Portugal, for its part, had been involved in conquering the Azores Islands, tiny islands in the Atlantic to the west of Portugal, in the years around the turn of the 16th century. The English had spent a few centuries attacking and colonizing Ireland, most recently in the mid-15th century. The French had a sort of continental colonization themselves in their seizing of eastern territories such as Burgundy and Picardy, which had been mortal enemies for many centuries. For all of these countries, experience was gained, lessons were learned, and techniques were sharpened in these colonization exercises. These experiences greatly aided in the success of much larger empires built in the Americas from the 15th to 18th centuries.

The Columbian Exchange

In the 1970s, a historian named Alfred Crosby wrote a book, *The Columbian Exchange*, that was a foundation for discussions of the European explorations. The book illuminated the system of trade, transference, and migrations that resulted from the European colonization of the Americas. According to

Crosby, the Columbian Exchange generated the transfer of organisms in both directions across the Atlantic. It fundamentally transformed both the New World and the Old World and the social, agricultural, biological, and cultural makeup of both Europeans and indigenous peoples. By exchanging animals, plants, goods, people, and diseases the Columbian Exchange significantly reduced the figurative size of the Atlantic Ocean that separated the New World from the Old World.

Key Facts about the Columbian Exchange

Animals, plants, and goods exchanged. First and foremost, many animals, plants, and goods were transferred from one place to another. The Europeans brought with them beasts of burden, horses, and military technologies like gunpowder, steel weapons, and heavy armor. They also brought animals like cows, chickens, pigs, and sheep. In terms of goods, some were cash crops, or goods useful for their trade value. The New World contributed tobacco, chocolate, vanilla, gold, and silver. In terms of staple crops, or food, the Europeans brought with them wheat, rice, sugar, and coffee, but discovered corn, tomatoes, potatoes, squash, and beans.

Culinary culture exchanged. The export of New World goods to the Old World had long-term effects in the culinary arts. In fact, many of the staple foods we associate with some Old World cultures did not even exist in those nations until the arrival of the Columbian Exchange. For example, tomatoes are a staple of Italian food, from tomato sauce in pizza to pasta, but they are native to the Americas. Peanuts are crucial to Thai food, but didn't exist in Asia until the Columbian Exchange. Ireland's cheap staple crop is the simple potato, which is native to the New World.

People relocated. The Columbian Exchange is often focused on goods, plants, and animals, but we should not neglect the movement of people, disease, and ideas. Many Europeans traveled to the New World from disparate parts of Europe to seek their fortunes, escape persecution, or gain a fresh start in life.

Diseases transferred. The transfer of diseases was mostly a one-way phenomenon. While the Europeans were harsh in their treatment of the native Indians of the Americas, most of the depopulation of these indigenous groups came from the invisible diseases Europeans brought, from smallpox and typhus to measles and the bubonic plague. The 16th-century spread of diseases caused the death of almost 90% of the native populations. Native Indians lacked the immunity and resistance to diseases that Old World people had built up for centuries. It seems that few diseases were exclusive to the New World; syphilis is one of the few that has been positively identified.

Slaves traded. Europeans traded slaves for agricultural and other labor. Slaves were taken, mostly from Portuguese and British port colonies in East Africa, and shipped across the brutal Middle Passage into the Caribbean colonies and from there to North America, the Caribbean, or South America.

Religion and politics transferred. Religion and politics were transferred back and forth between the two continents. It is well known that Europeans brought with them the ideologies of Christianity (in all denominations and forms), national sovereignty, and basic economic theories of exchange and money. Europeans also brought, in various locations and times, ideas of national sovereignty, individual rights, and the social contract. This is how democracy was forged in the crucible of the New World. However, what is often forgotten is that the people and lands of the New World also informed and affected the creation of new political ideas in Europe. The encounters between Europeans and natives affected the former's views about politics, the state, and individual freedom, while the experience of being in the vast wilderness of the New World helped to determine the conclusions that European philosophers and statesmen would make later.

The Commercial Revolution and Mercantilism

A commercial revolution emerged out of the wave of imperialism in the New World. While explorers and conquerors were the first to come to the Americas from Europe, the next groups were merchants and traders, many of whom made great fortunes.

Key Facts about Commercialism and Mercantilism

Early capitalism. The goods traded from the New World created much wealth, which could be invested as capital in new ventures and fields. This is where the earliest forms of capitalism began to emerge in more concrete forms. For example, wealthy traders made so much money from selling raw materials from American colonies that they could invest their surplus capital in entities such as joint-stock companies and other business ventures. The investors' fates went along with the company's venture. If the company went under, everyone lost their investments, but if it prospered, everyone would benefit in proportion to their investment. These types of economic innovations, caused by a great increase in wealth and population in Europe, meant that the foundations of European capitalism were laid.

Early mercantilism. As the commercial revolution took its course, the leading imperialist powers turned toward the economic policy of mercantilism. If we think about the spectrum between two types of trade policies, *free trade* (where companies and individuals can trade and sell as they like) as opposed to *protectionism* (where the government regulates trade to benefit its nation first and foremost), mercantilism is the historical precedent for current-day protectionism.

In the 16th and 17th centuries, mercantilism was created by the Spaniards. It was somewhat informal, but the French perfected mercantilism. It was then copied by the English and others. As the Spanish devised it, they focused on collecting gold and silver from the New World and transferring it to royal hands (from the colonies to Seville) and later Madrid. This was early capitalism. Mercantilism also created a singular market, where American raw materials were shipped to Spain, and manufactured goods were sold to the colonists from the motherland. Spanish colonists were, in theory, only allowed to buy goods from the mother country because allowing free trade could undermine the nation's economy to the benefit of foreigners. Military forces and naval powers upheld this system, which meant that it declined over time as Spain weakened and its rivals grew powerful. Other countries expanded this policy as their own high points of imperialism materialized.

Early free trade. Free trade was not popular with elite economists and kings, but it was popular with radical thinkers and revolutionaries, like the ones who had ideas for a new country—the United States in the 1700s.

Exploration Linked to the Scientific Revolution and Enlightenment

In the next chapter, we will review the closely linked Scientific Revolution and Age of Enlightenment.

HISTORIOGRAPHY. *It has been widely argued by historians that the timeline of the Age of Exploration and the Age of Enlightenment is no coincidence. In fact, some academics argue that the discovery and exploration of the New World by Europeans led to a shock in the epistemology that propelled European thinkers into new directions that governed Europe for centuries (epistemology refers to the organization and rules of knowledge as a system).*

Prior to the Age of Exploration, Western philosophers and scientists had discovered, cataloged, and written about people and events from the ancient Greeks to the turn of the 16th century. Many scholars might have felt confident in c. 1491 that the world was a known entity and there was not so much more to explore and discover. However, within a few decades the discovery of new tribes of people, new lands, new animals, new plants, new crops, new languages, and new ideas made it all too clear that the world was a vast place about which scholars knew very little.

The Scientific Revolution focused on *empiricism* (the use of direct observation as evidence for scientific conclusions). Since much of the work in the past had been discredited, there was a need to focus on a new means of gathering facts and information. The Enlightenment focused on *reason* as a means of discovering new truths and the importance of characterizing, describing, and cataloging everything about the natural world. What's certain, as we will see in the next chapter, is that these two movements transformed the European worldview mindset.

The Reformation (c. 1515 to c. 1650)

The Reformation was a movement aimed at a new way of thinking about Christianity—Protestantism. Protestantism challenged the powerful Roman Catholic authority and the political, social, and cultural face of 16th-century Europe. What started as a religious movement of discontent resulted in political rulers waging brutal religious wars throughout Europe. The reorganization of 16th-century Christianity splintered the Catholic Church and gave rise to Lutheranism, Calvinism, and Anglicanism (illustrated in the diagram that follows).

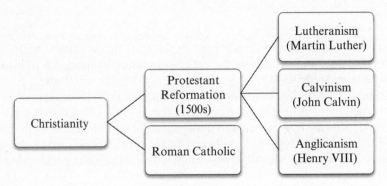

The Roman Catholic Church (Catholicism)

The Protestant Reformation was a political movement to take control of the Roman Catholic Church (the "Church").

Key Facts about the Reasons for Discontent with the Roman Catholic Church

The Catholic Church was stagnate. At the beginning of the 16th century, the Catholic Church was still politically strong, as it had been for much of the past centuries, but it had been mortally weakened by the loss of faith among many ordinary Catholics. As we saw earlier, the Black Death undermined faith in local priests and bishops, while the new ideas of humanism from the Renaissance posed a challenge to the Church's focus on the spiritual world. People throughout Europe started to question whether the papacy and the Church were quite as holy as they were supposed to be.

The Catholic Church scandals. Scandals and corruption exacerbated this crisis of authority. One example of a scandal was the sale of indulgences. The Church had long offered indulgences to the laypeople. These indulgences were meant to intervene on behalf of deceased loved ones who languished in purgatory, a place between heaven and hell where sinful souls had to wait and expunge their sins—through suffering and pain—before moving on to join the community of saints in heaven. This was a popular practice, given the Church's focus on good works combined with faith for salvation. Often, these indulgences were sold to incentivize the living to assist the souls of the beloved departed and to pay for church costs. The famous St. Peter's Basilica in Rome was rebuilt using precisely these funds. However, in the late medieval period, these sales began to be widely abused by middlemen contracted by the Church who charged exorbitant prices and fleeced the poor churchgoers by threatening damnation and pain for their loved ones. For many people, this sordid behavior was epitomized by Dominican priest Johann Tetzel, who was famous for his alleged saying, "As soon as a coin in the coffer rings, the soul from purgatory springs."

The Catholic Church's corrupt clergy. The sale of indulgences was not the only abuse of temporal power that Christians saw in the Catholic Church. There was also considerable consternation from the worshippers and reformers about the inadequacies and misdeeds of local clergy—gambling, drinking, and breaking vows. The Catholic clergy, from priests, monks, and nuns to bishops, cardinals, and popes, were required to be *celibate* (giving up marriage and sexual relations). They were also expected to be literate and well-educated enough to conduct the mass and tend to their (largely illiterate) flock of worshippers. While the Church, in a concession to human nature, recognized that all men are sinners and no man is perfect, the priesthood was considered a higher calling, which meant that clergy members were expected to be more moral and dutiful than laymen. Thus, the widespread rumors and, sometimes, overt display of sexual relations by clergy (even popes in some cases), of ignorance and negligence by many of them, and their flouting of the laws of God and man turned many against the Church, which some eventually came to see as corrupt as the Babylon in the Book of Revelations.

The Lutheran Church (Lutheranism)

Martin Luther (1483–1546) became one of the most important figures of world history. Luther's clerical career started in 1505 as an Augustinian monk in Germany. He was highly intelligent and morally conscientious as a young man who studied and learned all that he could about theology, philosophy, science, and law. Yet, Luther found that after a certain point, none of these subjects brought him closer to God.

Key Facts about Martin Luther

Luther questioned the Catholic Church's integrity. Long before Luther questioned Church doctrine publicly, he found himself disgusted by the corruptions of the Catholic Church. The sale of indulgences was a particularly sharp grievance. He became a professor of theology at the University of Wittenberg, a platform he used to criticize the sale of indulgences and the alleged greediness of some in the Church hierarchy.

Luther questioned the Catholic Church's teachings. Using his broad knowledge of the Bible, Luther began to question some of the Church's teachings. Reading St. Paul (who was a great source of inspiration for him), Luther argued that the Catholics were wrong in believing that man is saved through faith (believing the right things) and works (doing the right things). Instead, Luther asserted that man could be saved by faith and faith alone. According to Luther, if a Christian believed honestly and fully in God's message, then the righteous works would automatically follow. This meant that confession, the practice whereby Catholic priests forgive the sins of the laity in the name of God, was no longer an important sacrament to Luther. Luther also rejected the priesthood, and asked "why should there by a middleman between God and his children?"

Luther questioned the interpretation of the Bible. Luther came to question the whole role of the Catholic Church. Luther argued that the Church was not needed to forgive sins. In the age of the printing press, Luther argued that it was feasible to spread Bibles far and wide so that ordinary laymen could read them and interpret the Bible in their own way. Traditionally, in medieval Europe, where most laymen were illiterate, the Church used a mass and Bible that were in Latin, the universal language of the educated of Europe. Priests read the Bible to parishioners and interpreted the sermons. For Luther, this entailed another unnecessary middleman.

Luther rejected the Catholic Church's authority. If a man could read, he could interpret the Bible in his own way, without needing to be a priest or to possess a degree in theology. Thus, Luther argued that all believers could be priests, rather than a separation between the laymen and the priesthood. When Luther rejected the authority of the Church and its papacy, the pope excommunicated him.

The beginning of Lutheranism. Luther began to preach to his faithful, a luxury afforded to him by the support and protection of powerful German princes who wanted to use Luther as a bulwark against the strength of the pope and the Holy Roman Empire. Lutheranism began to spread throughout the German lands, but more radical reformers than Luther would build upon his teachings, as we shall see shortly.

Did you know? Students often wonder, "Did Luther actually nail *The 95 Theses* to the church door in Wittenberg?" This event, like many other famous and illustrative episodes or quotes in history, although widely circulated as true, did not actually happen. There are many apocryphal (of a story of questionable authenticity) moments in history. Marie Antoinette probably did not say, "Let them eat cake," and Julius Caesar likely did not accuse Brutus with "*Et tu,* Brute (and you, Brutus)?" Most Reformation historians believe that Luther did not actually nail the theses, but this story does serve to help students visualize and remember this event in history.

Luther's criticism of the Church's dogma and practice. When thinking about Luther's criticism of the Catholic Church, we should make an important distinction between a church's *dogma* and *practice*. This is the difference between what a church holds as beliefs, or dogma, and what a church does in the real world, or practice. We will also return to this distinction when looking at other Protestant movements as well as the response of the Catholic Church. Keep in mind that many reformers criticized the Church for corruption or scandal without ever truly questioning the dogma of Rome. Men like Erasmus tried to reform the Church from within without abandoning dogma and starting anew. Protestants like Luther broke away from the Church because of critiques of both Church dogma and Church practice.

Luther's revolutionary ideas provoked the Peasants' War. Luther's revolutionary preaching had unforeseen consequences. Armed with his radical beliefs, German peasants around Luther's hunting grounds began to question their repressed social status. If the mighty Catholic Church, 1,500 years old, could be challenged, why not the power of the German princes? German peasants in the south of the region, starting off in Luther's county of residence, began to denounce the clergy and aristocracy for persecuting, overtaxing, and oppressing the people. By 1524, peasants began to take up arms and attack the soldiers of the German princes. These peasants hoped that Luther, their messiah and savior, would come to their aid. Instead, Luther was horrified by the peasants' fighting. He condemned the peasant leaders as charlatans and demanded that the peasants be punished with harsh severity. The noble lords and their men at arms were all too happy to oblige. While the peasant rebellion was massive (about 100,000 peasants were killed) they were defeated because they were poorly armed and lacked military strategies. The rebellion was crushed in the summer of 1525. This event both pushed Luther from radicalism to a more conservative reformism, and tarnished his image among many poor and radical peasants throughout Europe.

The Calvin Church (Calvinism)

A generation younger than Martin Luther, the Frenchman **John Calvin** was influenced by Luther's message and eventually founded his own church after breaking with Rome in 1530.

Key Facts about John Calvin

Calvin denounced the material world. Calvin faced religious persecution in France, and so he fled to Switzerland, a location of relative tolerance in Europe. Calvin founded the eponymous (a person giving their name to something) **Calvinism,** which was a more extreme form of Luther's Protestantism. Calvin rejected many of the same things Luther rejected in the Catholic Church, such as corruption, excess spending, and unnecessary sacraments and ceremonies. However, Calvin went further, denouncing the material and secular world as evil and corrupt. For Calvin, music, dancing, drinking alcohol, and entertainment were expressly forbidden because they were distractions from the holiness and unity with God.

Calvin's divine predestination. Another key aspect of Calvin's teachings was the divine double predestination. Christians believe that God, having created human beings himself, knows who is predestined to go to heaven or hell, even before the person is born. Christians also allow for free will—men can make their own decisions about heaven and hell. Calvin's double predestination goes further. Calvin argued that God chose the ultimate fate for each man and woman after death. According to Calvin, free will was an illusion. Instead, humanity was divided between the many Damned, and the few Elect, who were destined to spend eternity with God.

Calvin's theocracy in Switzerland. Calvinism dominated in Geneva, Switzerland, which quickly became a Christian *theocracy* (a form of government in which the religion is the authority) under Calvin's leadership. The old separation between the Church and the state was removed, and religious police and councils took charge of enforcing Calvinistic morality among the population, willing or otherwise. The theory of double predestination meant that the Elect were uniquely holy men who could control others' lives, as opposed to the Catholic mindset in which priests, bishops, and the pope himself were mere sinners who could not presume to condemn others for sinfulness. Late in life, Calvin secured complete dictatorial control over Geneva, although his dominance there was tempered by hearing reports of Calvinist brethren being persecuted in his French homeland.

TEST TIP: Two important concepts about Calvinism on the AP EURO exam are: 1) Calvin's puritanical policies of enforcing public morality on people, and 2) Calvin's teaching of divine predestination. These two beliefs were not only important for shaping the political, social, and moral traditions of the Netherlands, Scotland, and other predominantly Calvinist areas of Europe, but they were also fundamental for the Pilgrims who landed in the Americas at Plymouth Rock. These beliefs were the foundation of the Massachusetts Bay Colony, and crafted the New England legacy that eventually became an indispensable part of the cultural fabric of the United States of America.

The Church of England (Anglicanism)

In 1521, King Henry VIII of England seemed a highly unlikely candidate to break from Rome and start his own church. That was the year that he wrote a book denouncing Luther and defending the papacy and the Church. The book was called *Defense of the Seven Sacraments,* and Henry was called a "Defender of the Faith" for this action.

Key Facts about King Henry VIII

King Henry VIII broke from the Catholic Church. In England, Protestant reform was prompted by the King's marriage. Henry's wife could not give birth to sons, a veritable offense for a queen at the time. To secure a male heir, the King asked the pope to annul (or cancel) his marriage so that he could wed again and father a legitimate male heir. When the pope repeatedly refused this request on principle, Henry decided to make himself the head of the Church of England and reject the authority of Rome. The papacy cut off ties with Henry, so the King responded by seizing lands owned by the Catholic Church and attacking Catholic followers like Sir Thomas More, who was executed.

King Henry VIII established the Church of England (Anglican Church). Henry opened up the floodgates of Protestant heresy in England, which brought forth the wide proliferation of vernacular Bibles, attacks on the privilege of Catholic clergy, and a variety of previously proscribed teachings. Not unlike Luther, Henry decided that his own reformation had gone too far and had become too radical. Henry stopped the most extreme variants of Protestantism and killed or jailed their leaders. Nevertheless, he could not, and would not, turn to Catholicism. Instead, he established the Church of England (or Anglican Church), which many historians consider to be a sort of middle ground between Catholicism and Lutheranism.

The Church of England established its doctrine. The Church of England had the king (or queen) of England as its religious and secular head. The authority of the pope was completely rejected. Other than the change at the top, however, the hierarchy remained. The Church of England had archbishops and priests, albeit priests who are allowed to marry (unlike their celibate Catholic counterparts). The Anglicans rejected five of the seven sacraments and agreed with all other Protestants in rejecting the Catholic conception of *transubstantiation* (the Eucharist literally becomes Christ's body and blood during the mass). The Anglicans also rejected the monastic orders of monks and nuns, and they were far less interested in devotion to the saints than were the Catholics. Despite all of these changes, however, many other Protestants viewed the Anglican Church as Catholic, especially in aesthetics. The Anglicans retained large, ornate churches, complex and orderly masses, two of the original seven sacraments, and even the clothing of clergymen.

Henry VIII died in 1547. Henry's son, Edward VI, and his daughter, Mary I, were conflicted about furthering Protestantism or going back to Catholicism during each of these rulers' short reigns. What really cemented the contentious religious settlement in England, however, was the long rule of their sister, Elizabeth I, who ruled from 1558 to 1603. We will return to her story later in this chapter (see p. 86).

The Catholic Response to Protestantism

In response to the rise of Protestantism, the Catholic Church initially made a series of mistakes and follies. While Luther, Calvin, and other reformers were using the printing press to issue pamphlets across Europe, both spreading news of their teachings and their arguments, the pope refused to engage them directly in printed media. The Pope was happy to use the age-old tools of Catholicism to counter heretics—from excommunication and banning to the papal Inquisition. Yet, the Pope considered it demeaning to engage these reformers directly, as that would mean treating them like equals. This meant that the Catholic Church lost the first several rounds of the propaganda war, about which many historians have recently written. Eventually, Catholic leaders came to the realization that the Protestant churches could not be defeated as easily as past heretical movements in previous centuries. Instead, something drastic would have to be done to prevent the breakup of the Catholic Church across Europe and to protect its holdings from further Protestant encroachments.

HISTORIOGRAPHY. *In response to the rise of Martin Luther, the title "The Catholic Response" was carefully chosen. This selfsame topic was loosely labeled "The Catholic Counter Reformation" for much of the past 250 years. Recently, however, historians have drawn attention to the bias inherent in this terminology. Pairing "The Protestant Reformation" with "The Catholic Counter Reformation" means implying several value judgments: that the Catholics were reacting to the Protestants, rather than making general reforms; that the Protestant movement was modern and the Catholic movement was retrograde; and that Protestants were moving forward in progress and the Catholics moving backward. These types of value statements were not a problem in the 19th century, when historians in places like Germany, England, and the United States were unabashed in their distaste and hatred of Catholics and the Church. But today, history is expected to be as objective as possible, so many historians have argued that we should substitute more neutral terms for "The Catholic Counter Reformation," such as "The Catholic Reformation," "Tridentine Catholicism," or "early modern Catholicism." It may take some time before these alternative terms filter down to textbooks, university lectures, and the tongues of history students, but what is important is that we are consistently thoughtful about using value-laden terms when dealing with areas of history that are still controversial to this day.*

The Catholic Council of Trent

In 1545, Pope Paul III called a Catholic Church Council to determine the proper response to the Protestant Reformation and its claims.

Key Facts about the Council of Trent

The Jesuits. Over the course of 18 long years, a generation of Church officials decided upon a process of reforming the Church to curb abuses, respond to Protestant attacks, and reaffirm the unique nature of the Catholic Church. The **Council of Trent** ushered in the creation of several new religious orders, but out of all of these, perhaps the most crucial to the Catholic response to the Protestant Reformation was the order of the Society of Jesus, better known as the *Jesuits*. The Jesuits were akin to foot soldiers for the Catholic Church. The Jesuits converted new members with zeal and combated the spread and influence of Protestantism. The Jesuits eventually became troublesome for the kings of Europe, being distrusted by both absolute monarchs and enlightened philosophers.

The Catholic Church did not compromise its doctrine. The Council of Trent refused to acknowledge any doctrinal mistakes by Rome (mistakes in Church doctrine), but they tacitly admitted to errors in practice among different dioceses and clergy throughout the Catholic world. The Church invested money and influence to clean up corruption and make sure that clergymen throughout the world were living up to their responsibilities. Nevertheless, the Council of Trent asserted that the Catholic Church was still the one and only true Church, and that religious truth could only be found through the Church. Ultimately, the Council of Trent reaffirmed Catholicism rather than compromising or diluting it. Many Catholic critics had hoped that the Church would make major compromises in order to protect its flock of worshippers. They were sorely disappointed by the ultimate results. In the end, both Catholic and Protestant leaders refused to significantly compromise, which entailed further decades of wars and millions of deaths.

TEST TIP: The AP EURO exam occasionally asks you to know the difference between Catholic and Protestant art in the 16th and 17th centuries. One way to remember the difference is to link the *aesthetic* with the *theological*. For example, Lutherans and especially Calvinists were not materialistic. They wanted simplicity in their churches because what really mattered to them was the word of God and the presence of the community of priests—worshippers. On the other hand, Catholics and Anglicans created ornate and grandiose churches to give greater glory and adulation to God. A good answer on an AP EURO art question might say that the Protestants were emphasizing God's closeness and familiarity to the layman, whereas the Catholics were emphasizing God's overwhelming majesty and power. See the section below to understand the Baroque style of art during this time period.

Religious Influences in Art and Music

An important aspect of the Catholic Reformation was the emergence of Baroque art and architecture. This art form spread throughout the Catholic world and is often associated with Spain, Portugal, and their American colonies, as well as Italy and Austria. Whether in church design, the building of statues, the painting of portraits, or the crafting of sculptures, Baroque art is characterized by ornate decoration, religious imagery devoted to the Holy Trinity or the saints, and a grandiosity that made everything seem triumphant and important. Catholic religious art and architecture had always been on the more complex side (think of Gothic cathedrals from the medieval period), but this went much further in that same direction. It was a response to the conscious simplicity of Protestant art. Just as in theology, in architecture the Church sought to emphasize the distinct identity of the Catholic Church.

The Baroque movement also affected music. Catholic composers wrote complex music with ornate melodies and a variety of differing parts, which is called *polyphony*. Professional or volunteer musicians took part in playing and singing this music at Catholic masses. This is in contrast to the Protestants, who (except for Anglicans) advocated simple, repetitive music that anyone could take part in singing during a church service. The Protestant church service was a more hands-on, interactive process, whereas the Catholic mass was more structured and orchestrated.

Religious Similarities and Differences

When it comes to religious or ideological differences, the AP EURO exam often requires you to compare and contrast, not only on longer free-response questions, but even on multiple-choice questions. In this case, it is a question of *religious dogma* (what the church believes is unequivocally true). You do not need to be an expert on the theology of the different churches, but you should have a rough idea about the Protestant criticisms of the Catholic Church, and how Catholicism and Protestantism differed, both in ideas and in practice.

Similarities	Differences
Prevented people from leaving the church. One similarity is that both Catholics and Protestants worked very dutifully to gain new converts and tried to prevent the faithful from questioning or leaving their churches. Both sides accomplished this violently or peacefully, depending on the circumstance. There were a rare few places of relative tolerance, such as in Holland, but in most places the members of the dominant faith lorded over their opponents, and the members of minority faiths bided their time and cursed their oppressors. **Confessionalization.** Another common thread between Catholicism and Protestantism is the process of what historians call *confessionalization*. This describes the process of fixing religious beliefs into set categories, or dogma. It was a form of "social disciplining." The churches used this to strengthen their dogmas, practices, and values. Whether in the "old church" (Catholicism) or one of the "new churches" (Protestantism), theologians, clergymen, and laymen all tried to maintain discipline. Confessionalization was practiced in order to strengthen the church against threats from outside (such as enemy armies or churches) and within (new heretical movements or schisms).	**Separation of church and state.** Catholics *did* separate church and state, but Protestants *did not* separate church and state. The most important contrast between Catholic and Protestant denominations is their respective approaches to the relationship between secular (state) authority and religious (church) authority. Separation of church and state was the long-standing stance of the Catholic Church, but the Protestants overturned this rule. **Catholicism: The Church takes precedence.** Few people would think of medieval Catholicism as an example; however, there was separation of religious and secular authority in Catholic Europe, only in a different direction. Today, the state is separate from religion, but the state takes precedence. In traditional Catholic Europe, the church was separate from the state, but the church had precedence. For example, consider Heinrich IV, Holy Roman Emperor in the 11th century, who got into trouble with the pope over *investiture* (who has authority) rights, was excommunicated, and ended up having to walk barefoot and without protection or shelter (according to the legends) to beg the pope for forgiveness and absolution. In the early modern era, popes maintained huge estates, employed armies, and even went to war with the kings and princes of Europe on a regular basis. In many ways, the papacy acted as a sort of super state, interacting with other nations on a basis that we would consider typical of a country. **Protestantism: The state takes precedence.** The Lutheran, Anglican, Calvin, and other reformed churches broke from the Catholic Church's millennium-long dominance of Western Europe. In the **Anglican** top-down reformation, the king of England took religious authority onto himself, supplanting the pope as religious head of Britain. **Calvin,** as we have seen, established a theocratic state in Geneva, with the merging of church and government. **Luther's** example is more complicated. On the one hand, Luther rejected the role of the papacy, and therefore actively sought powerful allies from some of the German princes like Frederick III of Saxony. These princes not only found religious inspiration in Luther's theology, but also sought to buttress their authority against the Holy Roman Emperor by rejecting Catholicism. After Luther's death, the Lutheran Church's relationship with the state was wildly inconsistent, reflecting the ebbs and flows of the politics of the Holy Roman Empire itself. Lutheranism often resisted the siren calls of the state, but later became close with Prussia and Imperial Germany. In many ways, the nature of these debates and controversies of the balance between church and state shaped the debates and controversies of the 18th, 19th, and 20th centuries. **Protestantism: Differences in denominations.** Lastly, you should consider the differences between the Protestant denominations themselves. Different Protestant denominations had different areas of focus. Calvinism focused on the moral and puritanical, Lutheranism on faith and the Bible, and Anglicanism on the power of the king or queen. Some denominations barely departed from the Catholic Church, such as the Anglicans, while others radically shifted from the Catholic Church. Some were top-down movements, such as Anglicanism, while others were more grassroots or at least local, such as the Lutherans and the Calvinists.

Religious Warfare in Europe

With the spread of Protestantism in the 16th and 17th centuries, religious differences sparked warfare throughout Europe. Although religious differences caused the start of wars, there were many other reasons for wars (power, territorial landholdings, economics, and natural resources).

Key Facts about King Charles V and the Wars of Religion

As we saw, Martin Luther's revolt against the Catholic Church began in Saxony, a region of what is today Germany. (Note: The term "Germany" was based on the Roman province of Germania, but there was no official nation of Germany until 1871. Germans were ruled by the Holy Roman Empire and later by the German Confederation until unification in 1871.)

Did you know? While historians and contemporaries at the time used the term "Germany," based on the Roman province of Germania and the language and cultural unity of Germans, there was no official nation of Germany. Germans were ruled by the Holy Roman Empire, and later the German Confederation. The formal unification of Germany did not occur until January 18, 1871.

King Charles V and the Holy Roman Empire. Germans were ruled by a supranational political entity called the Holy Roman Empire. Established in c. 800 by Charlemagne, the first Holy Roman Emperor, the Holy Roman Empire was a decentralized political entity that reigned in over 300 different states by c. 1500. These historic states shared political autonomy and control with the man who held the official position of Holy Roman Emperor, which was in theory an elected position. (It often comes as a surprise to students in the 21st century that elective monarchies were not uncommon in the medieval and early modern periods of Europe.) Despite its seemingly elected status, however, the Habsburg House of Charles V had ruled over the empire during the 1500s.

TEST TIP: The following quote from Voltaire might be useful when answering free-response questions about the Holy Roman Empire on the AP EURO exam.

Voltaire, the Enlightenment philosopher, famously quipped that the Holy Roman Empire was "neither Holy, nor Roman, nor an empire." With characteristic brilliance, he was pointing out that the Holy Roman Empire was not "holy" but a civic institution, and that it had little claim to the heritage of the Roman Empire. It was not a traditional unified empire, but more of a decentralized confederation.

King Charles V was one of the most important figures in European history. Through sheer happenstance, Charles became the ruler of the largest domain that *Christendom* (the Christian world) had ever seen. Because of the untimely death of his older relatives, Charles inherited four different realms from four different grandparents: Castile (and the Americas), Aragon (and much of Italy), Burgundy, and Austria. The inheritance of the first two realms brought him into conflict with the Ottoman Empire, the leading power of the Muslim world. The inheritance of Burgundy and Austria, and his accession to the post of Holy Roman Emperor in 1519, led Charles into religious conflict with the powers of Lutheranism in the German lands over which he ruled.

King Charles V led wars against Protestantism. Because of the power of the emperor, the line between opposition to him on religious grounds and opposition to him on political grounds began to blur. In 1531, Emperor Charles V took the step of demanding that Lutheranism and other Protestant sects be removed from the Holy Roman Empire. The Protestant princes united to form the *Schmalkaldic League,* a union of these princes to jointly hold off the power of the emperor. For the next two decades, the Catholic emperor and his allies fought the Schmalkaldic League. Charles achieved a near-total victory in 1547, but several of his allies became afraid that he had become too powerful, and betrayed him. For another decade, Charles continued to pour enormous amounts of money and manpower into these wars. By 1555, crippled with gout and close to death, the emperor realized that Lutheranism and other sects had spread too widely, and that they could not be wiped out by military force. Thus, he agreed to the Peace of Augsburg (see below). Charles divided his massive holdings into two empires: the Holy Roman Empire for his nephew, Maximilian, and the rest of his lands for his son Philip.

The Peace of Augsburg (1555)

The religious wars in Germany came to an end after Charles recognized the fact that he could not hope to triumph over his legions of enemies and undo the work of the Protestant Reformation. By 1555, Charles was getting old and was suffering horribly from gout and other medical problems. Exhausted and despondent, with even his Catholic allies pleading for peace and calm, Charles made an agreement with the German Lutheran princes for the coexistence of Catholicism and Lutheranisim. Charles decided to abdicate his throne and split up his realms between the German lands and the Spanish possessions. In Augsburg, Bavaria, they created the **Peace of Augsburg** (also called the Augsburg Settlement), which would put a new system into place in the Holy Roman Empire for the next half-century.

Key Facts about the Peace of Augsburg

The settlement created political and religious governance. The Peace of Augsburg set up a new system of political and religious governance in the Holy Roman Empire based upon the axiom, *cuius regio, eius religio* ("whose realm, his religion"). The Peace of Augsburg allowed princes throughout the empire to adopt Lutheranism or Catholicism and enforce religious unity within their holdings. This was not really religious freedom in the 21st-century sense, except perhaps limited freedom of religion for these elites. In fact, historians have drawn parallels between the Augsburg settlement and the Christianization of central and northern Europe in the early medieval period, where kings like Charlemagne would convert to Christianity and then force their subjects, largely pagan, to convert to Christianity.

The settlement only recognized Catholicism and Lutheranism. Despite the settlement nature of the Peace of Augsburg, there were also flaws that meant that some people were deeply unsatisfied. For one, while *cuius regio, eius religio* meant that Protestant princes could enshrine their religion in their realms, the settlement only recognized two faiths as legitimate: Roman Catholicism and Lutheranism. Calvinism, Anabaptism, and other Protestant dissident groups had no official recognition and were thus considered heresies, punishable by imprisonment or death. Needless to say, these religious groups felt sorely left out of the agreement.

The settlement was difficult to enforce. Another flaw of the Peace of Augsburg was related to the nature of the Holy Roman Empire itself. The empire was split among lands personally ruled by the emperor, secular lands (held by princes or lower nobles), church lands (held by bishops or other Catholic hierarchy members), and Free Cities (self-governing cities). This diversity of different types of state within the Holy Roman Empire made it very difficult to enforce the settlement. One particularly sticky point was an internal contradiction within the settlement's logic. What would happen if the Catholic bishop of an *ecclesiastical* (religious) state, like the Electorate of Cologne, decided to convert to Protestantism? Would he lose his bishopric and become a secular leader of that state? Would he be removed from the leadership? What would happen to the people of that state? This was not a moot point, because this actually happened in 1583 and led to a small war over the issue. Clearly, religious conflict was far from over in German lands.

The settlement only postponed religious conflict. Ultimately, despite the fact that it was a compromise, the Peace of Augsburg only postponed religious conflict in the Holy Roman Empire. Religious tensions between Catholics and Lutherans, not to mention among other dissident religious groups, continued to wax and wane, and eventually set the stage for the outbreak of the Thirty Years' War in the early-17th century.

Religious Wars in France

When we think of the division between Catholics and Protestants in Europe, it is natural to put France squarely in the Catholic camp. This was not a foregone conclusion in the 16th century. France could easily have been split between Catholics and Protestants, like Germany was later in the 19th and 20th centuries. The fact that it did not was a result of the *French Wars of Religion* that began in 1562 after a massacre of Huguenots (French Calvinists) by Catholics. The wars of religion raged on and off for a decade, until the occurrence of one of the most infamous events in European history. In 1572, French Huguenots and Catholics gathered in Paris for a royal wedding. Led by Catherine de Medici, the queen regent and mother of King Charles IX, Catholic leaders took advantage of the festivities to slaughter their guests. The Protestants were utterly caught by surprise and many of their most important leaders were killed, crippling their side in the war. This massacre paved the way for the final religious war in France, the interestingly named *War of the Three Henrys*.

In the 1570s and 1580s, the religious wars in France had become bloodier and uglier, as foreign nations began to intervene in France to take advantage of the disorder. Spain, hoping to curb French power, supported Henry of Lorraine to be the next king of France. Most French Catholics, who were anti-Spanish, supported the standing king, King Henry III, while Huguenots and their foreign allies (Elizabeth I of England) supported Henry of Navarre, a Huguenot leader. The war lasted for years until Henry III and Henry of Lorraine (Duke of Guise) were both assassinated within a short period of time. Without these two Henrys, there was only one left to claim the throne in Paris, Henry of Navarre.

The Edict of Nantes (1598)

Henry of Navarre, an underdog for the throne in Paris, became the king after the deaths of the other two Henrys. A cunning student of Machiavelli (see p. 60), he knew that most Frenchmen would never support a Protestant king. Henry gave up his Huguenot faith and adopted Catholicism as his religion. He is reported to have said that "Paris is worth a mass," a cynical assessment that religious allegiance did not matter and could be easily changed in exchange for what did matter—political power. (Note: Henry of Navarre became Henry IV after being crowned, did not actually utter this statement aloud, but it is useful to remember the choice that he made in order to become king.)

Henry IV was crowned in 1594, and 4 years later issued the **Edict of Nantes.** This law officially established Catholicism as the religion of France. The law also allowed partial toleration for Huguenots throughout the kingdom. It was a compromise that did not fully satisfy either side, but it did allow for decades of peaceful coexistence between Catholics and Protestants. The long decades of religious conflicts in France, which had become a perpetual force in the French kingdom, had finally come to an end.

> **TEST TIP:** When thinking about the role of religion between 1517 and the Thirty Years' War in 1618–1648, consider both *regions* and *periods*. For regions, you will want to break down different geographic areas and the religious conflicts—Anglicanism in England, the Huguenots against the Catholics in France, the Calvinists in Geneva, and the like. For periods, consider the states in power at the time of war, as opposed to the long (relative) peace between the signings of Augsburg and Nantes and the outbreak of the Thirty Years' War in 1618.

The Witch Craze (1580 to 1630)

When you think of witches and witch trials in European history, you might first think of the medieval period, when superstition and ignorance were commonplace. In fact, the peak of European witch hunting did not take place in the medieval period, but in the 1500s and 1600s. It was during this period that tens of thousands of women were accused, tortured, and killed for witchcraft in Europe.

First, do not confuse witchcraft with heresy. *Heresy* meant questioning the teachings of the faith (whatever faith was dominant in that state). *Witchcraft* was considered to be much worse in the sense that it meant consorting with the devil. Second, in this period official literature on witches and Satanism spread throughout Europe in both Catholic and Protestant lands.

The most likely targets of witch hunts and trials were elderly women, especially widowed women. Men were not immune to accusations of associating with the devil, especially in areas of Europe that had not been thoroughly Christianized. However, women were the likely targets because of societal notions that women were physically weaker, and therefore spiritually and morally weaker. Witch hunts frequently erupted in areas where there was religious conflict and fighting. It seems that religious strife drove fears and panic about witches and pacts with the devil.

Heads Up: What You Need to Know

The AP EURO exam examines the roles of gender throughout different time periods. When comparing and contrasting different eras or nations in terms of gender roles, it is important to avoid one of the most common fallacies of historical thinking—what is true today has always been true. It is tempting, and sometimes even comforting, to think that the beliefs, values, norms, and conceptions that are dominant in the 21st century have always been true. In fact, the opposite is often the case. Gender is an excellent example here. In the 15th century, women were considered morally weak and prone to sexual lust, while men were stronger and more virtuous. It was only a few centuries later, in the Victorian era, that gender roles had completely reversed. Women were seen as averse to sex and pure in mind, while men were impulsively lustful. This contrast provides a reminder of how fundamental social norms and beliefs can change over relatively short periods of time.

The Ottoman Empire

The Muslim world had threatened Christendom since the 700s when they conquered Spain. Relations between Muslim empires and Christian kingdoms waxed and waned over time, with some lulls during periods where one side was preoccupied with infighting or when relative religious tolerance was present in the Muslim world. In the early modern era, Islamic-Christian conflict heightened once again. In 1453, the Byzantine Empire, the Eastern Roman Empire that was founded by Constantine, was conquered by the Muslim Turks. A new Islamic threat had emerged in Western Europe—the Ottoman Empire.

Key Facts about the Ottoman Empire

Muslims defeated Christian nations. Building on their conquest of the Byzantines, the Muslims contested the Mediterranean Sea and the Christian powers. With an innovative navy and one of the most feared armies in the world, the Turks pummeled their way through enemy empires and became very powerful. In the 1520s, they struck fear into the hearts of all Europeans with massive conquests in the Balkans and Hungary, although they were halted at the gates of Vienna in the Holy Roman Empire. Things worsened in subsequent decades as the Turks swept up Djerba, Cyprus, and Malta, among others. The Christian navies tried to resist the Muslim onslaught, but they were smaller, inferior, and often preoccupied, as the Christian kings fought each other. It seemed that the Ottomans might be able to complete the work that previous Muslims had failed. Perhaps they could conquer Rome, lay Christendom low, and seize the heartland of Europe for Islam.

Muslims were defeated at the Battle of Lepanto. Then in 1571 came the *Battle of Lepanto,* one of the most important battles in the history of Islamic-Christian conflict. A Christian navy of combined Spanish, Italian, and papal forces confronted the Turks at the Gulf of Corinth in Greece. Their ships were both outnumbered and technologically inferior to those of the Turks, but in the battle they were able to turn things to their advantage by closing in on the Turkish navy and boarding their ships with soldiers. In brutal hand-to-hand combat, the Christian soldiers were able to crush the Turks, leading to a massive military upset and one of the greatest victories in European history. This battle not only destroyed an important Turkish fleet, but it also restored confidence to the rulers of Christian Europe.

Despite the momentous triumph of Lepanto, the Christian powers of the Mediterranean still had much to fear. While some worrying trends had begun to emerge in the Ottoman Empire's society and government, by 1648 the Ottoman Empire was still a military threat to all of Europe.

The Rise of New Monarchies (c. 1450 to c. 1550)

The power struggle within states resulted in political centralization and a decline in feudalism. New monarchies unified their nations, created a stable government, limited the power of the aristocracy, promoted trade, imposed religion, maintained military force, and established a taxation system.

This section covers the rise of new monarchies in Spain, England, and France.

TEST TIP: On the AP EURO exam, it is important to recognize the different types of European monarchies.

- Monarchies of Christendom and the Holy Roman Empire (Middle Ages): Monarchs were divine representatives of God. Monarchs were rulers, but were not lords over lands (see feudalism on p. 56).

- New monarchies (Renaissance): With the rise of nation-states, monarchs represented centralized power. Monarchs had the authority in both political and spiritual matters.

- Absolute monarchies (18th century): Monarchs ruled as the supreme authority of the state. For example, France's Louis XIV declared, "I am the state."

- Nationalist (enlightened) monarchies (18th and 19th centuries): Monarchs ruled on behalf of the people's aspirations, but kingdoms belonged to the monarchs.

- Constitutional monarchies (19th century–present): Monarchs were symbols of the state, but the authority was exercised by constitutional elected bodies of government.

Spain's Monarchies

As the trailblazers of an overseas empire, the Spaniards also paved the way for the modernizing and centralizing of monarchical power in Europe.

Key Facts about Spain's Monarchies

Ferdinand and Isabella. In the Iberian Peninsula, the process of centralization began with Ferdinand and Isabella of Spain, known by their title of "Their Most Catholic Majesties." Not only did they unite the country by completing the *Reconquista* in 1492 (Christian conquest in the Iberian Peninsula), but they enforced religious unity. During this time, Spain had a diverse religious population of Christians, Jews, and Muslim Moors. However, Ferdinand and Isabella used the Spanish Inquisition to execute, banish, or imprison people who had opposing religious views. Spain drove Muslims from the peninsula and expelled 200,000 practicing Jews from the peninsula. Some Jews avoided persecution by converting to Christianity and secretly remaining Jewish (called *Conversos*), but thousands died trying to reach safety. This established a key facet of the modernized monarchs: securing religious uniformity to unite the country. By 1525, all Spaniards were officially Roman Catholic.

The monarchs also brought their nobles under the heel of the throne by enhancing monarchical power and taking the power from aristocratic bulwarks, such as the *Cortes Generales* (a representative body of nobles). At the same time, they greatly strengthened the *Holy Brotherhood* (a peacekeeping police force that answered directly to the monarchs). Ferdinand and Isabella increased taxes in order to raise monarchical funds. They raised larger bands of soldiers, more ships, and more foundries for cannons. Lastly, despite their Catholic devotion, Ferdinand and Isabella enhanced their power over the Spanish Church, at the expense of Rome.

Philip II. The centralizing and modernizing tendencies of the Spanish monarchy continued under the next two kings of Spain, Charles V (Carlos I to the Spanish) and Philip II. Philip II enjoyed a long rule of over four decades, during a period when Spain was the wealthiest, most powerful, and most respected nation in Europe. As strong as it was, however, the empire began to decline, especially in the later years of Philip's rule. Philip was a very religious and zealous leader who believed he was destined to save Spain, and by extension, the rest of Europe, from the threats of Islam (which we have already seen) and Protestantism. Much of his foreign policy decisions were undertaken in this mindset. Remember that Philip inherited a massive empire from Charles, including the Low Countries (today's Holland and Belgium). This part of the empire, known as the Spanish Netherlands, saw large-scale conversions to Calvinism during Charles' reign. Rather than compromising, Philip asserted that he would rather lose all of his dominions than rule over heretics. He used brute force to crush Calvinism and political opposition in the Low Countries. This set off the **Eighty Years' War,** an extremely long conflict between Dutch Protestants and Spanish Catholics. At the beginning of this war in 1568, the Dutch were hopeless underdogs against the might of the Spanish Empire. Yet, by the end of the war in 1648, the roles had dramatically changed.

Spain's Cultural Golden Age. While Spain's monarchs were centralizing their power and tilting at windmills overseas, Spanish artists and writers were unleashing a cultural *Golden Age* that has rarely been surpassed. The Spaniards proved to possess some of the greatest art in early modern Europe. From El Greco and Diego Velazquez to Francisco de Zurbaran and Luis de Morales, Spanish artists set the standard for great art throughout Europe. The Spanish also contributed to literature and poetry. Miguel Cervantes became the first novelist in the world with his monumental *Don Quixote*. Poets and dramatists such as Lope de Vega and Francisco de Quevedo, while not as great as England's William Shakespeare, profoundly shaped European culture for over a century. Moreover, the Spaniards also proved themselves to be masters of the Baroque style. Whether composing beautiful religious music or creating majestic churches and palaces, the Spaniards exemplified Baroque style in Europe and also spread it to the New World through their colonies. From St. Augustine, Florida, to Bueno Aires, Argentina, the Western Hemisphere still bears testament to this Baroque inheritance even today.

England's Tudor and Stuart Monarchies

Key Facts about England's Monarchies

The restoration of Anglicanism: Elizabeth. As we saw earlier in the chapter, Elizabeth, daughter of Henry VIII, became the queen of England in 1558. When she first came to the throne, little was known about her. She replaced her sister, Mary, who had persecuted Protestants and attempted to turn England back to Catholicism during her short reign. After a period of uncertainty, Elizabeth restored Anglicanism to England. She was a realist who was more concerned with England's position than with religious dogma. Although she did persecute Catholics after failed attempts to assassinate her or remove her from the throne, she was more tolerant than Mary had been and tried to unify the country around her leadership.

Elizabeth ruled over people who harbored low expectations of her abilities, but she disproved these perceptions with her astute foreign policy. England was still very weak and vulnerable, so Elizabeth balanced the mighty power of Spain by sending aid to rebels against Spain (including the Dutch), by allying with Spain's enemies (such as Valois France), and by sending pirate ships to harass Spain's colonies and treasure fleets without declarations of war. These ingenious strategies eventually pushed things to a breaking point.

The conquest of Spain's armada: Elizabeth. As a Protestant ruler and a supporter of the Dutch rebels, Elizabeth earned the hatred of Philip II of Spain. Philip, in fact, had been the king consort of England during his short marriage to Mary I of England and had a zeal for Catholicism. The year 1588 proved to be the turning point of Elizabeth's reign. In that year, Philip II sent an armada (or fleet) with an invasion force to England in order to depose Elizabeth and restore the country to Catholicism under a new ruler. Despite overwhelming superiority on the Spanish side, brilliant English tactics and renegade storms ensured the smashing of the Spanish Armada. While Spain remained a dangerous foe to England, the destruction of the Armada ensured the viability of Elizabeth's reign, and England was not seriously threatened with invasion for over two centuries. England experienced a period of economic prosperity as well as a cultural outflowing epitomized by William Shakespeare, the best-known dramatist and writer in the history of the English language.

> TEST TIP: Because of Hollywood representations and widespread misconceptions, many people believe that the divine right of kings was established during the medieval era in European history. In fact, this theory was not viable during that period because of the power of the Catholic Church, which considered itself supreme over the state. It was not until the Reformation that the divine right to rule would become widely advocated, first in England by James I, and from there to France, Austria, and other continental lands.

The restoration of Protestantism: James I. Elizabeth died without an heir, so her reign was succeeded by James, King of Scotland and descendent of Henry VIII. He became James I of England and furthered the Protestant domination of England. James was a devout Protestant who penned the version of the Bible we now know as the *King James' Version*. He believed in the divine right to rule and strengthened monarchical power in both religious and political senses.

The restoration of Anglicanism: Charles I. James' son, Charles, became king of England in 1625. By this time, and much like what we will see in central Europe for this time period, old religious resentments had started to come to the surface in England. Charles I was a faithful Anglican, but religious dissident groups had come to criticize the Anglican Church as too close to Catholicism.

The rise of Puritanism. Calvinists wanted to purify the Church of England, and thus earned the name of Puritans. They objected to music and other frivolities, to the religious hierarchy of the Anglican Church, and to the sacraments of the church and its masses. The Puritans were also Presbyterian. They wanted more control of the church to be in the hands of local communities and commoners, rather than just the church hierarchy and the king. These religious objections became linked to political objections since Puritans were mostly middle-class commoners and rural townspeople who used the power of Parliament, England's elected legislature. This was done to resist the absolutist tendencies of the Anglican monarchy and its aristocratic allies.

The Puritan-dominated Parliament rose up against Charles I. Charles was a decent and honest man. However, his religious views caused conflict among the Puritan-dominated Parliament. Charles advocated the divine right to rule, tried to enforce religious uniformity, and married a Roman Catholic (birthing conspiracy theories spread about his being a secret Catholic himself). The Puritan-dominated Parliament protested against Charles and a civil war erupted in 1642. This conflict brought to the fore deep religious and political divisions in England and changed the course of English and European history. We will pick up with the **English Civil War** (1642–1651) in the next chapter (p. 126).

> TEST TIP: When answering free-response questions about the Reformation era on the AP EURO exam, keep in mind that politics and religion are a common thread that connects conflicts. In some nations, religious conflict took on a political character—for example, the *Peasants' War* in Germany. In many other nations, political conflicts took on a religious character. For example, in the Netherlands, the oppressive behavior of Spanish Catholics led many rebellious Dutch to turn to Calvinism. When the English Protestants invaded Ireland, they strengthened the connection between Irish identity and Catholicism, as the Irish held on to their faith as another means of resistance to foreign rule. We might also dwell on the German lords who wanted to subvert the Holy Roman Emperor's temporal power, and turned to Luther's teachings in order to do so.

France's Monarchies

In a previous section, we left off in France with the rule of Henry IV, the convert to Catholicism who ended the religious wars in France. When Henry IV was assassinated by a Catholic extremist in 1610, Louis XIII came to the throne in the House of Bourbon, France.

Key Facts about France's Monarchies

The centralization of the French monarchy: Louis XIII. From 1610 to 1643 Louis XIII, who later chose the cunning Cardinal Richelieu as his first minister, ushered in a period of centralization of the French monarchy. As in all countries at the time, strengthening the monarchy meant weakening the aristocracy. The two sets of interests were diametrically opposed. To centralize the monarchy, Richelieu increased taxes, strengthened the king's military forces, and established the intendant system.

The establishment of the intendant system: Louis XIII. France was divided into administrative systems ruled by noble governors. Richelieu replaced these men with intendants who answered directly to the crown.

The intendants were often middle-class commoners or "nobles of the robe." The latter designation contrasted men of wealth who bought aristocratic positions from the king with "nobles of the sword," ancient noble houses that had won their status through medieval combat. This intendant system allowed more direct control of France by the king, replacing the aristocrats as middlemen. Louis XIII and Richelieu combined this new approach to domestic politics with a new realism in international affairs, as we will see in the next section.

The *Fronde* civil war: Louis XIV. Louis XIII died in 1643, paving the way for his son, Louis XIV, who would become one of the most illustrious kings in world history. On the day of his succession, however, Louis XIV was only 5 years old. While we will discuss his adulthood and absolutism in the next chapter, the formative years of the young king are very important for shaping his style of rule. Shortly before Louis XIII died, Richelieu died as well. With both of these men gone and a child king in Louis XIV, the French nobles felt they could revolt to reassert aristocratic privilege and rein in the power of the monarchy. This revolt was called the *Fronde,* and soon engulfed most of France.

King Louis XIV's early childhood impressions shaped his reign. In 1648 came a critical episode in Louis XIV's life. French soldiers and commoners serving the rebellious aristocrats of the *Fronde* broke into the royal palace in Paris and stormed into the young king's room. Menacingly, they threatened him to his face. As a 10-year-old boy, Louis XIV learned lessons from this event that would shape the rest of his reign. Based on his early childhood experience, Louis XIV believed that the common people of France were disgustingly unruly and should be kept very far from the majesty of the king. The king also believed that nobles were potentially very treacherous and could rebel and seize power from the king whenever they wanted. Overall, the king believed that the world was a dangerous, unstable place that could only be safely navigated by a king armed with strength, confidence, and unquestionable authority. As we will see in the next chapter, these lessons stuck with Louis XIV until his dying day.

The Thirty Years' War (1618 to 1648)

In the decades after the Peace of Augsburg, tensions between Catholics and Protestants across central Europe reduced, but the rivalries among different faiths and polities never disappeared. Augsburg represented the acknowledgment by the Holy Roman Empire and his Protestant princes that neither side could achieve a complete religious and political victory over the other.

Key Facts about the Thirty Years' War

The Protestant Union. Ferdinand II of Spain was a different type of Holy Roman Emperor. Ferdinand rejected the longtime compromise between the faiths and thought that he could force religious and political unity on the Protestant powers of the Holy Roman Empire. He was somewhat arrogant and intolerant in this regard. The Protestants responded by forming a Protestant Union to counterbalance the power of the emperor and the Catholic Church. Memories of violent religious conflicts faded over the decades, neither Catholics nor Protestants were afraid to fight over this issue once again.

The Defenestration of Prague. In May 1618, tensions came to a head. Ferdinand sent representatives to Prague, which was in the extremely important province of Bohemia (today it's known as western Czecha and eastern Austria). The Protestant counselors had a disagreement with the two Catholic representatives and they were defenestrated (literally, "thrown out the window")! The Catholic representatives later claimed that they had been saved by angels from God that flew down and carried them to safety. More likely is the version told by the Protestants—the Catholic lives were saved by falling in horse manure.

Heads Up: What You Need to Know

Questions about the Defenestration of Prague frequently appear on the AP EURO exam. The Defenestration of Prague is a significant occasion in European history. As it has often happened throughout history, there was a powder keg of hatred, tensions, and resentments in Europe. In this case, it was the powder keg of religious conflict, never fully resolved, between Catholic and Protestant powers in the Holy Roman Empire. The Defenestration of Prague served as the match to this powder keg, setting off a massive war, which became the bloodiest and ugliest ever seen in Europe in the Christian era—The Thirty Years' War.

Source: The Defenestration of Prague (c. 1618).

No in-depth knowledge of military war history is required on the AP EURO exam, but you should know about the phases of the Thirty Years' War.

Phases of the Thirty Years' War	
Years	**Phase**
1618 to 1624	The Bohemian phase—known for the defeat of the Protestants in Bohemia and the triumph of the Spanish-Imperial forces.
1625 to1629	Catholic triumph—known for the invasion of Germany by the Danish, who were themselves crushed by the Catholics.
1630 to 1635	Swedish invasion—known for the invasion of Germany by the Swedes under the great Gustavus Adolphus.
1636 to 1648	French intervention—known for France's decision to fight against its Catholic brethren. Eventually the emperor was forced to relent in the war.

The Catholic forces of the Holy Roman Emperor and the King of Spain scored early triumphs, such as the *Battle of White Mountain* (1620) and the *Siege of Mannheim* (1622), in the process crushing the Bohemian revolt in a few short years. The defeat of the Protestants in Bohemia was quickly followed by the invasion of Denmark, another Protestant power, which scored some early victories but could not hope to turn the tide of the war in the long run. This phase of the war ended with the triumph of the Catholic powers, and in the process, the emperor of the Holy Roman Empire, Ferdinand II, passed the hugely controversial Edict of Restitution in 1629. Keep in mind that this edict was passed at the apex of Catholic triumphs of arms, after the Protestant powers of Bohemian lords and the kingdom of Denmark had been utterly destroyed. In this edict, Ferdinand restored lands and privileges of Catholic clergy members and princes and also reestablished Imperial rule from Vienna over states that had been secular and nominally independent for almost a century. This meant the dramatic expansion of both the Catholic Church and the Holy Roman Empire over the German states.

The Swedish and French invaded Germany. In response to the Edict of Restitution, the pride of the Holy Roman Emperor, and the persecution of Protestants in the domains held by Catholics, the Swedish invaded from the north across the Baltic Sea. Led by Gustavus Adolphus, one of the greatest military commanders in the history of Europe, the Swedes made huge inroads into Germany. Shortly thereafter, the French invaded, giving the Catholics further trouble. The French feared being encircled by the Spanish and Austrian Habsburgs, so they struck out against the House of Austria.

The end of religious wars (1648). The Thirty Years' War is often remembered for beginning as a war of religious differences between Catholics and Protestants in the Holy Roman Empire, and ending as a secular war fought over the balance of power in Europe. It has been called "the first secular war in Christian Europe." This statement is an oversimplification, but can help you remember its importance in this period. For a century, most European wars had been waged around religious issues, but since 1648, religion has played a minimal role in European wars. While perhaps best remembered for its religious conflict, its brutal atrocities, and its harvesting of millions of European lives, the Thirty Years' War also witnessed a revolution in the financing and maintenance of armies and navies.

Machiavellian realpolitik. We saw that France, a Catholic power, decided to attack the Spanish-Imperial Catholic forces. This decision was undertaken by Cardinal Richelieu, who, in addition to being the villain of the books by Alexander Dumas, was the foreign policy architect of Louis XIII for nearly two decades. At the time, many Catholics were shocked that a clergyman would take such a course. Richelieu was not the first European statesman to make alliances and war based on national interest rather than religion (the alliance of French King Francis I and the Ottomans in the 1520s comes to mind), but his realist decision was a turning point. Hereafter, more and more European diplomats and leaders would engage in Machiavellian realpolitik to increase their nations' power and wealth.

TEST TIP: On the AP EURO exam, you should be familiar with the term *realpolitik*. It is German for "realistic" or "practical." Realpolitik warfare is a system of politics based on practical rather than moral or ethical considerations. Realpolitik is often used throughout history when referring to amoral and ruthless warfare, as illustrated in Niccoló Machiavelli's *The Prince* (pp. 60–61).

The Decline of Power in Spain

The 17th century in general, and the Thirty Years' War in particular, are synonymous with the decline of the power of Spain.

Keep in mind that the Spanish monarchy had been the most innovative and cutting-edge monarchy under Ferdinand and Isabella (1469–1516). As we saw in the section on the Age of Exploration, gold, silver, and other resources and manual labor made Spain the greatest power of the 16th century and the envy of all of Christendom. True, Spain suffered major defeats, such as the loss of the Armada in 1588, but in 1600 it was still the richest, most powerful, and most respected state in Christian Europe. All of that would change in the 17th century, one of the ugliest and most humiliating centuries that one country has ever had to suffer through.

Even at the height of Spain's strength and prestige, its inner weaknesses had begun to make themselves known. During the 16th century, the country became dangerously overstretched in finances and manpower by fighting in Charles V's and Philip II's innumerable wars. There remained enormous shipments of silver coming into the peninsula from the New World, but Spain suffered from a shortage of perceptive economists who could manage expenditures. Spain's runaway inflation destroyed industries and crushed lives while enriching its creditors. In the 17th century, Philip's incompetent son and grandson further made a mess of things with wasteful spending and impulsive policies. The Thirty Years' War had started out so promisingly for the Spanish, with a string of victories in the 1620s against the German Protestants and the Dutch.

TEST TIP: On the AP EURO exam, you should be familiar with the causes of Spain's decline as a world power. Many factors contributed to Spain's decline including its crushing religious war defeats, internal rebellions, poor investments from its overseas wealth, high taxes, huge loans to finance religious wars, and disastrous twists of fate. These factors ensured that by 1648 Spain was a shadow of its previous self. It had lost Portugal as a subject state, had let the Netherlands go after 80 years of war, and had lost important territory to the French, its mortal enemy. Spain was politically, economically, and spiritually broken.

Heads Up: What You Need to Know

On the AP EURO exam, the **Peace of Westphalia** of 1648 is considered one of the most important treaties in world history. Be prepared for questions on the treaty (its winners and losers), as well as its long-term aftermath and consequences for the continent of Europe. (Note: Because it was a series of treaties, historians sometimes refer to this peace agreement as the Treaty of Westphalia.)

The Peace of Westphalia officially ended the Thirty Years' War and established the political system of Europe. Nation-states (rather than churches, multinational empires, or multistate leagues) became the center of international politics. It also enshrined the concept of the European balance of power, a system in which smaller powers would unite in coalitions to prevent one *hegemon* (a leading power) from dominating the continent. The balance of power would form the basis of Western diplomacy until well into the 20th century.

The Peace of Westphalia (1648)

Key Facts about the Peace of Westphalia

The aftermath of the Thirty Years' War. The year 1648 finally brought an end to the Thirty Years' War. It was the bloodiest war ever fought in Europe until that point. Decades of roaming bands of mercenaries, mass tortures, rapes, public executions, atrocities, and reprisals, and looting and pillaging armies had left their mark on a weary Europe. The devastation in central Europe was particularly horrendous with almost 8 million deaths. German territories were decimated, at least one-third of the population was killed, while in some regions the death rate was closer to 75 percent. Over half of all German towns were destroyed by the soldiers, and many towns, castles, and estates were sacked, burned, and ravaged over and over again as different armies came rampaging through.

The historical consequences of the Thirty Years' War. The Thirty Years' War resulted in several outcomes: 1) The war established several treaties, including the Peace of Westphalia; 2) Nation-states were free to practice any religion, and Calvinism became a politically accepted religion; 3) The Holy Roman Empire declined in power; and 4) France became the dominant European power.

Three different treaties to end religious wars. What we conveniently label the **Peace of Westphalia** was actually three different treaties. The first was the **Peace of Munster,** which ended the separate Eighty Years' War between Spain and Holland. This conflict had become subsumed within the larger conflict, but the Spanish-Dutch vendetta had been settled with Spanish capitulation. The other two treaties were signed on the same day: the **Treaty of Munster** (easily confused with the Peace of Munster), which ended the war between the Imperial powers and France, and the **Treaty of Osnabruck,** which ended the war between the Imperial powers and the Protestants.

The war was an abject defeat of Spain and the Holy Roman Empire. After so much bloodshed and chaos, the religious status quo in the lands of Germany had effectively been maintained. However, the actions of France and disgust with the carnage led Europeans down the course of turning away from religious, sectarian conflict and toward what would eventually emerge as *secularism* (the separation of church and state).

The rise of a modern age. The Peace of Westphalia ushered in the modern age.

- **Nation-state.** The treaty established nation-states as sovereign key players in foreign affairs and wars.
- **National sovereignty.** The treaty also established the conception of *national sovereignty,* which is the system where each nation has its own border, government, and makeup. For example, the kingdom of France was no longer merely defined by the king himself (including his finances, his familial relations, and his laws), but by the larger nation itself. Religion was still important in Catholic and Protestant nations, but sovereignty of the nation came before the cross-border authority of religious hierarchies or religious laws.
- **Reasons of state.** There was also the introduction of the idea of "reasons of state." Operating under a rational framework of interests, a nation had its own state interests that it would pursue based on necessities, without morality or honor being the primary considerations. We saw many examples of this during the course of the war itself. For example, the French government attacked the Habsburgs, their Catholic brethren, because the political interests of the state had come to dominate its religious considerations. From then on, even deeply conservative and religious states would begin to operate under national interests to a progressively more regular degree.

The era of secular nation-states would be a tumultuous one. As a testament to this, several of the Great Powers of 1648 had either become second-rate or had ceased to exist altogether by 1815, our next watershed date. For the former, consider Spain, Holland, Denmark, and Sweden; for the latter, Poland-Lithuania.

TEST TIP: On the AP EURO exam, you may be asked to discuss the unification of nations (i.e., Germany or Italy). During the 17th century, the lands of Europe were devastated by the Thirty Years' War, and some historians argue that the depopulation and destruction engendered by the war delayed the unification of Germany and Italy as nation-states by more than a century. As a reminder, these events did not occur in history until the second half of the 19th century, over 200 years after the end of the Thirty Years' War.

Germany was weakened. This is an important issue because Germany remained a vacuum of political and military power, a fact that allowed France to become powerful.

Chapter Review Practice Questions

Practice questions are for instructional purposes only and may not reflect the format of the actual exam. On the actual exam, questions are grouped into sets. Each set contains one source-based prompt (document or image) and two to five questions.

Multiple-Choice Questions

Questions 1 and 2 refer to the following reproduction by Jacques Callot.

Source: *The Great Miseries of War*, "The Hanging" (1632) by Jacques Callot.

1. Which of the following historical aspects of the Thirty Years' War is portrayed in Callot's illustration?

    A. Assaults of Spanish armies on the Aztec Empire
    B. St. Bartholomew's Day Massacre of French Huguenots
    C. Outbreak of mass atrocities and reprisals by opposing armies
    D. Repression of the Catholic Church by Romanian barons

2. Which of the following true generalizations best supports the impact of the conditions depicted in Callot's illustration?

    A. The Thirty Years' War was one of the bloodiest wars of all time.
    B. The code of noble chivalry was still popular in the mid-17th century.
    C. The Spanish Inquisition reached its apex in the 17th century.
    D. The Thirty Years' War began as a religious war but later became more political.

Questions 3 and 4 refer to the following passage.

> Therefore, let us now chiefly consider women; and first, why this kind of perfidy is found more in so fragile a sex than in men. And our inquiry will first be general, as to the general conditions of women; secondly, particular, as to which sort of women are found to be given to superstition and witchcraft; and thirdly, specifically with regard to midwives, who surpass all others in wickedness . . .
>
> And the first is, that they are more credulous; and since the chief aim of the devil is to corrupt faith, therefore he rather attacks them. . . . The second reason is, that women are naturally more impressionable, and more ready to receive the influence of a disembodied spirit; and that when they use this quality well they are very good, but when they use it ill they are very evil. . . . The third reason is that they have slippery tongues, and are unable to conceal from the fellow-women those things which by evil arts they know; and, since they are weak, they find an easy and secret manner of vindicating themselves by witchcraft.

> —*Malleus Maleficarum* by Heinrich Kramer and Jacob Sprenger, 1487.

3. Based on your knowledge of European history, which of the following aspects of the 16th-century witch hunts is best supported by the passage?

    A. More witch trials in Catholic countries existed than in Protestant ones.
    B. Suspecting converts from Judaism of false conversion
    C. Torturing suspected witches
    D. Targeting older widows with accusations of witchcraft

4. With which statement below would the authors most likely agree?

    A. Women are purer in spirit than men.
    B. Women are likely to become witches to increase their political power.
    C. Women should have an equal place in the church hierarchy with men.
    D. Women's sexual desires make them more open to the temptations of the devil.

Questions 5 and 6 refer to the following passage.

Upon this a question arises: whether it be better to be loved than feared or feared than loved? It may be answered that one should wish to be both, but, because it is difficult to unite them in one person, it is much safer to be feared than loved, when, of the two, either must be dispensed with. Because this is to be asserted in general of men, that they are ungrateful, fickle, false, cowardly, covetous, and as long as you succeed they are yours entirely; they will offer you their blood, property, life, and children, as is said above, when the need is far distant; but when it approaches they turn against you.

And that prince who, relying entirely on their promises, has neglected other precautions, is ruined; because friendships that are obtained by payments, and not by greatness or nobility of mind, may indeed be earned, but they are not secured, [. . .]

Nevertheless a prince ought to inspire fear in such a way that, if he does not win love, he avoids hatred; because he can endure very well being feared whilst he is not hated, which will always be as long as he abstains from the property of his citizens and subjects and from their women.

—*The Prince* by Niccoló Machiavelli, 1513.

5. Which of the following best supports realpolitik, or realism in politics, as presented in the passage?

    A. Religion should be the primary influence on political choices.
    B. A leader should expect the worst and immoral behavior from his opponents.
    C. Those with power will decide what morality really is.
    D. A nation should always ally with more powerful opponents.

6. Which historical figure's actions best emulate the advice given in the passage?

    A. Catherine de Medici's St. Bartholomew's Day Massacre of French Huguenots
    B. Ferdinand and Isabella expelling the Jews from Spain
    C. Pope Urban II calling for a crusade against the infidels
    D. Charles V agreeing to the Peace of Augsburg

Questions 7 and 8 refer to the following theses from Martin Luther.

Out of love for the truth and from desire to elucidate it, the Reverend Father Martin Luther, Master of Arts and Sacred Theology, and ordinary lecturer at Wittenberg, intends to defend the following theses and to dispute on them in that place. Therefore he asks that those who cannot be present and dispute with him through oration shall do so in their absence by letter. In the name of our Lord Jesus Christ, Amen. [. . .]

5. The pope neither desires nor is able to remit any penalties except those imposed by his own authority or that of the canons.

6. The pope cannot remit any guilt, except by declaring and showing that it has been remitted by God; or, to be sure, by remitting guilt in cases reserved to his judgment. If his right to grant remission in these cases were disregarded, the guilt would certainly remain unforgiven. [. . .]

36. Any truly repentant Christian has a right to full remission of penalty and guilt, even without indulgence letters.

37. Any true Christian, whether living or dead, participates in all the blessings of Christ and the church; and this is granted him by God, even without indulgence letters.

—*The 95 Theses* by Martin Luther, 1517.

7. Which of Luther's criticisms of the Catholic Church is best supported by the passage?

   A. Only two sacraments are legitimate, baptism and communion.
   B. The pope wastes money on projects like St. Peter's Basilica.
   C. Papal indulgences should not be sold.
   D. The pope is an Antichrist and false prophet.

8. Which theological innovation of Luther is best supported by the passage?

   A. The Holy Roman Emperor had no authority over religion.
   B. Laymen should have access to the Bible for their own interpretation.
   C. Man is saved through salvation alone.
   D. Forgiveness of sins can be attained without confession.

Questions 9 and 10 refer to the following reproduction by El Greco.

Source: *The Adoration of the Name of Jesus,* or *The Dream of Philip II* by El Greco, 1579.

9. Which of the following best reflects Philip II of Spain's reign as portrayed in El Greco's painting?

    A.   Philip's role as defender of the Catholic Church against Muslims and Protestants
    B.   Philip's conversion of native Indians in the New World
    C.   Philip's troubled relations with his son, Don Carlos
    D.   Philip's wars with the Valois of France

10. Which of the following characterizes El Greco's portrayal of Philip II of Spain?

    A.   His martial prowess and excellence in commanding armies
    B.   His love of glamour and demonstrations of kingly wealth
    C.   His solemnity and respect for the Church
    D.   His youth and vigor

Document-Based Question

1 question

60 minutes

Reading Time: 15 minutes (brainstorm your thoughts and organize your response)

Writing Time: 45 minutes

Directions: The document-based question is based on the seven accompanying documents. These documents are for instructional purposes only. Some of the documents have been edited for the purpose of this practice exercise. Write your response on lined paper and include the following:

- **Thesis.** Present a thesis that supports a historically defensible claim, establishes a line of reasoning, and responds to all parts of the question. The thesis must consist of one or more sentences located in one place—either the introduction or the conclusion.
- **Contextualization.** Situate the argument by explaining the broader historical events, developments, or processes that occurred before, during, or after the time frame of the question.
- **Evidence from the documents.** Use the content of at least three to six of the documents to develop and support a cohesive argument that responds to the topic question.
- **Evidence beyond the documents.** Support or qualify your argument by explaining at least one additional piece of specific historical evidence not found in the documents. (Note: The example must be different from the evidence used to earn the point for contextualization.)
- **Analysis.** Use at least three documents to explain the documents' point of view, purpose, historical situation, and/or audience relevant to the topic question.
- **Historical reasoning.** Use historical reasoning to show relationships among the documents, the topic question, and the thesis argument. Use evidence to corroborate, qualify, or modify the argument.

Based on the documents that follow, answer the question below.

Question 1: Based on your knowledge of European history, analyze reasons for Spain's characterization during the colonization of the New World from 1500 to 1650.

Document 1

> **Source: Anonymous, *Theatrum Orbis Terrarum*, the first New World atlas, 1654.**
>
>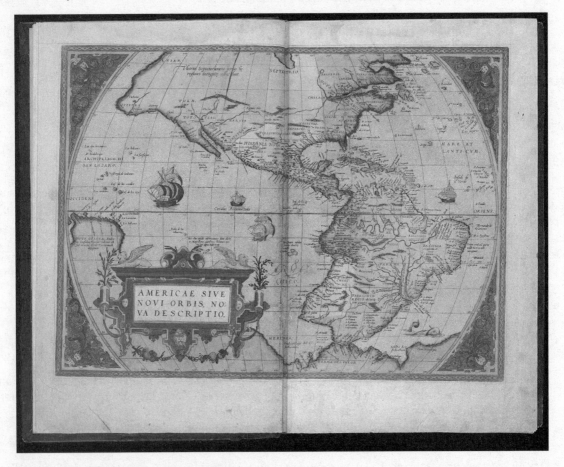
>
> Library of Congress Geography and Map Division.

Document 2

Source: Bartolomé de las Casas, *A Short Account of the Destruction of the Indies*, 1542.

Two principal and general customs have been employed by those, calling themselves Christians, who have passed this way, in extirpating and striking from the face of the earth those suffering nations. The first being unjust, cruel, bloody, and tyrannical warfare. The other—after having slain all those who might yearn toward or suspire after or think of freedom, or consider escaping from the torments that they are made to suffer, by which I mean all the native-born lords and adult males, for it is the Spaniards' custom in their wars to allow only young boys and females to live—being to oppress them with the hardest, harshest, and most heinous bondage to which men or beasts might ever be bound into. . . .

The cause for which the Christians have slain and destroyed so many and such infinite numbers of souls, has been simply to get, as their ultimate end, the Indians' gold of them, and to stuff themselves with riches in a very few days, and to raise themselves to high estates... [A]ll the Indians of all the Indies never once did aught hurt or wrong to Christians, but rather held them to be descended from heaven, from the sky, until many times they or their neighbours received from the Christians many acts of wrongful harm, theft, murder, violence, and vexation. . . .

Document 3

Source: Bernardino de Sahagún, *The Florentine Codex*, 1570.

Fifteenth chapter, where it is said how the Spaniards came from Itztapalapan when they reached Mexico.

[. . .]

And when Moteuczoma went out to meet them at Huitzillan, thereupon he gave various things to the war leader, the commander of the warriors; he gave him flowers, he put necklaces on him, he put flower necklaces on him, he girded him with flowers, he put flower wreaths on his head. Then he laid before him the golden necklaces, all the different things for greeting people. He ended by putting some of the necklaces on him.

Then [Cortés] said in reply to Moteuczoma, "Is it not you? Is it not you then? Moteuczoma?"

Moteuczoma said, "Yes, it is me." Thereupon he stood up straight, he stood up with their faces meeting. He bowed down deeply to him. He stretched as far as he could, standing stiffly. Addressing him, he said to him,

"Be doubly welcomed, enter the land, go to enjoy your palace; rest your body. May our lords be arrived in the land."

"Let Moteuczoma be at ease, let him not be afraid, for we greatly esteem him. Now we are truly satisfied to see him in person and hear him, for until now we have greatly desired to see him and look upon his face. Well, now we have seen him, we have come to his homeland of Mexico. Bit by bit he will hear what we have to say."

Thereupon [the Spaniards] took [Moteuczoma] by the hand. They came along with him, stroking his hair to show their good feeling. And the Spaniards looked at him, each of them giving him a close look. They would start along walking, then mount, then dismount again in order to see him. . . .

Document 4

Source: **Bernal Diaz del Castillo**, *The Conquest of New Spain*, 1547.

Our general and father Olmedo readily perceived that Moteuczoma would never give his consent to our erecting a cross on his chief temple, nor that we should build a chapel there. We had, upon our arrival in Mexico, fitted up some tables as an altar; but we were not satisfied with this, and therefore begged of Moteuczoma's house-steward to order his masons to build us a church in our quarters, who referred us to the monarch himself, upon which Cortes sent him with our interpretress and the page Orteguilla to Moteuczoma, who immediately gave his consent and issued orders accordingly.

In three days our church was finished, and a cross planted in front of our quarters. Mass was now regularly said every day as long as our wine lasted, which indeed was very short, as Cortes and father Olmedo, during their illness in Tlascalla, had used the wine destined for the mass. Nevertheless we went daily to church and prayed on our knees in front of the altar and before the holy images; because it was our Christian duty, and that Moteuczoma and his grandees might notice it, and become accustomed to these holy things, from seeing us kneel down in devotion before them, particularly when we repeated the Ave Maria.

Document 5

Source: **Lienzo de Tlaxcala**, *Battle of Otumba*, 1552. **The improbable Spanish victory over the Aztec warriors.**

Batalla de Otumba

Document 6

Source: Anonymous, *Las Castas*, a social-racial classification system used in Spanish American colonies, c. 1700.

Document 7

> **Source: Christopher Columbus, Journal of the First Voyage of Columbus, 1503.**
>
> Sunday, 14th of October
>
> . . . these people are very simple as regards the use of arms, as your Highnesses will see from the seven that I caused to be taken, to bring home and learn our language and return; unless your Highnesses should order them all to be brought to Castile, or to be kept as captives on the same island; for with fifty men they can all be subjugated and made to do what is required of them. . . .
>
> Sunday, 16th of December
>
> . . . your Highnesses may believe that this island (Hispaniola), and all the others, are as much yours as Castile. Here there is only wanting a settlement and the order to the people to do what is required. For I, with the force I have under me, which is not large, could march over all these islands without opposition. I have seen only three sailors land, without wishing to do harm, and a multitude of Indians fled before them. They have no arms, and are without warlike instincts; they all go naked, and are so timid that a thousand would not stand before three of our men. So that they are good to be ordered about, to work and sow, and do all that may be necessary, and to build towns, and they should be taught to go about clothed and to adopt our customs.

Answer Explanations

Multiple-Choice Questions

1. **C.** The Thirty Years' War took place in Europe, so choice A cannot be correct, and choice B references an event that took place in the previous century. Choice D references repression that took place much later in European history. The correct answer is choice C because of the mass violence and brutality of the Thirty Years' War in central Europe.

2. **A.** The torture and murder of prisoners of war or civilians violated the code of chivalry, so choice B does not make sense. The Spanish Inquisition was still strong in the 17th century, but it played no part in the fighting of the Thirty Years' War, so choice C can be eliminated. Choice D is an attractive distracter because it asserts a true statement that is also relevant to the topic, but it is not proven by or related to the image. Choice A is correct; the Thirty Years' War was superlatively bloody and witnessed enormous casualties and damage.

3. **D.** While this document was written by Catholic theologians, the zeal for witch hunting was no weaker among Protestants than among Catholics, so choice A is incorrect. While Jewish conversos could be punished by the Spanish Inquisition (choice B) and suspected witches could be tortured (choice C), neither is referenced in the document. Choice D is the best answer because the document does focus on the weakness of women and their vulnerability to the devil's charms.

4. **D.** The authors are clearly critical of women, so choices A and C are inherently bad answer choices. Choice B might have been a possible accusation against some women accused of witchcraft, but it has no justification in the document. Choice D is the best answer; the passage's authors see women's licentiousness and tendencies toward lust as their greatest weakness in terms of the devil's temptation.

5. **B.** Realism in politics means acting upon national interest without regard for religion, which excludes choice A. Choice D is not generally in keeping with realism; under that theory a nation should balance powerful opponents with alliances of weaker ones. Choice C is close to the amoral quality associated with

Machiavelli and realpolitik, but the best answer is choice B because it is supported by the passage. If a leader expects the worst, he will be prepared for betrayal, treachery, and subterfuge from his opponents.

6. **A.** The best answer is choice A, as the St. Bartholomew's Day Massacre was a power move by Catherine de Medici and her advisors to remove powerful opponents to her son's position on the throne. Contemporaries of her, especially Protestant ones, called her a murderer and an immoral follower of Machiavelli's theories. Choice B references a religious decision that increased Spanish unity at the expense of its economic power. Choice C is incorrect for the same reason as choice B, as it was religiously motivated. Charles' agreement to the Peace of Augsburg (choice D) was pragmatic, but it was made because of the emperor's weakness, not because of realism.

7. **C.** Theses 36 and 37 reference papal indulgences, so choice C is the best answer. Choice A is an accurate part of Luther's argument about the sacraments, but nothing is said about that in the passage. While Luther indeed did criticize the pope for wasting the funds of the Catholic faithful and undermined his authority, there is nothing in the passage to support choices B or D.

8. **D.** The passage does not mention the Emperor of the Romans, so choice A is incorrect. Laymen's access to translated Bibles (choice B) and salvation through faith (choice C) were of course crucial to Luther's reformed church, but neither is referenced in the passage. Choice D is justified based on theses 5 and 6 in the passage.

9. **A.** Philip II saw himself as defender of the one true faith against Muslim infidels and Protestant heretics. The religious iconography justifies choice A, without referencing choices B, C, or D, even though all three of the latter are important parts of Philip's reign as king of Spain.

10. **C.** Choice A is an attractive answer because Philip was a warring king. However, as often as Philip waged wars, he was not a great military commander like his father. Philip was known for his austere lifestyle, so choice B makes little sense. Choice D is incorrect because Philip is clearly an aged man in this portrait, a fact that El Greco does not attempt to conceal (although in fact by this point in history Philip may not have been physically able to kneel because of his gout). Choice C is the correct answer, as evidenced by the prominent religious symbolism of the portrait and by the solemnity of the simple black clothes for which Philip was known.

Document-Based Question

DBQ Scoring Guide

To achieve the maximum score of 7, your response must address the scoring criteria components in the table below.

Scoring Criteria for a Good Essay	
Question 1: Based on your knowledge of European history, analyze reasons for Spain's characterization during the colonization of the New World from 1500 to 1650.	
Scoring Criteria	Examples
A. THESIS/CLAIM	
(1 point) Presents a historically defensible thesis that establishes a line of reasoning. (Note: The thesis must make a claim that responds to *all* parts of the question and must *not* just restate the question. The thesis must consist of *at least* one sentence, either in the introduction or the conclusion.)	The response provides a well-developed thesis and responds with a historically defensible argument that characterizes Spain's aggressive nature. The essay is presented in the context of the 16th and 17th century time period. The line of reasoning throughout the sample response shows that the Spanish used brute force to conquer the native peoples of their New World colonies and utilized policies of racial differentiation and economic subjugation to keep them under control.

Continued

Scoring Criteria	Examples
B. CONTEXTUALIZATION	
(1 point) Explains the broader historical context of events, developments, or processes that occurred before, during, or after the time frame of the question. (Note: Must be more than a phrase or reference.)	The essay cites evidence from a broader historical context that is relevant and valid to the question prompt. All of these documents demonstrate the repressive nature of the Spanish imperial project. Spain may have presented its imperialism in religious or ideological terms as a benefit to the colonized peoples, but in reality it was a cynical and brutal method of controlling the population and exploiting them for economic gain and world dominance.
C. EVIDENCE	
Evidence from the Documents **(2 points)** Uses at least *six* documents to support the argument in response to the prompt. OR **(1 point)** Uses the content of at least *three* documents to address the topic prompt. (Note: Examples must describe, rather than simply quote, the content of the documents.)	To earn the highest point value, the essay response draws from at least six documents to support the thesis with evidence. For example, Document 1 shows a map of the Spaniard's vast colonization. Document 2 showcases the brutality for which the Spanish would become infamous thanks to the Black Legend of Spain. Documents 3 and 4 show how deception and violence were standard operating procedures from the beginning of colonization. Document 5 shows the Spanish using powerful horses to charge and conquer the Aztecs on the battlefield. Document 6 shows the racial castas system (a hierarchical system of race classification) through which the people of Spanish America were regulated.
Evidence Beyond the Documents **(1 point)** Uses at least one additional piece of specific historical evidence beyond those found in the documents that is relevant to the argument. (Note: Evidence must be different from the evidence used in contextualization.)	The essay extends the argument by incorporating outside evidence. For example, in the final paragraph, the sample essay compares the "average colonizing" to Spain. The Spanish were no more brutal than other imperialistic countries during 16th and 17th centuries. Sociology also tells us that racial relations are often a tool of power in the hands of the state.
D. ANALYSIS AND REASONING	
(1 point) Uses at least *three* documents to explain how each document's point of view, purpose, historical situation, and/or audience is relevant to the argument. (Note: References must explain how or why, rather than simply identifying.)	The essay response draws from at least three documents to support the documents' point of view. For example, the primary source authors of Documents 3, 4, and 5 illustrate first-hand accounts (in written and pictorial formats) of the Spaniards imperialistic intentions to dominate the native Aztecs. In addition, the author of Document 6 shows how racial divisions and differentiation was turned into a means of controlling the population and keeping them divided and conquered.
(1 point) Uses historical reasoning and development that focuses on the question while using evidence to corroborate, qualify, or modify the argument. (Examples: Explain what is similar and different; explain the cause and effect; explain multiple causes; explain connections within and across periods of time; corroborate multiple perspectives across themes; or consider alternative views.)	The essay focuses on the historical skill of *causation* to corroborate the argument. The sample response not only explains the causes for Spain's aggressive characterization, but it also explains the consequences of Spain's aggressive nature—imperialistic empires, Spanish economic gains, and world dominance.

Sample Response

In the 16th century, the Spanish became the first European power to explore and conquer lands in the New World of the Western Hemisphere. From Hispaniola and New Spain to Florida and Peru, the Spanish used imperialism, brute force, racial differentiation, and economic subjugation to conquer these lands because they wanted to develop new empires in Mesoamerica.

When the Spanish conquistador, Herman Cortés, arrived in Mesoamerica, he was met by the dominant warrior civilization in the region—the Aztecs. The Aztec natives had a well-developed social and tributary system, and believed that their gods had great powers. When the Spaniards arrived, the Aztecs thought Cortés was a reincarnation of their god Quetzalcoatl and welcomed Cortés into their capital, Tenochtitlan. The point of view by de Sahagun in Document 3 shows that the leader of the Aztecs, Montezuma, put flower necklaces on him and bowed down deeply to Cortes to welcome his new visitors.

The Spaniards took advantage of the Aztecs beliefs and their gullibility. Cortés deceived the Aztecs and used violence to conquer the peoples of their New World colonies. Cortés utilized policies of racial differentiation and economic subjugation to keep them under control. Historical evidence shows that the Empire of Spain was determined to exploit the economic resources of the New World using any means necessary, even brute force. In Document 7, Christopher Columbus describes the economic potential of the island of Hispaniola. Columbus recognized from the beginning the ability of this island to be harnessed to the benefit of the Spanish motherland, so long as extreme measures of slavery, property acquisition, and violence were accepted. The map in Document 1 shows the end result: the vast colonization of the New World to create a Spanish empire in the New World. The Spanish employed the means of their imperialistic nature shown in Document 6: using racial *castas,* the racial mixing of different types to keep the people in line and focusing on their immediate "superiors" and "inferiors" rather than on the overall Spanish overlords.

The Spanish used the most depraved forms of violence to carve up their new empire. In Document 2, Bartolomé de las Casas' perspective provides a vivid description of the most ruthless methods used by the Spanish in the conquest and rule of the Caribbean islands. Documents 3, 4, and 5, confirm the means used for subjugating the people of the Aztec Empire after the conquest of that polity by the armies of Cortés. In Document 3, the Spaniards benefited from the Aztec leader, Montezuma, believing that Cortés was sent from the Gods to be the Aztec's new ruler. The Aztec's did as the Spaniard's asked. As corroborated in Document 4, the natives built the Spaniard's sleeping quarters, and an altar and cross, where they could pray each morning. In the process, the Spaniard's aroused their appetite by discovering a hidden room filled with gold and treasures greater than anyone had ever seen.

If the Spaniards couldn't get what they wanted peacefully, they used weapons and brutal tactics never before witnessed by the Aztecs. Document 5, shows that in the *Battle of Otumba*. The Spaniards had prompted an attack and it escalated into a battle where 15 mounted horses were used to drive through the center of the Aztecs, leaving them confused. Cortes ordered his officers to focus on killing the new Aztec ruler and their leaders. Even though the Aztecs had about 100,000 to 200,000 men and Cortés only had 500 men, the Spaniards slaughtered the Aztecs and founded the New Spain in the center of the Aztec Empire, Tenochtitlan.

Spain provided the example of European colonization of the New World. The Spanish aggressions were no more brutal or murderous than the average colonizing country; they simply had the first chance to colonize and made full use of it. The fruits of their labors provide the perfect example of how colonization can succeed and take root.

Chapter 5

Historical Period Two: Enlightenment and Expansion (c. 1648 to c. 1815)

Period Two explores the emergence of modern-day Europe from the Scientific Revolution and the Age of Absolutism in the 17th century to the end of the French Revolutionary War and the reign of Napoleon in the 19th century.

- The Scientific Revolution (c. 1543 to c. 1700)
- The Age of Enlightenment (c. 1685 to c. 1789)
- European Powers of the 17th and 18th Centuries
- Europe's Economic and Social Changes in the 18th Century
- The French Revolution and the Pre- and Post-Revolutions (1789 to 1799)
- The Napoleonic Wars (1799 to 1815)

Heads Up: What You Need to Know

The Age of Enlightenment is also known as the Age of Reason because there was a radical shift in thinking in Western Europe—from blind obedience to rational reasoning based on scientific evidence. It paved the way for modern-day intellectual traditions around the world.

Overview of AP European History Period Two

As progressive ideas began to spread across Europe, the organization of political sovereignty, economic expansion, and scientific achievements changed the relationships among people and among nation-states. Monarchs became a symbol for absolutism in France, Spain, and Britain, and new philosophies ignited revolutionary wars across Europe.

The AP European History curriculum framework and key concepts explain the reasoning behind particular ideas and developments that emerged in Europe during this time period. The historical examples of significant themes, trends, events, and people support the recommended study topics that are specific to the AP EURO exam. As you study the key concepts, use the chart on the next page as a checklist to guide you through what is covered on the exam.

Visit http://apcentral.collegeboard.com for the complete updated AP EURO course curriculum and key concept descriptions.

AP European History Key Concepts (c. 1648 to c. 1815)	
KEY CONCEPT 2.1: NEW MODELS OF POLITICAL SOVEREIGNTY **Different models of political sovereignty affected the relationship among states, and between states and individuals.**	In much of Europe, absolute monarchy was established over the course of the 17th and 18th centuries. Challenges to absolutism resulted in alternative political systems. After 1648, dynastic and state interests, along with Europe's expanding colonial empires, influenced the diplomacy of European states and frequently led to war. The French Revolution posed a fundamental challenge to Europe's existing political and social order. Claiming to defend the ideals of the French Revolution, Napoleon Bonaparte imposed French control over much of the European continent, which eventually provoked a nationalistic reaction.
KEY CONCEPT 2.2: GLOBAL COMMERCE **The expansion of European commerce accelerated the growth of a worldwide economic network.**	Early modern Europe developed a market economy that provided the foundation for its global role. The European-dominated worldwide economic network contributed to agricultural, industrial, and consumer revolutions in Europe. Commercial rivalries influenced diplomacy and warfare among European states in the early modern era.
KEY CONCEPT 2.3: THE SCIENTIFIC REVOLUTION **The spread of Scientific Revolution concepts and practices and the Enlightenment's application of these concepts and the practices to political, social, and ethical issues led to an increased, but not unchallenged, emphasis on reason in European culture.**	Enlightenment thought, which focused on concepts such as empiricism, skepticism, human reason, rationalism, and classical sources of knowledge, challenged the prevailing patterns of thought with respect to social order, institutions of government, and the role of faith. New public venues and print media popularized Enlightenment ideas. New political and economic theories challenged absolutism and mercantilism. During the Enlightenment, the rational analysis of religious practices led to the demand for religious toleration. The arts moved from the celebration of religious themes and royal power to an emphasis on private life and the public good. While Enlightenment values dominated the world of European ideas, they were challenged by the revival of public expression of emotions and feeling.
KEY CONCEPT 2.4: EUROPEAN SOCIETY **The experiences of everyday life were shaped by demographic, environmental, medical, and technological changes.**	In the 17th century, small landholdings, low-productivity agricultural practices, poor transportation, and adverse weather limited and disrupted the food supply, causing periodic famines. By the 18th century, the balance between population and the food supply stabilized, resulting in steady population growth. The consumer revolution of the 18th century was shaped by a new concern for privacy, encouraged the purchase of new goods for homes, and created new venues for leisure activities. By the 18th century, family and private life reflected new demographic patterns and the effects of the commercial revolution. Cities offered economic opportunities, which attracted increasing migration from rural areas, transforming urban life and creating challenges for the new urbanites and their families.

Significant Themes

The significant themes related to the key concepts for Period Two should help you to think about *why* particular developments occurred in the context of the larger historical "big picture." The study questions give you important insights related to specific questions that will help you make mental connections between each given topic and the social, political, economic, and religious significance.

Glance through the study questions before you start the review section. Take notes, mark questions, and write down page number references to reinforce your learning. Refer to this list as often as necessary until you are confident with your answers.

Study Questions Related to Significant Themes in Period Two

Theme 1: Interaction of Europe and the World

1. How did European states establish and administer overseas commercial and territorial empires? (Hint: Slave-labor system, diplomacy, mercantilism, and warfare.)

2. What were the economic gains and losses for Europeans in overseas trade? (Hint: Think about mercantilism, diplomacy, expansion of transatlantic slave-labor system, increased social and cultural diversity, new consumer goods, introduction of disease, and global conflict.)

3. Did non-Europeans adopt or resist European values? (Hint: Think about cultural, political, and economic values and how these may have influenced the French Revolution.)

4. How did European expansion and colonization bring non-European societies into global economic, diplomatic, military, and cultural networks? (Hint: Revolution across the Atlantic, colonial rivalry, diplomacy, and slave trade.)

5. How did the impact of war and overseas colonization impact the balance of power until 1789? (Hint: Think about the dynastic wars, colonial wars, French revolutionary wars, and commercial rivalries.)

Theme 2: Poverty and Prosperity

1. How did the new wealth generated by new trading and manufacturing impact Europe's consumer economy? (Hint: Europe became dominant in a worldwide economic network. The new wealth created a commercial revolution and an agricultural revolution, which led to demographic changes, but also created commercial rivalries and warfare.)

2. What led to the increased migration from rural areas into cities from the 16th to the 19th centuries? (Hint: The commercial and industrial revolutions led to new demographic patterns and changes in the social structure, most notably a shift from land ownership to the commercial elite. This led to increased taxation and affected peasants across Europe.)

Theme 3: Objective Knowledge and Subjective Visions

1. How did the Enlightenment encourage Europeans to understand human behavior, economic activity, and politics as governed by natural laws? (Hint: Rational and empirical thought, new political and economic theories, and the revival of public sentiment.)

2. What helped to contribute to the new theory of knowledge and the conception of the universe? (Hint: Overseas exploration, Renaissance humanism, new print media, the scientific method, and rational and empirical thought.)

3. How did social inequality impact the 19th and 20 centuries? (Hint: Europeans challenged traditional values and ideas about gender roles, class structure, and political participation, and observed rational and empirical thought.)

4. How did the worldview of science and reason challenge social order and roles? (Hint: Arguments over the exclusion of women from political life.)

5. How did individualism, subjectivity, and emotion come to be valid sources of knowledge? (Hint: Europeans' emphasis on private life in the arts, the revival of public sentiment and feeling, and new political ideals in an emotional identification with a nation.)

6. What political and economic theories helped shape constitutional states, parliamentary governments, and the concept of individual rights? (Hint: Liberalism: John Locke and Adam Smith.)

Theme 4: States and Other Institutions of Power

1. Describe the changing relationship between states and ecclesiastical authorities regarding religious tolerance. (Hint: Think about absolutist religious policies, the French Revolution's attack on religion, and Napoleon and the Concordat of 1801.)

2. How did religious and secular groups attempt to limit monarchical power? (Hint: Think about the political action taken by England and the Dutch Republic, the French Revolution, Enlightenment ideals, and John Locke and Adam Smith—their theories of resistance to absolutism.)

3. How did religious reform in the 16th and 17th centuries challenge the control of the Church? (Hint: Religious tolerance of Christian minorities and Jews, emergence of civic venues such as salons and coffeehouses, expansion of printing to disseminate knowledge.)

4. How did nationalism change the European balance of power? (Hint: Think about *fraternité,* or brotherhood, and the citizen armies in the French Revolution and the Napoleonic Wars.)

5. How did new weapons, tactics, and military organization shift the balance of power? (Hint: Think about the French Revolutionary warfare and Napoleonic tactics and warfare.)

6. What were the causes and reactions of the French Revolution in Europe? What were the reactions around the world? (Hint: Think about non-European resistance to European cultural, political, and economic values and Napoleon's domestic reforms. Also, consider how the role of social inequality contributed to the French Revolution.)

7. What natural rights movements helped to redefine governments and citizenship? (Hint: Social and political equality such as feminism, anticolonialism, and immigrant's rights.)

8. Explain the emergence of representative government as an alternative to absolutism. (Hint: Think about the Enlightenment principles in politics and capitalism.)

Theme 5: Individual and Society

1. How did the growth of commerce and changes in manufacturing challenge the dominance of corporate groups and traditional estates? (Hint: Urban migration, poverty, the agricultural revolution, and the cottage industry.)

2. Why did the nature of the family change over time? (Hint: Consumerism, privacy in the home, and marriage.)

3. What events may have led to the tensions between women's roles and status in their private domain versus their public domain? (Hint: The French Revolution, the Napoleonic Code, Enlightenment, and natural rights.)

4. How did women participate in and benefit from shifting values of European society? (Hint: The French Revolution, Napoleonic era, Enlightenment, salons, commercial revolution, and family life.)

5. How were identities such as race and class defined in relationship to society? (Hint: Think about the slave revolt and independence of Haiti, nobles and absolutism, the French Revolution, and the attack on feudalism.) And why did Europeans marginalize certain populations? (Hint: The Reign of Terror, counterrevolution, and the Napoleonic Empire.)

Theme 6: National and European Identity

1. How and why did national identities develop and spread? (Hint: Absolutism and state centralization, war-inspired emotional attachments to nations, enlightenment values, and monarchs like Russia's Peter the Great and France's Louis XIV built on common language and cultural identity.)

2. How did political, economic, and religious developments challenge or reinforce the idea of a unified Europe? (Hint: Rivalry between Britain and France resulted in wars fought in Europe and colonies; growth of overseas trade; the French Revolution challenged Europe's social order; Peace of Westphalia.)

Important Events, Terms, and Concepts

The table that follows shows important events, terms, and concepts that you should be familiar with on the AP EURO exam. Please don't memorize each concept now. Place a check mark next to each topic as it is studied and refer to this list as often as necessary. After you finish the review section, reinforce what you have learned by working the practice questions at the end of this chapter. The answers and explanations provide further clarification into the perspectives of the people who lived in Europe about 200 to 400 years ago.

Events, Terms, and Concepts You Should Know					
Event	**Year/Brief Description**	**Study Page**	**Event**	**Year/Brief Description**	**Study Page**
The English Civil War	**1642–1649.** The English Civil War determined whether England would be an absolutist and theocratic government or a republican government.	p. 126	The American Revolutionary War	**1775–1783.** The American Revolution saw the implementation of European Enlightenment ideals in the New World.	p. 131
Battle of Vienna	**1683.** A turning point in history. It was the first time the Church and the Commonwealth combined forces to protect Europe from Muslim control.	p. 124	The Seven Years' War	**1756–1763.** The Seven Years' War transformed the global balance of power and heralded British world dominance for nearly two centuries.	pp. 130–131
The Edict of Nantes is revoked	**1685.** This edict ended the relative tolerance of Jews and Protestants in France.	p. 123	The French Revolution begins	**1789.** The French Revolution was one of the most important events in human history. Europe is still living in a world that is shaped by the legacy of the French Revolution.	pp. 134–139
The War of the Spanish Succession	**1700–1714.** This war transformed the face of European politics. It also set the stage for a century of cabinet wars.	pp. 128–129	Rule of Napoleon Bonaparte	**1799–1814.** Napoleon's rule was short-lived, but it transformed Europe's legal and political systems.	pp. 139–142
Denis Diderot published the *Encyclopédie*	**1751–1772.** This document epitomizes the Enlightenment school of philosophy and political thought.	p. 120	Napoleon is defeated	**1814–1815.** Napoleon's defeat ended his reign in Europe and reorganized the state of European diplomatic power. The military genius died in exile in 1821.	pp. 141-142

Chapter Review

Chapter 5 covers the rise of the modern world caused by the 1) Scientific Revolution, 2) the Age of Enlightenment, 3) the French Revolution, and 4) the Napoleonic era. The timeline on the next page illustrates AP EURO important events that happened gradually over time during this period. The timeline should help you visually and conceptually identify what preceded and what followed particular events.

The intellectual history of this period spotlights two key areas of study: the **Scientific Revolution** and the **Age of Enlightenment.** New perspectives of the natural world inspired European scientists, thinkers, and leaders to bring about revolutionary changes throughout Europe in science, philosophy, religion, and government. Great thinkers emerged with innovative contributions that drove Europe to world leadership.

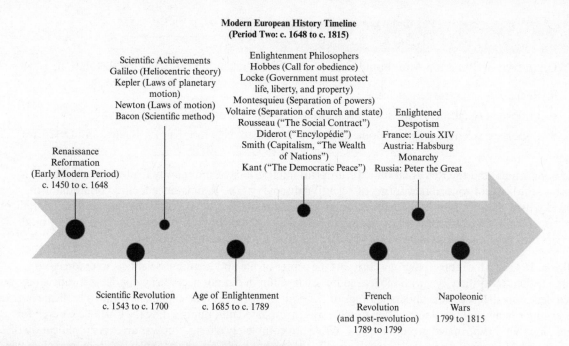

Modern European History Timeline
(Period Two: c. 1648 to c. 1815)

Scientific Achievements
Galileo (Heliocentric theory)
Kepler (Laws of planetary motion)
Newton (Laws of motion)
Bacon (Scientific method)

Enlightenment Philosophers
Hobbes (Call for obedience)
Locke (Government must protect life, liberty, and property)
Montesquieu (Separation of powers)
Voltaire (Separation of church and state)
Rousseau ("The Social Contract")
Diderot ("Encylopédie")
Smith (Capitalism, "The Wealth of Nations")
Kant ("The Democratic Peace")

Enlightened Despotism
France: Louis XIV
Austria: Habsburg Monarchy
Russia: Peter the Great

Renaissance Reformation (Early Modern Period) c. 1450 to c. 1648

Scientific Revolution c. 1543 to c. 1700

Age of Enlightenment c. 1685 to c. 1789

French Revolution (and post-revolution) 1789 to 1799

Napoleonic Wars 1799 to 1815

Heads Up: What You Need to Know

On the AP EURO exam, you must know that the Scientific Revolution and the Age of Enlightenment were influenced by the Renaissance and Reformation period for the following reasons: 1) breakdown of traditional feudal loyalties, 2) rise of powerful monarchies, 3) collapse of a single religious doctrine and the effects of the printing press, 4) discovery and exploration of the New World, and 5) reexamination of the science of the universe.

The Scientific Revolution (c. 1543 to c. 1700)

The foundation for the Scientific Revolution and the Age of Enlightenment was laid by the Renaissance and Reformation, which had undermined the unquestionable authority of the Church and the scholastic tradition. As you will see, the two are very closely intertwined.

Pre-Scientific Thinking

It may surprise you to learn that scientists did not always base their theories about the natural world on what we know today as scientific evidence. Instead, scientists long ago looked at two sources for knowledge: tradition and religion.

Key Facts about Pre-Scientific Thinking

Tradition. During the medieval period, before the Scientific Revolution, most of the scientific ideas were from inherited traditions of Aristotle. Aristotle, as you may remember, was a Greek philosopher who died nearly 2,000 years before the Scientific Revolution. Aristotle argued that Earth was the center of the universe (geocentric theory) and that Earth remained stationary while the stars and the heavens moved around it.

Heads Up: What You Need to Know

On the AP EURO exam, you should know the following related to the Scientific Revolution:

- Reasons for the rise of science.
- Important scientific terms: scientific method, empiricism, and inductive reasoning.
- Important scientific contributions: Copernicus, Galileo, Newton, Kepler, Bacon, and Descartes.

The Renaissance and the Reformation led European intellectuals to move away from the traditions of ancient scholars and toward new forms of scientific discovery. The Renaissance focused on humanism, individualism, and the scientific organization of knowledge. In the context of humanism and individualism, scientists soon had a desire for public recognition, and this paved the way for scientists to break through barriers into new areas of evidentiary study. The result was scientific methodology.

Religion. In the 17th century, religious faith was the center of life and learning. Scientists were forced to reconcile their scientific views with biblical sources. The Church did not necessarily oppose scientific study, but ruled decisively that scientific understandings of the natural world must be explained within a biblical context. For example, many people assumed that Galileo was investigated and punished by the Catholic Church for theorizing that Earth rotated around the sun. While not completely wrong, this was an oversimplification of the facts. The Church did not object to this specific theory, but it did object to Galileo's failure to explain why his theory did not complement biblical sources. This might seem like a small distinction to us in the 21st century, but it provides the historical context of medieval Catholicism. Religion was the utmost authority.

The Rise of Science

The 17th-century scientific achievements were spearheaded by Copernicus, who dared to question that the sun, not Earth, was the center of the universe. Scientists soon began to reevaluate the blindly accepted theories of ancient scientists like Ptolemy and Aristotle, and a new era of scientific thinking emerged.

Did you know? Many people believe that the Scientific Revolution started during the Age of Enlightenment. In fact, the myriad of scientists who worked on new scientific theories between c. 1543 and c. 1700 did not even see themselves as living through or taking part in a Scientific Revolution. In truth, the Scientific Revolution actually started much earlier in history with the notable contributions of scientists like Copernicus and Galileo.

Surprisingly, the notion of one specific time period was actually conceived by a historian in the late-18th century. It was later in history, while reconsidering the many different divisions of science, that historians named the Scientific Revolution of early modern Europe as a singular, discrete phenomenon. Given this vantage point, historians were able to clearly see that the scientific inventions and innovations of the 16th and 17th centuries laid the foundation for the modern world, with all of its technological wonders and scientific complexities.

Scientific Terms and Concepts

This section covers important scientific terms, famous scientists, and their contributions that you should know for the AP EURO exam.

Scientific method. The scientific method is the logical process of gaining knowledge through designing and performing experiments. The scientific method involves conclusions that are based on the observation and reproducibility of results. The five basic steps of the scientific method are 1) make an observation, 2) state the problem by forming a question, 3) develop a hypothesis, 4) test the hypothesis in an experiment, and 5) analyze the data to draw the conclusion. This ties to *empiricism,* which is a system of knowledge.

Did you know? The scientific method and empirical evidence contributions of the 16th and 17th centuries form the foundation for scientific study of our modern world today!

Empirical evidence. Empiricism is the study of knowledge derived through the observation of sensory experiences. As opposed to the study of other systems of knowledge, such as *ontology* (the study of the nature of being, or thinking through thought processes), empirical knowledge is learned by gathering and examining evidence of observable experiences in the physical world.

Inductive reasoning. Before discussing inductive reasoning, let's first define deductive reasoning. *Deductive reasoning* is the type of reasoning that detectives use when they deduce the facts to form ideas about what might be true. Their reasoning is a "top-down" approach of knowledge—from general to specific. Detectives examine general facts and then work their way down to form a specific conclusion about what might have occurred after considering all of the possibilities.

Inductive reasoning, on the other hand, is a "bottom-up" approach—from specific to general. It involves examining small sample groups of phenomena to make larger (general) observations or categorizations about the world. For example, a scientist might look at the positioning of the stars each night while using inductive reasoning to conclude that Earth revolves around the sun. Inductive reasoning is the basis of scientific knowledge, along with empiricism and the scientific method.

Scientific Achievements

Isaac Newton is probably the most well-known scientist during this time period, but when most people think of this time period they often think of astronomer Galileo Galilei. He not only proved Copernicus' heliocentric solar system, but he also stood up to the Catholic Church by refusing to recant his scientific views. Other scientists struggled with the question of certainty, like the philosopher Descartes, who became popular for the phrase *Cogito, ergo sum*—Latin for "I think, therefore I am." Descartes posed a question: "What can a person know for sure about the world?" He deduced that a person can only be unequivocally sure of one thing—his own existence.

The reference table that follows reviews some of the most important figures of the Scientific Revolution. Notice that these scientific contributions are listed in context of the times in which the scientists lived. Ancient writers like Ptolemy and Aristotle influenced some of these ideas, but other scientists went on to make some of the most important contributions in the field of science today.

For the AP EURO exam, be sure to know each of the scientists and what they invented, theorized, or proved.

Important Scientific Achievements		
Scientist	**Field**	**Famous For**
Nicolaus Copernicus (1473–1543)	Astronomer, mathematician	Instrumental in establishing a heliocentric theory (sun-centered universe). First to challenge the Church doctrine of the geocentric theory (Earth-centered universe).
Galileo Galilei (1564–1642)	Astronomer, physicist, mathematician	Law of planetary motion. Invented an improved telescope and provided first observational evidence in support of Copernicus' heliocentric theory, which caused him to stand trial for heresy against the Church.
Johannes Kepler (1571–1630)	Astronomer, mathematician	Three laws of planetary motion (math calculations regarding planetary orbits that supported heliocentric theory—planets follow elliptical paths, not circular paths).
Sir Isaac Newton (1642–1727)	Mathematician, astronomer, physicist	Laws of motion. Laws of gravity proved the force of Earth's gravity on the orbit of the moon. Provided final proof of Copernicus' heliocentric theory.
Sir Francis Bacon (1561–1626)	Philosopher, scientist, queen's lawyer	Continued the ideas of Aristotle and established the foundation for modern-day scientific inquiry. The scientific method (experiments). Inductive reasoning (empiricism). Knowledge is power.
Rene Descartes (1596–1650)	Mathematician, philosopher, scientist	Known as the father of modern philosophy, "I think; therefore I am" (*Cogito, ergo sum*). Applied logic to understand the natural world (i.e., deductive thought and rationalism).

The Age of Enlightenment (c. 1685 to c. 1789)

The empiricism of the Scientific Revolution and the humanism of the Renaissance set the stage for the innovative new thoughts of the Enlightenment and the rise of new political philosophies in the 17th and 18th centuries. The revolutionary ideas of these great writers radically changed the face of Europe during the period of Enlightenment. European thinkers believed that reason, logic, and knowledge could change the world.

This section reviews the causes for the rise of philosophical ideas, the new ideas related to Europe's political, social, and economic climate, and the important written contributions made by Europe's notable philosophers.

A new way of thinking about humanism started in the Renaissance when great thinkers began to reevaluate old beliefs of philosophy, government, and economics. Before reviewing the political *philosophes* (French term for "philosophers"), let's take a look at two important overarching concepts that frequently appear on the AP EURO exam: enlightened despotism and the Republic of Letters.

Enlightened Despotism

The ideas of the Enlightenment reached to the thrones of European monarchs. Monarchs who supported the ideals of the Enlightenment, yet remained powerful rulers, were called enlightened despots. **Enlightened despotism** refers to despotic (or tyrannical) monarchs who embraced some aspects of Enlightenment thought.

Many people are confused by the idea of enlightened despotism. After all, the philosophes seemed to undermine absolute monarchies. How could kings embrace their ideas? Simply put, enlightened despots chose to accept what they liked about the Enlightenment and ignored ideas that threatened their interests. Sometimes monarchs even exchanged correspondence with prominent philosophers and solicited their opinions about enlightened ideas. Most of all, monarchs emphasized the public use of reason to enhance the power and efficiency of the state. In exchange for reforms and changes, monarchs demanded absolute loyalty and obedience from their people. German philosopher Immanuel Kant proclaimed that these rulers said to their subjects, "Argue as much as you will, and about what you will, but obey!" For example, Frederick the Great of Russia said, "The people may think what they want, and I may do what I want."

The three primary enlightened despots you should be familiar with are:

- **Frederick the Great (Prussia):** Frederick adopted many ideas of the philosophers and frequently corresponded with Voltaire. Frederick was interested in scientific advancements and reformed the system of agriculture (crop rotation and iron plows), reformed taxation, and increased religious tolerance.

- **Catherine the Great (Russia):** Catherine supported Russia's cultural modernization through Western Europe's art, architecture, the printing press, and music. She restricted the cruel punishment of the poor (with mixed results), and when the French government banned the publication of Diderot's *Encyclopédie,* she offered to publish it.

- **Joseph II (Austria):** Joseph was the most progressive of all the monarchs. He attempted to abolish serfdom in Austria, reduced the power of the nobility, promoted religious tolerance, abolished torture, and made changes to the legal and judicial systems.

Republic of Letters

During the 18th century, philosophers were aware that they were living in revolutionary times with radical new ideas being created at an unprecedented rate. Keep in mind that some overbearing monarchs and governments considered new political thoughts dangerous. Intellectuals exchanged their philosophies through written communications called the **Republic of Letters.** It was through these letters that great thinkers could debate one another, inform one another, and craft blueprints for the future of an enlightened republic.

Enlightened Philosophy

Key Facts about Enlightened Philosophy

Reason and knowledge will transform society. Enlightenment is also known as the "Age of Reason." The Enlightenment was a philosophical movement that welcomed ideas suggesting that the conditions of society could be transformed through reason and knowledge. From politics and religion to economics and culture, the philosophers of the Enlightenment believed that reason could fix the problems of contemporary society.

Church and state must be separate. In line with sensible thinking, many philosophers criticized what they viewed as irrational or illogical. For example, Voltaire wrote articles, pamphlets, and books like his famous *Candide* that satirized irrational religion, inefficient monarchical government, and general ignorance. Many thinkers of the time were *deists* (meaning they believed in the existence of God, but that God did not intervene on behalf of mankind). Most philosophers believed that the Church and state should be separated, and that all men should enjoy freedom of religion (or lack of religion).

Government powers must separate into branches. Philosopher Baron Montesquieu sought to diminish the problems of society by proposing the separation of governmental powers into three branches: legislative, judicial, and executive. Rather than a government ruled by a monarchy (king or queen) or ruled by despot (dictator), Montesquieu believed that elected leaders must have government checks and balances in order to prevent corruption and the abuse of power.

Citizens deserve legal rights. Many philosophers believed in some form of a representative government, but fought to abolish torture and unlawful imprisonment. One of the most important political ambitions that nearly all Enlightenment philosophers believed in was the inalienable rights that all people deserved. This was reinforced in Jean-Jacques Rousseau's (and others') conception of a *social contract* (an agreement between rulers and ruled, in which there were mutual obligations and promises). Voltaire and many others contended that a free society could not truly exist if ordinary citizens did not possess the right to freedom of speech, press, assembly, and petition. Moreover, many of the Enlightenment thinkers wanted to guarantee a citizen's right to a fair trial, a jury of his peers, and the right to defend himself in a speedy trial against whatever charges had been brought against him.

Society must look to a better future. Philosophers not only criticized social injustices, but also explored the question, "How does someone build a better future?" John Locke proposed that a new society based on rational governance was possible using the concept of *tabula rasa* (the concept that humans are born into "clean slates" onto which values and morals can be written by society). Another perspective from Rousseau stated that a return to nature, which was pure, would allow men to remove the corruption and filth accrued from living in modern society.

Citizens needed all the information possible to secure their independence and make their own decisions. Denis Diderot compiled an encyclopedia (*Encyclopédie*) with thousands of articles about everything from democracy and secularism to stonemasonry techniques and cooking directions. Diderot's idea was that more information available to the ordinary man would enable him to be a strong citizen and a prepared democrat. Fortunately, Enlightenment philosophers had a strong belief in the inevitability of progress in an upward trajectory. This would eventually reach a state of utopian perfection. From a 21st-century perspective, the Enlightenment philosophers are often viewed as hopelessly naïve. However, during the Enlightenment, the belief in progress fueled enormous energies among philosophers, readers, and statesmen.

Society does not sufficiently address gender inequality. Regrettably, most Enlightenment philosophers ignored racial matters and gender inequality. Only a few liberal philosophers believed in eliminating the slave trade and providing beneficial reforms to nonwhites. Mary Wollstonecraft, a late-18th-century philosopher, however, was one of the first feminists to gain notoriety in European history for gender equality. Writing both works of fiction and political philosophy, she pointed out the irony that women were being deprived of their rights to independence and economic self-sufficiency. Wollstonecraft argued that women should have the birthright opportunities of education, inheritance, and work to be able to prove themselves equal to men in all matters of the public sphere.

Governments must apply new capitalistic economics. Great thinkers, like economics founder Adam Smith, applied the rationalism of the Scientific Revolution and Enlightenment principles to capitalism. Prior to Smith's revolutionary ideas, the success of a nation's economy was measured by its storage of gold and silver. Smith believed that a nation's wealth should be measured by production and commerce (now known as the GDP: gross domestic product), rather than pounds of gold and silver.

When most governments were practicing heavy-handed forms of mercantilism, Smith argued for *laissez-faire capitalism* (a system of economics in which the government did not interfere in the economy). Smith wrote about an "invisible hand" of the market, whereby the element of unseen economics starting with self-interest would achieve the greatest good for everyone. If a government did not interfere, the market would self-regulate and provide benefits for everyone. It may have seemed greedy for wealthy individuals to pursue their own self-interests, Smith admitted, but when they did, they inadvertently created wealth for everyone, not just themselves. Smith asserted that he "intends only his own gain, and he is in this, as in many other cases, led by an invisible hand to promote an end which was not part of his intention."

Political Philosophers of the Enlightenment

Use the reference table below to review some of the most important political philosophers of the Enlightenment and European history.

For the AP EURO exam, be sure that you know each of the philosophers and what ideas they theorized.

Enlightenment Political Philosophers		
Philosopher	Nationality	Famous For
Thomas Hobbes (1588–1679)	English	Life is nasty, brutish, and short. Called for obedience.
		The state must be powerful to protect people; *Leviathan*.
John Locke (1632–1704)	English	When man enters into a social contract with the government, he does not give up his rights to protect life, liberty, and property. Government by consent of the governed. Ideas influenced American colonists and the Declaration of Independence.
		Chief purpose of the government is to protect inalienable rights that can't be taken away.
		The *tabula rasa* (blank page); *Essay Concerning Human Understanding*.

Continued

Philosopher	Nationality	Famous For
Baron Montesquieu (1689–1755)	French	Separation of powers in government; *The Spirit of Laws.* A system of checks and balances to prevent corruption and absolutism.
Voltaire (1694–1778)	French	Freedom of conscience, religion, press, and assembly; *Letters Concerning the English.* Separation of Church and state.
Jean-Jacques Rousseau (1712–1778)	French	The general will guides democracy. End inequality among citizens by an agreement of general will; *The Social Contract.* Humanity should return to nature because it is pure.
Denis Diderot (1713–1784)	French	Published the *Encyclopédie.*
Adam Smith (1723–1790)	Scottish	Wrote the bible of capitalism and the first system of political economy, *The Wealth of Nations.* The invisible hand—a free market regulates itself.
Immanuel Kant (1724–1804)	Prussian	Democracies will not war with one another; *The Democratic Peace.* Metaphysical philosophy—universal principles of human reason gives moral law. Scientific knowledge, morality, and religious belief are mutually consistent: *Critique of Pure Reason.* Synthesized early modern rationalism and empiricism.
Mary Wollstonecraft (1759–1797)	English	The ideas of feminism started in the Renaissance, but Wollstonecraft originated modern feminism, calling for equality of women; *Vindication of the Rights of Woman.*

European Powers of the 17th and 18th Centuries

In the 16th century, the high point of Spanish dominance declined as quickly as it had appeared. As feudalism declined, the growth of nation-states increased in the 17th and 18th centuries, followed by a series of great political changes and power shifts. The shifting territorial boundaries created landholding exchanges throughout Western and Eastern Europe.

The Rise of France

By the mid-1600s, France's growing population size drove it to become the most powerful nation on the European continent. France's population boom from 1500 to 1750 surpassed any other European nation-state.

Nation	Year (c. 1500)	Year (c. 1700)
France	15 million	25 million
England	7 million	9 million
Spain	6 million	8 million

> **TEST TIP:** If you don't remember the specific historical details to answer a free-response question on the AP EURO exam, remember that you can take an educated guess. For example, France's population was almost three times greater than any other nation's. During this period, a nation with a large population size typically had a powerful economy, military, and government.

France's massive population overshadowed others with a strong economy, gained diplomatic power over other nations, and influenced cultures from around the world. Remember, this was a time when the army size still had a strong correlation to military power. France became the dominant military superpower of Europe that lasted for two centuries. It was during this time that France set the standard for the rest of Europe. Spain and Italy no longer made the greatest cultural contributions in art, music, philosophy, and language.

Louis XIV: The Sun King

Louis XIV was one of the most influential rulers in European history. He ruled for 72 years (from c. 1643 to c. 1715), starting at 4 years old—longer than any monarch in world history. One of Louis XIV's greatest achievements was the construction of the majestic **Palace of Versailles** that he built in the suburbs outside of Paris. Perhaps the most majestic and ostentatious palace in all the world, Versailles features massive sprawling gardens, ornate and winding fountains and ponds, and meticulously crafted and maintained shrubbery. It is a geometric model that celebrates the Scientific Revolution's spirit of orderliness and classification. It is also an example of *monumental architecture* (architecture built to demonstrate the power, wealth, and glory of the monarch), similar to the Taj Mahal in India or the Pyramids at Giza in Egypt.

Source: Hyacinthe Rigaud, *Louis XIV of France*, 1701.

Heads Up: What You Need to Know

On the AP EURO exam, you should know the following related to Louis XIV, who reigned over France during the Golden Age.

- Destabilized the power of the nobles.
- Believed in the divine right theory of government (the monarch's power is from God). His famous statement *Létat, c'est moi* ("I am the state") supported this belief.
- Engaged France in many territorial wars over foreign nations and established the first modern army.
- Expanded mercantilism to improve the economy.
- Revoked the Edict of Nantes.

Key Facts about King Louis XIV

Louis XIV destabilized the power of the nobles. As discussed in Chapter 4, during the medieval period, France was divided among different regions and ruled by a weak king who had to contend with the powerful influence of the nobles. The nobles sought to limit the powers of the monarchy, but Louis XIV changed the course of history by weakening the power of the nobles and ensuring that a powerful monarchy would rule France. Louis XIV embodied the power and majesty of 17th- and 18th- century **absolute monarchs** (the monarch [king or queen] had unrestricted power over the people).

Louis XIV led France's wars in pursuit of territorial expansion. France participated in numerous wars to conquer lands and expand French territories. Louis XIV's passion for "glory" led his massive army to quickly become the most powerful military in Europe and worldwide. Many other armies, like the Spanish and the Dutch, could not match France's innovative military tactics. Much like Charles V of Spain had done in the 16th century, Louis XIV conquered so many new territories, raising an empire so large and powerful in the process, that France became the dominant world power—a **universal monarchy** (meaning, one monarchy has supreme rule over most land).

France was at war for almost all of Louis XIV's rule. With threats looming, other nations put their differences aside and unified to fight against France. Between 1660 and 1700, France fought four major wars and over a dozen minor wars. Over time, more and more nations united against France, even mortal enemies such as Spain, Holland, and England. By 1700, France was the most powerful nation in the world, but it was also the most feared and hated nation in the world.

Did you know? Louis XIV declared himself the absolute authority over France. His famous assertion, "The state? I am the state." (*"Létat, c'est moi."*) reflected his belief that he embodied the state, had a divine right to rule, and had unlimited power. This statement is useful to remember as his authoritative point of view.

France did not have a powerful parliament or legislature, and Louis XIV continued to reduce the power of the nobles at the expense of the members of the *bourgeoisie* (middle class), whom Louis believed would be easier to control.

Louis XIV advanced mercantilism to improve the economy. Louis XIV pursued policies that would boost the economy followed by the dictates of **mercantilism.** Mercantilism was a new economic policy that centralized the control of all trade by the monarch by increasing exports and limiting imports. It emphasized accumulating a gold supply and favoring a balance of trade when dealing with foreign nations. Mercantilism placed high tariffs or taxes on imported goods in order to restrict foreign imports and boost France's manufacturing power.

Under King Louis XIV's rule, Jean-Baptiste Colbert served as France's controller of finances and increased France's balance of trade. Colbert was an important part of advancing France's economic reconstruction. In the end, Colbert's successful efforts fell short due to Louis XIV's costly war campaigns that ultimately depleted the French economy.

Louis XIV revoked the Edict of Nantes. The 16th-century Edict of Nantes, which had granted religious tolerance in France, was overturned by Louis XIV. He then enacted the *Edict of Fontainebleau* (1685) in an effort to eliminate the *Huguenots* (French Protestants inspired by John Calvin) and unify the Catholic religion. From this point on, Protestants, Jews, and other non-Catholics were theoretically considered enemies of the state. Although most people practiced secretly and were reluctantly tolerated in many areas of France, hundreds of thousands were driven out of France to England and the Netherlands. The Edict of Fontainebleau was historically important because France's economy and military declined after the edict when thousands of people were exiled.

Eastern Europe

Now that we've covered the most powerful European nation in the 17th and 18th centuries, let's review the important Eastern European nations: Prussia, Austria, and Russia.

Heads Up: What You Need to Know

On the AP EURO exam, you should know the following related to absolutism in the Eastern Europe nation-states during the Age of Enlightenment.

- Prussia: Cultivated an army of the state, which promoted Prussian nationalism.
- Austria: Survived the Ottoman onslaught and rebuilt its power and status.
- Russia: Achieved victories over the Ottomans and the Swedes; Peter the Great modernized Russia.

Prussia

In 1650, Prussia was a small and distressed northern kingdom in the Holy Roman Empire (today's northeastern Germany and northwestern Poland). Prussia's desolate wasteland was considered the poorest backwater in the Holy Roman Empire with no serious potential.

Key Facts about Prussia

Protestant movement. Although the Thirty Years' War weakened the Holy Roman Empire, it strengthened Prussia and the Hohenzollern rulers. Prussia emerged as a northern Protestant counterbalance to the Catholic Church.

Military force. In the 1650s, Prussians could not hope to compete with the cultural and economic pursuits of France and other European nations. Instead, Prussians focused on building a military powerhouse. Prussia could not rely on a superior army size against their opponents, so it ensured that its army had the best discipline, well-trained soldiers, and most innovative military tactics. For decades, Prussia's small, elite army honed its talents against Sweden, Poland, and other neighboring states. Soldiers were well paid and accorded an elevated status in Prussian society. This elevated status was similar to that of merchants in England or priests in Spain. By the mid-18th century, the militaristic Prussia became powerful enough to seriously compete with Austria for control of German territories.

Did you know? Two centuries after the Age of Enlightenment, Prussia became the most dominant military power on the continent on the cusp of German unification. Reflect upon continuities and changes over time in the 17th- and 18th-century history to understand how Prussia ultimately became so powerful.

Absolute monarchy. The Prussian kings ruled in absolute fashion, which they accomplished through close cooperation with the *Junkers,* a group of landed nobles in the eastern portions of the kingdom. In exchange for control over their serfs, the Junkers gave absolute control to the king and served in his armies.

Austria

The 17th century was a tumultuous time for the Austrian Habsburg monarchy. The end of the Thirty Years' War in 1648 was their low point, and things didn't get better because they still had to deal with the Ottoman Empire (Turkish Empire). The Ottomans had been prevented from conquering Europe in the 1520s at the Battle of Vienna, but in 1683 they again began to battle Vienna with a strong army. It appeared that the Turks were poised to invade the heart of Europe once again, but in fact the Habsburgs and the Holy Roman Empire, with help from the Commonwealth in central Europe, turned back the Ottomans and destroyed their military forces. The Turks soon began a quick retreat. While the Turks maintained territory in Europe until the 20th century, they never again posed a serious threat to the European great powers.

In the late-17th and early-18th centuries, the Austrian Habsburgs increased their dominance by reforming the army, updating their tax system, and limiting the power of the nobility. Austrians continued to use Catholicism to enforce religious uniformity and to persecute or expel religious minorities. The Habsburg monarchy may not have had the power to dominate the Holy Roman Empire as they once had, but they were instrumental in ruling their own lands as absolute monarchs.

Russia

For centuries, Russia had languished as Europe's most backward and divided land. Russians had suffered the oppression of the invading Mongols, who were not chased out of Russia until the end of the 15th century—the same time Italy was enjoying its Renaissance and Spain was discovering the New World. Russia was isolated from the rest of Christian Europe, and little of the latter's influence made its way into Russia. Russia increased its military power and size over the course of the next two centuries, but it was not until the reign of Peter the Great that Russia truly emerged on the European stage.

Peter the Great

Peter the Great, of the Romanov Dynasty that ruled Russia from 1613 to 1917, did more to modernize Russia than any leader until the Russian Revolution. Ruling from 1682 to 1725, his extraordinary vision propelled Russia from a backward nation to a modern European nation. Peter believed that if Russia did not become modernized and westernized, Russians would always be defeated. This belief was reinforced by his observations of other nations as he traveled in disguise through Western Europe in his youth.

Source: Paul Delaroche, *Peter der Grosse,* 1838.

Heads Up: What You Need to Know

On the AP EURO exam, you should be familiar with Peter the Great's breakthrough projects to modernize Russia's military, economy, government, and culture. It was not until the reign of Peter the Great that Russia truly emerged on the European stage. Keep Peter's modernization projects in mind as you compare the political and economic consequences of Russia's 20th-century lack of industrialization and modernization.

Key Facts about Peter the Great and His Modernization Projects

Military modernization. Peter transformed the Russian army by changing recruitment strategies, providing modern uniforms and weapons, and providing Western specialists to lead the troops, update Russia's forts, and implement new financing schemes. Peter also established a powerful Russian navy for the first time.

Economic modernization. Peter introduced Western European crops to Russia to enhance its ability to feed its burgeoning population. He imported economists who could sensibly guide Russia's finances in enlightened ways. Peter nationalized the treasury and modernized the tax system.

Cultural modernization. Peter wanted Russian monarchs and nobles to expand their cultural practices and embrace Western ideas. They needed to wear Western garb, listen to Western music, appreciate Western art, and speak Western languages like French. Famously, Peter even demanded that Russian nobles give up their traditional long beards, in which they had much pride. Nobles who refused to shave had to pay a "beard tax," and Peter sometimes sheared off a nobleman's beard with his own royal hand.

St. Petersburg. Peter built the city of St. Petersburg at the northwestern edge of the empire as a Western-looking city, both literally and figuratively. Thousands of workers died building this magnificent, massive city on the swamps of the Baltic coastline. St. Petersburg, which Peter made the capital of Russia (an honor it would retain until the Russian Revolution), was a modern city with a port that was open to trade and cultural exchange with the nations of Western Europe.

Peter's modernization programs paid dividends in a series of wars against Sweden and the Ottomans. Keep in mind that Sweden was a dominant world power in 1700, with control over all of Scandinavia and some of the south Baltic coastline. In the Great Northern War of 1700–1721, Russia soundly defeated Sweden for the first time and seized the Baltic shore and major warm-water ports. Russia also soundly defeated the Ottomans and came to challenge Poland as an Eastern European power.

England

Heads Up: What You Need to Know

On the AP EURO exam, you should know the following related to England during the 17th and 18th centuries:

- Oliver Cromwell and his role in the execution of Charles I and enforcing religious doctrine.
- Thomas Hobbes and his Leviathan theory.
- Outcome of the Glorious Revolution: The Bill of Rights and the end of state Catholicism.

The English Civil War (1642 to 1651)

When last we left England in Chapter 4, the country had fallen into a mass civil war between the supporters of King Charles I, called the *Cavaliers* (Anglicans and some Catholics), and the Protestants, called *Roundheads* (Puritans and other Protestant dissenters), who advocated for the power of the Parliament. The Cavaliers and Roundheads were fighting over religious and political differences between the king, who believed in absolutism, and the Roundheads, who wanted a stronger Parliament. The Cavaliers started strong, but within a few years the tide had turned.

Oliver Cromwell

Oliver Cromwell, an outspoken Puritan, took the reins of the Roundhead military forces and transformed their army with new weapons, tactics, and strategies into what was called the **New Model Army.**

Key Facts about Oliver Cromwell

Cromwell's role in the execution of King Charles I. At the end of the war, tensions began to rise between Charles I and Parliament. Charles I was captured by the Puritans and put on trial. In January of 1649, the Parliament leaders shocked the entire world by executing King Charles I in a public spectacle. It was not the first time a European king had been executed, but this had been more common in the most chaotic periods of the medieval period. In the more stable 17th century, it was a shock to the world.

Cromwell enforced a Puritan religion. After the king's execution, Parliament gained control over power in England. Cromwell became Lord Protector of England. As we were reminded of in the last chapter, Puritan faith demanded that the government enforce the moral code of religion. In keeping with this tradition, the government oversaw press censorship, the closure of pubs, and the prohibition of theater performances. During this period, the Puritan ideology reigned supreme and England became a *theocracy* (government ruled by the Church), wherein people who were Catholic, drank alcohol, danced to music, or failed to show up for Sunday service could be jailed. The power of the state and the church became one presiding authority.

Cromwell condemned the Leveller movement. The once-ostracized Puritans were not as tolerant as their Anglican and Catholic predecessors had been. Cromwell persecuted non-Puritan nonconformists and condemned the **Leveller movement** (informal alliance of reformers). Levellers sought democracy and tolerance and were committed to abolishing noble privileges.

Cromwell condemned the Irish. Cromwell used great brutality in his treatment of the Irish. Ireland had been invaded by the English at different times over centuries. Cromwell made a name for himself in the annals of Irish history by brutally repressing the Irish and ensuring the destruction of their resistance to English rule.

Thomas Hobbes

One of the most important intellectuals to live in 17th-century England was Thomas Hobbes (1588–1679). He was a mathematician and writer, and was best known for his political philosophy.

Key Facts about Thomas Hobbes

Hobbes believed that humans were brutal. After living through the tumult, violence, and destruction of the English Civil War, Hobbes was horrified by what he witnessed. He started seeing the worst in other people and in the world at large. Hobbes asserted that the natural order of the world was violent and human life was "nasty, brutish, and short." According to Hobbes, human beings took advantage or hurt other people whenever they could get away with it. Hobbes believed that, left to their own devices, most people would commit unspeakable evil in a perpetual attempt to gain advantages over other people.

Hobbes believed in absolutism. Hobbes' pessimistic view about human beings shaped his belief that people must be ruled and protected in order to prevent violence. Thus, there must be a powerful and mighty government to protect the people and curb their primitive instincts. In 1651, Hobbes expounded upon these views in his text, *Leviathan*. *Leviathan* was a metaphor from the Bible about a huge, terrifying sea monster. Hobbes believed that a Leviathan type of state could bring about civil peace and social order. The government must be terrifying and powerful to tame the common masses. According to Hobbes, people must exchange much of their personal liberties in order to gain safety.

Hobbes believed that the state had an obligation to protect its citizens. Hobbes' worldview might sound very repressive, but don't forget that Hobbes also believed that the government had an obligation to the people. Hobbes believed that the state had an obligation to protect the safety and rights of people, or the state should be forfeited and overthrown by the people.

The Glorious Revolution (1688 to 1689)

In 1658, Cromwell died. In search of a leader, Parliament's leaders decided upon calling Charles II, the son of the executed former king, from his exile in France. Charles II was not a popular leader, but his reign did ensure stability. After his death in 1685, however, problems returned to England. Since Charles II had no sons upon his death to inherit the throne, his brother, James, was brought to the throne.

Key Facts about the Glorious Revolution

King James II dethroned. James II became a hated monarch, because unlike his father, who had mostly ignored religious issues, James was a devout Catholic and sought to restore Catholicism. While the Catholic minority rejoiced at being freed from religious persecution, English Protestants objected to his reign because they remembered Mary Tudor's short but violent reign a century before. In 1688, Protestants overthrew James II and installed James' Protestant daughter, Mary, and her Dutch husband, William of Orange. The dethroning of James II was called the **Glorious Revolution** because it was achieved without bloodshed, unlike the English Civil War. Faced with capture and imprisonment, James II fled into exile.

Bill of Rights strengthened Parliament. The revolution established Parliament's authority over the monarchy. The leaders of Parliament wanted to ensure stability and prevent further absolutism, religious conflict, or civil war. The **Bill of Rights** of 1689 firmly enacted the permanence of Parliament and its power to regulate crown finances. This document was incredibly important to democracy in England and was the start of the constitutional monarchy that we know today. It was built upon the principles of the **Magna Carta** of 1215 (a cornerstone agreement that protected the rights of men from being victimized against the absolute monarchs), and limited the powers of the monarchy by ensuring that English kings could no longer rule as the absolute authority.

> TEST TIP: The English Bill of Rights also endorsed individual liberty by outlawing the arrest and imprisonment of people without a trial. This laid the foundation for the American Revolution and the U.S. Constitution a century later.

Spain: The War of the Spanish Succession (1701 to 1715)

Europe's 18th century started with a fateful and violent opening act that was triggered by the death of the Habsburg king of Spain, Charles II. Eventually the War of the Spanish Succession ensued between France, which supported a French claim to the Spanish throne, and those who feared the union of Spain and France into one powerful empire (Britain, Austria, Prussia, Holland, Portugal, and other minor powers). Needless to say, this was a highly unfavorable war for France because France was fighting alone against many great powers of Europe.

> **Did you know?** King Charles II was born after centuries of Spain's dynastic inbreeding. In spite of royal descendants dying at an early age due to severe physical and mental disabilities, Charles II defied all odds by living for nearly four decades until 1700. Charles II could not father a son. After his death, the great powers of the English, Dutch, and French descended upon Spain to seize its empire (this was a sticking point in European politics for decades).

Key Facts about the War of the Spanish Succession

The War of the Spanish Succession was one of the most important wars during Period Two for the following reasons.

The war shifted European powers. The war lasted for more than a decade and ended with the **Treaty of Utrecht** in 1713. A reorganization of powers emerged out of Utrecht. Holland, Spain, and Portugal were collapsing into third-rate European status, while England, Austria, and Prussia were strengthened. England gained Gibraltar, a naval outpost off the coast of Spain, and increased its naval power. Austria gained the Spanish lands in the Low Countries and Italy, and Prussia gained enormous prestige and military experience through the war.

The war caused Spain to surrender territories and power. Spain lost its valuable territories in Italy and the Low Countries. After the war ended, Spain's only overseas territories were outside Europe in the Americas and Asia.

The war forced France to limit territorial expansion. Even though France officially won the War of the Spanish Succession by putting a French Bourbon on the throne of Spain, France's opponents ensured that Spain and France could never be united into one vast empire. While France remained the dominant power on the continent, the limits of France's unbridled expansion had become clear. To make matters worse, Louis XIV died in 1715, and his 5-year-old grandson Louis XV took over the throne.

The Cabinet Wars (1648 to 1789)

From the end of the War of the Spanish Succession (1715) to the French Revolution (1789), European nation-states fought a series of very similar conflicts that were often called, in German, *Kabinettskriege,* or the Cabinet Wars. This term refers to the wars of the 18th century in Europe that were similar in methods, origins, and goals.

Key Facts about the Cabinet Wars

Balance of power. In this era, European nation-states wanted to preserve the balance of power. To preserve the balance of power, France, Austria, Prussia, and other great powers were continually shifting coalitions to balance perceived threats to the stability of the European power structure.

Secular wars. Religion did not play a part in the balance of power wars of Western and Central Europe. Catholic, Protestant, Orthodox, and even Muslim powers allied with each other freely without consideration of faith or creed. This truly was the inauguration of the period of the Peace of Westphalia.

Limited goals. This was not a time when massive empires and territories were conquered by European powers—that would transpire in the 19th and 20th centuries. Instead, the Cabinet Wars focused on small territorial gains in Europe or the New World.

Small professional armies. The Cabinet Wars were fought with small maneuverable armies of professional career soldiers who were extremely disciplined and skilled in warfare. Large armies of peasants or laborers who had never handled a musket, lance, or pistol were easily slaughtered by a small opposition of experienced soldiers. Note: It was not until Napoleon's innovations at the turn of the 19th century that this balance of military power began to change.

Extended alliance systems. Because the Cabinet Wars had small armies, nation-states often formed large coalitions to work together. Within these alliance systems, some "allies" often had very different objectives.

The War of the Austrian Succession (1740 to 1748)

One of the most important Cabinet Wars was the War of the Austrian Succession. A violent conflict that emerged to control the Habsburg Austrian throne. The Austrian king, Charles VI, Holy Roman Emperor (r. 1711–1740) realized that his daughter, Maria Theresa, would have to take the throne after his death.

Because Charles VI lacked a male heir, he proclaimed the **Pragmatic Sanction,** which granted the right for women to inherit the throne.

Key Facts about the War of the Austrian Succession

Pragmatic Sanction was not honored. Charles VI spent decades of his life traveling through Europe begging, bribing, and threatening other nation-states to accept the Pragmatic Sanction. When Charles VI died in 1740, his daughter Maria Theresa took the throne. Although European leaders had agreed to the sanction, many went back on their word and viewed this as an opportunity to gain control of the Habsburg Austrian throne and its territories.

Alliances formed (Prussia-France-Spain versus Austria-England). Led by Frederick the Great of Prussia, the War of the Austrian Succession started. Supported by France, Prussia seized the prosperous land of Silesia in the northeast of Bohemia. Much like the War of the Spanish Succession, the War of the Austrian Succession became a European war that created different nation-state alliance systems fighting for their own interests. While Prussia and Austria were fighting over German territories, France and Spain joined Prussia. The war was successful for the Prussian-French-Spanish alliance until Britain joined forces with Austria and made gains against France and Spain.

Treaty of Aix-la-Chapelle. The war ended in 1748 with a compromise of peace. In the treaty that ended the war, Prussia retained control of Silesia and accepted Maria Theresa's place in Habsburg Austria. (Note: As a woman, Maria Theresa was not able to head the Holy Roman Empire, but her husband, Emperor Francis, held the position.)

Consequences of the war. Prussia emerged as a German state and other nations enjoyed minor territorial gains, but France had a significant long-term impact. France's military performed extraordinarily well in the war and gained large territories in the Austrian Netherlands. However, France's King Louis XV made the stunning decision to give back all the French territorial conquests to Austria. This decision created a backlash against Louis XV by Frenchmen because France was furious about sacrificing Gallic blood shed during the war for no gain. Soon after, the prestige of the French monarchy diminished as Frenchmen lost respect for their king. Austria was hated by French citizens.

> TEST TIP: The consequences of the War of the Austrian Succession are historically important because of what happened next—the Seven Years' War. Prussia's contemptuous treatment of France angered the French government because Prussia tried to secure France as an ally of Austria.

The Seven Years' War (1756 to 1763)

The Seven Years' War initially started over the Prussian-Austrian competition for German territories, but it soon became a global war that reached Europe, North America, and Asia.

Key Facts about the Seven Years' War

New alliances formed (France-Spain-Austria-Russia versus Prussia-England). Between 1748 and 1756, Europe underwent a great diplomatic revolution. Offended by Prussia's conduct during the War of the Austrian Succession and fearful of Prussia's rising power, France and Spain joined an alliance with Habsburg Austria. Russia later joined the alliance. Britain joined an alliance with its former enemy, Prussia. The Seven Years' War ensued.

> **Did you know?** Prussia survived the Seven Years' War due to the **Miracle of the Hohenzollerns.** In Europe, Prussia faced certain defeat by its French, Austrian, and Russian enemies after losing almost half of its soldiers, but in a turn of events called the Miracle of the Hohenzollerns (Miracle of the House of Brandenburg), Prussia survived the war. The anti-Prussian Tsar of Russia died just as Russian troops were about to capture Berlin. The new Russian tsar was reluctant to continue the attack and withdrew Austrian and Russian troops. Prussia continued to survive, defend itself, and expand its territory through the course of the war.

British victory over France. British troops crushed French forces in India (1757) in the Battle of Plassey, which led to British authority in India until World War II. The British navy seized Spanish territories in Cuba, the Philippines, and the Caribbean. Spain and France were hopeless against the British military onslaught. The 1763 Treaty of Paris enforced British dominance over European powers in naval and overseas matters, while Prussia was established as the continent's dominant territorial power.

Paved the way for the American Revolution. The Seven Years' War paved the way for the American Revolutionary War (1775–1783). While 1763 seemed to be the apex of British imperial power, it also set the stage for the overthrow of the British Empire. Despite England's unquestionable triumph, the British faced tremendous economic debt. With few friends on the continent and newly acquired territories to defend, the British government decided to raise taxes and tariffs in the Thirteen Colonies of the New World. British troops were sent to the New World to prohibit colonists from settling in the American land recently seized from France. These measures formed the basis for the main grievances of the American revolutionaries against Britain—setting the course for a revolution that would change the course of world history.

TEST TIP: Do not spend your time trying to memorize each of the Cabinet Wars. You will not need in-depth knowledge of the battles of the War of Jenkins' Ear or the outcome of the War of the Polish Succession. Instead, you need to know the general characteristics of the Cabinet Wars and their significance to this period in European history, as a placeholder to compare to the murderous wars of early modern Europe and the mass national armies of the French Revolutionary Wars.

Europe's 18th-Century Economic, Social, and Cultural Changes

Economic Changes

The 18th-century revolution in agriculture led to Europe's increased economic growth. Prior to the 18th century, European peasants used the same system of farming for centuries, the **open-field system,** which revolved around the common use of designated farming and grazing lands. The emphasis was not on who owned the lands, but rather on the common benefit of all.

Agriculture changed in the 18th century with the rise of the **enclosure movement,** which entailed wealthy landowners, nobles, and speculators deciding that this common land was ripe for the taking. The wealthy aristocrats seized land for themselves, erected fences, posted guards, and hired lawyers to defend their legal "rights" to the lands.

Key Facts about Economic Changes

Agricultural production increased commerce. With the new lands now owned by wealthy landowners, a new system of **crop rotation** was used to maximize the efficiency of agricultural production. The enclosure movement allowed for large-scale agricultural production aimed at increased commerce. Crop rotation switched different crops into fields and allowed other fields to lie fallow so that the soil's fertility could be restored. Peasants operating common lands could not afford to implement such practices because they were producing agriculture for their own subsistence.

Commercial revolution. This was a period of the commercial revolution, also known as the *capitalist revolution*. The surplus wealth in the 17th century allowed for further investments and speculation in the 18th century. The larger joint-stock companies and new ventures became larger and more profitable across European countries. Prices continued to rise through inflation in most European countries and the medieval guilds that had monopolized trade and production were undermined by the genius of entrepreneurs who financed their own production and cottage industries.

Bourgeoisie capital. Some national governments such as France and Spain enforced strict mercantilism. Other governments such as England and Holland flirted with free-trade economics. In these economies, large numbers of investments and amounts of capital were placed in the hands of a new class: the **bourgeoisie.** The bourgeoisie referred to middle- and upper-class investors and speculators whose wealth was not based on landed estates and aristocratic privilege. Wealth was based on commercial interaction by using capital. The bourgeoisie class would come to undermine the old systems of European governance and continue through the 18th and 19th centuries.

Social Changes

Key Facts about Population Changes

Population explosion. The 18th century generated a rapid increase in Europe's population growth. In the 1700s, Europe's population was slightly above 100 million; by 1850, the population had more than doubled. Much of this growth took place in powerful countries like England, France, Prussia, and Russia. In other countries, such as Spain, Portugal, and some parts of Italy, the population stagnated due to endemic poverty and government corruption. In an era when population size strongly correlated with economic and military strength, the population trends reflected the rise of some nations and the fall of others.

As we sit in the 21st century, it's difficult to imagine that Europe hosted a population explosion. However, even while Europe's population remained marginal compared to that of Asia, the population of European nations increased significantly from the 18th century to halfway through the 20th century. At that time, Europe had a surplus population that emigrated to the overseas colonies, and later to what became the United States.

Heads Up: What You Need to Know

For the AP EURO exam, you should know the reasons for the 18th-century population explosion: 1) the agricultural revolution; 2) the Columbian Exchange, whereby cheap, stable crops like the potato and the tomato brought food surpluses to many European countries that had struggled to feed themselves for centuries; 3) the rise of the secular and limited Cabinet Wars (compared to the immensely bloody religious wars); and 4) the decline of plagues like the Black Death.

Key Facts about Family Changes

Family life. Along with the economic and population shifts in Europe, family life started to shift. Most of the 16th- and 17th-century traditional European cultures included extended families, with generations of grandparents, cousins, and children living with adult married couples. This can be traced back to Lutheranism and Napoleon's emphasis on the nuclear family being the core tenant of society. In some cultures, this is still the norm in the 21st century. In the 18th century, though, economic changes transformed family life. The new nuclear family consisted of children and their parents only, until the children moved out and started their own nuclear families. Extended family members no longer lived in the same household.

The child mortality rate continued to remain extremely high in 18th-century Europe. In fact, many 18th-century parents did not name their children for many years after their birth. This lack of bonding often resulted in an emotional disconnection between parents and their children. Deep emotional connections between parents and children were rare.

TEST TIP: When taking the AP EURO exam, remember not to write about the practice of teen marriages on an essay question about 18th-century family life!

Many high school students today have the impression that from the medieval era until the dawn of the 19th century, European men and women married very young. This is often confirmed by images of 14-year-old spouses on the Internet. In reality, the opposite is true. As late as the 1790s, the age that an average person got married in Europe was relatively mature—from ages 23 to 29.

The practice of young marriages did not actually begin until the Second Industrial Revolution of the 19th century.

Cultural Changes

Key Facts about Art History Changes

Early 18th-century art. The 18th century saw a transformation in European art from the Baroque period of the 17th century. The foundations of the great artists were from Italy and Germany, but they had many regional differences. Early-18th-century art reflected the Scientific Revolution, the Age of Enlightenment, the Counter-Reformation (against Protestantism), and the absolute monarchs. Many artists embraced not only the classical styles and techniques, but also incorporated neoclassical themes of art, such as dramatic spectator involvement, strong emotion, and grandeur. The neoclassic portrait shown here of the great *Oath of Horatii* is Jacques-Louis David's interpretation of a father handing swords to the Horatti brothers, while swearing allegiance to the state in ancient Rome. Ancient Greek and Roman mythologies also formed popular artistic subjects during this period.

Source: Jacques-Louis David, *Oath of Horatii,* 1784.

Late 18th-century art. A dominant art form associated with the late-18th century was the **Age of Rococo (1750–1800).** This was a period of dramatic social changes in Europe. Artists were influenced by the French Revolution and the Industrial Revolution. Classical French artists moved away from the dark colors and heroic subjects to themes of domestic life. Some historians have contrasted the "grand themes" of Baroque (whether religious imagery, monarchical portraiture, or martial portrayals) with the new sense of nationalism and "domestic themes" of Rococo, which illustrated such homely themes as fruit bowls, children at play, or the furniture of drawing rooms. Rococo art featured bright, colorful pastels, and while it was considered inferior by some critics of the time, it had a strong resurgence in the late-19th century. Most historians consider the Rococo style the quintessential 18th-century art style.

The French Revolution (1789 to 1799)

The French Revolution (1789–1799) stunned the world with a radical movement of the French people to protect liberty, equality, and fraternity (brotherhood). The Revolution marked the breaking point between the masses and the privileged aristocrats, which led to a **Reign of Terror** against the aristocrats. The historical importance of events of the Revolution was so profound that even today France celebrates every year on July 14 to honor the fall of the Bastille in Paris, France.

Did you know? The French Revolution is one of the most important events in the history of mankind, and the world is still living in its wake with its long-lasting consequences. Democracy and the recognition of individual rights are the result of the French Revolution and the revolutions in America and England. In fact, two centuries after the French Revolution, when the Chinese communist premier Zhou Enlai was asked about the legacy of the French Revolution, he said, "It is too soon to tell!"

Key Facts about the Causes of the French Revolution

Let's consider the causes of the Revolution so that we can understand how this event held Europe in its grip for a quarter of a century. The following causes came to a head in 1789.

Enlightenment ideology. The Enlightenment ideals, especially the new economic thoughts, filled the minds of the people. While most Frenchmen could not read or write, the ideals of the Enlightenment spread quickly throughout the educated class and eventually filtered down to the poor and illiterate.

Poor harvests. One of the coldest winters of the 18th century was in 1788. Crops failed throughout France. This made it much more difficult for the monarchy to feed its people, especially in heavily populated Paris. Even though there were food shortages, rising food prices, unemployment, and starvation, the government continued to collect taxes. Many of the pivotal moments of the Revolution occurred during the bread riots.

Unequal tax system. The tax system under the Bourbons was unfair and led to the discontent of Frenchmen. The nobles and clergy owned most of the property in France, but they did not pay taxes. The peasants did not own property, but they had the burden of paying most of the taxes. Not only was this tax system inequitable, but it also caused the peasants and the growing middle-class people to have immense hatred of the clergy and nobility for their privileges. People were fed up with high taxes and the privileged classes.

Government bankruptcy. France was severely in debt in 1787 because the government spent too much money on a series of wars, especially France's financial support of the American Revolutionary War. King Louis XVI was incompetent and unrealistic. He decided to raise taxes to pay off his debts, but realized that he did not have a representative assembly to help him solve France's financial problems.

Louis XVI and Marie Antoinette. France's weak leaders made for a weak government. Louis XVI was a timid, indecisive, and shy king who could not hope to inspire the respect and fear that his famous grandfather had received. The queen, Marie Antoinette, was from Habsburg Austria, the mortal enemy of France for centuries. She was despised by the French people, who believed she personally wasted much of the royal treasury on luxuries.

Timeline of the French Revolution

It's often helpful to conceptualize historical events in chronological sequence. The principal dates and events of the French Revolution—their causes and results—are listed by stages of the pre-revolution, revolution, and post-revolution from 1789 to 1799.

Heads Up: What You Need to Know

On the AP EURO exam, you may be tested on the following French Revolution terms, concepts, or events. The bullet points can be used as a checklist as you review and study the timeline of events.

- The Estates General
- The Tennis Court Oath
- The Storming of the Bastille
- The Declaration of the Rights of Man and of the Citizen
- The Jacobins and the Girondins
- The sans-culottes and the bourgeoisie
- The Committee of Public Safety
- The Reign of Terror
- The levée en masse
- The Directory

Pre-Revolution

Before 1789: Rising discontent. The middle class and peasants were burdened with abuses of the *Ancien Regime* (old regime) of the absolute monarchy and their abuses of power. The royal treasury was bankrupt, harvests had failed, starvation was widespread, and taxes were increasing for 90 percent of France's population. The new ideas of the Enlightenment and the American Revolution gradually gained momentum with the people to end the injustices of the French monarchy.

July 1788: The Estates General. Louis XVI called a meeting of the Estates General, a representative body that could grant further taxes to pay for France's national debt (even though the Estates General had not met in over 175 years). The Estates General was made up of delegates from three different groups of people. The First was made up of clergy, the Second of nobles, and the Third of everyone else, but mostly influential industrial and commercial leaders who were familiar with the Enlightenment philosophes (more than 90 percent of the population!). The Three Estates were not equally representative of the people since the votes from the First and Second Estates could overrule the Third Estate (remember, the clergy and nobility were exempt from paying taxes).

The Revolution

June 1789: The National Assembly. With a growing middle class excluded from political decision-making, the Third Estate broke away from the Estates General and declared itself the true National Assembly of France. To the chagrin of Louis XVI, the Third Estate (along with a few clerical and noble allies) decided to lock themselves in the tennis court of Versailles and took an oath, called the **Tennis Court Oath,** and refused to leave until a new constitution was created. Their goal was to create a constitution to allow for the election of a legislative assembly. This would lead to the forces that started the French Revolution.

July 1789: Storming of the Bastille. Louis XIV was determined to restate his authority and ordered a mercenary army to dissolve the National Assembly by force. Angry mobs were already protesting, and tensions were rising to a state of anarchy. As royal troops marched toward Versailles, an uprising of Parisian workers and peasants stormed the prison (and medieval castle) of the Bastille. The mob killed the few guards monitoring the Bastille, freed a handful of prisoners, and seized the Bastille's weapons. The Storming of the Bastille was a symbolically important act against the authority and legitimacy of the monarchy.

> **TEST TIP:** Here's a fact that will aid you in answering an essay question on the topic of the key events of the French Revolution. The French Revolution began with the Storming of the Bastille on July 14, 1789, but it is important to know that two different groups of people had different objectives about the revolt against the monarchy and aristocrats. 1) The motives of working-class and peasant radicals were aimed at using violence and direct action to revolt. 2) The middle-class and upper-class moderates desired gradual change and a peaceful reform. For differing reasons, both of these parallel "revolutions" proceeded simultaneously, but would routinely diverge from or conflict with one another in the decade following the Storming of the Bastille.

July 1789: The Great Fear. A mass hysteria swept throughout France and resulted in peasant attacks on the manors to destroy the feudal records of their rent obligations to the nobles. It was called the Great Fear. Nobles surrendered their privileges and fled the country.

August 1789: The Declaration of the Rights of Man and of the Citizen. The National Assembly was now recognized by Louis XVI as a legislative body of France. The Third Estate and its allies formed the National Convention, a legislative assembly led by Marquis de Lafayette (and Thomas Jefferson) crafted the Declaration of the Rights of Man and of the Citizen. Since there was no time to write a constitution, the document was modeled after the American Declaration of Independence and declared that "Men are born free and equal in rights," defined as fraternity, liberty, and equality. It was also based on the ideas of the Enlightenment philosophes—natural rights, natural law, and general will. A new constitutional monarchy was born whereby the king remained on the throne but his powers were limited by the constitution and by the legislature.

"The Declaration of the Rights of Man and of the Citizen."

Unfortunately, the Declaration of the Rights of Man and of the Citizen excluded women from legal, political, and social equality with men. Although Frenchwomen were allowed to own property, they were excluded from the declaration and did not have the right to vote or hold office. This did not cause a controversy for most Frenchmen. As we saw in the previous sections, most Enlightenment thinkers ignored the rights of women. However, a few French citizens stood up for women's equality, including **Olympe de Gouges,** who wrote plays, novellas, and political treatises. She was later executed on fabricated charges. Still, foreign women such as **Mary Wollstonecraft** continued her work by making eloquent defenses for the rights of women.

November 1789: Confiscation of the Church lands. The Catholic Church was also severely restricted, as its properties were seized by the government and its clerical privileges were taken away. Catholic clergy had to take an oath to serve the new government rather than serving the pope in Rome. (Note: Half of the Catholic clergy refused to take the oath, and many Catholics continued to be opponents of the French Revolution.)

December 1789: Government reformed. France was divided into 83 departments and local municipal governments were granted the right to levy and collect taxes. Thus, the French reforms created a constitutional monarchy.

June 1791: Louis XVI unsuccessfully attempts to flee France. Louis XVI disguised himself and tried to escape from France with his family to a foreign country. Louis was captured, and radicals in the new government abolished the monarchy and established a new democratic republic.

Post-Revolution

September 1791: The Jacobins and Girondins, and the Constitution of 1791. France's first constitution was written with a constitutional monarchy and provided a separation of powers among the executive, legislative, and judicial branches. It only stayed in effect for 1 year, but changed the Revolution. The legislative assembly was composed of 745 members, primarily representing the middle class.

The legislative assembly was divided between monarchists on one side and groups of Jacobins and Girondins on the other side. The Jacobins were a radical group that hoped to execute the king, abolish the monarchy, and radically transform French society. The Girondins were a less radical group that believed that the Revolution could serve as an example for other Europeans who favored absolutism. The Girondins hoped to abolish the oppression of tyranny throughout Europe; however, they did believe in individual rights and property rights.

April 1792: War with Austria and Prussia. The French Revolution had a vast impact on other European nations. A declaration by the King of Prussia and the Emperor of Austria (brother of Marie Antoinette) said they would intervene in French affairs. This was considered a threat by France. The leaders of Austria and Prussia declared that if any harm came to the royal family, war would ensue. This declaration did little to help the situation, but rather made it worse. Later that year, France declared war on Austria and Prussia. By July 1792, Austrian and Prussian forces invaded France to restore Louis XVI to the throne. France defeated Austrian and Prussian forces on the battlefield, but it led to economic turmoil and royalist betrayal.

August to September 1792: Sans-culottes and the end of monarchy. Chaos and violence erupted by the radical group of **sans-culottes** (poor men without breeches). The sans-culottes took advantage of the situation to slay clergymen, nobles, and monarchists. They stormed the Tuileries palace and massacred 600 of the king's guards and later slaughtered another 1,200 people who were against the Revolution. The royal family was placed under arrest, and Louis XVI was officially suspended from office. The radical group of sans-culottes took control over the French Revolution and ushered in the rule of the Jacobins, just as the war in Europe was turning against the French military.

Based on the principles of the Enlightenment, the leaders of the French Revolution wanted to change French society to build a nation of republicans. A new culture of republicanism was sought. French leaders did not make Catholicism illegal, but they did remove the estates of the Church, took away its privileges in education and taxes, and demanded that the clergy swear oaths to the republic. The old calendar, which largely revolved around Catholic holy days and liturgical seasons, was replaced with a new calendar that started with Year 1 and featured months named after seasons rather than religion. The government also penned a new national anthem, "The Marseillaise," created a new French tricolor flag (replacing the old white Bourbon flag), sponsored nationalist artwork, and inaugurated civic festivals and celebrations. The intent was to make republicans out of Frenchmen in order to protect and preserve the new republic.

December 1792: Louis XVI condemned to death. King Louis XVI was on trial for treason by the National Convention and was condemned to death by a vote of 361 to 360. He was executed on January 21, 1793. The queen, Marie Antoinette, was convicted by a vote of 693 to 0 and met the same fate in October 1793.

April 1793: Committee of Public Safety. Faced with foreign attacks and internal rebellion, the French government established the Committee of Public Safety (CPS), which was a governing council of 12 men (led by Maximilien Robespierre) who held supreme power over France for a year and ushered in the Reign of Terror.

June 1793 to July 1794: Reign of Terror. The Jacobins and the Girondins continually disagreed over the future course of action of the French Revolution. With the help of the sans-culottes, in 1793 the Jacobins took control over the French government. After executing Louis XVI and Marie Antoinette, they were viewed as enemies who threatened the survival of the republic. To make matters worse, England, Holland, and Spain joined with Prussia and Austria in the war against Revolutionary France, as all monarchical nations feared the spread of the revolutionary spirit throughout Europe. This was the start of the royalist uprisings. Royalist and clericalist Frenchmen in the conservative rural parts of the country rose against secularist republican rule. In 1794, French opponents to the CPS joined together to overthrow Robespierre and other Jacobin leaders, who were then executed for the massacres they had unleashed on the country. Unlike those later bloodbaths, however, the Reign of Terror lasted only 1 year.

August 1793: *Levée en masse*. The Jacobins established a proclamation of *levée en masse* (drafting of mass armies). Ordinary French citizens who had never even held a gun were drafted to serve in the military in the war against the European monarchies. Women and children were not exempt, but held positions serving in hospitals, sewing clothes, cooking, or running errands. While these men did not hold the same status as the professional soldiers from other European countries, they made up for it with patriotic zeal. French soldiers were not fighting for the king or the church, but for a nation of reform. The French attitude of nationalism changed the course of European warfare, as the mass armies of the French Republic eventually came to overpower the smaller professional armies of other European nations.

1793: Execution by guillotine. The Committee of Public Safety included famous, or infamous, names such as Maximilien Robespierre, Louis St. Just, and Bertrand Barère. With fears of invading foreign armies, conspiring traitors at home, and royalist or clerical emigres waiting to return and wreak havoc in France, the CPS began using a new innovation, the guillotine, to execute thousands of noblemen, clergy, spies, criminals, political opponents, and saboteurs. Because of the hysteria of the war and revolution, many of these thousands were executed with little to no evidence.

Did you know? Today, we often think of the guillotine as a ghastly and morbid device. Thanks to authors like Charles Dickens, the image of ragged sans-culottes presenting severed heads to raving crowds is strong in our collective memory. However, the guillotine was originally invented by an 18th-century scientist who viewed it as an eminently humane method of execution. Before you laugh at that idea, consider that under the Old Regime, public executions included hanging, dismemberment, boiling alive, and even breaking on the wheel. Compared to these medieval devices of execution, a quick execution by the guillotine was relatively painless. Another interesting fact: We associate the guillotine with the 1793–1794 Reign of Terror, but it continued to be used by the French long after the end of the French Revolution. The last execution by guillotine was in 1977!

HISTORIOGRAPHY. *The historiography of the French Revolution is one of the richest bodies of historical literature. In the 19th century, Karl Marx, the father of communism, used the French Revolution to support his theory of dialectical materialism. Marx believed that class conflict (over control of the means of production) drove history. Marx argued that the French Revolution uprising broke out because a new class (the bourgeoisie, or middle-class capitalists) arose to take control of the economy from the aristocratic class. This argument was widely believed for a time, and some still believe this today, but many have criticized it for being overly simplistic. Under close analysis, many French Revolutionary leaders were not members of the bourgeoisie, but more commonly came from the class of writers, lawyers, and even former landowners who stood little to gain from capitalism.*

1795 to 1799: The Directory. After the upheaval of the Reign of Terror by the radical Jacobins, France wanted to return to some semblance of normality. A conservative government known as the Directory controlled France for 5 years. Five men jointly shared the title of executive council director. The growing power of the wealthy members of the bourgeoisie controlled France. At first, they oversaw a period of moderation in contrast to the upheavals of the previous 5 years.

Although the French military armies were successful, political corruption, economic stagnation, and food shortages could not be solved by the Directory. The many military victories were largely due to **General Napoleon Bonaparte,** who achieved staggering successes and triumphs from the Italian Peninsula to the Low Countries. Rather than shoring up the support of the French people for the Directory, this simply strengthened the praetorian appeal of a great military leader like Napoleon. One contemporary of the Directory said that it was the only regime during this period in French history that never inspired French people. The Directory was certainly less tumultuous and violent than other regimes, but was also the most lackluster.

The Directory was overthrown by the young and aspiring General Napoleon Bonaparte in 1799.

The Napoleonic Wars (1799 to 1815)

Napoleon's Rise to Power

In 1799, Napoleon took power in France through a *coup d'état* (overthrow of the existing government). He was overwhelmingly supported by the armed forces and by many political leaders who welcomed an end to the Directory's mediocrity. Napoleon served as the first of three consuls who ruled over the nation.

Napoleon not only led the nation through his military prowess, he also enacted policies to reform the government and society of France into a modern nation.

Key Facts about Napoleon's Rule

The Napoleonic Code. Napoleon established the Napoleonic Code, the consolidation of local laws into one legal code to streamline the legal system throughout the nation and its territories. The legal code is the basis of French law today. The Napoleonic Code was patriarchal and afforded few legal or political rights to women. On the other hand, legal equality (among men) was guaranteed and aristocratic privilege was completely rejected.

Levée en masse. Napoleon was not the originator of *levée en masse* (the forced mass recruitment of national service), but he did enforce this law as a war strategy in defeating other nations. Napoleon was a military genius who changed military warfare by restoring France's old, small armies of professional, lifetime soldiers supported by the *levée en masse.* This type of military exists in France today.

Source: Jacques-Louis David, *Napoleon Crossing the Alps,* 1801.

Growing nationalism in Europe. Many European monarchs lost their power to Napoleon after being defeated by French army invasions. After being defeated, other nations had a greater sense of nationalism and were determined to unify to gain back self-government. Napoleon did not intend to inspire German and Italian nationalist movements, but that's exactly what happened when France invaded these nations and dissolved the Holy Roman Empire. Napoleon mistakenly fueled the unification of German nationalism because Germans felt demoralized by Napoleon's invasion. For example, in 1799, the Holy Roman Empire in Germany occupied over 300 states, but by 1815, it occupied only 30 states.

Modernization. In many ways, Napoleon exemplified the Enlightenment philosophes. He was an extremely shrewd negotiator and leader who was interested in policies to create an efficient, centralized government. Officials were chosen on the basis of merit and education. Napoleon helped to modernize France's military, economy, bureaucracy, and diplomacy.

The Concordat. In 1801, Napoleon crafted a peace treaty with the Catholic Church called the Concordat, which mended ties between the French nation and the papacy. The Concordat recognized the rights of Rome over the French Church and declared that the majority of Frenchmen were Catholics (although it did not establish Catholicism as the official religion in France). What did Napoleon get out of this bargain? In return, the papacy accepted his rule and ceased its constant attempts to undermine the French government, which had persisted since 1789.

Loss of freedoms. Napoleon's rule had many negative outcomes with losses of liberties. Napoleon restricted and censored the press, political opposition, and public demonstrations. Napoleon was not as brutal as the Jacobins, but he was not reluctant to jail or execute people who threatened his rule. Many people opposed Napoleon's policies but had trouble organizing resistance because Napoleon achieved stunning military victories. Most people were grateful to live in a stable and secure nation. By 1806, France controlled half of the continent.

From 1806 on, Napoleon took unprecedented steps to transform his rule. In that year, he made himself Emperor of France. He abolished feudalism throughout all holdings of the French nation in Europe, and consolidated the sprawling territories of the Holy Roman Empire into one Confederation of the Rhine. Napoleon soon invaded Spain to place his brother on the Spanish throne.

HISTORIOGRAPHY. *Historians do not usually ascribe to the Great Man Theory of history about Napoleon. This 19th-century traditional school of history focused on the events and movements driven by the decisions of great leaders: kings, popes, generals, and thinkers. Instead, many historians often look for larger, structural movers of history: economic, social, or even cultural. Napoleon Bonaparte might be one of the exceptions, as he was an unparalleled military genius who left his indelible mark on Europe, from military strategy and technology to economics and the law. He truly was a self-made great man who shaped world history with his own hands.*

Napoleon's Turning Point (1812 to 1813)

After conquering most of the European continent, by 1812 Napoleon was at the height of his power and appeared to be invincible. Napoleon's army was unparalleled to that of any other nation, but his desire for power led him to make three crucial mistakes.

1. **Continental System.** Of the great nations, only England and Russia resisted France. Napoleon lacked a navy to invade England, so he hoped to implement a Continental System to close all European ports to British ships. Napoleon was hoping to strike at the British economy by blocking British goods from being delivered to the lands under French rule. The problem was that Napoleon's ally, Russia, and its tsar, Alexander I, refused to stand by the Continental System.

2. **War with Spain (1808–1813).** Napoleon overthrew Spain's Bourbon rulers and installed his brother Joseph as the king of Spain. The Spanish population rose in rebellion, which started guerrilla warfare in Spain against France. French troops overran the country, but with the help of British troops led by the Duke of Wellington from Portugal, French troops were ambushed. In the next 5 years, France lost almost 250,000 soldiers through guerrilla warfare in Spain.

3. **Russian invasion (1812).** When Russia refused to stop British trade, Napoleon made the deadly decision to invade Russia with his Grand Army of 650,000 soldiers. Russia was disastrous for Napoleon's army. The French emperor hoped that he could quickly seize a few major cities and the capital, achieve stunning tactical victories, and defeat the leader of Russia (as he had done with so many other nations).

   Russian forces were outmatched by their French opponents, so they practiced *scorched earth* military tactics. Russians retreated from the mighty French forces and burned every city, village, and town in their path. This military tactic denied the enemy food and resources to continue their military invasions. Despite this challenge, Napoleon reached Moscow and captured the city, only to find that it was virtually abandoned because Tsar Alexander refused to surrender. Napoleon and his army retreated from Moscow in the bitter cold while being attacked by swarms of Russian opponents along their departure route. When Napoleon finally returned to friendly territory, his army of 650,000 had been diminished to fewer than 100,000 soldiers.

Napoleon's Fall from Power: The Hundred Days (1813 to 1815)

Napoleon's failure in Russia was a turning point and the coalition against France was growing: England, Austria, Prussia, Russia, and Sweden. After this humiliating defeat, Napoleon was forced to retreat to France, during which time many of France's alleged allies took advantage of the chaos to form a final, terminal coalition against Napoleon that united much of Europe. After these defeats, Napoleon surrendered to his opponents in the spring of 1814. The victorious coalition decided not to execute Napoleon, as they feared making him a martyr for liberalism throughout France and Europe. Napoleon was exiled to Elba, an island off the coast of Italy, not too far from Napoleon's Corsican birthplace.

Less than a year after his exile to Elba, Napoleon had grown restless and escaped the minimal British naval surveillance of Elba. *Hundred Days* is the name given to Napoleon's extraordinary return to power. He made his way to Paris with fewer than 1,500 soldiers, and although King Louis XVIII sent armies to confront Napoleon, the soldiers quickly switched sides and joined the emperor. Napoleon was once again Emperor of France. He offered peace to the crowned heads of Europe and hoped that European leaders would allow him to hold the French throne. However, an alliance of British, Prussian, Austrian, Russian, and other leaders raised an army of 1 million men under the command of the Duke of Wellington. The European alliance knew that they had to confront Napoleon and defeat him once and for all.

Napoleon's army of 120,000 moved into Belgium, hoping to defeat the Prussian army of 160,000, and then the British army of 106,000, before confronting the Austrian and Russian armies. Although Napoleon was initially successful, the **Battle of Waterloo (1815)** marked Napoleon's final defeat. After the final defeat of Napoleon, European leaders exiled Napoleon once again, but this time to the island of St. Helena in the middle of the Atlantic, where he died in 1821 at the age of 51.

Chapter Review Practice Questions

Practice questions are for instructional purposes only and may not reflect the format of the actual exam. On the actual exam, questions are grouped into sets. Each set contains one source-based prompt (document or image) and two to five questions.

Multiple-Choice Questions

1. Which of the following political developments did Baron Montesquieu support?

   A. Separation of the government into three branches
   B. Establishment of an absolute monarchy
   C. Social contracts between the government and the governed
   D. Society as a tabula rasa that could be shaped into a new democracy

2. Which of the following most directly influenced the rise of the Scientific Revolution?

   A. Patronage of the Catholic Church
   B. Scientific treatises of Martin Luther
   C. Adaptation of empiricism as a system of knowledge
   D. Artistic innovations of the Renaissance

3. All of the following were common Enlightenment views EXCEPT

   A. Consent of the governed
   B. Complete racial equality
   C. Individual liberty and property rights
   D. Freedom of religion and conscience

4. All of the following provide explanations for causes of the French Revolution EXCEPT

    A. Weakness in the personality of the French monarch

    B. An inequitable tax system

    C. The painful legacy of the Seven Years' War

    D. Invasion of France by Austria and Prussia

5. Which one of the following was part of Peter the Great's (of Russia) modernization plans?

    A. Abolition of serfdom

    B. Separation of church and state

    C. Shaving nobles' beards

    D. Partition of Poland

6. Which of the following is an example of theocratic rule in Europe?

    A. Cromwell's rule in England

    B. Spain under the Habsburgs

    C. France under Napoleon

    D. Hohenzollern Prussia

Questions 7 and 8 refer to the following passage.

The Revolution created in France overnight, although with less stability, what in Great Britain had taken more than a century of steady evolution: the institutions, which until then had been lacking, for critical public debate of political matters. Club-based parties emerged from which parliamentary factions were recruited; there arose a politically oriented daily press.

And already the Estates General successfully asserted the publicity of its deliberations. Beginning in August the daily Journal des Debats et des Decrets appeared, specializing in reports on parliamentary proceedings. At least as important as the factual institutionalization of the public sphere in the political realm was its anchoring in legal statutes. The revolutionary event was immediately interpreted and defined in terms of constitutional law; therein may lie the reason that on the continent the bourgeois public became so precisely aware of its political functions, actual or potential. [. . .]

From elements in the codifications of the French revolutionary constitution, the political functions of the public sphere were quickly transformed into slogans that spread all over Europe. The constitution of 1793 explicitly included freedom of assembly in the protection of freedom of expression: 'The right to communicate one's ideas and opinions, whether through the political Functions of the Public Sphere press or in any other manner, the right to assemble peaceably . . . cannot be refused.' It then added, as if to offer an excuse for this precaution, a reference to the *ancien regime*. [. . .] The Charter of June, 1814 (Article 8) also stated: "The French have the right to have their views published and printed, if they abide by the laws which are intended to prevent the abuses of this liberty."

—Jurgen Habermas, *The Structural Transformation of the Public Sphere.*
(Cambridge: MIT Press, 1961)

7. Based on your knowledge of European history, which of the following historiographical schools would the author most likely belong to, and why?

   A. The Great Man school; he focuses mostly on the leaders of the French Revolution

   B. The feminist school; he examines the way in which patriarchy led to a public sphere identified as masculine

   C. The postmodern school; he shows that the "political" public sphere was really an area of cultural discourse centered around texts and symbols

   D. The Marxist school; he emphasizes the role of class in the formation of the public sphere

8. Which of the following historical assessments does the passage support?

   A. The French Revolution cemented a public sphere of political debate, which the return of the Bourbon monarchy could not extinguish.

   B. The French Revolution was a Marxist revolt of the proletarians against the bourgeoisie.

   C. The French invented the public sphere, which had come out of the Enlightenment.

   D. King Louis XVI created the public sphere in France when he called the Estates General.

Questions 9 and 10 refer to the following map of territorial adjustments after the Treaty of Utrecht.

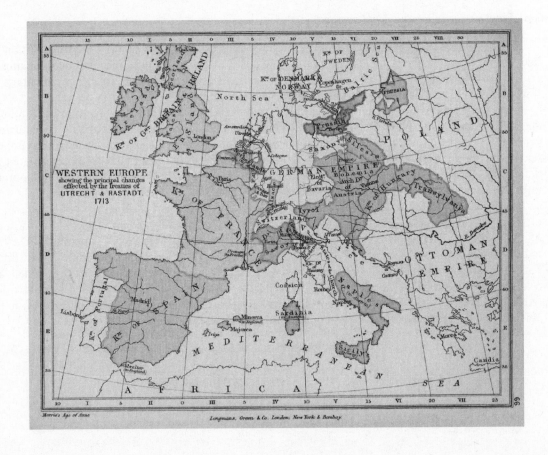

9. Based on your knowledge of European history, which of the following wars ended because of territorial adjustments after the Treaty of Utrecht?

   A. The Seven Years' War
   B. The War of the Spanish Succession
   C. The Napoleonic Wars
   D. The Great Northern War

10. Which of the following historical developments resulted from the Treaty of Utrecht?

   A. Competition between the Dutch and English merchant navies
   B. Spain's invasion of Portugal over colonial tensions
   C. Further conflict between France and Austria
   D. Creation of a unified German nation-state

Document-Based Question

1 question
60 minutes

Reading Time: 15 minutes (brainstorm your thoughts and organize your response)
Writing Time: 45 minutes

Directions: The document-based question is based on the seven accompanying documents. These documents are for instructional purposes only. Some of the documents have been edited for the purpose of this practice exercise. Write your response on lined paper and include the following:

- **Thesis.** Present a thesis that supports a historically defensible claim, establishes a line of reasoning, and responds to all parts of the question. The thesis must consist of one or more sentences located in one place—either the introduction or the conclusion.

- **Contextualization.** Situate the argument by explaining the broader historical events, developments, or processes that occurred before, during, or after the time frame of the question.

- **Evidence from the documents.** Use the content of at least three to six of the documents to develop and support a cohesive argument that responds to the topic question.

- **Evidence beyond the documents.** Support or qualify your argument by explaining at least one additional piece of specific historical evidence not found in the documents. (Note: The example must be different from the evidence used to earn the point for contextualization.)

- **Analysis.** Use at least three documents to explain the documents' point of view, purpose, historical situation, and/or audience relevant to the topic question.

- **Historical reasoning.** Use historical reasoning to show relationships among the documents, the topic question, and the thesis argument. Use evidence to corroborate, qualify, or modify the argument.

Based on the documents that follow, answer the question below.

Question 1: Based on your knowledge of European history, evaluate the causes of the 1789 French Revolution.

Document 1

Source: Cahier of 1789, *The Third Estate of Versailles*. A list of grievances prepared by the people of France to present to the Estates General.

Of the grievances, complaints and remonstrances of the members of the third estate of the bailliage of Versailles.

Art. 1. The Power of making laws resides in the king and the nation.

Art. 2. The nation being too numerous for a personal exercise of this right, has confided its trust to representatives freely chosen from all classes of citizens. These representatives constitute the national assembly.

Art. 3. Frenchmen should regard as laws of the kingdom those alone which have been prepared by the national assembly and sanctioned by the king.

[. . .]

Art. 5. The laws prepared by the States General and sanctioned by the king shall be binding upon all classes of citizens and upon all provinces of the kingdom. They shall be registered literally and accurately in all courts of law. They shall be open for consultation at all seats of municipal and communal government; and shall be read at sermon time in all parishes.

[. . .]

Art. 11. Personal liberty, proprietary rights and the security of citizens shall be established in a clear, precise and irrevocable manner. All *lettres de cachet* shall be abolished forever, subject to certain modifications which the States General may see fit to impose.

Art. 12. And to remove forever the possibility of injury to the personal and proprietary rights of Frenchmen, the jury system shall be introduced in all criminal cases, and in civil cases for the determination of fact, in all the courts of the realm.

[. . .]

Art. 23. All taxes now in operation are contrary to these principles and for the most part vexatious, oppressive and humiliating to the people. They ought to be abolished as soon as possible, and replaced by others common to the three orders and to all classes of citizens, without exception.

Document 2

Source: Edmund Burke, "Reflections on the Revolution in France," 1790. An intellectual criticism of the French Revolution written by a British statesman.

France, by the perfidy of her leaders has utterly disgraced the tone of lenient council in the cabinets of princes, and disarmed it of its most potent topics. She has sanctified the dark, suspicious maxims of tyrannous distrust; and taught kings to tremble at (what will hereafter be called) the delusive plausibilities of moral politicians. Sovereigns will consider those, who advise them to place an unlimited confidence in their people, as subverters of their throne; as traitors who aim at their destruction, by leading their easy good nature, under specious pretenses, to admit combinations of bold and faithless men into a participation of their power. This alone (if there were nothing else) is an irreparable calamity to you and to mankind. [. . .] For want of these, they have seen the medicine of the state corrupted into its poison. They have seen the French rebel against a mild and lawful monarch, with more fury, outrage, and insult, than ever any people has been known to rise against the most illegal usurper, or the most sanguinary tyrant. Their resistance was made to concession; their revolt was from protection; their blow was aimed at a hand holding out graces, favours, and immunities.

Document 3

Source: The Declaration of the Rights of Man and of the Citizen. Approved by the National Assembly of France, August 26, 1789.

The representatives of the French people, organized as a National Assembly, believing that the ignorance, neglect, or contempt of the rights of man are the sole cause of public calamities and of the corruption of governments, have determined to set forth in a solemn declaration the natural, unalienable, and sacred rights of man, [. . .] Therefore the National Assembly recognizes and proclaims, in the presence and under the auspices of the Supreme Being, the following rights of man and of the citizen:

Articles:

1. Men are born and remain free and equal in rights. Social distinctions may be founded only upon the general good.
2. The aim of all political association is the preservation of the natural and imprescriptible rights of man. These rights are liberty, property, security, and resistance to oppression.
3. The principle of all sovereignty resides essentially in the nation. No body nor individual may exercise any authority which does not proceed directly from the nation.
4. Liberty consists in the freedom to do everything which injures no one else; hence the exercise of the natural rights of each man has no limits except those which assure to the other members of the society the enjoyment of the same rights. These limits can only be determined by law.
5. Law can only prohibit such actions as are hurtful to society. Nothing may be prevented which is not forbidden by law, and no one may be forced to do anything not provided for by law.

[. . .]

9. As all persons are held innocent until they shall have been declared guilty, if arrest shall be deemed indispensable, all harshness not essential to the securing of the prisoner's person shall be severely repressed by law.

Document 4

> **Source: Jean-Marie Roland de la Platière, The State of the French Economy, 1789. A French industrial scientist who became a moderate bourgeois French Revolutionary leader.**
>
> I have seen eighty, ninety, a hundred pieces of cotton . . . stuff cut up, and completely destroyed. I have witnessed similar scenes every week for a number of years. I have seen manufactured goods confiscated; heavy fines laid on the manufacturers; some pieces of fabric were burnt in public places, and at the hours of market: others were fixed to the pillory, with the name of the manufacturer inscribed upon them, and he himself was threatened with the pillory, in case of a second offence.
>
> All this was done under my eyes, at Rouen, in conformity with existing regulations, or ministerial orders. What crime deserved so cruel a punishment? Some defects in the materials employed, or in the texture of the fabric, or even in some of the threads of the warp.
>
> I have frequently seen manufacturers visited by a band of satellites who put all in confusion in their establishments, spread terror in their families, cut the stuffs from the frames, tore off the warp from the looms, and carried them away as proofs of infringement; the manufacturers were summoned, tried, and condemned: their goods confiscated; copies of their judgment of confiscation posted up in every public place; fortune, reputation, credit, all was lost and destroyed. And for what offence?

Document 5

> **Source: Abbé Sieyes, "What is the Third Estate?" 1789. Writing a script for the Revolution, Sieyes' ideas challenged traditional conceptions of nation and government.**
>
> [. . .] If privileged persons have come to usurp all the lucrative and honorable posts, it is a hateful injustice to the rank and file of citizens and at the same a treason to the public.
>
> Who then shall dare to say that the Third Estate has not within itself all that is necessary for the formation of a complete nation? It is the strong and robust man who has one arm still shackled. If the privileged order should be abolished, the nation would be nothing less, but something more. Therefore, what is the Third Estate? Everything; but an everything shackled and oppressed. What would it be without the privileged order? Everything, but an everything free and flourishing. Nothing can succeed without it, everything would be infinitely better without the others.
>
> It is not sufficient to show that privileged persons, far from being useful to the nation, cannot but enfeeble and injure it; it is necessary to prove further that the noble order does not enter at all into the social organization; that it may indeed be a burden upon the nation, but that it cannot of itself constitute a nation.
>
> [. . .]
>
> What is a nation? A body of associates, living under a common law, and represented by the same legislature, etc.

Is it not evident that the noble order has privileges and expenditures which it dares to call its rights, but which are apart from the rights of the great body of citizens? It departs there from the common law. So its civil rights make of it an isolated people in the midst of the great nation. This is truly imperium in imperia.

Document 6

Source: Marilyn Butler, ed., *Burke, Paine, Godwin and the Revolution Controversy* (Cambridge: Cambridge University Press, 1984, pp. 31-32). A British debate over the French Revolution.

What an eventful period this is! I am thankful that I have lived to see it . . . for mine eyes have seen thy salvation. I have lived to see a diffusion of knowledge, which has undermined superstition and error—I have lived to see the rights of men better understood than ever; and nations panting for liberty, which seem to have lost the idea of it. I have lived to see 30 MILLIONS of people, indignant and resolute, spurning at slavery, and demanding liberty with an irresistible voice; their king led in triumph, and an arbitrary monarch surrendering himself. . . . After sharing in the benefits of one revolution, I have been spared to be witness to two other revolutions, both glorious. And now . . . I see the love for liberty catching and spreading, a general amendment beginning in human affairs; the dominion of kings changed for the dominion of laws, and the dominion of priests giving way to the dominion of reason and conscience.

Be encouraged, all ye friends of freedom, and writers in its defense! The times are auspicious. Your labours have not been in vain. Behold kingdoms, admonished by you, starting from sleep, breaking their fetters, and claiming justice from their oppressors! Behold, the light you have struck out, after setting America free, reflected to France, and there kindled into a blaze that lays despotism in ashes, and warms and illuminates EUROPE!

Tremble all ye oppressors of the world! Take warning all ye supporters of slavish governments. . . . Call no more reformation, innovation. You cannot hold the world in darkness. Struggle no longer against increasing light and liberality. Restore to mankind their rights; and consent to the correction of abuses, before they and you are destroyed together.

Document 7

Source: *The Third Estate carrying the Clergy and the Nobility on its back,* **Bibliothèque Nationale de France.**

A FAUT ESPERER Q'EU'JEU LA FINIRA BEN TOT

Answer Explanations

Multiple-Choice Questions

1. **A.** Montesquieu is best known for the proposal of governmental separation of powers into executive, legislative, and judicial branches, choice A. Choice B is incorrect because Montesquieu rejected absolutism and the ideas of placing too much power with one individual or group. Choice C, the social contract, is associated with Rousseau. Choice D, the tabula rasa (or clean slate), is a term coined by John Locke.

2. **C.** The Catholic Church largely rejected the Scientific Revolution, so choice A is clearly not true. Luther wrote no treatises about science, so we can also reject choice B. The Renaissance did influence the Scientific Revolution, but more in its humanism and focus on new forms of learning (choice D). Thus, choice C is the clear answer, as empiricism laid the foundation for the Scientific Revolution.

3. **B.** The Enlightenment philosophers certainly did not agree on everything, but there were some areas of consensus. The social contract (choice A), individual and property rights (choice C), and freedom of religion and conscience (choice D) were all widely accepted and fundamental to the Enlightenment. On the other hand, while there were some Enlightenment thinkers who questioned racism and thought

that nonwhites could be civilized, the belief in complete racial equality (choice B) was nearly nonexistent in 18th-century Europe.

4. **D.** Choices A, B, and C are all accurate reasons, while choice D, the Austrian and Prussian invasions of France, came *after* France had its Revolution, established a republic, and executed the king.

5. **C.** Peter the Great strengthened the system of serfdom (which was not abolished until the 19th century!), so choice A is incorrect. Far from separating church and state (choice B), he tied the two even closer together under the caesaropapism of the Russian monarchy. The Russian Empire certainly did partake in the partitions of Poland (choice D), but the first one did not occur until decades after Peter's death. On the other hand, choice C is correct, even though it might seem like a trivial aspect of modernization. Peter believed Russia could not be modern until Russians acted modern, which included the fashion of the nobility, who, after all, set examples for the Russian nation. Since modern Western Europeans did not wear long beards, Peter ordered Russian nobles to shave their traditional facial hair. He even occasionally did the barber's work himself.

6. **A.** While Spain was perhaps the most religious and conservative state in early modern Europe, it was not a theocracy, choice B. The Church was powerful in Spain, but the monarchs held their own power and, despite their religious devotion, often butted heads with the popes. Napoleon was a secularist who saw religion as a tool to be used in holding power, so choice C is wrong. Prussia under the Hohenzollern Dynasty was religious but no theocracy, so choice D is incorrect. Choice A is correct because, under Cromwell's rule from 1653 to 1658, Puritan religion and state law became one. This was the most theocratic period in English history.

7. **D.** We can eliminate choice A because the author does not focus on great men, but on laws and political structures. While it is true that feminist scholars would later build upon his argument, as choice B describes, the author himself did not do so. Choice C is similarly false, as postmodern scholars have tried to utilize the author's theoretical framework while shifting the focus from political and class to culture, but this was decades after the author's passage was written. Choice D is correct because the author was in fact a structuralist Marxist, and his theory of the public sphere was in this passage tied, albeit briefly, to the bourgeoisie as a class.

8. **A.** We see that choice A is correct because the author is showing that the French public sphere was created *after* the French Revolution (which eliminates choice C), and that a public sphere is not something that can easily be destroyed. This was demonstrated when the Bourbons returned to rule France in 1814–1815; despite their return, they could not hope to re-establish the absolute monarchy. Choice B is incorrect because the proletariat (industrial working class working for wages) did not exist in the 18th century, and the bourgeoisie had scarcely begun to exist themselves. Choice D might seem correct, because it is true that Louis opened a Pandora's box by allowing the Estates General to come to Versailles and debate his rule. However, he did not create the public sphere himself; the passage states that would come later.

9. **B.** The Treaty of Utrecht (1714) ended the War of the Spanish Succession, choice B. If you forget the date, you can also infer this from looking at the map: The war was about possession of the Spanish Empire, and that empire was split because the war ended inconclusively. The Seven Years' War (choice A) was decades later and primarily focused on Franco-British rivalries. The Napoleonic Wars (choice C) did touch Spain, but at that point Spain had long lost its territories in the Low Countries and Italy. The Great Northern War (choice D) was fought, as the name indicates, in Northern Europe between Russia and Sweden.

10. **C.** While Anglo-Dutch commercial competition (choice A) certainly took place, it was more pronounced in the 17th century and had little to do with the War of the Spanish Succession. We can eliminate choice B because Spain did not invade Portugal in conjunction with the Treaty of Utrecht. The nation of Germany was not created until 1871 (choice D), and had nothing to do with the War of the Spanish Succession. Our best answer here is choice C, and the territorial adjustments on the map can help to indicate this. After the Treaty of Utrecht, France and Austria found their territories very close to one another; France had long been threatened by the Spanish Netherlands, Milan, and Naples, all of which were taken by Austria after the War of the Spanish Succession. Of course, Franco-Habsburg conflict was hardly new in 1714, but it was intensified by Austrian inroads into former Spanish territories.

Document-Based Question

DBQ Scoring Guide

To achieve the maximum score of 7, your response must address the scoring criteria components in the table below.

Scoring Criteria for a Good Essay	
Question 1: Based on your knowledge of European history, evaluate the causes of the 1789 French Revolution.	
Scoring Criteria	**Examples**
A. THESIS/CLAIM	
(1 point) Presents a historically defensible thesis that establishes a line of reasoning. (Note: The thesis must make a claim that responds to *all* parts of the question and must *not* just restate the question. The thesis must consist of *at least* one sentence, either in the introduction or the conclusion.)	An effective thesis should develop a historical claim that follows a line of reasoning about the key distinctions between at least two primary causes of the French Revolution, which are sometimes easy to confuse. For example, a good essay can differentiate the economic causes of the revolt (given the class-based grievances and remedies of the revolution) and the intellectual causes (given the role of Enlightenment beliefs in causing and guiding the revolution).
B. CONTEXTUALIZATION	
(1 point) Explains the broader historical context of events, developments, or processes that occurred before, during, or after the time frame of the question. (Note: Must be more than a phrase or reference.)	The essay cites evidence from a broader historical context that is relevant and valid to the question prompt. The French Revolution was keenly watched by the rest of Europe and had a vast social and political impact on other European nations. In addition, a good response will have something to say about the long-term significance of the French Revolution. After all, many historians would argue that no one event was as important in shaping the modern Western world in which we live. The legacy of the revolution is still being decided over two centuries later: As Chinese premier Zhou En Lai declared when asked about the legacy of the French Revolution, "it's too soon to tell."

Scoring Criteria	Examples
C. EVIDENCE	
Evidence from the Documents **(2 points)** Uses at least *six* documents to support the argument in response to the prompt. OR **(1 point)** Uses the content of at least *three* documents to address the topic prompt. (Note: Examples must describe, rather than simply quote, the content of the documents.)	To earn 2 points, the essay response should be able to reasonably provide evidence from six or seven of the documents presented on this topic (including references to three documents with the documents' point of view). Supporting references might include Documents 1, 4, and 7 (describing the economic causes of the French Revolution); Documents 5 and 6 (showing the intellectual causes and principles of the revolution); Document 3 (showing some of the goals of the revolution as espoused by its founders); and Document 2 (showing the negative reaction from conservative Europe). Per Document 2, written by conservative Edmund Burke of Britain, other monarchical nations feared the "revolutionary spirit" spreading democracy to their nations. Before France could stabilize politically, it underwent a period of a "Reign of Terror," whereby the enemies of the Revolution were executed.
Evidence Beyond the Documents **(1 point)** Uses at least one additional piece of specific historical evidence beyond those found in the documents that is relevant to the argument. (Note: Evidence must be different from the evidence used in contextualization.)	The essay should extend the argument by incorporating one piece of outside evidence. Specific examples of outside evidence might include, 1) "The Declaration of Rights of Man," stating that "men are born free and have equal rights," but this document did not include women (cite the work of Mary Wollstonecraft in shaping future rights for women); or 2) France's first constitution was written as a result of the French Revolution, separating powers into executive, legislative, and judicial branches (with the help of the Thomas Jefferson from the United States).
D. ANALYSIS AND REASONING	
(1 point) Uses at least *three* documents to explain how each document's point of view, purpose, historical situation, and/or audience is relevant to the argument. (Note: References must explain how or why, rather than simply identifying.)	The essay response draws from at least three documents to support the document's point of view, purpose, historical situation, and/or audience. For example, a good essay might reference 1) Document 1: an outline of the grievances over oppressive taxes and unfair economic mercantilism of the French government. 2) Document 2: Burke's contrasting views of the revolt. Burke attacked the principles of the French Revolution and opposed the values of his contemporary revolutionaries, calling them "traitors who aim at their own destruction." 3) Document 3: The National Assembly recognized that all men had equal rights including liberty, property, and freedom of religion. 4) Document 7: The illustration of "The Third Estate Carrying the Clergy and Nobility on its Back" depicts the historical context of the unfairness of the tax system under the Bourbons. The Third Estate (peasants and the middle class) had the burden of paying the majority of taxes, while the Church and aristocrats were exempt or paid little in taxes.
(1 point) Uses historical reasoning and development that focuses on the question while using evidence to corroborate, qualify, or modify the argument. (Examples: Explain what is similar and different; explain the cause and effect; explain multiple causes; explain connections within and across periods of time; corroborate multiple perspectives across themes; or consider alternative views.)	The essay focuses on the historical skill of *causation* to corroborate the argument. Essays earning an acceptable response show an understanding of the origins/outbreak of the French Revolution—for the people to have equal rights and eliminate aristocratic/monarchical oppression. This well-developed essay explains the social, economic, cultural, and political significance of the French Revolution while outlining the causes of the outbreak.

Sample Response

The French Revolution was one of the most important events in European history, as it served as the reason for propelling Europe into the modern age of democracy, human rights, and nationalism. The historiography of the French Revolution is complicated, because the event itself had several different features, periods, and themes. The documents illustrate historical context.

The path to the Revolution was paved with intellectual and economic developments. The ideals of the Enlightenment, such as Jean-Jacques Rousseau's social contract or Voltaire's freedom of conscience, filtered down from elites to the middle classes and sometimes even to the poor. In Document 5, Abbé Sieyes makes the clear argument of Enlightenment values: For Sieyes, France is not made up of the king and his subjects. It is a nation of different classes with free and independent rights. The Third Estate, just like the nation as a whole, deserves a legislative body that actually represents it, rather than the sham represented by the Estates General. Documents 1, 3, 4, and 6 follow Sieyes' line of reasoning and support his revolutionary viewpoints.

The economic factors were also key here. Document 1: Article 23, shows the unrest in Bourbon France over the unjust taxes and unfair economic mercantilism of the French government, while Document 4 shows how French overregulation and overbearing mercantilism hurt, rather than helped, French industries and put an enormous strain on the national economy. When combined with the famines of 1788 and the resulting shortages of bread in 1789, this made France primed for a revolution. Moreover, in Document 7, we have a powerful pictorial interpretation of the unfairness built into the French tax code. The poor Third Estate had to pay the lion's share of taxes, while the clerical First Estate and aristocratic Second Estate were essentially freeloading. The French monarchy understood this problem and tried repeatedly to rationalize the tax system, but the vested powers of the church and nobility stood in the way. Louis XVI, in desperation, called the Estates General to rectify the tax code, ushering in his own death and his monarchy's destruction in the process.

The nature of the French Revolution became clear in the pivotal years 1789–1795. Document 3 was the founding document of the French Revolutionary government and it presents both the intellectual heritage of the Enlightenment and also the economic grievances of the bourgeoisie against the monarchy, church, and aristocracy.

The French Revolution was watched by the rest of Europe. Document 2, written by British conservative Edmund Burke, presents a view of the French Revolution as being too radical, throwing away the value of tradition and authority, only to replace it with a far inferior equality and democracy. The legacy of this revolution is still being decided over two centuries later: As Chinese premier Zhou Enlai declared during President Nixon's visit to China in 1972 about the legacy of the French Revolution: "It's too soon to tell."

Chapter 6

Historical Period Three: The Age of Nationalism (c. 1815 to c. 1914)

Period Three explores the "long 19th century" that lasted from the end of the Napoleonic Wars in 1815 to the outbreak of the First World War in 1914.

- The Age of Metternich (1814 to 1848)
- 19th-Century European Revolutions
- Great Britain and the Victorian Age (1837 to 1901)
- The Age of Romanticism (c. 1795 to c. 1850)
- The Age of Nationalism (c. 1850 to c. 1919)
- The Industrial Revolution (c. 1840 to c. 1914)
- The Unification of Nations (1854 to 1871)
- The Belle Époque (1871 to 1914)
- The New Second Wave of Imperialism (1870 to 1914)
- The Road to World War I (1871 to 1914)

Overview of AP European History Period Three

The rise and fall of the Napoleonic era contributed to a significant turning point in European history. Many monarchs lost their thrones to France's armies, but after Napoleon's defeat, Britain, Russia, Austria, and Prussia became key European powers. The ideals of the French Revolution were permanently embedded in the minds of Europeans—liberty, justice, and equality. These ideals gave rise to the competing ideologies of democracy and nationalism that intensified revolutionary movements in 19th-century Europe.

The AP European History curriculum framework and key concepts explain the reasoning behind particular beliefs and developments that emerged in Europe during this time period. The historical examples of significant themes, trends, events, and people support the study topics that are specific to the AP EURO exam. As you study the key concepts, use the chart on the next page to guide you through what is covered on the exam.

Visit http://apcentral.collegeboard.com for the complete updated AP EURO course curriculum and key concept descriptions.

AP European History Key Concepts (c. 1815 to c. 1914)	
KEY CONCEPT 3.1: THE INDUSTRIAL REVOLUTION SPREADS **The Industrial Revolution spread from Great Britain to the rest of the continent, where the state played a greater role in the promotion of industry.**	Great Britain established its industrial dominance through the mechanization of the production of textiles, iron, and steel, as well as new transportation systems in conjunction with uniquely favorable political and social climates. Industrialization took root in continental Europe (following the British example), sometimes with state sponsorship. During the second Industrial Revolution (also known as the Technical Revolution, c. 1870–1914), more areas of Europe experienced industrial activity, and industrial processes increased in scale and complexity.
KEY CONCEPT 3.2: CHANGES IN EVERYDAY LIFE **The experiences of everyday life were shaped by industrialization, depending on the level of industrial development in a particular location.**	Industrialization promoted the development of new classes in the industrial regions of Europe. Europe experienced rapid population growth and urbanization, leading to social dislocations. Over time, the Industrial Revolution altered the family structure and relations for bourgeois and working-class families. A heightened consumerism developed as a result of the second phase of the Industrial Revolution. Because of the persistence of primitive agricultural practices and land-owning patterns, some areas of Europe lagged in industrialization while facing famine, debt, and land shortages.
KEY CONCEPT 3.3: IDEOLOGICAL CHANGES **Political revolutions and the complications resulting from industrialization triggered a range of ideological, governmental, and collective responses.**	Ideologies developed and took root throughout society as a response to industrial and political revolutions. Governments, at times based on the pressure of political or social organizations, responded to the problems created or exacerbated by industrialization. Political movements and social organizations responded to the problems of industrialization.
KEY CONCEPT 3.4: INTERNATIONAL UPHEAVAL **European states struggled to maintain international stability in an age of nationalism and revolutions.**	The Concert of Europe (or Congress System) sought to maintain the status quo through collective action and adherence to conservatism. The breakdown of the Concert of Europe opened the door for movements of national unification in Italy and Germany, as well as liberal reforms elsewhere. The unification of Italy and Germany transformed the European balance of power and led to efforts to construct a new diplomatic order.

KEY CONCEPT 3.5: THE SECOND WAVE OF IMPERIALISM A variety of motives and methods led to the intensification of European global control and increased tensions among the great powers.	European nations were driven by economic, political, and cultural motivations in their new imperial ventures in Asia and Africa. Industrial and technological developments (i.e., the second Industrial Revolution) facilitated European control of global empires. Imperial endeavors significantly affected society, diplomacy, and culture in Europe and created resistance to foreign control abroad.
KEY CONCEPT 3.6: THE ROMANTIC MOVEMENT European ideas and culture expressed a tension between objectivity and scientific realism on one hand, and subjectivity and individual expression on the other.	Romanticism broke with neoclassical forms of artistic representation and with rationalism, placing more emphasis on intuition and emotion. Following the revolutions of 1848, Europe turned toward a realist and materialist worldview. In the late 19th century, a new relativism in values and the loss of confidence in the objectivity of knowledge led to modernism in intellectual and cultural life.

Significant Themes

The significant themes related to the key concepts for Period Three should help you to think about *why* particular developments occurred in the context of the larger historical "big picture." The study questions give you important insights related to specific questions that will help you make mental connections between each given topic and the social, political, economic, and religious significance.

Glance through the study questions before you start the review section. Take notes, mark questions, and write down page number references to reinforce your learning. Refer to this list as often as necessary until you are confident with your answers.

Study Questions Related to Significant Themes in Period Three

Theme 1: Interaction of Europe and the World

1. How did scientific and intellectual advances facilitate European interaction with other parts of the world? (Hint: New technologies, new communication, and new transportation—including railroads—resulted in a global economic network; search for raw materials and markets.)

2. How did cultural beliefs overseas change over time? (Hint: Ideology of cultural and racial superiority; "The White Man's Burden"; social Darwinism.)

3. What was the extent of, and causes for, non-Europeans adopting or resisting European cultural, political, or economic values? (Hint: Latin American revolutions; Imperialist motives, racial Darwinism.)

Theme 2: Poverty and Prosperity

1. How did wealth generated by new trading, financial, and manufacturing practices create a market and then a consumer economy? (Hint: Economic institutions and human capital—inventors, engineers, and capitalists—helped Britain lead industrialization through private initiatives.)

2. How did geographic, economic, social, and political factors affect the timing and nature of industrialization? (Hint: The industrial dominance in Great Britain and the second phase of the Industrial Revolution.)

3. What was the role of colonization, the Industrial Revolution, total warfare, and economic depression in changing the government's relationship to the economy? (Hint: Britain's parliamentary government promoted commercial and industrial interests because they were the interests of the Parliament.)

4. How did the government and nongovernmental reform movements respond to poverty and other social problems in the 19th and 20th centuries? (Hint: Political movements and social organizations; government labor laws and social welfare programs; governments tried to manage the market through monopolies, banking practices, and tariffs.)

Theme 3: Objective Knowledge and Subjective Visions

1. How did a worldview based on science and reason challenge and preserve social order and roles—especially the role of women? (Hint: Feminist movements; radical and republican advocates of suffrage and citizenship; cult of domesticity; liberals emphasized popular sovereignty, individual rights, and enlightened self-interest.)

2. How did the emergence, spread, and questioning of scientific, technological, and positivist approaches address social problems? (Hint: People turned toward a realist and materialist worldview; socialists called for a fair distribution of society's resources and wealth evolving from a utopian to a Marxist scientific critique of capitalism.)

Theme 4: States and Other Institutions of Power

1. Describe the emergence of civic humanism and new conceptions of political authority. (Hint: Growth of regulatory states, political movements, political ideologies; various private nongovernmental reform movements tried to lift up the deserving poor and end serfdom and slavery.)

2. How did the new ideas of the Enlightenment challenge absolutism and shape the development of constitutional states, parliamentary government, and the concept of individual rights? (Hint: Mass political movements and reform; national unification and nation-building; ideologies of change.)

3. How did the roles of nationalism change the European balance of power? (Hint: Nationalists encouraged loyalty to the nation including Romantic idealism, liberal reform, political unification, radicalism, and chauvinism justifying national aggrandizement.)

4. Explain the emergence of representative government as an alternative to absolutism? (Hint: Ideologies of liberation; mass movements and reform; revolutions from 1815 to 1848; nationalism and unification.)

Theme 5: Individual and Society

1. How did the nature and role of the family change? (Hint: Bourgeois families became focused on the nuclear family with distinct gender roles for women. Wages and the quality of the lives of the working class improved to restrict the labor of women and children, introduce new social welfare programs, and promote use of birth control. The notion of a companion marriage—rather than economic motivations—was adopted by the working class.)

2. How did identities such as ethnicity, race, and class have a defined individual relationship to society? (Hint: Industrialization and class; middle- and working-class families, post-1815 ideologies, mass political movements and governmental reform, interaction with colonies.)

3. How and why did Europeans marginalize certain populations defined as "other"? (Hint: Nationalism, anti-Semitism, chauvinism, persistence of serfdom and feudalism, racial Darwinism, "The White Man's Burden," imperial-influenced art and colonial independence movements, and social Darwinism.)

Theme 6: National and European Identity

1. How and why were national identities created, developed, and challenged? (Hint: Imperial expansion in the 19th century; ideologies as responses to industrialization; Concert of Europe; nationalist movements; German and Italian unification; governments' responded to social/political pressures; mutual aid societies and unions were formed.)

2. How did cultural, regional, and other social identities coexist with national identities and sometimes challenge the notion of a unified nation (or empire)? (Hint: Concert of Europe; increasing economic globalization; industrialization; emerging class consciousness; radical political thought and the rise of Zionism; conservative suppression of nationalism; the revolutions of 1848; nationalist movements in the colonies.)

Important Events, Terms, and Concepts

The list below shows important events, terms, and concepts that you should be familiar with on the AP EURO exam. Please don't memorize each concept now. Place a check mark next to each topic as it is studied and refer to this list as often as necessary.

Events, Terms, and Concepts You Should Know					
Event	Year/Brief Description	Study Page	Event	Year/Brief Description	Study Page
The Congress of Vienna	**1815.** Reshaped the map and character of Europe after the Napoleonic Wars.	pp. 160–162	German unification	**1871.** Prussia won the Franco-Prussian War with ease and was able to unite the new Germany.	p. 176
Year of Revolutions	**1848.** Revolutions erupted in almost every European country.	pp. 162–165	The Berlin Conference	**1884–1885.** Conference that split up Africa into European colonies.	p. 182
The Crimean War	**1853–1856.** The Crimean War fundamentally shook up the balance of power in Europe and set the stage for German unification.	pp. 174–175	Revolution in Russia	**1905.** This revolution shook Russia to its core and forced the tsar to yield to his people.	p. 179
Italian unification	**1861.** Italy was unified after a victorious war against Austria with French support.	p. 175	World War I erupts	**1914.** World War I was the culmination of conflicts and secret pacts after 40 years of peace.	pp. 183–184

Chapter Review

Period Three is known for three key areas of study: the realignment of the European balance of power, the outpouring of European nationalism, and Europe's dominance as a world leader.

The following timeline illustrates AP EURO important events that happened gradually over time during this period. The timeline should help you visually and conceptually identify what preceded and what followed particular events.

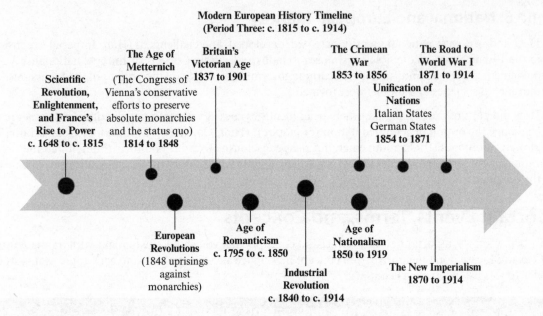

**Modern European History Timeline
(Period Three: c. 1815 to c. 1914)**

The Age of Metternich (1814 to 1848)

After Napoleon's defeat and 25 years of nearly uninterrupted revolutions, wars, and upheavals, European leaders decided to meet at the **Congress of Vienna** (1814–1815) to create a new order in Europe that would ensure stability and peace for the foreseeable future. The leaders of the strongest nations—Austria, Prussia, Russia, and England—formed a coalition to preserve stability in Europe and redraw Europe's boundaries. Each of these nations had drastically different objectives. After all, England was an advanced constitutional government, but the other three nations had despotic monarchies. Even though their differences caused conflicts during the conference, all nations agreed to end the upheaval and war that had scourged Europe for so long.

Heads Up: What You Need to Know

On the AP EURO exam, you should know that this period is often referred to as the *Age of Metternich*. **Klemens von Metternich** (1773–1859) founded the Concert of Europe and was probably the most important figure who epitomized the goals of the Congress of Vienna. Metternich was the foreign minister of Austria; he brought an aristocratic and conservative spirit to the conference. In a way, this was the last hurrah of Austria, which had had its troubles in the 18th century and was doomed to suffer greatly through the 19th century. Metternich became a symbol of preserving the status quo and restoring absolutism.

The Congress of Vienna led to discontentment throughout Europe. In an attempt to protect each nation's sovereignty and territorial integrity, the **Concert of Europe** was established as a system of diplomacy to enforce the decisions of the Congress of Vienna and create a balance of power. (Note: The Concert of Europe was successful in creating a foundation for international order in Europe until 1871.)

Key Facts about the Congress of Vienna

Promoted principles of peace. The Congress of Vienna was created to ensure peace in Europe.

Restored conservatism. Metternich headed the Congress of Vienna and opposed the ideas of the French Revolution: to protect liberty, equality, and fraternity (brotherhood). After the violence of two and a half decades of liberalism, many longed for conservatism and the rejection of societal reform. Like Metternich, many people believed in turning back the clock to restore former absolute rulers and their strict boundaries.

Reduced fears of nationalism. The creators of the Congress of Vienna viewed the nationalism that spread in France during the Napoleonic era as a threat to European stability. They sought to use monarchical absolutism as a counterweight against the ideology of nationalism. This was especially important for monarchies that ruled over many nationalities, such as those of Russia and Austria. As you will learn, the Congress of Vienna could not permanently suppress nationalism in Europe.

Restored the legitimacy of monarchy and the Church. The French Revolution overran the authority of the monarchy and the Church, and replaced it with the will of the people. Russia, Austria, and Prussia, in particular, wanted to see monarchical legitimacy and the Church restored across the face of the European continent.

Restored a balance of power. France had become a powerful nation during the 17th and 18th centuries. To rebalance the power, the diplomats of the Congress of Vienna, chaired by Metternich of Austria, took away most of the territories France gained during the French Revolutionary Wars and established monarchies around France. France was weakened so that it could no longer threaten other nations and rise to dominate Europe.

Leaders in Britain, Russia, and Austria did not realize that they had gone too far in the other direction and might antagonize France, as they would learn later in the century. As much as the Congress of Vienna sought to balance France's power, they did not intend to utterly humiliate France. The Congress of Vienna divided France into smaller states and imposed crushing territorial demands, but also sought to bring France back into the European state system as a moderate and reliable partner.

Created the Holy Alliance. In 1815, the powers of Russia, Austria, and Prussia established the **Holy Alliance.** This three-nation alliance was one of conservatism and monarchical legitimacy. The Holy Alliance served two purposes: to maintain conservatism throughout Europe, and to protect conservative legitimacy within the three member states. Fearing their own populace, these three emperors went so far as to promise aid to each other. For example, if an uprising occurred in Russia, Austria and Prussia would send their troops to maintain order and protect the Russian tsar. This was the ultimate expression of conservatism and the rejection of nationalism.

Did you know? The Congress of Vienna was established to promote European stability. In fact, the consequence of the Congress of Vienna's strict conservative principles caused the opposite to emerge—instability and revolutions. The 19th century became a period of violent upheavals and extremism.

People hoped for the spread of Enlightenment ideals, but saw that the absolutist monarchs of Eastern Europe held the most influence. Many liberals and reformers across Europe who had decried the radicalism of the Jacobins and the militarism of Napoleon turned to radicalism when they saw themselves deprived of legitimate power in their governments. As it turned out, diplomatic treaties and the military force of the Holy Alliance could not fully extinguish the light of liberty from Europe's people. Instead, it merely convinced many reformers that violent revolutions were the only way that Enlightenment ideals could survive.

19th-Century European Revolutions

By 1848, uprisings swept across the continent, causing instability and social chaos throughout Europe. Almost every nation had a revolution, but most were unsuccessful and not well coordinated. European monarchs were threatened as middle and working classes sought to establish a voice in government. The first revolution started in Paris, France and brought down King Louis-Philippe; the revolutions then spread from Paris to other countries. This section discusses the causes and consequences of the revolutions in France and other nations.

Heads Up: What You Need to Know

Common themes for 19th-century revolts across Europe include:

1. **Economic crisis.** Poor agricultural harvests, increasing food prices, and unemployment caused panic and unruliness (i.e., the "hungry forties" that struck Northern Europe).
2. **Political and social reform.** Citizens were dissatisfied with leadership and sought to establish new forms of government to change political, economic, and social structures.
3. **Romanticism.** People revolted against the Enlightenment ideals of rational laws and rules. Remember, Romantics emphasized the assertion of individual rights and self-determination.
4. **Nationalism.** Nations asserted conservative unification, autonomy, and supremacy of their ethnic or cultural group to defeat liberal ideals. (Note: The ideologies of socialism and communism were on the fringes of emerging.)

Note: The specific reasons for each nation's rebellion are listed in the tables on pp. 163–164.

France's Revolutions

Believe it or not, France's political history was nearly as tumultuous from 1830 to 1848 as it had been from 1789 to 1815. Remember that after Napoleon's defeat, Louis XVIII was restored to the French throne. The elderly king died in 1824 and was succeeded by his younger brother, Charles X. King Charles X was a reactionary ruler and upset the fragile balance of French politics by trying to turn France back to absolutism.

Revolutions in France		
Date/Ruler	**Cause**	**Consequence**
1830: King Charles X	**Revolt against repression.** The French people resisted a complete return to the old regime of monarchical absolutism and revolted in 1830, forcing King Charles into exile. The 1830 revolution proved to be the first of many in 19th-century France.	The revolution was successful. King Charles was replaced by a more acceptable liberal alternative, King Louis-Philippe.
1832: King Louis-Philippe	**Revolt against monarchical corruption.** Some students and radicals were unhappy with the 1830 revolution, as they felt they had exchanged one corrupt king for another. In 1832, they rose up in the June Revolution, and were quickly crushed by the government forces.	The revolution failed due to lack of public support, but the heroic naiveté became immortalized in Victor Hugo's *Les Miserables* (there have been both musical and film adaptations of this epic story).
1848: King Louis-Philippe	**Revolt against poor economic conditions.** The year 1848 became a year of revolutions in almost every corner of Europe, starting in France as the epicenter of a violent revolution against King Louis-Philippe. Louis-Philippe was known as the "bourgeois king" because he supported the upper middle class. He became increasingly disliked in the 1840s due to worsening economic conditions and repressing the industrial classes. Louis-Philippe outlawed political demonstrations and increased military force to crack down on political organizations against his regime. This backfired, and a revolution broke out in Paris once again.	King Louis-Philippe fled to Britain in exile. The French Second Republic was established, but much like the First Republic, it did not last long. A struggle between classes developed.

Conservative Leaders Fear Another French Revolution

The uprisings in France led to many fears in conservative European nations. Leaders of other nations grew concerned about another French Revolution spreading the flame of liberalism across Europe. Conservative nations became vigilant of possible threats and struggled to establish order. The following two examples illustrate how two other conservative nations dealt with threats of liberty revolts that started in the early 19th century.

German and Russian Turmoil		
Nation	**Cause**	**Consequence**
German Confederation 1819: Carlsbad Decrees	**Rebellion against Austrian domination.** Metternich of Austria found himself having to work hard to safeguard his Concert of Europe. In this period, the Italian states rose against Austrian domination, and Metternich quickly sent in troops. Metternich was not willing to lose valuable Italian possessions to the modern force of nationalism. When liberalism emerged in Austria itself, radical students began organizing political clubs that opposed the regime.	Metternich issued the **Carlsbad Decrees,** which banned nationalist student associations, imposed media censorship, removed liberal university professors, and enforced police repression. Metternich and successive Austrian leaders hoped that brute military force and the heavy hand of the state could prevent liberalism and nationalism from spreading in Austria. This repression only prolonged the inevitable.

Continued

Nation	Cause	Consequence
Russia 1825: Decembrist Revolution	**Demands for constitutional reforms.** To understand the cause of the Decembrist Revolution, first look at the events that led up to the revolution. Even though Russian troops were sent to defeat Napoleon's troops in 1815, when they returned to the stark despotism of Russia, some aristocratic generals who were captivated by liberalism secretly met to discuss enlightened ideals. The Decembrist Revolution was led by these enlightened military officers, who hoped to move Russia into the modern age. When the Russian tsar died in 1825, Russian officers rose in rebellion, demanded constitutional reforms, and demanded the abdication of the new tsar, Nicholas I, who was known for his extreme absolutist views.	The "Decembrists" did not find widespread public support. Nicholas' response was brutally revengeful. His army used artillery fire on the besieged rebels. Once the surviving rebels surrendered, they were executed or imprisoned. Nicholas I would rule Russia for three decades. He proved to be its most autocratic (dictatorial) tsar since Peter the Great. During Nicholas' reign and his successor's reign, Russia became a symbol of absolutism and reactionary politics for all of Europe.

European Revolutions in 1848

France's revolutions are noted on p. 163 and Britain was spared from the revolts, but there were many significant revolutions in various nations throughout Europe in the fateful year of 1848. Most of the revolutions outside of France failed because of the resilience of the European monarchies and the disintegrating informal partnerships between groups of people who were not natural allies, such as the bourgeoisie and working classes, and the nationalist minorities and liberals.

> TEST TIP: On the AP EURO exam it is important to know the long-term consequences of the 1848 revolutions (think about historical changes over time). Despite their immediate failures, these revolutions laid the foundation for long-term changes that would emerge much later—for example, the unification of Italy and the unification of Germany, the establishment of representative democracy, and the abolition of censorship.

In the immediate aftermath, however, the year 1848 seemed to be an exercise in the futility of radical change and violent revolutions.

European Revolutions in 1848		
Nation	**Cause**	**Consequence**
Austria	The national minorities of Austria (a majority of the population) rose up in conjunction with German liberals to demand changes from the Habsburg monarchy.	Metternich, still in power at this point, fled to exile in England. In honor of the Holy Alliance, Russia eventually sent in military troops to help the Habsburgs put down the rebellion. Changes eventually materialized, including the abolishment of serfdom in the Austrian Empire.
Italy	To establish unified nation-states, Italians rose up in rebellion against Austrian domination and the rule of local monarchs.	Italians were easily defeated by Austrian military forces, but the revolution laid the foundation for Italian unification two decades later.

Nation	Cause	Consequence
German Confederation	Riots ensued in Berlin guided by liberal German students who demanded rights, unity, and a representative democracy in Germanic states. Rebels were later aided by some of the middle and working classes of Germany.	Frederick William IV mobilized Prussian troops and the rebellion was quickly crushed. Although Frederick initially allowed an assembly to draft a constitution, "Declaration of the Rights of German People," the threat to power was too great for Frederick and he decided to dissolve the Prussian assembly, impacting the future of Germany.
Poland Territories	Poland had been dismembered by Prussia, Austria, and Russia in the 18th century. In 1848, Prussia's army imprisoned Poles to reduce Russia's strength. Many Poles rose in a nationalist revolution and rebellion against their foreign overlords. Unfortunately, the Poles and Prussians ended in conflict.	The Poles were put down when Prussian troops were sent in.
Denmark	Denmark was ruled by an absolute monarch, and liberals and reformers arose with some support among army officers and the rank and file.	Unlike most of the revolutions, this revolt was successful. Because of the crucial element of (some) military support, the Danish revolutionaries were able to successfully force a constitutional monarchy upon the king of Denmark.

Great Britain and the Victorian Age (1837 to 1901)

In 1837, the king of England died and was succeeded by the young Victoria. Queen Victoria ruled England for nearly 64 years. This era was known as the Victorian Age. Queen Victoria presided over the *Pax Britannica* (the period in which the British dominated the world).

Key Facts about the Political Changes During Queen Victoria's Reign

The 19th century saw many dramatic changes in England. Below are the key political features of Queen Victoria's reign (we will return to economics and culture later).

Slave trading ends (1833). Slavery was abolished by Britain in 1833, and most other European nations followed suit. (Note: To give perspective, slavery was not abolished in the United States until 1865.) During Victoria's reign, Britain used its military force and economic leverage to combat slavery around the world. Slave fortresses were attacked on the African coast and slaves were set free from foreign combatant nations.

Chartist Movement to reform the working class (1838). A mass movement called the **Chartist Movement** was formed by Britain's working class. Britain's parliamentary system was unrepresentative of the working class in 1837. In addition, the vast majority of men could not vote because they did not own land. Chartism sought to solve the problems of the working class by changing government policies. In 1838, working-class activists created The People's Charter, demanding universal adult-male suffrage, electoral changes, compensation for members of Parliament, and protections for workers. Followers of the movement became known as Chartists. The Chartists gained millions of signatures on petitions to Parliament, and enjoyed widespread support among the public, but their demands were rejected as radical by the British government.

Famine in Ireland (1845–1849). In the mid-1840s, a terrible famine struck Ireland because of *blight* (disease) among the potato crop, the cheap food staple on which the Irish poor had depended for over a century. British landowners and officials who were used to repressing the Irish did little to help, and worldwide opinion emerged in an outcry against this humanitarian crisis. Over 1 million Irish died, and many more fled to the United States to escape destitution and starvation, leading to two decades of immense Irish immigration to the U.S. Hatred of the British ensued for ignoring the plight of the Irish, which led to Irish support for independence from Britain. Ireland did not become independent from Britain until 1922 (Northern Ireland is still under British rule).

Empire in India (1877). The British had lost most of their overseas empire in the American Revolutionary War, but still retained footholds in India. During Victoria's reign, Britain greatly expanded these holdings through commerce and military force, and by 1877 it controlled enough of India for Victoria to be crowned as Empress of India. Britain also held important lands in Burma (Myanmar), Formosa (Taiwan), and the Pacific Islands.

Territorial conflict with the United States (1895). Britain remained hostile toward the United States long into the 19th century due to the American Revolution. Britain was at war with the United States during the War of 1812, opposed American attempts to take Cuba, and came very close to intervening in the American Civil War on behalf of the Confederacy. For decades Britain feared American conquest of Canada and resented American economic growth. At the end of the century, though, a territorial crisis emerged in Venezuela with Britain in 1895. Referencing the **Monroe Doctrine** (the 1823 policy that opposed further European colonization in the Americas), Venezuela sought United States intervention against Britain. Britain and Venezuela agreed to American leadership's request for arbitration. This was the last noteworthy foreign policy conflict between Britain and the United States.

The Age of Romanticism (c. 1795 to c. 1850)

Something new emerged from the culture of the 18th century—Romanticism. The Age of Romanticism was an artistic movement that swept across Europe for most of the 19th century and left its imprint on the way people thought and believed well into the 20th century. Romanticism was a revolt against logic and reason from the previous century. Romanticism was a reaction against science, rationalism, social convention, and industrialization (the machinelike world of the Industrial Revolution). Instead, it stressed individual imagination, inner knowledge, and the mysteries of power coming from the natural world. Romanticism influenced all areas of European culture and was expressed in art, music, literature, religion, and philosophy.

TEST TIP: In each uniquely different historical time period, patterns of social thinking were expressed in the fine arts. People thought about and responded to historical events through their works of art. For this reason, the works of artists, composers, poets, writers, and philosophers living during the Age of Romanticism were very different from those living in the Age of Enlightenment. Even if you don't remember the details about specific artists, it is important to include this fact in an essay answer. For more information about art movements, refer to the tables on pp. 7–8 and p. 180.

Since Romanticism is one of the most important areas of study in the field of 19th-century modern European cultural history, let's take a closer look at some of its most important characteristics. To help you respond to questions on the AP EURO exam, each characteristic listed below provides an illustrated category for your consideration (i.e., art, music, literature, religion, or politics). The characteristics are not limited to one category, but may also apply to other areas of study. For example, European painters often used nature and emotion when portraying their works of art.

- Focus on nature
- Focus on individualism and unique genius

- Focus on emotion and imagination
- Focus on romanticizing the Middle Ages (medieval period)
- Focus on nationalism

Key Facts about the Age of Romanticism

Art: Focus on nature. Romantics had a renewed focus on the beauty of nature. This marked the end of the Baroque artistic movement and the beginning of the realism (and later Impressionism) artistic movement. Artistic nature was seen as something to be marveled at, rather than something to be conquered and controlled. Romantic painters reveled in portraying beckoning landscape wildernesses, tempestuous seas, and abandoned buildings overtaken by nature. Romantics believed that human beings and their civilizations were *interlopers* (people in a place where they did not belong) in the natural world. Famous Romantic visual artists included Delacroix, Goya, and Friedrich. Delacroix painted scenes of political revolutions and social upheavals. Goya portrayed chilling and sometimes shocking depictions of myth and history.

TEST TIP: Friedrich was perhaps the best-known German artist in Romantic history. When responding to a 19th-century free-response question, use Friedrich's socio-historical work as an example of the cultural reflections of the Age of Romanticism. Friedrich's well-known painting below depicts subjectivity (individualism), mystery (divine inspiration), and the symbolism of a man positioned at the apex of the natural world (man's profound respect for the genuineness of nature and beauty).

Source: Caspar David Friedrich, *Wanderer above the Sea and Fog,* 1818.

Music: Focus on individualism and unique genius. While the Renaissance and the Enlightenment eras certainly had their fair share of brilliant minds, the Romantic era celebrated individual uniqueness in the fine arts— for example, the genius of the first Romantic composer, Ludwig van Beethoven. Artists, musicians, and poets were not merely beneficiaries of aristocrats, nobles, and bishops like artists of past eras; they were celebrities among the masses, especially the working classes. Individual genius was the highest principle in the school of Romanticism. Famous Romantic composers include Beethoven, Chopin, Wagner, Mendelssohn, Schumann, and Tchaikovsky.

Literature: Focus on emotion and imagination. Romantics focused on subjective emotions, internal thoughts, feelings, and imagination. In literature, this was expressed in poetry, stories of love, adventure, life, and tales of fantasy. Famous Romantic writers include Goethe, Wordsworth, Hugo, Eliot, Tolstoy, Dostoyevsky, Dickens, and Jacob and Wilhelm Grimm.

Religion: Focus on romanticizing the Middle Ages. Romantics sought out the beautiful, the mysterious, and the noble aspects of history. While the Enlightenment philosophers searched the ancient past of the Greeks and Romans for wisdom and knowledge, Romantics turned to the medieval era for inspiration of heroes and unsolved mysteries. (Remember that enlightened thinkers rejected beliefs of the medieval era due to its superstition, ignorance, and religious fanaticism.)

Politics: Focus on nationalism. The Romantics were fervent believers in nationalism, especially of historically oppressed or maligned people. They found the old folklore, customs, and traditions to be delightful sources of nationalist pride and unity. Romantic artists from powerful nations such as England and Austria eagerly embraced the clothes and music of Hungarians, Greeks, and Lithuanians, members of the "little nations" of Europe.

> **TEST TIP:** On the AP EURO exam, you may be asked to compare and contrast historical events. For example, compare and contrast the basic views of the Age of Enlightenment and the Age of Romanticism. Use the following chart as a quick reference for differences between these two time periods.

Comparing Enlightenment and Romanticism	
Enlightenment	**Romanticism**
Emphasized rationalism and intellectualism to understand human nature.	Emphasized individualism and self-expression using emotions, senses, mood, and mysteries to understand human nature.
Emphasized scientific empiricism (reason and observation).	Emphasized individual senses and genius; rejected science.
Emphasized deism. Enlightened thinkers replaced religion with science and reason. They believed in God, but believed that God did not interfere with human beings' ability to reason.	Emphasized divine wisdom. Romantics believed that inner knowledge was manifested by God's divine inspirations.
Emphasized social conventions and well-defined laws. Enlightened thinkers believed in the ideas of democracy (i.e., a social contract between the state and the people, a separation of powers, and a separation of church and state).	Emphasized nationalism and liberalism. Romantics revolted against the rules and laws in favor of self-determination and unrestrained behavior.

The Age of Nationalism (c. 1850 to c. 1919)

Recall that Napoleon's invasion of Germany united a few hundred German Confederation states into fewer than 40 states. The largest of these states was Prussia. Napoleon's oppression of the Germanic people inspired German nationalism as a force of resistance (not unlike how British oppression of the Irish inadvertently led to surging Irish nationalism).

Heads Up: What You Need to Know

The term *nationalism* is an important historical ideological concept and frequently appears on the AP EURO exam. Nationalism is a form of patriotism and the love for one's nation. It is a group's supreme loyalty formed by shared interests and a common identity: ethnicity, language, customs, traditions, or culture.

In the 19th century, nationalism was the powerful force that transformed and unified European nations. The spirit of nationalism was closely tied to Romanticism. While the Romantic artists and scholars were connecting with nature, nationalists focused on the past culture of the Middle Ages and sought to restore its political ideals.

It may surprise you that many 19th-century citizens identified with the nationalistic beliefs of "us versus them." Think about explaining these ideological changes over time on the AP EURO exam. For example, even though the principles of nationalism were important during the 18th-century French Revolution and the 19th-century unification of Italian and German states, by the 20th century, nationalistic attitudes had become associated with backward politics. In fact, extreme nationalism became one of the primary causes of World Wars I and II.

Italian States' and German States' Unification

In the beginning of the 19th century, there were no nations called Italy or Germany. Italian states and German states consisted of many separate groups and regions. Each group had its own language, culture, laws, and economy. These nation-states were unified only in the minds of their people because they were not yet sovereign nations due to the political disunity of the German lands and the Austrian dominance of the Italian peninsula. The unification of Italian states and German states took place during the Age of Nationalism and altered the balance of power in Europe. The unification will be discussed later in the section "The Unification of Nations (1854 to 1871)" (p. 173).

The Industrial Revolution (c. 1840 to c. 1914)

The Industrial Revolution began in Britain, but soon spread into France, Germany, and other countries. The Industrial Revolution of the 19th century would eventually extend to the United States, and from there to the rest of the world into the 20th century.

Heads Up: What You Need to Know

The Industrial Revolution had a dramatic impact on the world's social, economic, and political history. On the AP EURO exam you will need to know that industrialization did not take place all at once. It gradually emerged in phases during the 19th and 20th centuries as new inventions were developed.

The first phase of the Industrial Revolution was based on coal and iron. While industrialization arguably started when James Watt invented the steam engine in 1769, it did not gain momentum until c. 1840 to c. 1870, when machinery improved the commercial manufacturing of goods. It was during this time that coal replaced wood for fuel, and the power of iron machines replaced wooden machines and the hand tools used by humans.

The second phase of industrialization began around c. 1870 to c. 1914—the Technical Revolution. It focused on oil, electricity, and fuel. The rapidly increasing industrial developments generated new sources of inventions, and with the discovery of electricity, the mass production of goods was possible. Changes in military technology, economic policy, and social structure also arose during this phase of industrialization.

TEST TIP: On the AP EURO exam, you may be asked *where* and *why* the Industrial Revolution first started.

Where: Britain was the first to industrialize, followed by France, then Prussia/Germany. Russia, Austria, and Italy were very late in implementing industrial modernization. As a result, these countries suffered in both economic competition and military hardships. If you have trouble remembering which countries industrialized earlier or later, just think of the economic conditions in today's Europe. The wealthy north and west and poorer south and east of today correspond well to their historical precedents of a century ago.

Why: Use the Key Facts below to point to key issues that explain why the Industrial Revolution started in Britain.

Key Facts about the Causes of the Industrial Revolution

The conditions in Britain favored industrialization. By 1850, Britain was a world leader in manufacturing: two-thirds of the coal, one-half of the iron, and one-half of the cotton industry.

Agricultural movement. As we saw in the previous chapter, the enclosure movement not only changed agriculture in Britain, but it also spurred new technological innovations by landowners who became prosperous, so they could afford to experiment by investing in new methods of technology.

Innovations. Inventions and mechanizations that resulted from the Scientific Revolution were applied to mechanics, engineering, and technology. Inventions were the machine that drove innovations in manufacturing, productivity, and transportation.

Displacement. Displaced farm workers and rural peasants from the enclosure movement caused people to relocate into cities, which became the centers of booming industrialization. Relatively small cities like Manchester and Birmingham became sprawling metropolises as landless people searched for work in factories. Most early factories were in the textile (clothing) industry because factory-produced clothing was cheap to make and could be sold across the world at a cheaper rate than hand-sewn clothing.

Cheap labor. Cheap labor was plentiful with an increased number of poor rural peasants who were available to work at reduced rates.

Natural resources. Britain had abundant natural resource deposits of coal and iron required for industrial production.

Transportation. Britain was a world colonial and maritime power that could easily manufacture, market, and ship raw and finished products. The island nation had access to ports and waterways through which products could be shipped more cheaply than using land transportation.

Capital investments. Compared to continental powers that had economically dwindled after a century of fighting almost endless wars, Britain had remained economically stable and had large amounts of capital for investments. Wealthy landowners and other British investors had a great deal of extra wealth that could be invested in industrialization.

Government. Britain's stable government helped to pass laws and reforms to protect businesses, making it easier for businesses to produce and sell goods. The government also instituted a good business banking system.

Inventions

Several important technological inventions helped to shape the Industrial Revolution.

Inventions That Shaped the Industrial Revolution	
Invention	**Importance**
Steam Engine and Steam Locomotive	The steam engine truly transformed the world. It shifted energy and power away from animal-drawn power, watermills, and manual power. The steam engine dramatically changed iron and steelmaking, textile production, and, most of all, transportation. The steam engine was used to develop the first steam locomotive, which resulted in the construction of railroads across countries. Railroads improved ground transportation for shipping goods and improved social traveling, strengthening national unity.
Cotton Gin	The cotton gin, invented by Eli Whitney, one of the most famous of the industrial inventors, sped up the process of weaving cotton to make clothing. The cotton gin mechanically separated seeds from the cotton fiber. This reduced the cost of clothing so that even the poorest populations could afford to wear cloth.
Flying Shuttle	The cotton textile industry was well established in Britain, but required lots of labor and time. The flying shuttle was a cloth-weaving machine that was an enormous timesaver in the textile industry. It doubled the productivity to allow weavers of cloth to work much faster.

Key Facts about the Impact of the Industrial Revolution

Increase in productivity. The result of the Industrial Revolution showed a dramatic increase in the production of modernized goods, particularly textiles, and a rise of factory manufacturing.

Demographic changes. The first years of the Industrial Revolution were difficult for millions of people who were forced to change their lifestyles when they moved from rural communities to urban centers. For example, the population of London more than doubled from c. 1800 to c. 1850.

Division of classes. The Industrial Revolution created enormous and unprecedented amounts of wealth for elite classes, and divided social classes between the rich and the poor. Other social classes were beginning to take shape during this period: the working class (known as the *proletariat*) and the middle class (known as the *bourgeoisie*).

Poor living and working conditions. Little was done to improve conditions for the working-class and poor populations.

- Factory workers had few legal protections, and the government showed little interest in helping the poor alleviate their problems.
- People living in industrial cities witnessed horrible, unsanitary working and living conditions.
- Workers were being injured in unsafe working factories.
- Workers were forced to work 12- to 14-hour shifts.
- Workers included women and children.
- The housing for the families of wage-earners consisted of dark, crowded tenements.

Protests. Workers and their reform supporters had many different responses to the ravages of industrial capitalism. Some turned to religion, focusing their efforts on churches that embraced social justice, like the Methodists or the Unitarians. Others tried to petition the government to ensure greater fairness in the law and the economy. Still others, such as the **Luddites,** protested these changes. The Luddite textile workers were artisans whose skills required decades to learn, but in the advent of industrialization their skills became obsolete. Despairing, they decided to destroy the evil machines that were ending their livelihoods, but their efforts were pointless. The change toward industrialization was inevitable. Today, the term "Luddite" is an insult, used to describe someone who unrealistically stands in the way of inevitable change.

Socialism. The greatest and longest-lasting impact of industrialization was socialism. While historical precedents exist for socialism from the early Christians, socialism was a response to industrial capitalism that emerged in the second half of the 19th century. Socialists rejected capitalism as an economic system, favoring a system of communal ownership of land and economic equality. There were two main types of socialists: Utopian socialists and Marxist socialists.

- **Utopian socialists,** including Robert Owen and Charles Fourier, who advocated for working people to go off into the countryside and build perfect societies that exemplified socialistic cooperation instead of capitalistic competition. To utopian socialists, this was the most efficient and humane system of economics. (Think of the hippies who built communes in the wilderness in the 1960s.) These experiments tended to be unsuccessful, and utopian socialism remained largely academic.
- **Marxists.** The other type of socialists were scientific socialists, or the Marxists, founded by Karl Marx, who asserted that most of the problems in a society were due to unequal wealth and social classes. Marx advocated for a violent overthrow of the social-economic system of government to form a classless society. Karl Marx and Friedrich Engels wrote *The Communist Manifesto* (1848) that advanced theories of modern scientific socialism.

  Although Marx's writings have many points, three important features of Marxism to remember for the AP EURO exam are listed in the chart that follows.

Important Features of Marxism	
Feature	**Description**
Governments should abolish social classes and unequal wealth.	The most important feature of Marxism is that social problems are the result of unequal economic class struggles. Marx wrote, "The history of all hitherto existing societies is the history of class struggles."
Governments should abolish capitalism.	In capitalism, a dominant group (capitalists) possesses the economic means of production, distribution, and exchange. In order to stay economically competitive, capitalists must acquire as much labor from proletariats (wage-earners) as possible and pay as little as possible. Proletariats only possess the capacity to work for survival. According to Marx, capitalism should be abolished because it leads to a class struggle.
Inequality leads to rebellion (dialectical materialism).	Marx's theory of *dialectical materialism* argues that the economic inequalities between classes gives rise to class struggles, which drive the society forward into an inevitable rebellion. The rebellion brings about social change when the existing class structure can no longer be sustained. According to Marx, in a capitalist society proletariats will be destined to overthrow capitalism and establish socialism. Hence, a new opposing class will be inadvertently created in the process. For example, during the Middle Ages the aristocracy held the means of production (farmland), but they were overthrown by the rising bourgeoisie, who established capitalism with the new means of production (capital). The advent of capitalism created the landless, urban, wage-working proletariat, who was destined to overthrow the bourgeoisie and establish socialism. Marx argued that a class struggle between the bourgeoisie and the proletariat might lead to a dictatorship of the proletariat, to be replaced by communism.

Heads Up: What You Need to Know

On the AP EURO exam, **Marxism** frequently appears as a test question. You should be able to identify the important features of Marxism, as provided in the chart above. Recognize that while Karl Marx's economic theories were discredited in the 20th century (when his theories were attempted in the Soviet Union, China, and other countries), Marx's theory of class struggle as the central element in the analysis of social change has remained influential in the study of social and economic history, even today. We have Marx to thank for understanding class analysis in examining history and historiography.

The Unification of Nations (1854 to 1871)

Until the 19th-century revolutions, most attempts of smaller territories to separate from their ruling European dynastic empires were crushed by force, except for Greece and Belgium. The independent territories of the Italians, Germans, Hungarians, Poles, and Turks sought separation from their ruling empires. The Italians, Germans (Prussians), Hungarians, and Poles were ruled by the Austrian Empire; the Turks were ruled by the Ottoman Empire; and some other Pole territories were ruled by the Russian Empire. After the 1848 revolutions, however, a nationalistic spirit was inspired throughout Europe and several smaller territories sought to establish individual unified nation-states and freedom from their dynastic empires. Starting with the Crimean War, this section will discuss the struggles that each territory faced to attain separation and eventually unification.

The Crimean War (1853 to 1856)

The Crimean War was the first major European war since the Congress of Vienna (1815). France and Britain, among others, felt that Russia was threatening the balance of power in the Turkish-ruled Jerusalem Holy Land.

The Crimean War (1854–1856)		
Nations	**Causes**	**Consequences**
Russia France England Ottoman Empire Sardinia-Piedmont	**Controversy over Holy Land.** The controversy was over the control of sacred Christian Holy Land sites in Jerusalem. Decades after Napoleon's defeat, Russia was still considered a powerful nation in Europe. Russia tried to control the holy sites in Turkish-ruled Jerusalem and tried to intimidate Turkey into giving Russia protection for Christians in the Holy Land. **Russia wanted access to the Mediterranean.** One of the primary objections to Russia controlling the Holy Land was that if Russia controlled the Holy Land, this would give it serious domination over Turkey and an entrance into the Mediterranean by occupying Istanbul. France and Britain opposed this change, and thus instigated the Crimean War against Russia. **Prussia and Austria refused to help Russia.** Russia resented Prussia and Austria for refusing to help because Russia counted on the support of their Holy Alliance allies. Russia was particularly angry with Austria since the Russians had dispatched soldiers to protect the Austrian monarchy in 1848. **Russia lacked technology.** Russia lacked the railroads to move soldiers, lacked the factories to feed and clothe soldiers, and lacked competent generals to lead soldiers. The Russians were humiliated by the allied forces in Crimea, and before long the Russians had to admit defeat and surrender before the heartland of Russia was subjected to another invasion.	The Crimean War was important because Russia's appearance of invincibility after the Napoleonic Wars was shattered. Russia had enormous potential in size, population, military, and energy, but it had fallen hopelessly behind in economic, social, and technological matters compared to the other great European powers. For example, Russia did not have railroads. Under Tsar Alexander II, Russia took radical steps to modernize itself, including the abolition of serfdom in 1861. Russia sullenly withdrew from European affairs to focus on rebuilding its forces. One of the most important consequences of the Crimean War was that it drove a wedge between Russia and its Prussian and Austrian neighbors with unresolved tensions. It was difficult to foresee at the time, but this left Austria vulnerable to future German and Italian nationalistic movements.

> **Did you know?** During the Crimean War, more than 500,000 people died, but most did not die from battle casualties. Most people died from unsanitary hospitals and disease. **Florence Nightingale (1820–1910)** and a team of other nurses who were working during the Crimean War were recognized as guiding forces to improve the unsanitary conditions in hospitals. Nightingale sanitized linens, bathed soldiers, and secured clean drinking water for the soldiers. Mortality rates dramatically improved. She was known as the "Lady with the Lamp" because she carried a lamp during her late visits to tend to patients.

Wars of Unification: Italian and German States

Two significant European developments occurred during the 19th century: the unification of Italy and the unification of Germany (called the German Confederation). Italian unification was accomplished through Sardinia (Piedmont) and German unification was accomplished through Prussia. The common obstacle to unification for both nations was Austria, which had controlled central Europe since the Congress of Vienna.

Unification of Italy (1859–1861)	
Cause	**Consequences**
After the Crimean War, Italian nationalists again began to agitate for a unified and independent Italy (similar to the revolt that was attempted in 1848). Metaphorically, Italy was the David, facing the Goliath powers of Austria, France, Italian *plutocrats* (tycoons), and the pope. With this opposition, nationalists in Piedmont in the northwestern part of Italy (industrialized and famed for military traditions), favored allying with outside powers such as France to drive out the Austrians. In 1859, the Piedmontese used their French alliance to defeat Austria.	Italy became one unified nation. After removing the Austrian influence, the Italians quickly united their different states through diplomacy and force. Through the efforts of politician **Camillo di Cavour,** Italy was unified under the monarchy of Sardinia. In 1861, the unification (*Risorgimento* in Italian) of the Kingdom of Italy was officially proclaimed. Unification was complete except for Rome (held by the pope) and Venetia (held by Austria). Venetia was ceded to Italy in 1866. The anti-Italian papacy still controlled the Papal States, including Rome and the Vatican. The pope was hostile to the new Italian nation-state because of its nationalism, modernism, and (relative) secularism. French troops remained in Rome to protect the pope from Italy until 1871, when they were hastily removed to defend France against a foreign invasion by Prussia.

TEST TIP: On the AP EURO exam, keep in mind that the sprawling Austrian Empire included many different ethnicities: Poles, Ukrainians, Serbians, and Croatians. Austrian-Germans formed a small minority within the empire. Forming the Austro-Hungarian Dual Monarchy was a necessary compromise to placate one of the largest minorities, the Hungarian Magyars. The rest of the minorities, still on the outside of power, remained discontent. Many historians view Austria-Hungary in the 19th and 20th centuries as an *anachronism* (an example of medieval monarchical legitimacy holding its ground against the forces of modernism and nationalism). In this version of events, it was inevitable that Austria-Hungary would not last much longer.

In the mid-19th century, German territories consisted of fewer than 40 independent German states, the largest of which was Prussia. During the next 7 years, Prussia fought three main wars to unify what is known today as Germany, crafting a unified German nation-state.

Unification of the German Confederation		
War	**Cause**	**Consequences**
Danish-Prussian War (1864)	The first war was against Denmark. The conflict was fought over two disputed border provinces, Schleswig and Holstein.	Danish forces were small and weak, and Prussia was able to easily defeat Denmark and take the land that it wanted.
Austro-Prussian War (1866)	In 1866, the Prussians went to war with Austria for control over the smaller German states. Russia refused to help Austria, as the tsar was still furious about Austria's betrayal during the Crimean War.	Austria was larger, more populous, and had near universal support among the smaller German states, but Prussia's railroad infrastructure, superior military tactics, arms, and superior military leadership allowed the Prussians to crush Austria in only 7 weeks. Prussia was able to dominate other German lands. Austria was humiliated, and 1 year later created a **Dual Monarchy** between Austria and Hungary to placate domestic unrest.
Franco-Prussian War (1870–1871)	Prussia invaded France to shift the European balance of power. The wars of national unification ended with the Franco-Prussian War. It started in 1870 over the pretense of a German insult to France concerning the succession to the throne of Spain. In fact, the leader of Prussia's foreign policy, **Otto von Bismarck,** had brilliantly engineered a crisis in which France would declare war on Prussia, ensuring that no countries would join the French "aggressors." Shortly after the outbreak of hostilities, the Prussians took the first step by invading France with massive armies. France's Napoleon III rallied his empire to combat the Prussian invasion. He rushed to the eastern frontier to face the Prussians, but at the *Battle of Sedan* his armies were trapped and he himself was captured. This was less than 8 weeks from the start of the war. Napoleon III met with Bismarck, who treated him cordially but demanded that he surrender to Prussia.	The peace settlement to end the war was harsh. The eastern provinces of Alsace and Lorraine surrendered to Prussia, and heavy reparation payments would be paid to Prussia for decades. France was humiliated and ashamed by this rapid and stunning defeat at the hand of the Prussians, and many Frenchmen spent the next four decades swearing *revanche* (revenge). At the end of the war, the Prussians staged a ceremony in the Hall of Mirrors at Versailles, which inaugurated the Prussian king as Emperor of the German Empire. The territories of Germany united into one German Empire. The work of centuries—French balance of power politics and English, Russian, and even Spanish designs—had been undone. As early as the 16th century, Machiavelli had warned against the power and possibilities of the united peoples and states of what was loosely called "Germany."

Shift in the European Balance of Power: Germany's Rise to Power

The year 1871 marked a tremendous shift in the European balance of power. Because of Russia's aloofness, Germany had united into the wealthiest and most powerful nation on the continent. France and Austria had been hopelessly weakened, and a weak Italy and Russia were hardly ready to take their places. All across the continent, European leaders and the public were aghast at the sudden rise of Germany, but the fact was now unavoidable. The German Confederation was destined to be the strongest power in Europe and would soon begin to flex its muscles abroad—laying the groundwork for both world wars.

Heads Up: What You Need to Know

Otto von Bismarck (1815–1898), the "Iron Chancellor," comes up often on the AP EURO exam. Bismarck was a notable statesman who helped Germany become a modernized, unified nation. Not only did he brilliantly manipulate his European rivals to unite and make Germany a world leader, but he was also a master of *realpolitik* (politics based on realism in international diplomacy, rather than on moral principles). He approached difficulties and problems from a pragmatic point of view. He always did what was most beneficial to his country's interest, without regard for ideological or moral considerations.

Source: Anton von Werner, *The Proclamation of the German Empire,* 1884. On January 18, 1871, the German Empire is proclaimed in the Hall of Mirrors of the Palace of Versailles.

The Belle Époque (1871 to 1914)

After the defeat of France and the advent of Germany's power in 1871, a new era in Europe known as the Belle Époque began. This section discusses important events in politics and culture during the Belle Époque.

Did you know? Belle Époque translates to "Beautiful Era." Belle Époque is a term that was coined in France in retrospect for the period after the end of the Franco-Prussian War (1871) to the start of World War I (1914). As the name suggests, this was a period of relative calm, peace, and security in international affairs. No major European wars were fought during this period. During the Belle Époque, there was a tremendous outflowing of industry, technology, and cultural growth, as well as changes in the domestic politics of European nations.

Key Facts about European Politics from 1871 to 1914

Mass politics. In this period, more men could vote than ever before, although women still did not have the right to vote. In every advanced European nation, most men were able to vote by 1910. Property qualifications were no longer legal, and new political parties were formed that appealed to ordinary people on a mass scale. Middle-class and working-class people took part in political protests and debates.

Welfare. Faced with the threats of socialism, many European governments decided to placate the working classes with state welfare and reform systems. This included unemployment insurance and labor reforms, and greatly expanded the size of governments while alleviating the pressure on the economic system of capitalism.

Women's suffrage. While men were gaining the right to vote in unprecedented numbers, women began to demand equal rights to vote and the rights to run for a government position. Initially, the suffrage participants were only radicals and extremists, but the movement began to take on momentum as the century turned.

TEST TIP: For the AP EURO exam, you should be familiar with the women's suffrage movement in Britain. The women's suffrage movement split between radical suffragists and moderate suffragists. The majority of European women had to wait until 1928, after World War I, to gain equal suffrage, but in 1893 in the British colony of New Zealand, women gained the right to vote. (Note: In 1918, only British women over 30 years old secured the right to vote.)

The New Woman. Gender norms varied widely and changed frequently throughout European history. During this period, gender norms were often linked to wider societal changes. The "New Woman" rejected conventional womanhood. People were shocked and intrigued by women riding on bicycles, going out unattended, smoking cigarettes, flirting with men, wearing pants, and taking part in politics and theater. These New Women were targets for cheap mockery, but they also paved the way for a fundamental rethinking of a woman's role in European society.

Social Darwinism. Biological Darwinism brought about an unpleasant feature during the Belle Époque—social Darwinism. Social Darwinism is the theory that the strongest group prevails after the weaker group drops out. Herbert Spencer applied Darwin's theories to human beings and argued that some people (wealthy, white northern Europeans) were superior to others (poor, southern-eastern, nonwhite, non-Christian Europeans). Some northern Europeans thought that to ensure the proper social balance, superior humans should dominate weak humans. This led to **eugenics,** a policy of sterilizing or otherwise preventing "undesirables" from breeding. These elements of coercion began a pathway; the terminal point was the gas chambers of Germany's Third Reich in World War II.

TEST TIP: Social Darwinism is an important concept that may appear on the AP EURO exam. It is based on the theory of natural evolution and argues that certain groups of human beings are superior to other groups. This theory fueled the 20th-century ideologies of fascist Germany and imperialistic Japan.

The chart below describes nation-specific political developments from 1871 to 1914.

Political Developments	
Nation	Events
France	The **Dreyfus Affair** gripped France in the 1890s, when a Jewish army officer was convicted as a traitor for selling secrets to the Germans (Dreyfus was later exonerated). The Affair became a battleground for the cultural wars of France. Intellectuals, politicians, and ordinary Frenchmen were taking sides.
Britain	In Britain, the question of **Irish home rule** loomed among the population. Liberals wanted to give autonomy or even independence to the Emerald Isle (Ireland), while conservatives wanted to maintain British dominance. This issue became more and more controversial until it nearly led to a civil war in 1914, a fate that was only avoided by the sudden outbreak of World War I.
Germany	In Germany, Bismarck was removed from power in 1888 by the impetuous new Kaiser Wilhelm II. Wilhelm II rejected Bismarck's cautious *realpolitik* (policy based on the primary given circumstances, rather than on moral or ethical principles), and decided upon a new policy of *weltpolitik* (world policy). In weltpolitik, Germany would attempt a global empire that would challenge and overtake the British Empire. Germany would need to become involved in overseas colonization, build a powerful navy to defeat Britain's dominant navy, and confront other global powers to enhance Germany's bargaining power. Germany continued to build its economic and military power, and by 1900 it was the dominant power on the European continent.
Russia	Russia, meanwhile, was struggling with the rigidity of its absolutist monarchy with the growing demands for political representation. The Russian tsars faced moderate liberals and dangerous radicals, such as the anarchists who managed to assassinate one of the tsars, Alexander II (and the communists who sought to provoke revolution and bring down the entire regime). A revolution against the tsar occurred in 1905 when Russia was defeated in the Russo-Japanese War. Workers rose up in every major city and crippled the Russian economy with general strikes. The new (and last) tsar, Nicholas II, was forced to choose between slaughtering his people and giving them a *duma* (parliament). Reluctantly, the conservative Nicholas II chose the latter.

Key Facts about European Cultural Changes from 1871 to 1914

Mass culture. Just as with politics, culture became a popular phenomenon during this period. The phenomenon was not only experienced by wealthy devotees of art, but it was also a middle-class and even a working-class phenomenon.

Modernity. Modernity refers to the "modern" viewpoints of the people who lived during the prevailing time period. Artists sought to create new styles of art that emphasized modernity to show new techniques that reflected perspectives from their generation. Modern artists of this period took great pleasure in rejecting the norms of society and the old standards of art from past eras and epochs.

Modern music. Composers and musicians began to reject both the formalism of classical music and the untamed emotions of Romantic compositions. They began to question the very foundations of music, creating unharmonious and experimental works that pushed the lines further than ever before.

Modern Art			
Style	Characteristics	Influential Artists	Historical Period
Realism (1848–1900)	After the invention of the camera, realists sought to create art that was similar to a photograph—without illusion. Colors, lines, and perspective were created so that paintings depicted the real world as seen by the naked eye. Still life was a popular subject for realist painters. Art often reflected the working class or peasants. For example, Daumier's *The Third Class Carriage* focused on a group of peasants.	Courbet, Millet, Daumier, Rousseau	Revolutions of 1848
Impressionism (1865–1900)	Impressionism started in France. Impressionists wanted to change the way art was captured, as if someone "caught a glimpse" of the subject. They used natural light and color on objects, but also introduced the technique of single-point perspective. The emphasis was on vivid colors and small brushstrokes to make paintings seem to breathe life and reflect light as seen by observers. Impressionists often depicted the daily life of subjects: leisure activities and public spaces.	Manet, Monet, Renoir, Cassatt, Degas, Rodin (sculpture)	Franco-Prussian War Unification of Nations (Italy and Germany) Belle Époque
Post-impressionism (1885–1910)	Post-impressionists tried to depict the outdoors through swirling color and thick applications with complementary colors—for example, van Gogh's *Starry Night*.	van Gogh, Gauguin, Cezanne	
Cubism (1900–1920)	If impressionism ignited the art world, cubists revolutionized the Belle Époque. Cubism changed European art that had dominated Western art for four centuries. Cubism portrayed overlapping jagged geometric forms to analyze subjects through multiple perspectives. Pablo Picasso was the most famous of the cubist artists, although he initially began as a more traditional painter.	Picasso, Braque, Boccioni	Pre- and Post-World War I Russian Revolution

Did you know? Futurism was an artistic movement that started in Italy around 1909, but it lasted only about a decade. In actuality, futurism was more of a social or political movement than an artistic movement. Why was futurism important? Because futurism embodied the historical concerns of the early 20th century. It conveyed a glimpse of fascism and totalitarianism that would not reach Europe until after World War I. Futurists were lovers of modernism, and emphasized the speed, technology, and machinery of modern-day life. Their paintings showed life from a variety of perspectives, but unlike the cubists, the futurists glorified industrial power and machinery. Artists portrayed military strength and weaponry. Futurists developed a *Futurist Manifesto*, arguing that art existed for the furtherance of state power and that Italy must rise up and take its proper place as a great power. Most ominously, just as fascists did three decades later, the futurists argued that war not only brought out the best in humanity, but it was also a way to sanitize society.

The painting below depicts the tension and violence between clashing anarchists and police when the Italian anarchist, Angelo Galli, was killed by police during a strike in 1904.

Source: Carlo Carrà, *Funeral of the Anarchist Galli,* 1911.

The New Second Wave of Imperialism (1870 to 1914)

Imperialism was the practice of building an empire by taking control over a foreign territory through military force or economic control. Since ancient times, imperialism has taken the form of political control. The First Wave of European imperialism had taken place in the developed colonies of the Americas, parts of Asia, and the footholds along the coasts of Africa roughly between c. 1500 to c. 1800 during the Age of Exploration. It was led by Portugal, Spain, Holland, England, and France.

A Second Wave of European imperialism occurred between 1870 and 1914. The leading great powers of this period, Britain and France, made the largest additions to their colonial domains, but Belgium, Germany, Austria-Hungary, Russia, and Italy also turned their sights to the other continents of the world in Africa and Asia. The Second Wave of imperialism involved some of the same powers, but Spain and Portugal were minor powers in the Second Wave. Even the United States was not immune to imperialistic fever and moved across the Pacific to seize the territories of Hawaii and the Philippines.

Key Facts about the Causes of the Second Wave of Imperialism

Economics. The conquest of Africa was centered on the exploitation of economic resources on the Dark Continent (the name given to Africa by Henry Stanley, who wrote about the underexplored and mysterious region), and was made possible by technological advances from the Industrial Revolution. It was called a "new imperialism" because the basis was the economic domination of an underdeveloped country, rather than political domination. Quinine (a medication to treat malaria) allowed white colonists and soldiers to travel to the continent that had long been known as the "white man's graveyard."

Social Darwinism. Europeans believed they were superior to Africans. Europeans ruled over and repressed the Africans, stole their lands, exploited their natural resources (diamonds, gold, and rubber), and forced religious beliefs on people throughout the continent. The European imperialists told themselves that they were more liberal and enlightened than their early modern predecessors, a sentiment that was partially hypocritical and partially an accurate contrast between the two different waves of imperialism.

Civilizing missions. Tied to European designs for African resources, as well as interest in coaling stations and military outposts, was the **civilizing mission.** This describes the semireligious fanaticism that Europeans had for civilizing Africans. Europeans believed that they had reached the highpoint of human civilization, but Africans (and other underdeveloped peoples of the world) could be improved through education and instruction acquired from Europeans. The zeal for civilizing missions was put into poetic form by Rudyard Kipling in his famous poem, "The White Man's Burden," which argued that Americans and Europeans had a responsibility to civilize primitive people of the developing world.

The scramble for control of Africa reached a highpoint with the **Berlin Conference** of 1885. European leaders met at this conference to divide up Africa amongst themselves to avoid war over disparate imperial interests. By 1914, every corner of Africa had been carved up by European nations except for Liberia, a tiny free state, and the ancient empire of Ethiopia (later conquered by the Italians in the 1930s).

At the same time, European countries made inroads to Asia. These colonies were split between direct control of large empires, such as Britain in India and France in Indochina, and indirect, economic control over spheres of influence, most notably in China.

Heads Up: What You Need to Know

On the AP EURO exam, you may be asked to compare and contrast the Second Wave of European imperialism and the First Wave of European imperialism. Other than the obvious geographic differences, here are five key points:

1. The First Wave was centered on domination of the New World, whereas the Second Wave was centered on economic exploitation of Africa's raw materials, lands, and profitability.
2. The First Wave had an influx of immigration to the colonies, but it was greatly reduced in the Second Wave.
3. The First Wave involved direct domination of colonies, while the Second Wave involved a combination of direct (such as in Africa) and indirect (such as in parts of Asia) control.
4. The First Wave was often motivated by religious conversion, sending missionaries to deliver the message of Christianity (especially for Spain), whereas the civilizing missions was a secondary consideration for the secular empires of the Second Wave.
5. The First Wave did not have the advances made possible by technological and scientific discoveries. The Second Wave had steamships to transport goods, rapid-fire weapons to overpower natives, the telegraph to exchange messages, and medicine (quinine) to treat malaria.

The Road to World War I (1871 to 1914)

Chapter 7 will cover the causes and consequences of World War I, but this section discusses some of the crises that led up to the war.

Source: Edward Linley Sambourne, "The Rhodes Colossus Striding from Cape Town to Cairo." Punch, 1892.

Pre-War Anxiety

The first 14 years of the 20th century was a perplexing time in Europe. On the one hand, Europe was undoubtedly the dominant political, economic, cultural, and intellectual power. The European influence was unparalleled and its power unmatched. On the other hand, the people of Europe were coping with extreme unease and uncertainty. Some contemporaries likened the pre-war angst in Europe to a train gathering more and more speed, trembling with immense power and potential, but in danger of running off the rails at any moment.

Why were the people of the world so anxious? A great many changes took place in Europe during the period from 1871 to 1914. The outstanding achievements in science and technology transformed cities into electrical-powered grids and bright centers of culture and entertainment. Military weaponry and naval armaments had become increasingly powerful. But no one could have predicted that the 20th century would lead nations to demonstrate that their civilizations were not far removed from the violence and destruction of the Dark Ages. In 1914, World War I erupted in Europe and shook the world to its foundation.

European Crises

From 1898 to 1914, the great powers of Europe underwent a series of crises that threatened war. Some of these crises took place for colonial reasons, such as the 1898 Anglo-French conflict over Fashoda in the Sudan, or the two Franco-German crises over Morocco. Others had European origins, such as the Boulanger Crisis of 1888 over the near-election of a French revanchist, or the 1913 Constantinople Crisis over German influence at the Porte.

Do not memorize the above crises. Instead, consider the following three main aspects of the crises.

1. The crises became increasingly common and brinkmanship became increasingly severe as time went on. Each time war was averted, it emboldened European leaders to push the envelope even further the next time.

2. None of the crises erupted into actual war.

3. Each of these crises featured different nations and different alliance systems. It was not known that World War I would be fought using particular alliance systems. Britain, France, and Russia fought together in 1914, but Britain had been a mortal enemy of France for several centuries. Britain and Russia were rivals in Central Asia, East Asia, and the Baltic. Given a slight change in circumstances, war might have broken out in 1898 between Britain and France, or in 1904 between Russia and France, and so forth.

The avoidance of war throughout these crises gave European leaders a false sense of security. Country leaders came to feel confident that they could come close to war while avoiding it at the last minute (almost like a game of chicken). However, a series of factors converged in 1914 to determine that the July Crisis of 1914 would lead to a war, one that would fundamentally change not only Europe, but the entire world.

Chapter Review Practice Questions

Practice questions are for instructional purposes only and may not reflect the format of the actual exam. On the actual exam, questions are grouped into sets. Each set contains one source-based prompt (document or image) and two to five questions.

Multiple-Choice Questions

1. Which of the following was NOT a cause of the scramble for Africa in the early-20th-century second wave of imperialism?

    A. The religious conversion of the natives
    B. The exploitation of gold, rubber, and diamonds
    C. The competition with other European powers
    D. The civilizing missions

2. Which of the following was NOT an aspect of art and music during the 19th-century Age of Romanticism?

    A. Romanticizing elements of the historical past
    B. Using nature as a subject
    C. Emotional emphasis
    D. Focus on science and rationalism

3. Based on your knowledge of European history, how was Germany unified into one empire?

   A. A reformist plan from the Prussian Kaiser
   B. The liberal revolution of 1848
   C. Three wars from 1864 to 1871
   D. A great war against Britain and France

4. Which of the following best describes the view of capitalism espoused by Karl Marx?

   A. Capitalism unfairly steals the product of the proletariat's labor.
   B. Capitalists unfairly discriminate against Africans and Asians.
   C. The capitalist economy fails to provide for political democracy.
   D. Capitalism is a corrupt system tied to repressive religious institutions.

5. Which of the following was NOT a reason for Britain's leading role in the Industrial Revolution from c. 1840 to c. 1870?

   A. Britain's abundance of coal and iron
   B. Britain's support for mercantilism
   C. A massive demand for textile production
   D. Britain's large navy and status as an island nation

6. Which of the following was the main reason for the Holy Alliance established by Russia, Austria, and Prussia in 1815?

   A. Support for the spread of Catholicism throughout Europe
   B. Support for enlightened despotism as a form of government
   C. Opposition to legitimacy as a basis for monarchical rule
   D. Opposition to nationalism as a replacement for legitimacy

Questions 7 and 8 are based on the following passage.

The excavation of the sewer of Paris has been no slight task. The last ten centuries have toiled at it without being able to bring it to a termination, any more than they have been able to finish Paris. The sewer, in fact, receives all the counter-shocks of the growth of Paris. Within the bosom of the earth, it is a sort of mysterious polyp with a thousand antennae, which expands below as the city expands above.

Beginning with this epoch, of which we shall shortly speak, the work was usefully and energetically resumed and prosecuted; Napoleon built—the figures are curious—four thousand eight hundred and four *metres*; Louis XVIII., five thousand seven hundred and nine; Charles X., ten thousand eight hundred and thirty-six; Louis-Philippe, eighty-nine thousand and twenty; the Republic of 1848, twenty-three thousand three hundred and eighty-one; the present government, seventy thousand five hundred; in all, at the present time, two hundred and twenty-six thousand six hundred and ten *metres*; sixty leagues of sewers; the enormous entrails of Paris. An obscure ramification ever at work; a construction which is immense and ignored.

—Victor Hugo, *Les Miserables,* 1863, on the construction of France's sewage system, which was symbolic for underlying political changes over time.

7. Based on your knowledge of European history, which of the following aspects of French history is supported by Hugo's passage?

    A. The long succession of different French governments in the 19th century
    B. The cruel rule of the *Ancien Régime*
    C. The occupation with sewage embodied in modern art
    D. The sewer construction projects of Napoleon III in Paris

8. Which of the following rulers would most likely have been responsible for changing the sewage system at the time of the events described in Hugo's passage?

    A. Charles X
    B. Louis-Philippe
    C. Napoleon III
    D. Georges Clemenceau

Questions 9 and 10 are based on the following image.

Source: Paul Delaroche, *Napoleon Crossing the Alps*, 1849.

9. The painting, *Napoleon Crossing the Alps*, depicts which of the following artistic movements?

    A. Impressionism
    B. Futurism
    C. Cubism
    D. Realism

10. Based on your knowledge of European history, which of the following events during Napoleon's reign is portrayed here?

    A. His invasion of Russia in 1812
    B. His incursion into the Vendée, France in 1796
    C. His defeat at Waterloo, Belgium in 1815
    D. His invasion of northern Italy in 1799

Document-Based Question

1 question

60 minutes

Reading Time: 15 minutes (brainstorm your thoughts and organize your response)

Writing Time: 45 minutes

Directions: The document-based question is based on the seven accompanying documents. These documents are for instructional purposes only. Some of the documents have been edited for the purpose of this practice exercise. Write your response on lined paper and include the following:

- **Thesis.** Present a thesis that supports a historically defensible claim, establishes a line of reasoning, and responds to all parts of the question. The thesis must consist of one or more sentences located in one place—either the introduction or the conclusion.

- **Contextualization.** Situate the argument by explaining the broader historical events, developments, or processes that occurred before, during, or after the time frame of the question.

- **Evidence from the documents.** Use the content of at least three to six of the documents to develop and support a cohesive argument that responds to the topic question.

- **Evidence beyond the documents.** Support or qualify your argument by explaining at least one additional piece of specific historical evidence not found in the documents. (Note: The example must be different from the evidence used to earn the point for contextualization.)

- **Analysis.** Use at least three documents to explain the documents' point of view, purpose, historical situation, and/or audience relevant to the topic question.

- **Historical reasoning.** Use historical reasoning to show relationships among the documents, the topic question, and the thesis argument. Use evidence to corroborate, qualify, or modify the argument.

Based on the documents that follow, answer the question below.

Question 1: Evaluate the changing roles of European women from 1815 until 1914.

Document 1

> **Source: Franz Xaver Winterhalter, *The Royal Family in 1846* (Queen Victoria).**
>
>

Document 2

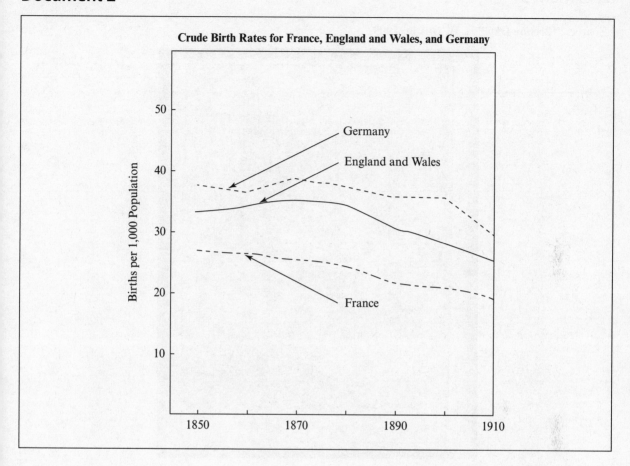

Crude Birth Rates for France, England and Wales, and Germany

Document 3

Source: "Election Day!" E. W. Gustin, 1909.

Document 4

Source: Isabella Beeton, "Mrs. Beeton's Book of Household Management," 1861.

38. WHEN FRUIT HAS BEEN TAKEN, and a glass or two of wine passed round, the time will have arrived when the hostess will rise, and thus give the signal for the ladies to leave the gentlemen, and retire to the drawing-room. The gentlemen of the party will rise at the same time, and he who is nearest the door, will open it for the ladies, all remaining courteously standing until the last lady has withdrawn. Dr. Johnson has a curious paragraph on the effects of a dinner on men. "Before dinner," he says, "men meet with great inequality of understanding; and those who are conscious of their inferiority have the modesty not to talk. Thanks, to the improvements in modern society, and the high example shown to the nation by its most illustrious personages, temperance is, in these happy days, a striking feature in the character of a gentleman. Delicacy of conduct towards the female sex has increased with the esteem in which they are now universally held, and thus, the very early withdrawing of the ladies from the dining-room is to be deprecated. A lull in the conversation will seasonably indicate the moment for the ladies' departure.

Document 5

Source: Anonymous, *Le Frou* political cartoon, 1900.

— Est-elle ridicule, cette femme, avec ses seins énormes ?
— Il paraît que ça se porte encore, en province.

Translation: "Large breasts may be okay in the provinces, but not in Paris!"

Document 6

> **Source: John Stuart Mill, *The Subjection of Women*, 1869.**
>
> Some will object that it's not fair to compare the government of the male sex with the other forms of unjust power that I have discussed, because it is natural while the others are arbitrary and brought about by mere usurpation. But was there ever any domination that didn't appear natural to those who possessed it? There was a time when the division of mankind into a small class of masters and a large class of slaves appeared, even to the most cultivated minds, to be the only natural condition of the human race! Conquering races hold it to be Nature's own dictate that the feebler and more unwarlike races should submit to the braver and more manly, or, to put it more bluntly, that the conquered should obey the conquerors. The smallest acquaintance with human life in the middle ages shows how supremely natural the dominion of the feudal nobility over men of low condition appeared to the nobility themselves, and how unnatural the conception seemed, of a person of the inferior class claiming equality with them or exercising authority over them. And it seemed almost as natural to the class held in subjection: the emancipated serfs and citizenry, even in their most vigorous struggles, never claimed a share of authority; they only demanded some limitation to the power of tyrannising over them. So true is it that "unnatural" generally means only "uncustomary", and that whatever is usual appears natural. The subjection of women to men is a universal custom, so any departure from it quite naturally appears unnatural!

Document 7

> **Source: Winnifred Harper Cooley, *The New Womanhood*, 1904.**
>
> [. . .] The finest achievement of the new woman has been personal liberty. This is the foundation of civilization; and as long as any one class is watched suspiciously, even fondly guarded, and protected, so long will that class not only be weak, and treacherous, individually, but parasitic, and a collective danger to the community.
>
> Although individual women from pre-historic times have accomplished much, as a class they have been set aside to minister to men's comfort. But when once the higher has been tried, civilization repudiates the lower. Men have come to see that no advance can be made with one-half humanity set apart merely for the functions of sex; that children are quite liable to inherit from the mother, and should have opportunities to inherit the accumulated ability and culture and character that is produced only by intellectual and civil activity.
>
> The new woman, in the sense of the best woman, the flower of all the womanhood of past ages, has come to stay—if civilization is to endure. The sufferings of the past have but strengthened her, maternity has deepened her, education is broadening her—and she now knows that she must perfect herself if she would perfect the race, and leave her imprint upon immortality, through her offspring or her works.

Answer Explanations

Multiple-Choice Questions

1. **A.** Exploitation of economic resources (choice B), competition with other European nations (choice C), and the idealism of the civilizing missions (choice D) were crucial to the scramble for Africa. However, while religious conversion was part of the colonizing efforts (choice A), it was never the primary cause, even for countries such as France that sent missionaries.

2. **D.** The medieval era, among other historical epochs, was romanticized by the Romantics, eliminating choice A. Romanticism emphasized the role of nature, from literature to fiction, so we can eliminate choice B. Nature was seen as pure and uncorrupted by human civilization. Emotion was the cause most celebrated for Romantics, so choice C can also be eliminated. Choice D is the best answer because the Romantics rejected the rationality of the Enlightenment.

3. **C.** Germany did see reformist plans from some Prussian kaisers (choice A), and there was a failed liberal revolution in 1848 (choice B), but neither caused Germany's unification into one empire. Germany did not fight against Britain and France together until World War I, so choice D is not accurate. Choice C is correct because Germany was unified from three wars: against Denmark (1864), Austria (1866), and France (1870–1871).

4. **A.** Choice A is correct because it gives the core of Marx's critique of capitalism in *Das Kapital*. Marx wrote almost nothing about racism, so choice B is incorrect; nor did he advocate any form of democracy (choice C). He also had precious little sympathy for religion (choice D), but his criticisms were of religion and of capitalism were separate in his written tracts.

5. **B.** Choices A, C, and D are all accurate: Britain did have valuable natural resources needed for industrialization (choice A), had a valuable market for its textile goods (choice C), and its powerful navy and isolated geography (choice D) guaranteed decades of relative peace and stability that created a fertile environment for investment and returns. Choice B is the correct answer. While Britain did support the economic theory of mercantilism until the 1840s, mercantilist policies did not help, but rather hurt, the process of industrialization achieved through protectionism.

6. **D.** The Holy Alliance featured a Catholic, Orthodox, and Protestant power (Austria, Russia, and Prussia, respectively), so choice A is incorrect. Choice B is incorrect because enlightened despotism was rejected by this generation of Russian, Austrian, and Prussian leaders. The Holy Alliance was in *support* of legitimacy, so choice C is incorrect. Choice D is the correct answer. Nationalism posed a threat to all three powers, both for its threat to monarchical legitimacy and for its threat to minority rule in Austria or multinational rule in Prussia and Russia.

7. **A.** This passage covers the series of rulers who governed France after the fall of Napoleon Bonaparte, making choice A the best answer. This is after the *Ancien Régime* collapsed, so choice B is incorrect. This is well before modern art emerged, so we can eliminate choice C. While Napoleon III is mentioned, choice D is problematic because it takes the discussion of sewage a bit too literally. The purpose of the passage is not to discuss sewage, but to discuss the symbolism of political change over time.

8. **C.** Charles X and Louis-Philippe ruled from 1824 to 1830 and 1830 to 1848, respectively, so neither choice A nor B could be correct. Georges Clemenceau (choice D) was the prime minister during World War I in the 20th century. Instead, this question calls up knowledge of Napoleon III's remaking of Paris during his reign, 1852 to 1870, choice C.

9. **D.** Choice D is the correct answer because this portrait of Napoleon crossing the Alps, in contrast to the more famous (and majestic) 1805 painting, shows a realistic portrayal of the emperor crossing the Alps on a mule. Realism, rather than imperial grandeur, is stressed in this painting.

10. **D.** The portrait presents Napoleon crossing the Alps, so the best answer is choice D. The painting connects Napoleon to the invasion of Italy by Hannibal, who also did so by crossing the Alps, in 218 B.C.E. The terrain certainly does not resemble the Vendée or the Low Countries, so choices B and C cannot be correct. Russia does feature rocky, freezing terrain such as that portrayed here, but not on the route that Napoleon took to invade Russia in 1812 (choice A). Remember, when evaluating images look at the context of the artwork. Don't be confused by the date when the artwork was painted. Rather, look for the historical context.

Document-Based Question

DBQ Scoring Guide

To achieve the maximum score of 7, your response must address the scoring criteria components in the table below.

Scoring Criteria for a Good Essay	
Question 1: Evaluate the changing roles of European women from 1815 until 1914.	
Scoring Criteria	**Examples**
A. THESIS/CLAIM	
(1 point) Presents a historically defensible thesis that establishes a line of reasoning. (Note: The thesis must make a claim that responds to *all* parts of the question and must *not* just restate the question. The thesis must consist of *at least* one sentence, either in the introduction or the conclusion.)	A good response to this question will have a central thesis that historically shows how women's roles changed from the start of the 19th century to the start of the 20th century. The line of reasoning should include how women saw their roles expand as they took on political and economic functions that were unthinkable a century before.
B. CONTEXTUALIZATION	
(1 point) Explains the broader historical context of events, developments, or processes that occurred before, during, or after the time frame of the question. (Note: Must be more than a phrase or reference.)	A good response should include the historical context of broader developments relevant to women's roles. Because of the wide range of themes in the documents, it might be useful to bring in extra information about Document 2, for example: The French government used the facts summarized in the graph to illustrate how women were pressured to have more children, mainly because the government feared that depopulation would weaken France's military position relative to Germany. In the case of Documents 3 and 7, you might bring in extra details about the archetype of the New Woman and how it aroused fears among many men about women's place in society.

Scoring Criteria	Examples
C. EVIDENCE	
<u>**Evidence from the Documents**</u> **(2 points)** Uses at least *six* documents to support the argument in response to the prompt. OR **(1 point)** Uses the content of at least *three* documents to address the topic prompt. (Note: Examples must describe, rather than simply quote, the content of the documents.)	To earn 2 points, a good essay should provide evidence from at least six documents to support the main thesis. The evidence should be relevant to European women during the 19th century. For example, Document 2 shows the pressures brought to bear on women in this way with the decline in birth rates when women started working outside their households, while Documents 3 and 5 show negative portrayals of the New Woman by its opponents. The new political view of women can be seen in Documents 3, 6, and 7 as women's movements began to emerge throughout Europe.
<u>**Evidence Beyond the Documents**</u> **(1 point)** Uses at least one additional piece of specific historical evidence beyond those found in the documents that is relevant to the argument. (Note: Evidence must be different from the evidence used in contextualization.)	The essay extends the argument by incorporating outside evidence. Your essay must provide at least one piece of historical evidence from your knowledge of 19th-century European history. In this case, a good example might include describing the gradual change in women's rights (i.e., voting, equality, political positions) and their role over the course of "the long 19th century." You might also reference feminist theory, the first feminist, Mary Wollstonecraft, and women's history as a way of understanding how patriarchy can be overcome through understanding history.
D. ANALYSIS AND REASONING	
(1 point) Uses at least three documents to explain how each document's point of view, purpose, historical situation, and/or audience is relevant to the argument. (Note: References must explain how or why, rather than simply identifying.)	To receive full credit, a good essay must cite the point of view or purpose from three documents. For example, the artist of Document 1 is portraying the traditional ideal of womanhood as embodied by Queen Victoria herself. It was common for 19th-century artists to depict realist art (realism) as shown in Queen Victoria's role as a mother with her children in the royal family. Remember, when analyzing documents, focus on grouping documents into categories or themes. This will help you understand documents' overlapping points of view. The categories should be grouped by main themes and specific themes. For example, main themes might include how women's roles were defined during this period. Specific themes might include women's roles during industrialization or the women's suffragist movement.
(1 point) Uses historical reasoning and development that focuses on the question while using evidence to corroborate, qualify, or modify the argument. (Examples: Explain what is similar and different; explain the cause and effect; explain multiple causes; explain connections within and across periods of time; corroborate multiple perspectives across themes; or consider alternative views.)	To qualify your argument, the essay should focus on the historical skill of *continuity and change over time*. Ask yourself, "What was similar and what was different for women during this time period?" The social, economic, and political roles of women were changing at a drastic rate from a patriarchy society to a modern society. For example, to support your argument you can explain the similarities and differences in women's roles compared to men's roles in equality, employment, or voting rights in the context of the century between 1815 and 1914.

Sample Response

When the 19th century began, the roles of traditional European women were distinctly different from the roles of men. Women were expected to live more private lives at home and had almost no political or economic rights (Documents 4 and 6). Women were expected to be the family household caregivers including child rearing, cooking, and house cleaning and did not have the same opportunities for employment, education, and political rights. Women were not even allowed an education after grade school, and were not allowed to inherit property.

In the broader historical context, gaining women's rights and equality was a hard fought struggle in Europe until the 20th century. Advocating for women's equality started as early as the late-18th century when women like Mary Wollstonecraft and Olympe de Gouges called for gender equality, but the European majority opinion was very much against them. Wollstonecraft's important work, the *Vindication on the Rights of Woman,* was published a century before society could accept her radical, but reasonable, views about equal relations of women within a society (Documents 3, 5 and 7).

Early in the 19th century, gender roles were clearly defined, and the ideal of womanhood was a very clear social role that impacted all economic classes of European women (Documents 1, 4, 6). For example, the author's point of view in Document 6 suggests that it is "natural" for women to be dominated. In Document 4, written in the early 20th century, the author suggests that ladies should be "good hostesses for their gentlemen." Even female monarchs were subjects of being overshadowed by male superiority. As depicted in Document 1, women could hold the throne, but it was usually because it was an exception due to the death of a male heir to the throne. As the image of Queen Victoria depicts in Document 1, even the Queen was expected to play the traditional role of a woman who is the perfect exemplar of femininity and womanhood. This was expected at the time because she was first and foremost a mother and a wife, despite her ostensibly important political role as queen. Even today, the Queen of England is referred to as Queen Elizabeth, "The Queen Mother."

In the historical context of Documents 2, 3, 5 and 7, however, we see change in women's roles in Europe from a patriarchal society to a modern society. Document 2 shows a graph detailing the declining birth rates among Europeans at the time. With the arrival of industrialization during the period from 1815 to 1910, things began to change for women, as the demand for a greater role in the public sphere helped women take on new political, economic, and social roles in Europe (Documents 2, 3, 5). During industrialization when the demands for women in the workplace increased, many men, especially government leaders, blamed women for this decline and sought to further control women's reproduction and economic independence in order to make up for this drop in the birth rate.

Women began to demand new rights during the period of 1815 to 1910, and women's movements began to emerge. Women began to secretly meet to discuss women's issues and organize protests, particularly in Britain and France. Women's suffrage movements argued that women were equal to men intellectually and deserved an equal role in society (Documents 3 and 7). Gradually the women's movement gained supporters. In the artist's rendering of the political cartoon in Document 3, we see the historical context of a 19th-century woman being able to exert more of an influence in shaping men's behavior. This could even include something as simple as influencing the use of alcohol at dinner. In Document 6, we see a resolute justification for the equality of women in the political area. Winnifred Cooley's essay in Document 7, exemplifies women exerting equality in terms of the right to vote and the need to make their voices heard politically.

Despite advances that women made during this time, their stand for their rights often led to serious backlash, even imprisonment. When imprisoned, women suffragettes were known to undergo hunger strikes in protest. Even though food was brought to them in prison, they refused to eat. The government intervened and force-fed the women, which was a painfully horrific ordeal. In Document 3, the portrayal of the New Woman makes it seem like she is a mannish rogue who is forcing her husband to do all the supposedly "womanly" work. In Document 5, the artist mocks the unfeminine appearance of the New Woman and implicitly accuses the New Woman of subverting "normal" gender norms.

The 19th century started with no place for women in the public arena. European women made great sacrifices to overcome traditional values and to fight for equal rights during this time period. Although the state of European women in 1914 was completely different from the century past, and World War I saw a temporary decline in the women's movements, women continued to struggle for equality throughout the 20th century. A few countries had already given women the right to vote, but it was a long road before women through Europe gained the right to vote. For example, France waited until 1945. Women had gained important economic rights and even some degree of independence from men, the requisite for having a chance for equality. While the project of gender equality is still not perfectly achieved even today in the 21st century, the long 19th century was tantamount to a quantum leap forward in the status of women and women's rights.

Chapter 7

Historical Period Four: Global Wars to Globalization (1914 to present)

Period Four explores Europe's turmoil in the 20th century.

- World War I (1914 to 1918)
- The Russian Revolutions and the Rise of Communism (1917)
- The Interwar Years (1919 to 1938)
- The Aftermath of the War (1920s)
- The Age of Extremism and the Road to World War II
  - The Great Depression (1929 to 1939)
  - The Rise of Fascism
  - The Rise of Mussolini's Power (Italy)
  - The Rise of Stalin's Power (Soviet Union)
  - The Rise of Hitler's Power (Germany)
- World War II (1939 to 1948)
- The Cold War (1945 to 1955)
- Decolonization (1947 to 1997)
- The Khrushchev Era (Soviet Union; 1956 to 1964)
- The Brezhnev Era (Soviet Union; 1964 to 1982)
- Gorbachev (Soviet Union; 1988 to 1991)
- PAX Americana (1990s)

Overview of AP European History Period Four

In the 20th century, Europe witnessed two world wars, a Cold War between two superpowers, the emergence of genocide, mass destruction, globalization, and the rapid overturning of nations and international systems. Although Europe was the most powerful continent in the world at the start of this time period, growing nationalism and social tensions led to conflicts, grievances, and wars that ended Europe's Golden Age.

The AP European History curriculum framework and key concepts explain the reasoning behind particular beliefs and developments that emerged in Europe during this time period. The historical examples of significant themes, trends, events, and people support the study topics that are specific to the AP EURO exam. As you study the key concepts, use the chart on the next page as a checklist to guide you through what is covered on the exam.

Visit http://apcentral.collegeboard.com for the complete updated AP EURO course curriculum and key concept descriptions.

AP European History Key Concepts (1914 to Present)	
KEY CONCEPT 4.1: TOTAL WAR AND POLITICAL INSTABILITY **Total war and political instability in the first half of the 20th century gave way to a polarized state order during the Cold War and eventually to efforts at transnational union.**	World War I, caused by complex interaction of long- and short-term factors, resulted in immense losses and disruptions for both victors and vanquished. The conflicting goals of the peace negotiators in Paris pitted diplomatic idealism against the desire to punish Germany, producing a settlement that satisfied few. In the interwar period, fascism, extreme nationalism, racist ideologies, and the failure of appeasement resulted in the catastrophe of World War II, presenting a grave challenge to European civilization. As World War II ended, a Cold War between the liberal democratic West and the communist East began, lasting nearly half a century. Nationalist and separatist movements, along with ethnic conflict and ethnic cleansing, periodically disrupted the post–World War II peace. The process of decolonization occurred over the course of the century with varying degrees of cooperation, interference, or resistance from European imperialist states.
KEY CONCEPT 4.2: ECONOMIC COLLAPSE AND IDEOLOGICAL BATTLES **The stresses of economic collapse and total war engendered internal conflicts within European states and created conflicting conceptions of the relationship between the individual and the state, as demonstrated in the ideological battle between and among democracy, communism, and fascism.**	The Russian Revolution created a regime based on Marxist-Leninist theory. The ideology of fascism, with roots in the pre–World War I era, gained popularity in an environment of postwar bitterness, the rise of communism, uncertain transitions to democracy, and economic instability. The Great Depression, caused by weaknesses in international trade and monetary theories and practices, undermined Western European democracies and fomented radical political responses throughout Europe. Postwar economic growth supported an increase in welfare benefits; however, subsequent economic stagnation led to criticism and limitation of the welfare state. Eastern European nations were defined by their relationships with the Soviet Union, which oscillated between repression and limited reform, until Mikhail Gorbachev's policies led to the collapse of communist governments in Eastern Europe and the fall of the Soviet Union.

KEY CONCEPT 4.3: QUESTIONING OF OBJECTIVITY AND RELIGION During the 20th century, diverse intellectual and cultural movements questioned the existence of objective knowledge, the ability of reason to arrive at truth, and the role of religion in determining moral standards.	The widely held belief in progress, characteristic of much of 19th-century thought, began to break down before World War I; the experience of war intensified a sense of anxiety that permeated many facets of thought and culture, giving way by the century's end to a plurality of intellectual frameworks. Science and technology yielded impressive material benefits, but also caused immense destruction and posed challenges to objective knowledge. Organized religion continued to play a role in European social and cultural life, despite the challenges of military and ideological conflict, modern secularism, and rapid social changes. During the 20th century, the arts were defined by experimentation, self-expression, subjectivity, and the increasing influence of the United States in both elite and popular culture.
KEY CONCEPT 4.4: DISRUPTIONS OF EVERYDAY LIFE Demographic changes, economic growth, total war, disruptions of traditional social patterns, and competing definitions of freedom and justice altered the experiences of everyday life.	The 20th century was characterized by large-scale suffering brought on by warfare and genocide as well as tremendous improvements in the standard of living. The lives of women were defined by family and work responsibilities, economic changes, and feminism. New voices gained prominence in political, intellectual, and social discourse. European states began to set aside nationalist rivalries in favor of economic and political integration, forming a series of transnational unions that grew in size and scope over the second half of the 20th century.

Significant Themes

The significant themes related to the key concepts for Period Four should help you to think about *why* particular developments occurred in the context of the larger historical "big picture." The study questions give you important insights related to specific questions that will help you make mental connections between each given topic and the social, political, economic, and religious significance.

Glance through the study questions before you start the review section. Take notes, mark questions, and write down page number references to reinforce your learning. Refer back to this list as often as necessary until you are confident with your answers.

Study Questions Related to Significant Themes in Period Four

Theme 1: Interaction of Europe and the World

1. What was the political and economic impact of Europe with other parts of the world after the world conflicts? (Hint: The relationship of Europe to the world shifted significantly with the globalization of conflict, the emergence of the United States as a world leader, and the overthrow of European empires.)

2. What was the United States' economic and cultural influence on Europe during this period? (Hint: United States' influence on elite and popular culture, the Cold War, world monetary and trade systems, geopolitical alliances, emergence of the United States as a world power, Marshall Plan.)

3. How did non-European peoples increase European social and cultural diversity and affect attitudes toward race? (Hint: Increased immigration into Europe, anti-immigrant agitation and extreme nationalist political parties developed, national self-determination.)

4. What were the roles of overseas trade, labor, and technology in making Europe a part of the global economic network? (Hint: Postwar reconstruction of industry and infrastructure, Marshall Plan, consumerism, new communication and transportation technologies.)

Theme 2: Poverty and Prosperity

1. How did wealth generated from new trading, financial, and manufacturing practices create a market and consumer economy? (Hint: Postwar economic growth, increased imports of United States' technology and popular culture, mass production, new food technologies, and industrial efficiency.)

2. How did socialist, communist, and fascist efforts develop responses to capitalism? Why did these efforts gain support during times of economic crisis? (Hint: In Russia, World War I exacerbated long-term problems of political stagnation, social inequality, incomplete industrialization, and food and land distribution, all while creating support for revolutionary change.)

3. What were the social and economic causes and consequences of the Great Depression in Europe? (Hint: Increased popularity of fascist ideology, World War I debt, nationalistic tariff policies, overproduction, depreciated currencies, disrupted trade patterns, and speculation created a weakness in the global economy.)

Theme 3: Objective Knowledge and Subjective Visions

1. How did new theories of government and political ideologies provide an explanation for human behavior? (Hint: Fascist rejection of democracy, glorification of war, and nationalism.)

2. How did science and reason challenge and preserve social order and roles? (Hint: Economic changes, gay and lesbian movements, feminism, and family responsibilities.)

Theme 4: States and Other Institutions of Power

1. How did new ideas of political authority and the failure of diplomacy lead to world wars and the establishment of totalitarian regimes in the 20th century? (Hint: Fascism and communism led to aggressive nation-states in Europe and the remaining democracies failed to adequately deal with these threats diplomatically.)

2. What were the anticolonial and nationalist responses to European imperialism and their impact? (Hint: Consider how the anticolonial and independence movements got their strongest wind after World War I devastated Europe and undermined its moral authority.)

3. How did ideological groups undermine democracy through the establishment of regimes? (Hint: Nazi aggression, the communist party's Bolshevik Revolution, the rise of fascism, and Stalin's rise to power.)

4. How did the introduction of new mechanized weapons change warfare? (Hint: The scale of deaths in the world wars, introduced nuclear weapons and the Cold War, guerrilla warfare, and genocide war.)

Theme 5: Individual and Society

1. Why did totalitarian and nationalist movements seek to eliminate those they labeled as "outsiders," sometimes by means of genocide? (Hint: Any person outside of the sphere was seen as an unperson—Nazi racist movements, the Holocaust, post-war nationalism, separatist movements, genocides, gays and lesbians, and immigrants.)

2. How did the role of technology transform society? (Hint: Technology improved society, but it also was destructive to society in wartime and environmentally after industrialization.)

3. How did worldview of the 20th century challenge or preserve social order and social roles? (Hint: Think about economic changes, feminism, women's rights, and gay and lesbian movements.)

Theme 6: National and European Identity

1. How were national identities created and challenged? (Hint: Nationalism; radical nationalism; fascist ideology; Nazism; communism; dissolution of Austro-Hungarian Empire; and the new nationalism in Eastern and Central Europe.)

2. How did cultural and social identities coexist with national identities? (Hint: Versailles Treaty; League of Nations; decolonization; Marshall Plan; Postmodernism; globalization; and postwar immigration.)

3. How did political, economic, and religious developments challenge or reinforce the idea of a unified Europe from 1450 to the present? (Hint: Fascism; radical nationalism; Cold War; ethnic cleansing; self-determination; economic modernization of the Soviet Union; impact of the Depression; and transnational identities.)

Important Events, Terms, and Concepts

The list below shows important events, terms, and concepts that you should be familiar with on the AP EURO exam. Please don't memorize each concept now. Place a check mark next to each topic as it is studied and refer to this list as often as necessary.

Events, Terms, and Concepts You Should Know					
Event	Year/Brief Description	Study Page	Event	Year/Brief Description	Study Page
World War I	**1914–1918.** World War I completely transformed Europe and the rest of the world.	pp. 205–210	The Cold War begins	**1946 1/n–1948.** A series of crises, misunderstandings, and provocations caused the United States and the Soviet Union to fall out with one another.	pp. 227–229
The Treaty of Versailles	**1919.** The Treaty of Versailles ended World War I and tried to form a new international order.	pp. 213–215	The Great Depression	**1929–1939.** A worldwide economic collapse that triggered social unrest and political radicalization.	pp. 217–218
The Russian Revolutions	**1917.** The Russian Revolutions brought communism to Russia and set the stage for the Cold War.	pp. 210–213	The Helsinki Accords	**1975.** The Helsinki Accords ratified the boundaries of post-World War II Europe. This was the high point of détente.	p. 230

Continued

Event	Year/Brief Description	Study Page	Event	Year/Brief Description	Study Page
The Kellogg-Briand Pact	**1928.** The Kellogg-Briand Pact was designed to ensure world peace after the brutality of World War I. While it failed, it represented the hope for a better world.	p. 217	Mikhail Gorbachev comes to power	**1985.** Gorbachev was the Soviet Union premier who would reform, and ultimately and inadvertently bring down, the Soviet Union.	pp. 230–231
World War II	**1939–1945.** World War II completed the decline of traditional European powers in the world.	pp. 223–227	End of the Cold War	**1989–1991.** When the Cold War ended with the collapse of the USSR, a new era of unprecedented hegemony by the United States was ushered in.	pp. 232–233

Chapter Review

Period Four is known for three key areas of study: 1) the destruction caused by total war (World War I and World War II) in the first half of the 20th century, 2) the economic and political power vacuum that led to the Cold War and the division of Europe, and 3) the founding of the transnational **European Union** (EU).

The following timeline illustrates AP EURO important events that happened gradually over time during this period. The timeline should help you visually and conceptually identify what preceded and what followed particular events.

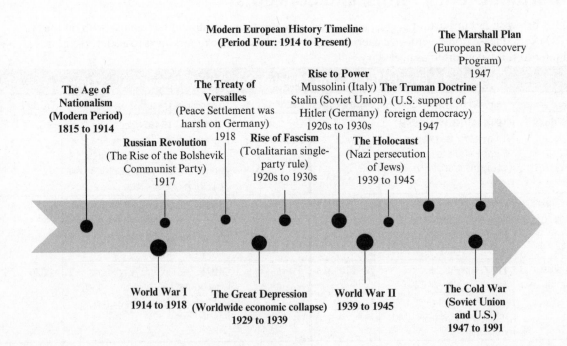

Modern European History Timeline (Period Four: 1914 to Present)

The Age of Nationalism (Modern Period) 1815 to 1914

Russian Revolution (The Rise of the Bolshevik Communist Party) 1917

The Treaty of Versailles (Peace Settlement was harsh on Germany) 1918

Rise of Fascism (Totalitarian single-party rule) 1920s to 1930s

Rise to Power Mussolini (Italy) Stalin (Soviet Union) Hitler (Germany) 1920s to 1930s

The Truman Doctrine (U.S. support of foreign democracy) 1947

The Holocaust (Nazi persecution of Jews) 1939 to 1945

The Marshall Plan (European Recovery Program) 1947

World War I 1914 to 1918

The Great Depression (Worldwide economic collapse) 1929 to 1939

World War II 1939 to 1945

The Cold War (Soviet Union and U.S.) 1947 to 1991

World War I (1914 to 1918)

The 20th century propelled many scientific and technological advancements, but the political and social tensions leading up to World War I, "The Great War," were intensifying. Working-class people and minorities demanded equal rights. Women rejected the old standards of gender-specific behavior and wanted to take on new roles in society. Socialism and rebellion posed enormous threats, as socialists controlled many seats in European parliaments and anarchists assassinated European monarchs and statesmen. Nationalism seemed to be reaching a boiling point, and countries spewed hatred against one another. Even art and music seemed to be out of control, with concerts sparking riots and paintings causing protests.

In the past, fears about various impending wars had been averted, but due to several forces converging, World War I appeared to be inevitable. Although there were several causes of the war, the immediate reason was the assassination of Archduke Franz Ferdinand of Austria. Other factors include militarism, alliances, imperialism, and nationalism. Let's examine each of these in further detail below to consider causes and consequences.

TEST TIP: On the AP EURO exam, consider the "main" long-term causes of World War I. The acronym MAIN is useful for remembering—militarism, alliances, imperialism, and nationalism.

Key Facts about the Causes of World War I

<u>M</u>ilitarism (increased war readiness). As alliances divided Europe and military technology advanced, European nations came to embrace militarism. Each great power prepared battle plans in readiness of war. Germany had the most powerful military in the world; before World War I, Germany's kaiser built a fleet of technologically advanced navy ships. This added to the mood of hostility in Europe. Germany's growing and powerful military was observed as a threat, especially to Britain. European leaders and their citizens came to see military force as the best option to resolve emerging diplomatic crises.

<u>A</u>lliances (secret pacts). Secret and entangled political and military alliances divided nations, and there were no international organizations (i.e., the United Nations) to help settle disputes. The great powers of Germany, Austria-Hungary, and Italy formed an alliance called the **Triple Alliance.** France, Russia, and Britain formed an alliance called the **Triple Entente** (*entente* is French for agreement). Secret pacts and political double-dealing among nations created an atmosphere of distrust. As a result, the Balkan crisis between the Austrians and the Serbs in June 1914, provoked a world war almost immediately.

<u>I</u>mperialism (colonial conflicts). In 1914, Europe was a world power, but European nations desired to control the remaining free territories of the world for increasing new markets and raw materials. The struggle for larger empires led to colonial rivalries. With rival colonies in Africa, Asia, and the Middle East, European powers approached the brink of war several times. Rivalry was especially contentious between Britain and Germany in Africa and between France and Germany in Morocco.

<u>N</u>ationalism (patriotism). As we saw in Chapter 6, strong ties to one's nation had stirred passionate nationalistic emotions by the turn of the 20th century. The emotional desire for national unity and political independence was particularly high in the Balkans and in Austria-Hungary. It reached a fever pitch in the years before World War I, especially along the borders with existing grudges, such as the French-German rivalry and the Serb-Austrian animosity.

Timeline of World War I

Crisis in the Balkans (1912–1914). The fuse that lit the powder keg of conflicts preceding World War I turned out to be the **Balkans** in southeast Europe. The Balkans were sandwiched between the imperialistic nations of Austria, Russia, Italy, and the Ottoman Empire (with a large peninsula between four seas: the Black Sea, Mediterranean Sea, Adriatic Sea, and Aegean Sea). The Balkans had historically been a magnet for violence and oppression in Europe and were previously ruled by Austrian, Hungarian, and Turkish powers. Religious groups included Muslim, Catholic, and Protestant groups (along with many ethnic nationalities). Tensions grew between Austria and Serbia, and in 1912–1913 two wars erupted for control of the Balkan regions. By 1914, the Balkans became known as the "powder keg" that ignited World War I.

Assassination of Archduke Franz Ferdinand (June 28, 1914). In June, Archduke Franz Ferdinand, the fiery and controversial heir to the throne of Austria-Hungary, was traveling with his wife to Sarajevo, the capital of Bosnia-Herzegovina. Ferdinand and his wife were assassinated by Serbian nationalists called the "Black Hand," and the state of Serbia was duly blamed when it was discovered that Gavrilo Princip, Ferdinand's assassin, had been acting with the support of high-level Serbian officials.

Austria-Hungry declared war on Serbia (July 28, 1914). The Austrians issued a series of excessive demands that they knew the Serbians would never accept in order to provoke a war with the small country. The Austrians hoped to destroy Serbia since the small country had long stirred up nationalism and rebellion among the Austrian-Hungarian Empire's Slavic minorities.

Germany declared war on Russia and France (August 1–3, 1914). As the largest Slavic nation in the world, Russia took measures to protect little Serbia and threatened to defend it in war. To make matters worse, the Germans offered a *carte blanche* (blank check) to their allies in Austria. This emboldened Austrian leaders to provoke Serbia, as they could rely on German armies to defend them against the Russians. However, the French had a 20-year-old alliance with Russia, which obliged them to take a stand with Russia.

Schlieffen Plan. To deal with the two-front war, the Germans developed the **Schlieffen Plan.** This was a precautionary plan that was developed many years before. The Schlieffen Plan allowed German armies to advance the majority of their forces to quickly sweep across the western border and take northern Paris. The plan had the expectation that France would be overcome in a matter of a few weeks. The goal of the first front was to defeat France. By the time the sluggish and massive Russian army prepared to mobilize, Germany would have defeated France and turned all of its forces back on the eastern front to deliver a blow to the Russian second front. The one problem with the Schlieffen Plan was that the first-front war required the invasion of a neutral nation, Belgium, en route to Paris, France.

Germany invaded Belgium, causing a global war (August 4, 1914). The Schlieffen Plan resulted in the invasion of neutral Belgium. This caused a chain of reactions. The subsequent "atrocities" committed by the Germans against Belgian civilians caused Britain to declare war on Germany. The war became global between Britain, France, and Russia on one side and Germany and Austria-Hungary on the other side. Italy claimed that Germany had begun an offensive, not defensive, war so they did not honor the Triple Alliance. Italy later joined the Triple Entente in 1915.

HISTORIOGRAPHY. *The historiography of the outbreak of World War I is one of the most written-about topics in European history. For a century, historians have debated the short-term causes of the war. You do not need to know the details of this literature, but you should know that historians have debated which nation(s) held most of the responsibility for the outbreak of war. Was it Germany's fault for giving the carte blanche to Austria? Was it Germany's fault for invading neutral Belgium? Was it Russia's fault for supporting Serbia? Was it Austria-Hungary's fault for wanting to exterminate Serbia? Was it Serbia's fault for financing the assassination of Ferdinand? Some historians have even blamed Britain, France, and even smaller nations.*

THE BOILING POINT.

Source: "The Boiling Point" Punch, 1912. Reproduced with permission of Punch Ltd.

Did you know? **Trench warfare** was a type of static land warfare tactic that was exercised at an unprecedented level during World War I. Ditches were dug into the ground in order to conduct battle at close range. Trench warfare helped both sides hold their line of defense without losing ground. Trench warfare was necessary because mobility was limited and both sides were unable to advance and overtake the other. Unfortunately, armies suffered enormous casualties during offensive maneuvers, and battle lines scarcely moved, even with millions of lives lost.

Outbreak of World War I

Britain advanced troops to help France, and France scrambled to defend Paris against the onslaught of Germany. At the **Battle of the Marne,** German troops reached so close to Paris that they could see the

Eiffel Tower from their trenches. However, they were not able to break through the British-French lines to defeat Paris. Instead, Germans were bogged down in **trench warfare.** Soon, Germany found itself in the same type of static warfare on the eastern front against the Russians. Germany, France, Russia, Austria-Hungary, and Britain had entered World War I, believing in a quick and easy victory. As it turned out, the war would be a vicious stalemate for 4 long years.

Key Facts about the Characteristics of World War I

World War I changed the way wars were fought.

Total war. World War I was the first "total war" in modern European history. All elements of each combatant nation were mobilized in the war efforts, whether it was soldiers on the front line, women working in wartime industries, or people at home rationing items and saving money to help with the war efforts. While the Western Front saw few civilian casualties, on the Eastern Front and in the Balkans civilian blood surged as religious groups and nationalities took vengeance on rivals.

New technology. World War I used newly advanced technology. The defensive trench warfare became the dominant way of fighting because of advanced machine guns, rifles, artillery, and even barbed wire, which turned frontal assaults into bloodbaths. Rudimentary airplanes provided reconnaissance, while submarines terrorized the seas. Poison gas killed relatively few, but made up for this with its horrifying effects, and flamethrowers cleared out the trenches. At the end of the war, even tanks emerged to stalk the battlefields.

Outdated tactics. The new technologies of the early-20th century did not carry over to new military strategies, which had scarcely changed since the Crimean War. Generals still utilized frontal assaults and charges to break through the enemy lines, which resulted in huge numbers of deaths because of the machine guns and rifles of the defenders. Millions of lives were lost or men were wounded because military leaders did not update their military tactical operations.

Massive casualties. World War I was one of the deadliest wars in world history. The casualties of the war were unprecedented, even when compared to the bloodletting of the Thirty Years' War. Over 10 million soldiers died in the war, and over 20 million military soldiers and civilians were wounded. These unthinkable casualties included the Battle of the Somme, where nearly 100,000 deaths occurred in one day. The Battle of Verdun saw nearly 1 million casualties. The Battle of the Marne saw 500,000 casualties in one week. Russia had the greatest number of casualties, with more than 2 million deaths by the end of the war.

Many minor powers. As the Great Powers waged their war, many minor powers entered the war. Minor powers were hoping to gain a seat with the victors at the bargaining table for little effort. Bulgaria and the Ottoman Empire joined with the Central Powers, while Romania, Italy, Portugal, and others joined with the Triple Entente. The minor powers increased the casualties of the war but did little to change the war's stalemate.

New roles for women. During the war, women began to work outside of their homes in large numbers. Many women occupied positions at traditionally held male jobs such as factory production or construction, while others worked in agriculture or government administration. Regardless, there was a vast awakening for women in the workforce, and people realized that women were as integral to the nation as men. This helped to spur women's suffrage, which was granted after World War I in most countries.

The End of World War I

Key Facts That Led to the End of World War I

Through 1915 and 1916, both sides of the conflict engineered massive offensives to try to break through the enemy lines and end the brutal stalemate. All of these, from the Battle of Verdun to the Battle of the Somme, failed utterly, as millions of lives were squandered for a mile or two of territory on the Western Front.

Germany commanded the seas. Naval battles were scarce because Germany protected its ports with a fleet of ships equipped with advanced weaponry. Germany sent out submarines to attack British merchant ships and sank over 6 million tons of British merchant goods (totaling 14 million tons by the end of the war). The German commander expressed regret, but said "war is war."

United States joined the war (April 6, 1917). Germany's aggressive, unrestricted use of submarine warfare and overtures to Mexico provoked the United States into joining the war efforts on the side of the Triple Entente (Britain and France). This was the final straw for Germany. Germany nearly single-handedly held off Britain and France in the west and toppled Russia in the east. Now, with thousands of fresh American troops arriving on the Western Front, it was only a matter of time before Germany had to surrender.

Bolshevik Revolution in Russia (October 24–25, 1917, Julian calendar, in contrast to the Gregorian calendar used by other powers). In 1917, Russia fell into revolution, a topic that we will discuss in the next section. Russia's revolution would soon knock Russia out of the war. Russia's new communist leaders sought a peace treaty favoring the Germans.

Peace negotiations started (January 8, 1918). In the United States, President Woodrow Wilson announced a blueprint for peace called *The Fourteen Points*. One million fresh American troops landed in France between March and July.

The Treaty of Brest-Litovsk (March 3, 1918). Russia signed the **Treaty of Brest-Litovsk** between Russia and Germany's Triple Alliance (also called *Central Powers*). The treaty ended Russia's participation in the war and forced it to surrender massive amounts of Russian territory in Europe (Poland, Latvia, Estonia). Russia agreed to forfeit territory, natural resources, and populations. The agreement was called "an abyss of defeat and humiliation" by Russian leader Vladimir Lenin. The treaty was the opposite of what had been envisioned in the Schlieffen Plan, which had called for France to be defeated first. However, the treaty freed up German armies to be sent to the Western Front and in late March to August, Germany launched the Great Spring Offensive, Germany's final effort for victory in the west.

Germany surrendered (November 11, 1918). In November, the German war efforts fell apart. Many German soldiers deserted the military, and naval soldiers caused mutiny on a German fleet. A revolution formed by socialists and anarchists erupted in Munich. On November 9, 1918, German Kaiser Wilhelm II abdicated and fled to Holland. The kaiser and his military staff had been completely discredited. German citizens had put all of their faith in the kaiser in 1914, and they felt betrayed by his failure to deliver a quick and easy victory as promised. In a moment of treachery that would have long-term effects for Germany and the world, the German generals and officials who had overseen the loss of the war resigned. While German troops still occupied foreign territory, these men knew that the war was a lost cause at this point. Instead of taking responsibility for the defeat, the blame was given to the new democratic leaders of Germany, the Marxist **Social Democrats (SPD).** The SPD were unfairly blamed for Germany's defeat and surrender in 1918.

Heads Up: What You Need to Know

The consequences of World War I changed the course of world history. Aside from the millions of people who were killed and wounded, the war caused Europe to lose its seat as a world power. The European political, social, and economic impacts of the war that you should be familiar with for the AP EURO exam include: 1) radical social changes (population decline, women gained the right to vote), 2) economic collapse—especially for losing nations like Germany because the Entente Powers (called *Allies*) wanted them to pay for reparations, and 3) political changes—four monarchs lost their thrones (the tsar of Russia, the kaiser of Germany, the emperor of Austria, and the sultan of the Ottoman Empire).

Important consequences of World War I that impacted the future of Europe:

1. The balance of power shifted, new nations were formed, and territories changed.
2. Political resentments formed, which planted the seeds for the Second World War 20 years later.
3. The Communist Party was formed in Russia.

The Russian Revolutions and the Rise of Communism (1917)

Russians rallied to the flag in 1914 during World War I, but in 1917 two revolutions moved through Russia to end imperialism and began the formation of the **Bolshevik Party** and **communism.**

Key Facts about the Russian Revolutions

World War I caused the Russian Revolution. During World War I, Russia's industrialization and modernization lagged behind the rest of Europe. Russia did not have the railroads to quickly move its massive armies to the front line. The lack of factories meant that artillery pieces, rifles, ammunition, and even uniforms were often in short supply. Poor military leadership had a disastrous impact. Although the mammoth Russians outnumbered the Germans and Austrians, the Russians lost victory after victory. Ill-equipped Russian soldiers suffered inexcusable casualties—more than 6 million by 1916. As the days darkened, some Russian sources reported that soldiers were being ordered to charge at German machine guns armed with bayonets, spades, or knives.

A new Russian democracy was formed under Alexander Kerensky (February 1917). Russia was losing the war and civilians were starving at home for lack of bread. Russians became disillusioned with Tsar Nicholas II's government because corruption became shockingly evident. As soldiers began to desert the front lines in masses, a civilian revolution broke out in Petrograd, Russia (St. Petersburg, rechristened with a less Germanic name). The soldiers, who were peasants themselves, refused to fire back at the rebels. The tsar's most loyal and disciplined troops and officers were all dead, squandered in the bloodbath of 1914–1917. The revolution quickly spread, and the ineffectual Tsar Nicholas II was forced to abdicate the throne. A new Russian democracy was formed under the socialist Duma deputy Alexander Kerensky. This was the February Revolution.

An unstable Provisional Government. Under Alexander Kerensky, the Provisional Government of Russia offered hope for a nation that had never known democracy. Kerensky and his Socialist Party offered major land reforms, educational reforms, and political changes to make Russia a better place for its underprivileged classes. However, despite the popularity of these domestic proposals, the Provisional Government decided to continue the war effort. Russian leaders feared giving up on the Allies and did not want to humiliate Russia's national pride. This was a major miscalculation. Although Russians welcomed the end of a dictatorship, their hatred of the war overrode their support for domestic changes. As a result, the Provisional Government became increasingly unstable.

The Bolshevik Revolution (October 1917). Conflicts came to a head with the October Revolution. Vladimir Lenin and Leon Trotsky led the communist Bolshevik Party, and engineered a revolution in Petrograd that seized control over the state. The Bolsheviks were a small Marxist party that had no support outside of Russia's large western cities.

The Bolsheviks believed that an *intelligentsia* (well-educated group of leaders) could lead peasant farmers into a revolution. By taking control of the government, they unleashed the Russian Civil War. This war pitted the *Whites* (monarchists and other anti-Bolsheviks) against the *Reds* (Bolsheviks and their allies). It lasted for 2 years and witnessed increasingly gruesome atrocities on both sides, mostly against the civilian population. Britain, France, the United States, and Japan tried to help the Whites by sending supplies and troops, but the Whites were undone by their own disunity and unpopularity among the peasants. In 1920, the Whites were dismantled and communist rule was firmly established. In order to safeguard their rule and prevent a return of the monarchy, the Bolsheviks brutally murdered Tsar Nicholas II and his family.

TEST TIP: It is easy to forget the difference between the two Russian Revolutions because many people think there was only one revolution. Dates can be confusing because there was a difference between our Gregorian calendar and the Russian Julian Calendar that was used in 1917. (According to our Gregorian calendar, the February Revolution actually took place in March 1917, and the October Revolution actually took place in November 1917!) To clarify the two revolutions, connect the political chronology of the revolutions. In a nation that had been ruled by an absolute monarchy for its entire existence, it makes sense that the first revolution would overthrow the tsar to establish a moderate republic, while the second revolution was more radical and established a communist dictatorship.

The Rise of Communism

While Russia's Civil War came to an end, Vladimir Lenin instituted a communist rule throughout Russia.

Key Facts about Vladimir Lenin (1917–1924)

Vladimir Lenin became known as the founder of communism in Russia. He promised social and economic equality and many people hoped that this new form of government would generate a perfect society—a communist empire. In 1922, the Union of Soviet Socialist Republics (USSR or Soviet Union) was declared a communist utopia. A union of "republics" was essentially a totalitarian rule under a communist version of the Tsarist Russian Empire. All decisions were made from Moscow (the new state capital).

The vanguard party. According to the new republic, only one class had political power: the *proletariat* (the wage-earner). As we saw in Chapter 6, Karl Marx proposed a social-economic system of communism through a dictatorship of the proletariat. Lenin argued that since Russia's proletariat was not yet developed, the Bolshevik Party should rule as the leading party, as sort of a placeholder for the eventual proletariat rule. Effectively, this meant a dictatorship of the party and of whoever ruled the leading party. There was no separation of powers (legislative, executive, or judicial).

The Politburo. The Communist Party was only a tiny percentage of the total Russian population, but it was completely controlled by the *Politburo* (the highest policy-making authority). Members of the Politburo included Vladimir Lenin, who had complete control; Leon Trotsky, who was the war commissioner; and Joseph Stalin, who was the secretary general of the Communist Party.

The Treaty of Brest-Litovsk. As discussed in a previous section, Lenin demanded an immediate end to World War I, which he saw as imperialistic. In March 1918, Lenin engineered a peace treaty between Russia and the European Central Powers of Germany, Austria-Hungary, Bulgaria, and Turkey. Lenin was buying time by surrendering land because he believed that Germany, and other monarchies, were bound to collapse.

World revolution. Lenin and Bolshevik leaders were extremely hopeful, believing that the Russian Revolution was only the beginning. The Bolsheviks anticipated that workers throughout Europe would follow Russia's example and overthrow capitalism, and lead to a world revolution. To move this along, the Bolsheviks sent spies, provocateurs, and organizers throughout other European nations.

Lenin targeted enemies. Lenin secured his power by unleashing a ruthless campaign to eliminate his opposition called the *Red Terror*. Lenin set a threatening precedent for communist Soviet rule by brutally repressing and murdering "enemies of the state." Over a million monarchists, nobles, clergymen, anti-communists, republicans, and political dissidents had been tortured or killed by the time Lenin died in 1924.

Source: "Lenin during the Russian Civil War," *Encyclopedia Britannica,* 1917.

A struggle for power after Lenin's death. When Lenin died in 1924, the initial battle for the leadership came between Leon Trotsky and Nikolai Bukharin. Trotsky believed in *collectivization* (a method to overcome the food shortage by forcing households to combine farms, land, and labor as a collective agricultural operation). Bukharin believed in *cooperatives* (a method that forced households to cooperatively work together on their respective farms, but people were allowed to keep their privately owned farms and pay lower government tax rates).

Although Trotsky seemed the favorite because he was an intellectual and a well-loved charismatic type, Trotsky and Bukharin were outmaneuvered by Joseph Stalin and his conspiracies and Machiavellianism. Stalin moved himself into the position of General Secretary, an office that allowed him to place allies in lower-level bureaucratic offices. This was not a flashy office, but it gave Stalin an enormous body of support among lower-level party officials. The General Secretary position became the unofficial head of the Soviet Union.

By 1928, Stalin had taken firm control over the Soviet state and its governmental apparatus. He was not yet an unchallengeable dictator, but he had outmaneuvered all of his opponents and had eliminated credible threats to his rule. As you will see in the discussion about Stalin on p. 221, things would only get worse, much worse, as Stalin became more and more secure in his rule and ultimately became the dictator of the Union of Soviet Socialist Republics from 1929 to 1953.

The Interwar Years (1919 to 1938)

Europe's interwar years is the period between World War I and World War II (1919 to 1938).

The Treaty of Versailles

After the 1918 truce was enacted, European and world leaders came to Paris to discuss the peace treaty. The Treaty of Versailles officially ended World War I and started Europe's interwar years.

Heads Up: What You Need to Know

The **Treaty of Versailles** and the **Fourteen Points** are key concepts that frequently appear on the AP EURO exam. Free-response questions may ask you to compare and contrast (comparison), explain reasons (causation), and recognize consistent patterns (continuity over time) that accompany major turning points in history, such as the next global conflict—World War II. As you look at the big picture, some of the reasons for World War II started with how the Entente Powers (Allies) dictated unfair peace negotiations with Germany in the Treaty of Versailles.

The Peace Settlement: Fourteen Points

Before discussing the Treaty of Versailles, it is important to understand what led up to the treaty. U.S. President Woodrow Wilson was an idealist who envisioned a world organization to protect nations and prevent future wars. He proposed a plan to preserve postwar world peace and diplomacy called the **Fourteen Points.** Wilson felt that the balance of power and secret treaties had caused World War I and wanted to prevent Europe from returning to old habits. No other world leader had ever declared such a proposal for global cooperation and world peace.

Wilson delivered high hopes and aspirations to Europeans who were weary of war, but he did not have enough leverage against the European Allies to enforce all of the points. In the American Congress, Wilson's proposal failed, and the United States refused to approve the Treaty of Versailles and did not become a member of the League of Nations. Wilson knew that the treaty might conceivably antagonize Germany into a future war.

For the AP EURO exam, you do not have to memorize each of the Fourteen Points, but it's important to understand some of the general ideas of Wilson's key points.

- Open diplomacy ("transparency"), rather than secret alliances
- Freedom of the seas. Remember, this was a problem in World War I when German ships attacked merchant civilian ships.

- Free trade
- Arms reduction
- Self-government. Wilson believed that citizens should have the right to determine who controls their government.
- The establishment of a general association of nations, *League of Nations,* to ensure collective security for nations of the world

Although parts of the Fourteen Points became a blueprint for the Treaty of Versailles, the plan failed for several reasons. Some nations were not interested in democracy. The idea of national self-determination inflamed Eastern Europe, Asia, and the Middle East. But probably the most important reason that the Fourteen Points failed was that the British and French wanted to punish Germany for aggressive acts during World War I. This was a critical point in history because the Treaty of Versailles was one of the primary causes that led to Germany's increased nationalism and war again almost 20 years later.

Key Facts about the Treaty of Versailles (1919)

With the hatreds of the war still boiling over, the Allies did not allow Germany and Austria-Hungary to take part in the Versailles Peace Conference. Russia was also not invited, as the Russians were seen as traitors to the Allies' cause. The main participants at the conference were Britain, France, Italy, and the United States.

Although the Treaty of Versailles sought to restore the balance of power in Europe, much to President Wilson's disappointment, French Premier Georges Clemenceau and British Prime Minister David Lloyd-George had different positions than Wilson. France wanted to make sure that Germany would never again be a threat, and Britain wanted naval and commerce supremacy. As a result, the treaty was extremely harsh on Germany.

Germany was punished. Germany gave up a good deal of its European territory and all of its colonial territories to Britain and France, disbanded its navy, was forced to limit its army, and was forced to compensate an astronomical sum of money for war reparations to the victorious powers. Most importantly, **Article 231** forced Germany to accept complete responsibility for starting the war—"war guilt." Allied leaders failed to foresee how Germans from all political affiliations would universally view this as an affront to German national honor. All of these terms infuriated the Germans for decades and weakened their nation beyond its natural level of strength.

New nations were formed. Out of the adjustment of German borders and the dissolution of Austria-Hungary came a series of minor powers in central Europe from Germany, Italy, and Russia. Some were ancient states, such as Poland and Romania, while others were newly created nations such as Yugoslavia and Czechoslovakia.

The League of Nations was formed. The League of Nations was created, as Wilson had hoped. This international organization was created with the mission of preventing another great war. However, Germany and Russia were not allowed to join at the time, and the United States decided not to join because of isolationism. The League of Nations was a politically weak organization until after World War II when it became the **United Nations** in 1946.

Italy and Japan were disrespected. Italy and Japan were on the winning Allied side, but were treated condescendingly at the peace table. In fact, Italy's Premier Vittorio Orlando walked out of the conference. Japan was mistreated because Europeans had imperialistic ambitions in Asia and also believed they were racially superior. Italy was considered inferior because of its minimal contributions during the war. Italy failed to gain its desired massive Mediterranean/Adriatic empire, while Japan could not attain its desired massive Asian empire. Italy and Japan's resentment set the stage for World War II.

Europe's map was redrawn. Like the Peace of Westphalia and the Treaty of Vienna, the Treaty of Versailles redrew the face of Europe. The new territories severely weakened Germany, and the treaty did little to establish a means for protecting this system. The League of Nations might have helped, but only if members cooperated. Ultimately, Germany's weakness could only be maintained through military force by Britain and France.

The Aftermath of the War (1920s)

The 1920s saw major cultural shifts in Europe. To understand these changes and what followed, we must consider the significance of the First World War. In 1914, Europe was considered the dominant leader in the world with scientific, technological, industrial, and cultural advancements. Europe was not perfect in 1914, but it was evolving in an upward trajectory of progress. The bloodshed and senselessness of the war had erased the promising future of Europe.

How could Europe call itself civilized and superior to other cultures if it was at the forefront of terrible destruction? Europe's sense of confidence and identity was profoundly shaken.

Key Facts about the Cultural Changes

The Lost Generation. The young men and women who had experienced World War I were extremely disillusioned in the old truths they had been taught to believe by their elders. Writers and artists were extremely cynical and expressed contempt for the society that had sent them off to war. They were especially uncertain of their future.

Modern literature. Beyond the disillusionment of the lost generation, Modern literature stressed the alienation of human beings from society and the isolation of the human mind. Modernists also rejected traditional literary conventions, whether it was poets forgoing rhyme and verse or novelists writing in a stream of consciousness style, meant to emulate the way the brain actually works. Moreover, the Modernists rejected 19th-century values and assumptions, forging their own in ad hoc fashion.

TEST TIP: The AP EURO exam will ask you to make connections between historical developments and different time periods using examples of primary and secondary sources. During the aftermath of World War I, German writer Erich Maria Remarque wrote *All Quiet on the Western Front,* a simple yet profound fictional text about antiwar and antimilitary feelings following the war. The book had few political *polemics* (written debates); instead, it depicted the utter brutality of the war. It was considered one of the greatest war novels relevant to postwar sentiments. The book became an embodiment of the senselessness of the war and the illegitimacy of the civilization of pre-war Europe.

Another book that gave a voice to postwar sentiments was written by American Ernest Hemingway called *The Sun Also Rises.* It was based on the men and women who came of age during World War I. *This Lost Generation* (coined by Gertrude Stein) represented people who lacked motivation or purpose for a better future due to the horrific atrocities experienced during World War I.

Modern art: Surrealism and Dadaism. The cubist trend popularized before World War I continued to grow, and other radical art forms emerged along with it. **Surrealism** began in the early 1920s. It was a cultural movement that depicted bizarre and impossible scenes that were contrary to reality. Artists painted depictions of dreams, irrational scenes, and juxtapositions. The **Dadaism** (1916–1923) art movement emerged as antiwar sentiments grew. It was a form of "anti-art" to express the horrors of World War I. Dadaists reveled in painting absurd "shock art."

Key Facts about Changes in Science, Psychology, and Philosophy

Cultural upheaval and uncertainty also influenced the sciences and philosophy.

Science. Age-old certainties of the Enlightenment and Scientific Revolution came under serious scrutiny. In the sciences, physics led the way when physicists undermined old axioms and assumptions of science. **Albert Einstein** made notable contributions in the field of science when he developed his theory of relativity. Einstein took the most seemingly absolute things, time and space, and showed that they were relative. His equation $E = mc^2$ (energy = mass × the speed of light squared) revolutionized science and changed our conception of time and space forever. Einstein's work, and the work of other physicists, paved the way for the splitting of the atom and nuclear fission.

Psychology. The founder of psychoanalysis, **Sigmund Freud,** revolutionized psychology during this period. The Austrian psychologist rejected the Enlightenment ideals of logic and reason. Freud believed that humans were driven by self-interest and powerful unconscious impulses. Using the metaphor of an iceberg, Freud theorized that the rational conscious mind is the tip of the iceberg above the ocean, while the unconscious mind is the massive section concealed under the water that motivates human behavior. Although some of Freud's theories and practices have been discredited over time, his most powerful argument, that unconscious desires drive much of human behavior, remains current in psychology today.

HISTORIOGRAPHY. *Historians' interpretations of Freud's theory will give you insights into the changes over time that were influenced by particular events of the 20th century. Although before World War I Freud focused his primary theory on unconscious motives, thoughts, and dreams that actualize human behaviors, after the war Freud modified his theory. After witnessing World War I, Freud described a theory of unconscious psychological tensions between individuals and society outlined in his book,* Civilization and Its Discontents, 1929. *According to Freud, humans have a primitive instinct to brutalize and dominate others in society through extreme violence. Needless to say, historians believe that Freud's theory was influenced by the bloodshed of the war.*

Philosophy. The philosophical ideas of "slave morality" by German philosopher **Friedrich Nietzsche** were popularized during this time. Although Nietzsche died in 1900, his ideas were too radical in the late-19th century and did not become widespread until after World War I. Nietzsche argued that European society had become corrupt from Christian notions of good and evil, which he called the *slave morality*. His philosophy was based on the ideology that some men were smarter or more gifted than others. According to slave morality, rationalism and democracy were confined to a few stronger men, the *Übermensch* (supermen), to benefit the majority of the population—the weaker men. Enlightened rationalism and democracy just furthered the elevation of the weak and the enslavement of the strong. According to Nietzsche, the only way society could advance is if the supermen were freed up to exercise their natural superiority and dominance over the world. Nietzsche's ideology aligned with the same sentiments that led to social Darwinism and *eugenics* (the practice of improving the genetics of the human population).

TEST TIP: Why are the contributions of psychology and philosophy historically important? Both theories lay the groundwork for German ideology and the rise of Nazi power in World War II. Nietzsche's theory of slave morality inspired the fascist movement—in particular, Adolf Hitler. Even though Nietzsche fiercely condemned anti-Semitism and racialism, the Nazi Regime carefully modeled much of its ideology on Nietzsche's theory. Freud's theory about powerful unconscious tensions between individuals and civilizations aligned with the Nazi Regime's desire to brutalize others through extreme violence.

A Hope for Peace

During the 1920s, European countries enacted treaties to preserve peace and order to avoid resorting to war.

Dawes Plan (1923). To achieve peace, it was important to reintegrate Germany into Europe as a peaceful partner. The United States and European powers agreed to enact the Dawes Plan in 1923. This plan provided loans from the American government to be allocated to Germany for war reparations. The Dawes Plan would help infuse the German economy and help to repay British and French reparation payments. Britain and France would then pay back interest and principal on their war loans from the United States. The Dawes Plan would create an interdependent financial system of reparations, but also increased the risk that a financial crisis in one country would quickly spill over to the others.

Locarno Treaty (1925). In 1925, Britain, France, Germany, and Italy signed the Locarno Treaty. This treaty guaranteed the western borders of Europe, particularly between France and Germany. The treaty marked an important turning point toward peace between France and Germany for the future. However, the treaty did not mention the eastern borders of Germany. Many historians believe that Britain and France seemed to be giving Germany a blank check because they were taking on international rivals to the east, the Soviet Union.

Kellogg-Briand Pact (1928). European leaders came together for the Kellogg-Briand Pact of 1928 to "renounce war as an instrument of national policy." While sometimes viewed as hopelessly naive today, this treaty was an important proclamation in the spirit of most Europeans at the time. In this pact, the majority of nations in the world, including all of the Great Powers, promised to not use war as an instrument of diplomacy. The idea was to end war by mutual accord. After the bloodshed of 1914–1918, many Europeans were eager to accept any agreement of future peace.

The Age of Extremism and the Road to World War II

The Great Depression (1929 to 1939)

Much of the history of fascism, Nazism, and World War II is unthinkable without considering the Great Depression. Certainly there were warnings of the future, even before 1914 (i.e., futurism), but as late as 1928, Nazi-style radicalism was only on the fringes of countries like Germany. Until the Great Depression, the only Germans who showed much support for radicalism were those who were extremely disgruntled, economically desperate, or prejudiced. But the economic destruction triggered by the Great Depression radicalized millions of Europeans.

> **Did you know?** In the 1928 German election, the Nazis won only 2.6 percent of the vote. A mere 4 years later in 1932 during the Great Depression, the Nazis won 37 percent of the vote, making them the largest party in the *Reichstag* (German Parliament) and paving the way for the ascension of Hitler as leader.

Key Facts about the Causes of the Great Depression

The Great Depression wreaked havoc on Europe. It caused panic and the economic destruction of millions of middle-class and working-class families' savings overnight. Nations initiated massive tariff policies, which merely deepened the Depression. Governments were forced to take their currencies off of the gold standard. National deficits made it impossible for governments to provide aid to the millions of unemployed and homeless people. Radicalism of both left and right sprang up everywhere, but the right-wing extremists proved to be the most popular.

So how did the Great Depression begin? Let's examine the causes.

Oversupply and lack of demand. Technological changes caused goods to be produced quickly and modestly. This sounds like it would be an advantage to competitive markets, but when the supply greatly overtakes demand, the conditions lead to a collapse in prices. The oversupply forced many manufacturers out of business, which was especially severe in the agricultural sector. As more and more manufacturing factories closed, unemployment spiked. People tried to withdraw their savings from their bank accounts.

Failed investment speculations. Theories and practices of financial market speculations that created a "stock market bubble" in the years before 1929 failed. These speculations generated good financial returns on investments for a while, but when the stock market bubble burst, speculative investments created losses in many different markets.

Stock market crash (1929). European and American families had been advised to buy goods and homes on credit in the 1920s. Many people relied on credit due to debt from the First World War. When the market was good, consumers were unaffected. When the stock market crashed in 1929, however, many people were unable to pay off their purchases and home loans. Home values depreciated. People lost their possessions, and even their homes. The stock market crash caused the United States to discontinue capital flow to Europe.

Lack of regulation. *Laissez-faire* (transactions free from government regulations) economic government policies worsened the Great Depression. Because bank deposits were not backed up by the government, banks collapsed and were unable to pay back the money saved for millions of families. Speculation was rampant in financial markets because governments did not regulate these irresponsible maneuverings.

The Rise of Fascism

Fascism emerged in Europe in the 1920s and the 1930s. It was a form of **totalitarianism**—a system in which government has complete control over every aspect of the lives of people. Since totalitarianism took both extreme left-wing and extreme right-wing forms, let's examine the ties that bound both sides.

Heads Up: What You Need to Know

On the AP EURO exam, you should be able to explain, cite examples, and compare/contrast the differences between the political ideologies of totalitarianism, fascism, and communism.

Totalitarianism is a single-party dictatorship. In totalitarianism, the ruling political party dominates and exercises complete authority over its citizens (activities, beliefs, and values). Opposition is not permitted, and anyone who disagrees with the ruler is killed or imprisoned (the *axe rule*). For example, Russia led by Stalin (1925–1953).

Fascism is a subcategory of totalitarianism—it's a way to organize society so that the government is the absolute authority. Fascism is a form of radical, extreme nationalism and is extremely militaristic so that people can be controlled by fear. Fascists believe in national or racial supremacy to all other nations (or races). Fascists do not accept democracy. Citizens are not allowed individualism. Democracy is seen as a sign of moral weakness. For example, Italy and Germany in 1919–1945.

Communism is a social-economic system of government of a classless society. It stresses social equality, rather than political equality. All decisions are made by a one-party state and the party is the custodian of the nation. Communism eliminates social classes, capitalism, unequal wealth, and all forms of religion. For example, the USSR (today known as the Russian Federation) was a communist nation, where all major decisions were made by the one-party state.

Key Facts about Totalitarianism and Fascism

Single-party rule. In totalitarianism and fascism, only one party is allowed to rule the government (i.e., the Communist Party of the Soviet Union or the National Socialist Party of pre–World War II Germany).

Glorification of the dictator. Totalitarian and fascist governments have no opposition. Dictators of these governments often form *cults of personality* that make themselves seem indispensable to their citizens. Cult of personality is when an authority figure uses propaganda to create a flattering image of him- or herself for the purpose of adulation. Dictators spread false biographies of themselves, erect statues, or hang portraits of themselves across the country. Fascist dictators are initially appealing because cults of personality show dictators as appearing charismatic, projecting confidence, and being admired by citizens. Before World War II, fascism was appealing to citizens in Germany because the country was struggling and people initially believed that nationalism, unity, and a sense of belonging would help the country become a safer place to live.

Individuals existed to serve the state. Inspired by the efforts during World War I, totalitarian governments demanded complete mobilization of all citizens at all times, during war and during peace. Under totalitarianism, citizens existed to serve the state's interests. In fact, citizens of totalitarian states could not often distinguish wartime from peace time because censorship, food rationing, and their involvement in public works did not change.

Censorship and surveillance. While absolutist rulers tyrannized their people for a millenium, dictators used modern technology to eliminate citizens' privacy; in theory, 24 hours a day. Citizens had no civil or political rights. Audio recordings, photographs, and video cameras were used to keep their citizens under control.

Necessity of enemies. Fascists, totalitarians, and communists were anti-democratic. The fascists had communists as mortal enemies, while the communists had fascists and monarchists as enemies. In extreme regimes, it was often necessary to have enemies to target in order to justify extreme violence and militarism.

Terror. Totalitarian and fascist nations used torture and murder to eliminate rivals and eradicate opposition to the regime. The old democratic virtues of persuasion and diplomatic debate with one's enemies were rejected. Opponents were dehumanized, brutalized, or eliminated.

Did you know? Most people think of Nazi Germany first when considering the rise of fascism, but keep in mind that the Italians turned to fascism even before the Great Depression. In 1922, Italy formed the "Italian National Fascist Party" ("fasces"). Italy existed under a fascist regime from 1922–1943.

The Rise of Mussolini's Power (Italy)

Italians of all political affiliations were unhappy about their nation's poor treatment in the Treaty of Versailles. They desired great lands on the Adriatic and Mediterranean, and the traditional political parties of Italy were heavily discredited by the settlement.

Benito Mussolini (1883–1945) was a former socialist pacifist who embraced the futurist-style politics during and after the Great War. Mussolini organized the fascist *Blackshirts* and rallied for an Italian nationalist response. Supported by Italian industrialists and wealthy landowners through fear of communism, the Blackshirts were thugs who attacked and sometimes killed political opponents and protesters. The socialists and communists of the far left were always the prime targets. Mussolini organized the **March on Rome** in October 1922, consisting of about 50,000 fascist Blackshirts, to seize power for himself and the Fascist Party. Mussolini became premier and then demanded dictatorial powers from the king in 1923. He then transferred all power to the Fascist Party, and by 1926 Italy had become a fascist state under the dictatorship of Mussolini.

Source: Mussolini and Hitler, 1936.

Mussolini began to organize his government by exercising violence and intimidation of his political opponents, strengthening the Italian military, censoring the media, and putting the economy on a nationalist course of rejuvenation. He also paid the Catholic Church to establish a treaty in the **Concordat** of 1929 in exchange for public support of his regime (think Napoleon's analogous Concordat).

The Rise of Stalin's Power (Soviet Union)

During this period, **Joseph Stalin** (1878–1953) was strengthening his steel grip over the Soviet Union. Stalin's rule lasted for almost 30 years.

Key Facts about Stalin's Rule (1925–1953)

The Great Terror. In the 1930s, Stalin ushered in a new extreme, the **Great Terror** *genocide* (mass killings). The Great Terror started with the targeting of political dissidents and class enemies, much as had happened under Lenin, but soon expanded with arbitrary and random terror. The secret police in each city or region were given quotas of people to arrest, torture, and execute. Those who posed threats to the regime were preferred, but soon anyone could be targeted without provocation. This arbitrary murderousness was meant to solidify Stalin's rule by keeping the population in perpetual fear. Citizens were too terrified to oppose the regime.

Stalin even turned his terror against his own government and military, purging most of the Old Bolsheviks (who had fought in the revolution), murdering most of the high- and low-ranking military officers, and killing secret police members. About 1 million people had been slaughtered by 1939. Stalin's rule became absolute and unquestionable, but the country's economy, military, and sciences were incredibly weakened.

Five-Year Plan. Beyond the Terror, Stalin also sought to modernize the Soviet economy. Stalin knew that the USSR's economy was a century behind the West's, so he instituted the **Five-Year Plan** to develop the national economy. The plan set the standards of industrialization and production to be met in a short amount of time. These standards were unrealistic and could only be met by using fraud and cheating. However, the Soviet Union did manage to modernize its economy in the 1930s, at enormous cost to human life and the environment.

Socialism in One Country. At the same time, Stalin announced the idea of **Socialism in One Country.** As opposed to Lenin and Trotsky's Permanent Revolution, Stalin's conception acknowledged that communist revolutions were not going to transpire across the European continent any time soon. Instead, Socialism in One Country meant that the USSR would build an economic powerhouse, and a free and equal society, and people across the world would see from Russia's example that communism was eminently superior to capitalism and democracy. The short-term focus, then, had to be on building up the Soviet Union. Spreading the word about communism in foreign countries was limited, at least until the end of World War II.

The Rise of Hitler's Power (Germany)

In 1923, an ambitious young World War I veteran, **Adolf Hitler** (1889–1945), attempted to overthrow the new German **Weimar Republic.** He sought to inspire a German version of Mussolini's March on Rome, but failed. Hitler and other conspirators were quickly arrested because Germany did not support the use of violence. Hitler learned this lesson well.

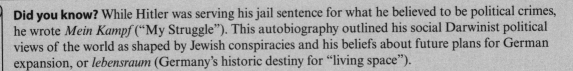

Did you know? While Hitler was serving his jail sentence for what he believed to be political crimes, he wrote *Mein Kampf* ("My Struggle"). This autobiography outlined his social Darwinist political views of the world as shaped by Jewish conspiracies and his beliefs about future plans for German expansion, or *lebensraum* (Germany's historic destiny for "living space").

Mein Kampf later became known as the "Nazi bible" during Hitler's rule. Hitler also wrote about his rage against the European system and the unfair treatment of Germany in the Treaty of Versailles. Hitler's outrage elevated his popularity because Germans unanimously hated the Treaty of Versailles and sought to overturn it.

Key Facts about Hitler's Rise to Power

Hitler was leader of the Nazi Party. Released from prison, Hitler took control of an already existing party, the Nazi Party, which was officially called the Nationalist Socialist Worker's Party (NSDAP). He used modern technology (such as telephones and cameras) as well as his own remarkable oratorical skills to recruit Germans to his cause. Anti-Semitism was not popular in Germany at the time, so he expertly crafted his argument to focus on a more popular topic, the railing against the Treaty of Versailles and the restoration of the German ego. Hitler's real success did not come until the Great Depression, when the German middle class was destroyed. This caused millions of Germans to reject traditionalism and democracy. Germans were seeking radical solutions for the economic and political problems that plagued their country.

Hitler's stab-in-the-back myth. Earlier, we discussed that many Germans believed their country had surrendered in World War I in 1918. Many people believed that German armies still had a chance to win the war, but this was not true. It seemed to make common sense to millions, since German troops were still in France when the cease-fire was given. German territory was never seriously invaded. Hitler and his allies exploited this misconception with the **stab-in-the-back-myth,** which held that the German army could have won in 1918 if the army had not been betrayed by the **November Criminals,** Marxists and Jews. Political cartoons spread like today's Internet news, portraying caricatures of communists and Jews, literally stabbing the German soldiers in the back. It is impossible to overestimate how powerful these images were in Germany and how much this myth discredited the Marxists and Jews in the Social Democratic Party (SPD), and by extension, the Weimar Republic.

The Third Reich. After the Great Depression, Hitler's Nazi Party became much more popular and took over the government through democratic elections in 1932 and 1933. Although German President Paul von Hindenburg refused to appoint Hitler as chancellor, he had no choice because the Nazi Party became the largest party in Germany. Conservatives viewed Hitler as an agitator with little intelligence who could easily be controlled. Instead, Hitler seized power in 1933, and Germany was ruled by the **Third Reich** (Nazi Party) in his image. Hitler began to modernize the German economy, rebuild the military, target his political opponents, and target the mentally and physically disabled, who were viewed as financial burdens on the state's economy.

The spread of fascism. Inspired by Germany and Italy, smaller nations such as Romania, Hungary, and Greece became fascist governments between 1933 and 1945. In other countries such as France, Belgium, and Holland, major fascist parties rose up and tried to use violence to threaten the stability of each country. Even Britain had a fascist party, led by the charismatic Oswald Mosley, but the small party became almost nonexistent when fascist thugs attacked protesters at a rally. The British, perhaps more so than any other European nation, had zero tolerance for political violence.

World War II (1939 to 1948)

Heads Up: What You Need to Know

On the AP EURO exam, you may be asked to identify the main causes and events that led up to World War II. Let's summarize some of the underlying causes that we have discussed so far:

- The Great Depression.
- The rise of anti-democratic ideologies: fascism in Germany, totalitarianism and fascism in Italy, socialism in the Soviet Union, and imperialism in Japan.
- German, Italian, and Japanese resentments about the unfair treatment in the Treaty of Versailles.

The next section will cover what transpired from 1934 to 1939 to cause World War II.

- **German rearmament.** Germany violated the Treaty of Versailles by rearming.
- **Appeasement.** Nations like Britain and France hoped to keep peace at any cost and did not enforce sanctions when Italy, Japan, and Germany invaded sovereign countries.
- **Nazi-Soviet Non-aggression Pact.** Germany and Russia formed an alliance.

The Path to War (1934 to 1939)

In 1934, it seemed inconceivable that a war would again grip Europe, but the rise of nationalism and the totalitarianism of single-party nations contributed to the outbreak of World War II. It took 5 years before World War II began.

So what happened in the meantime in the years from 1934 to 1939? A series of diplomatic and military moves brought Europe from peaceful inactivity to the brink of war. Let's review the essential points.

Key Facts about the Path to War

German rearmament (1935–1936). Under Hitler, Germany openly violated the Treaty of Versailles by building up Germany's military and remilitarizing the Rhineland, an area adjacent to France. This action could have provoked war as early as 1936. European nations, like Britain and France, failed to enforce the Treaty of Versailles because they hoped to appease Hitler and keep peace.

Mussolini's invasion of Ethiopia (1935). In 1935, Mussolini acted upon his militarist rhetoric by invading Abyssinia (today's Ethiopia). With brutal tactics and modern technology, Italy pummeled this primitive African nation into submission. The League of Nations protested Italy's actions, but was too weak to stop Italy from brutalizing a league member. This exposed the fatal flaw in the collective security logic of the League of Nations—it had no real power.

The Spanish Civil War (1936). In 1936, the fragile Spanish Republic erupted into a civil war between nationalists (fascists and monarchists) and republicans (liberals, socialists, and communists). This became a practice run for World War II, as the Soviets supported the republicans while Germany and Italy supported the nationalists. All three intervening powers were able to send in troops and even tested their new bombers, tanks, and artillery pieces in live combat. In 1939, the nationalists triumphed and established a fascist dictatorship in Spain that lasted until 1976.

The Austrian Anschluss (1938). Hitler demanded that Austrians join the Third Reich with their fellow ethnic Germans. In 1938, the two fascist powers signed an alliance treaty called the *Anschluss* (annexation of Austria), an act that strengthened Germany and also brought Italy closer to Germany.

The Czechoslovakian crisis (1938). Later in 1938, Hitler demanded that Czechoslovakia surrender the Sudetenland (a border region that was taken away from Germany in World War I that was populated by ethnic Germans). When the Czech leaders refused, Britain and France decided to meet with Hitler by calling for a **Munich Conference.** The Soviets and even the Czechs themselves were not invited to this conference. To avoid war and appease Hitler, Sudetenland was handed over to Germany. Hitler promised that he had no further demands after the Sudetenland, but he soon broke his promise. In 1939, Hitler's troops seized the rest of Czechoslovakia.

Nazi-Soviet Nonaggression Pact (1939). At this point, French and British leaders realized that Hitler could not be stopped, but they did not try to seek an alliance with the Soviets. Stalin feared that capitalistic nations would team up against the Soviet Union as they had in 1918–1920, so in 1939 Stalin sought out an agreement with Hitler, the **Molotov-Ribbentrop Pact.** In this pact, Germany and the USSR promised not to attack each other and agreed to split up Eastern Europe between the two nations.

Did you know? Modern readers are often baffled as to why British and French leaders initially elected to appease Hitler. How could they yield to a madman like Hitler?

Remember that the leaders did not have the benefit of hindsight. Some believed that Hitler's hyperbolic (exaggerated) rhetoric and eccentric claims were not sincere. The British and French publics were extremely opposed to war, and were not willing to fight over Austria or Czechoslovakia. That's not to say that there were not those who opposed Hitler's invasions. The strongest voices opposing Hitler were Britain's Prime Minister Winston Churchill and the English historian A.J.P. Taylor. Both men argued that Hitler was a dangerous madman who could not be appeased. Churchill and Taylor turned out to be right!

Key Facts about the Events of World War II

Germany invaded Poland (1939). After the Munich Conference, Hitler was sure that Germany could invade Poland without a challenge from Britain and France. Hitler was unstoppable. Germany invaded Poland in September 1939. After the invasion, Nazi Germany executed over 60,000 Polish officers and activists, and Hitler and Stalin partitioned Poland's territory. To Hitler's surprise, Britain and France honored their agreement and declared war on Germany if Germany would not withdraw its troops from Poland. This ushered in World War II.

Germany conquered France, Belgium, and Scandinavia (May 1940). As soon as his armies had triumphed in the east, Hitler turned west against the British and French. In a stunning reversal of the events of 1914, Germany was able to use *blitzkrieg* (lightning-war) to quickly crush the French armies and chase the British out to sea. Within a few weeks, Paris was captured and the French Republic surrendered. Hitler occupied half of France. In the other half of France, Hitler established the *Vichy Regime in France* (a fascist pawn state meant to support the German overlords) and Vichy France broke off relations with Britain. Hitler then overwhelmed Belgium and Scandinavia.

Germany attacked Britain (August 1940). The British were outnumbered by the Germans, but refused to give up. The British Royal Air Force (RAF) fought daily battles with the Germans. Germany's aerial bombardment of Britain did not fully succeed in softening up British defenses because the RAF was not defeated.

The United States became an "arsenal of democracy" (January–March 1941). The United States was neutral in the **Neutrality Act of 1939,** but President Franklin Roosevelt signed the **Lend-Lease Act** with Britain to supply the British and Free France with stocks of arms, ammunitions, and aircraft in exchange for 99-year leases to eight defense bases. Secret U.S. and British talks about the U.S. engaging in the war started in January 1941.

Germany invaded the Soviet Union (June 1941). Hitler vacillated between launching an amphibious invasion of Britain or breaking his pact and invading his "ally," the Soviet Union. Hitler decided upon what he thought was the path of least resistance, **Operation Barbarossa,** the massive invasion of the Soviet Union that was designed to quickly crush Soviet forces, conquer the communist state, and exploit its resources to support Germany's war efforts. In June, the plan went into effect with a lightning-quick surprise attack on the Soviet Union's frontier. However, just like Napoleon had found in 1812, the Nazi forces found themselves bogged down in the Russian winter. The Germans struggled to move through a land subjected to the scorched earth policy and intermittent guerrilla warfare attacks. The invasion broke the non-aggression pact of 1939 between Germany and the Soviet Union.

The Grand Alliance (December 1941). After the Soviet Union was attacked by Germany in June 1941 and the United States was attacked by Japan on December 7, 1941, Britain, the Soviet Union, and the United States formed an alliance—"The Big Three."

TEST TIP: It is important to remember the key players of World War II.

- The Allied Powers (called the *Allies*). The big three Allies included Great Britain, the United States, and the Soviet Union (joined in 1941 after Germany's betrayal). Other nations included Belgium, the Netherlands, Denmark, Norway, Greece, Yugoslavia, Poland, nationalist China, Canada, Australia, New Zealand, and France (until 1940).

- The Axis Powers: Germany, Italy (joined 1940 until 1943), Japan, Hungary, Bulgaria, Finland, and Romania.

The Allies conquered Italy and northern Africa (May–July 1943). Several battle campaigns were sparked throughout Europe from 1940 to 1943. Military strategies by the Allies were primarily conceived by the United States and Britain. The year 1943 proved to be the major turning point in the war. In the west, American and British troops took part in the invasion of Italy and major victories in northern Africa. In the east, the Soviets finally stemmed the Nazi onslaught at Stalingrad, near the southern entryway to the Caspian Sea and the Baku oil fields so desperately needed by the Nazis. On both the Western and Eastern fronts, the Allies began to push back against the Nazis, who suddenly seemed less than invincible.

The invasion of Normandy (June 1944). The northern Africa strategy succeeded and Italy proved to be very weak and easy to remove from the war. The Allies continued their campaigns to invade through the west. The British and Americans conducted the largest seaborne invasion in history when they landed on the beaches of Normandy, France, on June 6, 1944, "D-Day." The invasion was extremely difficult and almost failed. Hitler's forces had entrenched themselves in concrete bunkers on Normandy's coast. Even after a massive U.S. artillery bombardment from battleships, the Allied forces faced the cliffs at Normandy. Still, the invasion succeeded, and the Allied forces drove through Europe into Germany, defeating the German armies. This marked the beginning of the liberation of German-occupied Europe. At this point, the Allies began a two-way race to meet in Berlin.

The end of World War II in Europe (May 7, 1945). The war came to a close in Europe in 1945 as the Allies closed in on Germany from all sides. (Note: The war continued in the Asian-Pacific with Japan until August 1945 when the U.S. dropped atomic bombs on the Japanese islands of Hiroshima and Nagasaki.) During this period, Allied leaders met to discuss the postwar settlement. From the very beginning, the Big Three of the Grand Alliance—Franklin Delano Roosevelt (U.S.), Winston Churchill (Britain), and Joseph Stalin (Soviet Union)—were adamant to weaken Germany, but not to allow a resurgent Germany to rise up from the cinders to cause a World War III. Germany was to be disarmed, demilitarized, and de-Nazified. Nazi leaders were taken to court and tried as war criminals. German resources were to be used to repair damages inflicted on other nations.

The Yalta Conference (1945). The Allied war conferences sought to create a strong alliance system and a version of the League of Nations, but with more teeth to impart security in Europe. At the **Yalta Conference,** the Big Three agreed, in principle and also in some specifics, to split up Europe between Soviet spheres of influence and British spheres of influence. This set the stage for the dividing up of Europe and Germany.

Source: From left to right: Winston Churchill (United Kingdom), Franklin D. Roosevelt (United States), and Joseph Stalin (Union of the Soviet Socialist Republics) at Yalta Conference, 1945.

The Holocaust

Persecution of the Jews had begun before the war, reaching a peak in *Kristallnacht* (Night of Broken Glass) in 1938. After a Jewish assassin killed a Nazi diplomat, the German government unleashed the terror of this night by having its henchmen and eager civilians destroy Jewish synagogues, businesses, and homes. Property destruction and intimidation of innocent people spread across the country, bringing great shame upon Germany in the international sphere, but also strengthening public support for Hitler's extreme anti-Semitism.

Things became much worse during the war. Hitler's belief in fascism convinced many German citizens that Jews were an inferior race. Hitler's terrifying Nazi destruction and propaganda did not stop on the battlefields. As Germany fought against its enemies, Hitler and his henchmen enacted the **Final Solution** to the "Jewish problem," attempting the genocide of the Jews of Europe. Hitler set up death camps across Nazi-occupied Europe that engineered the death of over 6 million Jews, along with other undesirables such as homosexuals, gypsies, the disabled, Slavs, and others.

> **TEST TIP:** While Nazism is most strongly associated with anti-Semitism, and with good cause, the systematic persecution of Jews on a national scale in Germany did not begin until 1938. Keep this in mind, as students often lose points for mistakenly arguing that Jews were persecuted as early as 1933 when Hitler took control of Germany.

The Cold War (1945 to 1955)

Key Facts about the Causes of the Cold War

The Cold War was between the two superpowers: the United States and the Soviet Union. They had been enemies since the Russian Civil War, when the U.S. backed the White Army against the Communist Red Army. While 1945 brought the end of World War II, a new conflict was already in the making. The Soviets were determined to permanently protect Russian borders against another recurrence of German betrayal and aggression. The Soviets wanted to secure communism and dismantle Germany of its ability to ever harm Russia again. World War II cost the Soviets more than 20 million Russian lives. Stalin wanted to protect Russian borders and placed soldiers in defending areas of Russia. Meanwhile, Britain and the United States wanted to help rebuild and revitalize Germany to avoid another war.

The Cold War officially began with the United States' adoption of a policy of the containment of communism, the Truman Doctrine, the Marshall Plan, the Berlin Blockade and Airlift Crisis, and the Iron Curtain.

Key Facts about the Basic Causes of the Cold War

Stalin enforced communist rule (1945–1946). After 1945, Stalin's military and secret police enforced communist rule throughout the Soviet Union and expanded communism by undermining democracies in some countries and simply abolishing them in others.

Germany divided. After Germany's defeat, Germany was divided into "zones" of occupation by the Soviet Union, United States, Britain, and eventually France. The American, British, and French zones occupied approximately two-thirds of western Germany. Located deep within the Soviet zone was Germany's capital, Berlin. Berlin itself was divided into four "sectors," with the United States, Britain, and France sectors occupying approximately the western sector, known as West Berlin, and the Soviets occupying the eastern sector, known as East Berlin.

The Division of Germany and Berlin

The Iron Curtain (1945–1991). Stalin's suspicions about Western intentions grew, and Europe was divided nearly in two by what was called an **Iron Curtain.** Winston Churchill described the Iron Curtain as a boundary that symbolically and physically divided Europe into two competing ideologies: Western democratic liberalism and Eastern totalitarian rule represented by the Soviet Union and its allies. The borders of the Iron Curtain were heavily guarded and militarized. Two German states emerged in 1949, commonly known as West Germany (the Federal Republic of Germany) and East Germany (the German Democratic Republic).

The Truman Doctrine (1947). The Truman Doctrine was an initiative of the United States to "support free peoples who were resisting the attempted subjugation by armed minorities or by outside pressures." The Truman Doctrine stated that the U.S. would provide political, military, and economic support to all democratic nations under threat from authoritarian forces. The Doctrine's first test was a civil war in Greece. The United States sent in military troops to prevent a communist victory.

The Marshall Plan (1947). The United States had lost hundreds of thousands of men in the war, but had not endured the costs associated with being invaded. Therefore, the United States had the stability and money to invest in the **Marshall Plan** (called the European Recovery Program). The Marshall Plan was an American initiative to give 13 billion dollars (in today's economy, it would be 130 billion dollars) to invest in rebuilding the European nations—both Allies and formerly Axis nations. The plan would help to stimulate European economies and rebuild the infrastructure destroyed from World War II. Americans had learned their lessons from World War I. By stabilizing the European economies, European nations might be less likely to radicalize and turn to fascism—or more urgently, to communism.

Tensions build. Britain and the United States combined their two occupation zones and were later joined by France to more efficiently coordinate Germany's reconstruction. They also issued a new currency for the combined zones. Coupled with the Truman Plan and the Marshall Plan, the Soviets felt threatened. The situation began to peak as Westerners came to see the Soviets as enemies rather than allies, and vice versa.

Berlin Blockade and Airlift Crisis (1948). In 1948, the situation came to a head when Stalin tried to enforce Soviet demands in Germany through a blockade of the United States, Britain, and French sectors of Berlin, and what came to be known as West Berlin. This set off the **Berlin Blockade and Airlift Crisis.** The Soviets began to block all water, railroads, and roads into West Berlin. After all, the city of Berlin was deep within Soviet-occupied East Germany, so Stalin felt it was okay to use medieval-era tactics to hold West Berlin hostage. Unfortunately for the Soviets, the principal allies of the U.S. (Britain, Canada, and Australia) used airplanes to deliver food and supplies to the people of West Berlin. Stalin had no more leverage, and near the end of 1949 he had to give in, having gained nothing but turning Germans against Soviet rule.

The NATO Alliance and the Warsaw Pact (1955). The American allies in Europe formed the **North Atlantic Treaty Organization (NATO),** a collective security alliance that was formed to protect democracies, large and small, from Russian aggression. The Soviets followed suit in 1955 with the **Warsaw Pact,** which unified the Soviet Union with its communist eastern European nations (Poland, East Germany, Czechoslovakia, Hungary, Romania, Albania, and Bulgaria) in a defensive alliance against the United States and its allies.

Decolonization (1947 to 1997)

Among the most important outcomes of World War II and the Cold War were the independent movements of nations from the developing world toward decolonization.

African and Asian colonies sought independence. For some time, Britain, France, and other European nations hoped to retain their own colonies. But the physical destruction resulting from two world wars, along with the demoralization of European spirits that accompanied them, ensured that independent movements arose in the African and Asian nations that Europe had gained in the 19th and early-20th centuries. Britain decided to voluntarily give up its colonies, such as India in 1947, most of the African colonies in the 1960s, and even Hong Kong in 1997. On the other hand, the French and the Portuguese decided to fight wars to keep their colonies. The French started the **War of French Indochina,** which attempted to preserve Vietnam, Cambodia, and Laos. The **Algerian War** was politically divisive, leading to large groups of dissident students and peace movements.

TEST TIP: For free-response questions on the AP EURO exam that deal with this period of European decolonization, consider the differences between nations that decided to give up their colonies peacefully, as opposed to nations that decided to fight wars to keep their colonies.

Suez Crisis. In 1956, the nationalist leader of Egypt, Gamal Abdel Nasser, declared the nationalization of the **Suez Canal,** a waterway that was still of vital importance to the British navy and to their trade. This set off the **Suez Crisis,** as Britain teamed up with France and Israel (the Israelis were concerned with the growing Arab threat to their country) to attack Egypt and overthrow the government. As it happened, though, the United States confronted these three powers and demanded that they withdraw from Egypt or face serious consequences. Britain, France, and Israel duly retreated. The Suez Crisis showed that Britain and France were no longer independent Great Powers. The world was split between the superpowers of the Soviet Union and the United States.

The Khrushchev Era—Soviet Union (1956–1964)

Joseph Stalin died in 1953, and his successor, **Nikita Khrushchev,** tried to reform the Soviet Union after three decades of Stalinist depredations. In a 1956 speech that soon became public knowledge, Khrushchev criticized Stalin for murdering millions of citizens and destroying the Communist Party. Many Soviet citizens welcomed Khrushchev's apparent transparency and his willingness to tell the truth in government after nearly four decades of communist rule.

Khrushchev realized he had opened up Pandora's box when a revolution broke out in Hungary that same year. These revolutionaries tore down Stalin's statues, but also threatened communist rule in Hungary. Faced with the consequences of his de-Stalinization program, Khrushchev decided to send in the tanks and restore order.

> ## Heads Up: What You Need to Know
>
> On the AP EURO exam, you should be able to identify and explain the **Berlin Wall** (1961–1989). The Berlin Wall symbolized the injustice of communism and the Cold War. After World War II, Berlin was located within the Soviet zone of occupation, becoming known as East Berlin in 1949. While Khrushchev was dealing with Stalin's legacy, he also took a radical step in Germany. Ever since the establishment of communism in East Germany, citizens had been fleeing to freedom in West Berlin. In 1961, Khrushchev and the East German leader elected to build a wall encircling West Berlin to prevent emigration. Not only did it stem the tide of East Germans fleeing the country, but it also served as a symbol for the brutality of communism.

The Brezhnev Era—Soviet Union (1964–1982)

After the tumultuous Khrushchev era, the rule of **Leonid Brezhnev** was one of stability, albeit with economic and cultural stagnation. The year 1968 was an important year in Europe, as radical student protests, taking much of their cue from American student movements, were inspired by Maoism (an anti-revisionist political theory in the form of Marxism-Leninism) and anarchism. Protestors rose up throughout the continent. In France, communist student protests almost brought down the government with massive rallies, while in Czechoslovakia anti-communist protesters managed to take control of the government in what was called the Prague Spring. Like Khrushchev before him, Brezhnev sent in the military and restored communist rule, solidifying what became known as the **Brezhnev Doctrine** (the Soviet Union could and would use force to maintain communist governments in the Warsaw Pact).

The 1970s saw major economic stagnation for the Soviets, which Brezhnev hoped to compensate for by seeking *détente* (the relaxing of tensions) with the West. To improve relations between the communist bloc and the West, the **Helsinki Accords** were enacted to recognize the borders of Europe as they had been at the end of World War II. This largely came in the form of unprecedented arms agreements, including **SALT I** and **SALT II,** in which the Soviet Union and the United States eliminated some nuclear weapons in their arsenals and agreed to their limitations. Détente fell apart after 1979 when the Soviet Union invaded Afghanistan, which brought condemnation from the West.

Gorbachev—Soviet Union (1988–1991)

Brezhnev died in 1982, and his two heirs died quickly within 3 years. Yuri Andropov and Konstantin Chernenko were deceased by 1985 when **Mikhail Gorbachev** took over the reins of the Soviet Union. Gorbachev was a full generation younger than his previous four predecessors, and the first Russian leader born after the Russian Revolutions.

Let's examine the key aspects of Gorbachev's short but portentous rule as the leader of the Union of Soviet Socialist Republics.

Key Facts about Gorbachev's Rule

A reformer's spirit. Gorbachev was an idealist who believed that the Soviet Union could reform itself into being a more humane and a more equitable country. Gorbachev imagined that he could transform the Soviet Union into a socialist democracy, like Sweden or Denmark.

***Perestroika* (the Soviet Union's policy of restricting the economic and political system).** Gorbachev attempted to resuscitate the Soviet economy by introducing market reforms and the profit motive, as well as removing corrupt managers from Soviet industries. The uncertainty of *perestroika* actually hurt the Soviet economy and sent it into a tailspin from 1986 forward.

***Glasnost* (openness).** This term described Gorbachev's desire to open up the Soviet society to democratic debate by eliminating censorship and curbing the power of the secret police. By 1988, Gorbachev was even advocating limited democratic elections. He hoped that the Russian people would be thankful to the Communist Party for reforming itself. He was hoping that the Russian people would willingly vote the Communist Party back into power. Instead, once he opened up elections, he saw the unpopularity of communism, as it had always been in the Soviet Union, going back to Lenin's time.

New thinking in foreign policy. Gorbachev wanted to change the way Moscow dealt with the West. Détente was not enough. Gorbachev surprised U.S. President Ronald Reagan time and time again by simply capitulating on everything the Americans wanted. The leader became a popular celebrity in the West, well-loved because of his willingness to abandon Soviet state interests.

Communist rulers lost control. Gorbachev rejected the Brezhnev Doctrine, believing that each communist country was sovereign. He also rejected the use of secret police and military to stop protests and maintain communist rule; this point was incredibly important for the year 1989, when nationalist and democratic protesters, encouraged by Gorbachev's openness, began to take direct action against Warsaw Pact nations. Protests began in Poland, where gas shortages were causing people to freeze in the winter and wages were falling. This spread to Hungary and East Germany. The pivotal moment came when Hungary opened the border with Austria, which meant that East Germans and other Warsaw Pact citizens could flee to Hungary and from there to freedom in the West.

When pro-democracy protests had happened before in 1956 and 1968, the Soviet Union kept the protests under control by sending in the tanks. However, Gorbachev refused to use force, which meant that the communist rulers in Warsaw Pact nations lost power in a matter of weeks.

> **TEST TIP:** When considering the outcome of 1989 in the *Eastern Bloc* (communist countries of Europe), a bit of world perspective can make for an important contrast. Consider that in 1989, communist China saw similar pro-democracy protests en masse. Just as Gorbachev had done, the Chinese leadership had spent years experimenting with capitalistic reforms, and they too had to decide how to react to existential threats of power. The main difference, and this highlights the importance of Gorbachev's personality in his statesmanship, was that China decided to use military force to put down the protests to sustain the party rule at any cost, leading to the massacre at Tiananmen Square in Beijing.

Source: "November 10, 1989, Tearing down the Berlin Wall"
http://www.year1989.pl/dokumenty/zalaczniki/18/18-23338.jpg

Pax Americana (1990s)

After the upheaval of 1989, it was only a matter of time before the Soviet Union collapsed. In 1989–1990, nationalist protests erupted in most of the non-Russian republics. In the Baltic states, nationalists demanded an end to 40 years of Soviet rule, while the Caucasus states (Georgia, Armenia, and Azerbaijan) arose in ethnic violence and reprisals. Despite the fact that his country was clearly falling apart, Gorbachev refused to sanction the use of military force against the protestors. As a result, the Soviet Union dissolved itself in December 1991.

Source: Russia Insider, 2010.

The end of the Cold War meant a new era for the world. While the European Union brought Europe together economically and politically for great bargaining power, the utter collapse of Russian military power has meant that the post-1991 world has seen the first era since the 1500s in which Europe did not dominate world affairs. Europe has taken a back seat to the power of the United States. Time will tell whether American hegemony will last as long and cause as much progress, pain, glory, and destruction as Europe's time at the helm.

Chapter Review Practice Questions

Practice questions are for instructional purposes only and may not reflect the format of the actual exam. On the actual exam, questions are grouped into sets. Each set contains one source-based prompt (document or image) and two to five questions.

Multiple-Choice Questions

1. Based on your knowledge of European history, which of the following years was the turning point in the ending of the Cold War?

   A. 1948
   B. 1968
   C. 1989
   D. 2001

2. Which of the following Soviet rulers was most responsible for the heightening of political tensions in Europe and the world?

   A. Konstantin Chernenko
   B. Mikhail Gorbachev
   C. Leonid Brezhnev
   D. Nikita Khrushchev

3. Which of the following best characterizes the Bolsheviks' justification for their dictatorship in Russia?

   A. The Bolsheviks were the vanguard party that ruled in the proletariat's stead until working people were ready to rule themselves.
   B. Democracy was a bourgeois fad, not a legitimate form of government.
   C. Russian Orthodox religion in Russia threatened communist rule and necessitated dictatorship to protect the people.
   D. Communism would usher in a classless society in which economic differences between the people ceased to exist.

4. Which of the following did NOT contribute to the outbreak of World War I?

   A. A series of diplomatic crises that did not result in war
   B. Increasing nationalism in European countries
   C. Extreme militarism among countries' populations
   D. The view of war as hygienic for the human race

Questions 5 and 6 refer to the following image.

Source: Anonymous, postcard, 1919.

5. Based on your knowledge of European history, which of the following historical events does the political cartoon represent?

   A.   The July Crisis, 1914
   B.   The Battle of Verdun, 1916
   C.   The armistice of November 11, 1918
   D.   The Treaty of Brest-Litovsk

6. Which of the following political sentiments best represents how this political cartoon may have helped to undermine the Weimar Republic?

   A.   By portraying Jewish leaders as selfish and incapable of leading the armed forces
   B.   By insinuating that the ruling Social Democrats were allied with Jewish traitors
   C.   By arguing that Jews had not done their part on the battlefield
   D.   By opposing the Balfour Declaration in support of a Jewish homeland in Israel

7. Based on your knowledge of European history, which of the following European leaders was aided by the "encapsulated" idea?

   A.   Benito Mussolini
   B.   Adolf Hitler
   C.   Joseph Stalin
   D.   Leon Trotsky

Questions 8–10 refer to the following excerpt from a poem.

[. . .] Gas! Gas! Quick, boys!—An ecstasy of fumbling,
Fitting the clumsy helmets just in time;
But someone still was yelling out and stumbling
And flound'ring like a man on fire or in lime . . .
Dim, through the misty panes and thick green light,
As under a green sea, I saw him drowning.

In all my dreams, before my helpless sight,
He plunges at me, guttering, choking, drowning.

If in some smothering dreams you too could pace
Behind the wagon that we flung him in,
And watch the white eyes writhing in his face,
His hanging face, like a devil's sick of sin;
If you could hear, at every jolt, the blood
Come gargling from the froth-corrupted lungs,
Obscene as cancer, bitter as the cud
Of vile, incurable sores on innocent tongues,—
My friend, you would not tell with such high zest
To children ardent for some desperate glory,
The old Lie: "Dulce et decorum est; Pro patria mori."
[Translation: "It is sweet and fitting to die for one's country."]

—Source: Wilfred Owen, "Dulce et Decorum Est," 1916

8. Wilfred Owen's poem is most critical of which of the following groups of people?

   A.   The generals who failed to bring the war to a quick conclusion
   B.   The women who shamed men into enlisting into the army
   C.   The political leaders who failed to stop the outbreak of war
   D.   The older generations of people who urged young men to enlist in the army

9. Which of the following World War I battles would most likely have been the setting for Owen's poem?

   A.   The Battle of Passchendaele
   B.   The Battle of Jutland
   C.   The Battle of Gallipoli
   D.   The Second Battle of Ypres

10. Which of the following postwar phenomena would be supported by this poem?

   A.   The rise of fascism in Europe
   B.   The rise of feminism
   C.   A new interest in existentialism
   D.   The Lost Generation of authors

Document-Based Question

1 question
60 minutes

Reading Time: 15 minutes (brainstorm your thoughts and organize your response)
Writing Time: 45 minutes

Directions: The document-based question is based on the seven accompanying documents. The documents are for instructional purposes only. Some of the documents have been edited for the purpose of this practice exercise. Write your response on lined paper and include the following:

- **Thesis.** Present a thesis that supports a historically defensible claim, establishes a line of reasoning, and responds to all parts of the question. The thesis must consist of one or more sentences located in one place—either the introduction or the conclusion.
- **Contextualization.** Situate the argument by explaining the broader historical events, developments, or processes that occurred before, during, or after the time frame of the question.
- **Evidence from the documents.** Use the content of at least three to six of the documents to develop and support a cohesive argument that responds to the topic question.
- **Evidence beyond the documents.** Support or qualify your argument by explaining at least one additional piece of specific historical evidence not found in the documents. (Note: The example must be different from the evidence used to earn the point for contextualization.)
- **Analysis.** Use at least three documents to explain the documents' point of view, purpose, historical situation, and/or audience relevant to the topic question.
- **Historical reasoning.** Use historical reasoning to show relationships among the documents, the topic question, and the thesis argument. Use evidence to corroborate, qualify, or modify the argument.

Based on the documents that follow answer the question below.

Question 1: Evaluate the changing developments of the Cold War from its beginnings, to its shifts, to its ending.

Document 1

Source: Leslie Gilbert Illingworth, "Soviet Russia," 1947. British cartoonist depicting Stalin reaching across Europe to plant the Soviet flag, marking communist expansion.

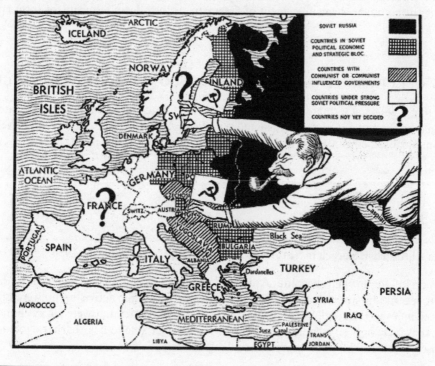

Document 2

Source: Yalta Conference Protocols, 1945.

III. DISMEMBERMENT OF GERMANY

It was agreed that Article 12(a) of the Surrender terms for Germany should be amended to read as follows:

"The United Kingdom, the United States of America, and the Union of Soviet Socialist Republics shall possess supreme authority with respect to Germany. In the exercise of such authority they will take such steps, including the complete dismemberment of Germany as they deem requisite for future peace and security."

[. . .]

IV. ZONE OF OCCUPATION FOR THE FRENCH AND CONTROL COUNCIL FOR GERMANY

It was agreed that a zone in Germany, to be occupied by the French forces, should be allocated to France. This zone would be formed out of the British and American zones and its extent would be settled by the British and Americans in consultation with the French Provisional Government.

Document 3

Source: Nikita Khrushchev, Speech to Session of the Twentieth Party Congress, 1956.

The Commission [of Inquiry] has become acquainted with a large quantity of materials in the NKVD archives. . . . It became apparent that many Party, Soviet and economic activists who were branded in 1937–1938 as enemies were actually never enemies, spies, wreckers, etc., but were always honest Communists; they were only so stigmatized, and often, no longer able to bear barbaric tortures, they charged themselves with all kinds of grave and unlikely crimes. . . .

Lenin used severe methods only in the most necessary cases, when the exploiting classes were still in existence and were vigorously opposing the revolution, when the struggle for survival was decidedly assuming the sharpest forms, even including a civil war.

Stalin, on the other hand, used extreme methods and mass repression at a time when the revolution was already victorious, when the Soviet state was strengthened, when the exploiting classes were already liquidated and Socialist relations were rooted solidly in all phases of national economy. It is clear that here Stalin showed in a whole series of cases his intolerance, his brutality and his abuse of power. Instead of proving his political correctness and mobilizing the masses, he often chose the path of repression and physical annihilation, not only against actual enemies, but also against individuals who had not committed any crimes against the Party and the Soviet government. . . .

Document 4

Source: Bill Sanders, "And Then There Were Three!" © 1989 Milwaukee Journal Sentinel, Inc. Reproduced with permission.

"...and then there were three!"

Document 5

Source: Leonid Brezhnev, ideological speech to the CPSU, 1976, to promote communism and caution against détente.

Contacts with socialist and social democratic parties have broadened. . . . It goes without saying that there can be no question of ideological rapprochement of scientific communism with the reformism of the social democrats. Among social democrats there are not a few whose whole activity is premised on anti-communism and anti-Sovietism. There are even parties where people are punished for having contact with communists. We will fight against any such phenomena, since they only play into the hands of reaction. . . .

Détente does not and cannot abolish the class struggle. No one can expect that under conditions of détente the communists will reconcile themselves to capitalist exploitation or that the monopolists will become revolutionaries. Thus the strict observance of the principle of non-interference in the affairs of other states, respect for their independence and sovereignty—this is the indispensable condition for détente. . . .

We do not hide the fact that we see in detente the road to the creation of more favorable conditions of peaceful socialist and communist construction. This only goes to show that socialism and peace are inseparable.

Document 6

Source: Mikhail Gorbachev, Vladivostok Speech, proposing a good-neighboring policy with the United States, 1986.

Six regiments will be returned home from Afghanistan before the end of 1986—one armored regiment, two motorized rifle regiments and three antiaircraft artillery regiments—with their integral equipment and armaments. These units will be returned to their areas of permanent deployment in the Soviet Union, in such a way that anyone interested can easily verify it.

[. . .]

Our approach to relations with the United States is well known. We stand for peaceful, good-neighborly relations and for mutually beneficial cooperation, which has incidentally considerable opportunities also in the Far East and in the Pacific.

A few words about the most important thing in our present relations, the termination of the arms race. After the Geneva meeting, the Soviet Union put forward major proposals on the entire range of problems of reducing and eliminating arms and of verifying the process. We have not seen any movement to meet us halfway.

Document 7

Source: George Kennan, the American in charge of Moscow affairs, "The Long Telegram from Moscow to the U.S. State Department," 1946. The 8,000-word telegram declared that the Soviet Union could not foresee a permanent, peaceful solution with the West.

At the bottom of the Kremlin's neurotic view of world affairs is a traditional and instinctive Russian sense of insecurity. Originally, this was the insecurity of a peaceful agricultural people trying to live on a vast exposed plain in a neighborhood of fierce nomadic peoples. To this was added, as Russia came into contact with the economically advanced West, fear of more competent, more powerful, more highly organized societies in that area. But this latter type of insecurity was one which afflicted the Russian rulers, rather than Russian people; for Russian rulers have invariably sensed that their rule was relatively archaic in form, fragile and artificial in its psychological foundation, unable to stand comparison or contact with the political systems of Western countries. For this reason they have always feared foreign penetration, feared direct contact between the Western world and their own, feared what would happen if Russians learned truth about world without or if foreigners learned the truth about the world within. And they have learned to seek security only in the patient but deadly struggle for total destruction of rival power, never in compacts and compromises with it.

It was no coincidence that Marxism, which had smoldered ineffectively for half a century in Western Europe, caught hold and blazed for the first time in Russia. Only in this land which had never known a friendly neighbor or indeed any tolerant equilibrium of separate powers, either internal or international, could a doctrine thrive which viewed economic conflicts of society as insoluble by peaceful means. After establishment of the Bolshevist regime, Marxist dogma, rendered even more truculent and intolerant by Lenin's interpretation, became a perfect vehicle for sense of insecurity with which Bolsheviks, even more than previous Russian rulers, were afflicted. . . . Basically this is only the steady advance of uneasy Russian nationalism, a centuries old movement in which conceptions of offense and defense are inextricably confused. But in the new guise of international Marxism, with its honeyed promises to a desperate and war torn outside world, it is more dangerous and insidious than ever before.

Answer Explanations

Multiple-Choice Questions

1. **C.** Each of the years was important for different reasons: choice A for the beginnings of the Cold War, choice B for the Prague Spring and for radical protests throughout the West, and choice D for the ending of Pax Americana with the upheaval of the September 11, 2001, atrocities against the U.S. Choice C is correct, though, because 1989 saw the end of communism in the Warsaw Pact nations and the fall of the Soviet Union from superpower status in the world.

2. **D.** Konstantin Chernenko (choice A) scarcely had time to do anything, much less instigate new problems with the West, and Gorbachev (choice B) and Brezhnev (choice C) oversaw periods of détente. Therefore, Nikita Khrushchev (choice D) is correct. Khrushchev built the Berlin Wall, instigated the Cuban Missile Crisis, gave incendiary speeches, and generally amped up the heat in the Cold War.

3. **A.** The Bolsheviks excoriated democracy, but that was not their justification for a dictatorship, so choice B can be eliminated. Choice C is incorrect because religion had nothing to do with the communist dictatorship. Choice D is an excellent summary of Bolshevik views of eventual communist triumph, but it does not justify dictatorship in and of itself. Choice A is correct because it sums up Lenin's adaptation of Marx's dictatorship and control of the proletariat to account for Bolshevik party rule.

4. **D.** Choice A is incorrect because this was one of the short-term causes of war between 1898 and 1914. Choices B and C are incorrect because these were long-term causes of the outbreak of war in 1914. Choice D is correct because the view of war as hygienic was associated with fascist movements in Italy and Germany that did not arise until after World War I.

5. **C.** This picture represents the German stab-in-the-back legend, which revolved around the armistice announced by the warring powers and agreed to by the German government on November 11, 1918. Choice C is correct.

6. **B.** This image relates to the German stab-in-the-back legend. It is not so much a critique of Jewish leaders of Germany (of which there were precious few), choice A, but, as a critique of the alleged Jewish influence in the Social Democratic Party, so choice B is correct. The Nazis and their sympathizers certainly would have agreed that Jews had not done their part in the war (choice C) and that the Balfour Declaration was wrongheaded (choice D), but neither relates to the legend or to the Weimar Republic.

7. **B.** This postcard is one representation of the German stab-in-the-back legend created by right-wing German extremists, which claimed that Jews and Marxists betrayed the German army by surrendering when Germany was still capable of winning the war. Adolf Hitler (choice B) is correct; while Hitler did not invent this legend, he did help to propagate it and certainly exploited it to aid in his rise to power.

8. **D.** While the author would certainly have held extreme contempt for the generals of the war (choice A), they are not directly criticized in this poem. While there were women who used white feathers to shame men into enlisting in the war effort, particularly in Britain, they are certainly not referenced in the poem, which eliminates choice B. While the poet would have held political leaders responsible for the outbreak of war (choice C), the direct condemnation in this poem is of the men who used Horace's *Dulce et decorum est* aphorism to urge young men to enlist and do their patriotic duty, so choice D is correct.

9. **D.** The Second Battle of Ypres in 1914 (choice D) was the first to see the mass-scale use of poison gas on the battlefield. The Battle of Passchendaele (choice A) did not see the use of poison gas, and, taking place in 1917, transpired after this poem was written. Choice B is incorrect because Jutland was the

largest, and one of the very few, naval battles of the war. Gallipoli was a military campaign fought in the Ottoman Empire. It was known for poor knowledge of terrain and fierce fighting by the Turks, not the use of chemical warfare, so choice C does not apply.

10. **D.** This anti-war poem has nothing to do with feminism (choice B) or existentialism (choice C). While the violence of the war certainly had its effect on the angry young men who would eventually form the basis of fascist Blackshirt and Brownshirt forces, choice A is a bit too disconnected from the poem itself. On the other hand, the anger, disillusionment, and rejection of traditional society that we see in this poem are exactly what motivated Lost Generation authors such as Ernest Hemingway, F. Scott Fitzgerald, and Erich Maria Remarque; choice D is correct.

Document-Based Question

DBQ Scoring Guide

To achieve the maximum score of 7, your response must address the scoring criteria components in the table below.

Scoring Criteria for a Good Essay	
Question 1: Evaluate the changing developments of the Cold War from its beginnings, to its shifts, to its ending.	
Scoring Criteria	**Examples**
A. THESIS/CLAIM	
(1 point) Presents a historically defensible thesis that establishes a line of reasoning. (Note: The thesis must make a claim that responds to *all* parts of the question and must *not* just restate the question. The thesis must consist of *at least* one sentence, either in the introduction or the conclusion.)	A good essay should clearly present a strong thesis statement that historically explains the political, ideological, and economic changes from the beginnings, course, and ending of the Cold War. The essay should follow a logical line of reasoning about the course of the Cold War and the world political and ideological developments surrounding the Cold War.
B. CONTEXTUALIZATION	
(1 point) Explains the broader historical context of events, developments, or processes that occurred before, during, or after the time frame of the question. (Note: Must be more than a phrase or reference.)	A good response should discuss the historical context of the Cold War. The documents themselves mostly feature the beginning period (1946–1950) and the ending (1985–1991) of the Cold War. The in-between period will have to be filled in as much as possible with historical examples based on your knowledge of European history and outside information. For example, the political, social, and ideological differences in Western democratic nations and Eastern communistic nations.

Scoring Criteria	Examples
C. EVIDENCE	
Evidence from the Documents **(2 points)** Uses at least *six* documents to support the argument in response to the prompt. OR **(1 point)** Uses the content of at least *three* documents to address the topic prompt. (Note: Examples must describe, rather than simply quote, the content of the documents.)	To earn the highest point value, an effective essay on this topic should be able to reasonably provide relevant evidence from the six or seven documents presented. Supporting references might include Documents 3, 5, and 6, which deal with the Soviet perspective, as well as the American and Western European perspectives from Documents 1, 4, and 7. An effective essay should also include the similarities and differences between the West (American perspective) and the East (Soviet perspective) and how these differences impacted the politics, ideologies, societies, and the economies of these nations.
Evidence Beyond the Documents **(1 point)** Uses at least one additional piece of specific historical evidence beyond those found in the documents that is relevant to the argument. (Note: Evidence must be different from the evidence used in contextualization.)	This part of the essay should bring together and connect content from the essay and outside information. For example, Stalin's reaction to the containment of communism outlined in the Marshall Plan. In addition, the Cold War was the most important political development of the second half of the 20th century. A good essay might comment on this important fact and the ongoing significance of Cold War politics in the post-1991 world. The rivalries created during the Cold War continue to exist even today, even with the interventions of NATO to resolve nuclear threats. In some ways, the world is still shaped by Cold War forces and ideologies, as stated in Fukuyama's writings.
D. ANALYSIS AND REASONING	
(1 point) Uses at least *three* documents to explain how each document's point of view, purpose, historical situation, and/or audience is relevant to the argument. (Note: References must explain how or why, rather than simply identifying.)	The essay response draws from at least three documents to support the document's point of view. For example, the artist in Document 1 shows Stalin "reaching across" to spread communism which further divided the Eastern and Western tensions leading to the Cold War. Document 2 shows the historical situation of the agreement made at the Yalta Conference to physically divide Eastern and Western political ideologies in Germany after World War II (communist socialism versus democrat capitalism). The author of Document 7, George Kennan, wrote a "long telegram," to declare that the Eastern divisions with the U.S. were "permanent," not temporary.
(1 point) Uses historical reasoning and development that focuses on the question while using evidence to corroborate, qualify, or modify the argument. (Examples: Explain what is similar and different; explain the cause and effect; explain multiple causes; explain connections within and across periods of time; corroborate multiple perspectives across themes; or consider alternative views.)	The essay focuses on the historical skill of *continuity and change over time* to corroborate the phases of the Cold War. What developments connected the different phases of the Cold War and what developments modified the Cold War outcome? The sample response should distinguish between these different phases of the Cold War, as well as between specific events and particular nations. The essay should also identify why certain changes happened in the context of the broader historical perspectives of competing world political ideologies of the liberal democratic West and the communist East nations.

Sample Response

The Cold War began as the Second World War came to an end and two previous allies, the Soviet Union and the United States fell into opposition. The changes and continuities of this conflict began with the separation of Europe into Eastern communist and Western noncommunist camps, and it was only able to end after communism gave up its socialist role as an alternative ideology to democratic capitalism. In the context of history, the four major changing phases of the Cold War were: the struggle for European territorial control in war-torn Europe after World War II; the Western containment of communism throughout the world; the East and West military tensions at the height of the Cold War including the Korean War and the Cuban Missile Crisis, with the threat of nuclear war; and the nonproliferation treaty and the collapse of communism to end the Cold War.

Document 1 presents the conventional wisdom at the outbreak of the Cold War. The creator of Document 1 shows that the Cold War began with the brutal dictator of the Soviet Union, Joseph Stalin, "overreaching" to take over the nations of Europe following the defeat of Nazi Germany. Poland, Czechoslovakia, and Bulgaria fell to communist control. The Soviets began to stretch out their influence, octopus-like, which gained the attention and anger of the United States. Document 2 provides the context for the growing tensions leading to the Cold War, as it shows the way in which the spoils of World War II were divided by the Yalta Conference in 1945. Europe quickly became a battleground for communist or anticommunist influence as Germany and the city of Berlin were divided into zones of occupation between the Soviet Union, United States, Britain, and France. Soviet tensions increased as the Western nations (the United States, Britain, and France) occupied the majority of Germany's zones.

Threatened by communism, the United States pledged military support in the Truman Doctrine to offer a containment strategy and aid any nation that was threatened by communism. During this second phase, the United States wanted to contain communism by reaching out to less developed European nations. The author of Document 7, George Kennan, illustrates the intellectual backdrop against which the Americans entered the Cold War, armed with Kennan's understanding of Russian history and outlook that Russia would never want peace. His cynical view of "Marxist dogma," illustrates how communism offered "honeyed promises," to a war-torn world. Kennan's writing portrays Russian history and Russian motivations as relentlessly evil, hostile, and menacing, which helped to shape the American mistrust of the Soviet Union during the conflict itself. The Soviets responded by enclosing the city of Berlin with what was called "The Berlin Wall" in East Germany in 1961 to isolate West Berlin from East Germany. This was a physical symbol of the division of the two opposing political ideologies. The Soviets also prevented the East Germans from escaping to West Berlin.

After Stalin's death in 1953, Khrushchev criticized Stalin (Document 3) and led the Soviet Union back to a Marxist-Leninism communist regime. During the height of the Cold War, when China and North Korea fell to communism, Western alliances aided the United States. However, by 1962 a "balance of terror," between the two Eastern and Western superpowers came to a highpoint in a nuclear arms race, and Khrushchev placed ballistic missiles in Cuba. The two superpower leaders barely avoided a nuclear holocaust.

Détente existed in the third phase (Document 5), and the political leaders were able to branch out of the traditional roles of each nation and shape new foreign policy trends. For example, Documents 3 and 6 show changes in Kremlin policy, from Khrushchev condemning Stalinism to Gorbachev calling for an end to the Cold War, and to stop the conflict and constant difficulties over ideology. These show that the Cold War was rarely inactive and often took new forms over the course of decades.

The image in Document 4 represents the last phase, the end of the Cold War, as the Soviet Union and eastern European satellite states collapsed, leaving only China, North Korea, and Cuba as major communist states. The Cold War came to a roaring end in Europe, but in China, Cuba, and North Korea it has continued (today, Vietnam and Laos are communist). American political scientist Francis Fukuyama claimed that history had come to an end because all alternatives to capitalist democracy had been exhausted. In fact, new alternatives have since emerged, but he was correct to note that communism in the historical context of the Soviet Union was no longer a viable alternative to a capitalist democracy.

Chapter 8

Full-Length Practice Exam

This chapter contains a full-length practice exam that will give you valuable insight into the types of questions that may appear on the AP EURO exam. The practice exam is for instructional purposes only, and some of the document sources may be longer than those on the actual exam. As you take this practice exam, try to simulate testing conditions and time limits for each of the following sections:

- Section I: Part A—Multiple-Choice Questions
- Section I: Part B—Short-Answer Questions
- Section II: Part A—Document-Based Question
- Section II: Part B—Long-Essay Question

Answer Sheet

Section I – Part A: Multiple-Choice Questions

1 A B C D	31 A B C D
2 A B C D	32 A B C D
3 A B C D	33 A B C D
4 A B C D	34 A B C D
5 A B C D	35 A B C D
6 A B C D	36 A B C D
7 A B C D	37 A B C D
8 A B C D	38 A B C D
9 A B C D	39 A B C D
10 A B C D	40 A B C D
11 A B C D	41 A B C D
12 A B C D	42 A B C D
13 A B C D	43 A B C D
14 A B C D	44 A B C D
15 A B C D	45 A B C D
16 A B C D	46 A B C D
17 A B C D	47 A B C D
18 A B C D	48 A B C D
19 A B C D	49 A B C D
20 A B C D	50 A B C D
21 A B C D	51 A B C D
22 A B C D	52 A B C D
23 A B C D	53 A B C D
24 A B C D	54 A B C D
25 A B C D	55 A B C D
26 A B C D	
27 A B C D	
28 A B C D	
29 A B C D	
30 A B C D	

Section I

Part A: Multiple-Choice Questions

Multiple-choice questions are grouped into sets. Each set contains one source-based prompt (document or image) and two to five questions.

55 questions

55 minutes

Questions 1–4 refer to the following passage.

> Undeniably, there is much to be said about the theories of the long-term government structural processes that played a substantial role in the outbreak of World War I. But none of these theories, even though they demonstrated the likelihood of an early-20th-century European war, can satisfactorily account for *why* the war broke out, *when* it broke out, and the *manner* in which it broke out. That can only be accounted for by looking closely at decisions of the handful of men who had the power to avert or launch a war. For various reasons these men decided to do the latter and unleashed what Fritz Stern rightly called, "the first calamity of the 20th century, the calamity from which all other calamities sprang."
>
> Historians do not normally indulge in the temptation of superficial or counterfactual history. However, when we consider the significance of the First World War, it is difficult to imagine a 20th century where the names of Hitler, Stalin, and Mao passed unknown to humanity. But these imaginings of an idyllic 20th century were not destined to be true. We can, therefore, only futilely wonder how the world might have been without the decisions of the handful of men who held supreme power in the July 1914 crisis.
>
> —Source: Malcolm Mafi, "A Swan Song for the West," 2015.

1. Based on your knowledge of European history, which of the following best summarizes the author's argument about early-20th-century Europe?

    A. World War I broke out because of structural trends.

    B. World War I was the first total war in European history.

    C. World War I led to many events that were inevitable.

    D. World War I cannot be understood by only examining its long-term causes.

2. Which of the following examples of evidence, if true, would most undermine the author's argument?

    A. France called up its military reserves before the assassination of Franz Ferdinand.

    B. German leaders had meticulously planned to attack France and Russia for over a decade.

    C. A crisis similar to the July 1914 crisis occurred in 1880, but it did not lead to war.

    D. World War II led to more social changes than World War I.

3. Which one of the following historiographical approaches best describes the author's argument?

    A. The Marxist school

    B. Counterfactual history

    C. Rankean history

    D. The Feminist school

4. Which of the following explains why the author contemplates the counterfactual history of World War I?

   A. To show the superiority of counterfactual history
   B. To demonstrate the inexorability of the war's breaking out
   C. To show the absurdity of engaging in counterfactual history
   D. To illustrate the watershed importance of World War I for ushering in radical changes

Questions 5–8 refer to the following passage.

The Taxed Cake
GIVE, give, they cry—and take!
　　For wilful men are they
Who tax'd our cake, and took our cake,
　　To throw our cake away.

The cake grows less and less,
　　For profits lessen, too;
But land will pay, at last, I guess,
　　For land-won Waterloo.

They mix our bread with bran,
　　They call potatoes bread;
And, get who may, or keep who can,
　　The starved, they say, are fed.

Our rivals fatten fast,
　　But we are free to pay;
And dearly they shall pay, at last,
　　Who threw our cake away.

Lend, lend thy wing, oh, steam,
　　And bear me to some clime
Where splendid beggars dare not dream
　　That law's best fruit is crime!

Oh, Landlord's Devil, take
　　Thy own elect, I pray,
Who tax'd our cake, and took our cake,
　　To throw our cake away.

　　　　　—Source: Ebenezer Elliott, "The Taxed Cake," England, c. 1830.

5. This 19th-century British poem, "The Taxed Cake," was criticizing which of the following law(s)?

   A. The Corn Laws
   B. The Factory Act
   C. The Poor Laws
   D. The Cat and Mouse Act

6. Based on your knowledge of 19th-century European history, which of the following political movements would most likely have agreed with the sentiments in Elliot's poem?

    A. The Jacobite movement
    B. The Chartist movement
    C. The Suffragist movement
    D. The Abolitionist movement

7. Which of the following economic philosophies led to the 19th-century circumstances described in the poem?

    A. Communism
    B. Mercantilism
    C. Keynesianism
    D. Classical economics

8. Which of the following 19th-century populations would have been most likely to directly prosper from the circumstances described in Elliot's poem?

    A. Rural peasants
    B. Urban bourgeoisie
    C. Aristocratic landowners
    D. Anglican clergy

Questions 9–11 refer to the following passage.

Oath of Supremacy

I . . . do utterly testify and declare in my conscience, that the Queen's Highness is the only supreme governor of this realm, and of all other of her Highness's dominions and countries, as well as in all spiritual or ecclesiastical things or causes, as temporal, and that no foreign prince, person, prelate, state or potentate, hath, or ought to have any jurisdiction, power, superiority, preeminence, or authority ecclesiastical or spiritual, within this realm; and therefore I do utterly renounce and forsake all foreign jurisdictions, powers, superiorities, and authorities, and do promise that from henceforth, I shall bear faith and true allegiance to the Queen's Highness, her heirs and lawful successors, and to my power shall assist and defend all jurisdictions, preeminence, privileges and authorities granted or belonging to the Queen's Highness, her heirs and successors, or united and annexed to the imperial crown of this realm. So help me God, and by the contents of this book.

—Source: Oath of Supremacy mandated in Ireland, 1559.
This was part of the Penal Laws of England and its dominions under Elizabeth I.

9. Based on your knowledge of 16th-century European history, the Oath of Supremacy expressed by Elizabeth I of England resulted in which of the following?

    A. To require Catholics to recognize the leader of the Church of England over the Roman Catholic pope
    B. To require the Irish to pay feudal dues to their English landowners
    C. To require the Irish to surrender their land to the English monarchy
    D. To require the Irish to pay for indulgences from the Church of England

10. Based on your knowledge of European history, which of the following events was most closely related to the 16th-century Penal Laws of England?

    A.   The Gunpowder Plot
    B.   The suppression of the Jesuits
    C.   The War of the Roses
    D.   The Glorious Revolution

11. Based on your knowledge of European history, which of the following 19th-century decrees ended the Penal Laws of England described in the passage?

    A.   The Act of Union
    B.   The Navigations Acts
    C.   The Home Rule Act
    D.   The Catholic Emancipation Act

Questions 12–15 refer to the following image.

Source: Anonymous, "Peace and Freedom in the Soviet Union," 1918. A propaganda poster depicting the Soviet leader as Satan.

12. The political cartoon portrays which of the following 20th-century Soviet leaders?

    A.   Leon Trotsky
    B.   Vladimir Lenin
    C.   Joseph Stalin
    D.   Nikita Khrushchev

13. Which of the following 20th-century historical events is depicted in the political cartoon?

    A. The Reds' mass murder of political opponents
    B. The Whites' use of foreign mercenaries
    C. Lenin's false promises to end the First World War
    D. Stalin's exploitation of slave labor in the gulags

14. Based on your knowledge of European history, which of the following political attitudes is expressed in the political cartoon?

    A. The implication that the Bolsheviks are non-Whites, or others who are foreign to Russia
    B. The connection of communism to anarchist assassins
    C. The criticism of Stalin as a radical leader of the Bolsheviks
    D. The criticism of the White Army for its violence during their Civil War

15. Based on the political cartoon, which of the following would have likely been echoed in Nazi propaganda?

    A. The portrayal of communists as mass murderers
    B. The connection between Bolshevik communism and Judaism
    C. The image of Jews as the destroyers of Christianity
    D. The need to exterminate Asians

Questions 16–20 refer to the following image.

Source: Otto Dix, "Storm Troops Advancing Under a Gas Attack," from the Der Krieg (the War) Collection, 1924. Five soldiers advancing an enemy line while under poison gas attack.

16. The 20th-century sentiment characterized in Dix's illustration was LEAST influenced by which of the following?

    A. The brutality of World War I
    B. The horror of gas attacks during World War I
    C. The atrocities against civilians during the war
    D. The dehumanization of soldiers during the war

17. Which of the following best describes the portrayal of the soldiers in Dix's illustration?

    A. Terrifying industrial-age monsters
    B. Disciplined German soldiers
    C. The average brave soldiers
    D. Enemies of liberty and the Allies

18. Based on your knowledge of 20th-century European history, the artist of this illustration, Otto Dix, would most likely have opposed which of the following?

    A. The Brest-Litovsk Treaty
    B. The Kellogg-Briand Pact
    C. The remilitarization of Germany
    D. The Locarno Pact

19. Based on your knowledge of European history, which of the following 20th-century wars does the above illustration depict?

    A. World War II
    B. The Franco-Prussian War
    C. The Italian invasion of Abyssinia
    D. World War I

20. When Adolf Hitler came to power in 1933, which of the following would have likely been Hitler's attitude toward Dix's illustration?

    A. Hitler would have proclaimed its usefulness as a recruiting tool.
    B. Hitler would have decried the illustration as too conventional and safe.
    C. Hitler would have praised the artist as an exemplar of the German avant-garde.
    D. Hitler would have denounced the illustration as degenerate art.

Questions 21–26 refer to the following chart.

The Ancestry of King Charles II of Spain (1661–1700)

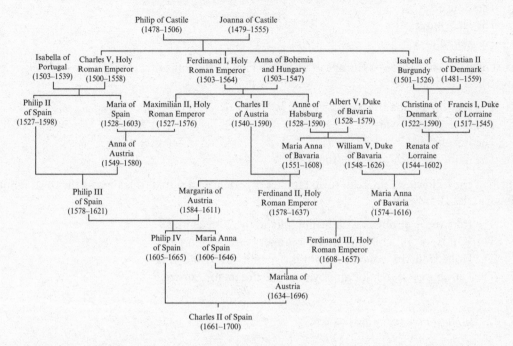

Source: "The Ancestry of King Charles II of Spain." The intermarriage of the royal Spanish monarchy.

21. All of the following events took place during the years reported in the Spanish monarchs' genealogical timeline EXCEPT:

   A. The conquest of the New World
   B. The Thirty Years' War
   C. The French Revolution
   D. The failure of the Spanish Armada

22. The timeline shows the ancestry of King Charles II of Spain. Based on your knowledge of European history, which of the following best describes the life of Charles II of Spain?

   A. Charles II was physically and mentally disabled.
   B. Charles II was Europe's greatest leader of the age.
   C. Charles II was devoutly religious and spread Catholicism throughout Europe.
   D. Charles II built strong alliances with England and Austria.

23. Which of the following best describes the importance of this genealogical timeline to Spain?

   A. Spain's rulers were exceptionally skilled at statecraft.
   B. Spain's royal bloodlines were weakened from generations of inbreeding.
   C. Spain's royal marriages strengthened its diplomatic position.
   D. Spain's succession of monarchs would likely be long-lived and healthy rulers.

24. Which of the following royal families does Spain's genealogical timeline represent?

    A.   The Trastamara
    B.   The Bourbons
    C.   The Habsburgs
    D.   The Romanovs

25. Based on your knowledge of European history, which of the following events is most closely related to King Charles II's ancestry?

    A.   The War of the Spanish Succession
    B.   The Seven Years' War
    C.   The Reconquista
    D.   The founding of the Spanish Inquisition

26. Which of the following European royal families experienced a similar dilemma as the royal family of King Charles II of Spain?

    A.   The Romanovs' problem with hemophilia in the 20th century
    B.   The Windsors' difficulty in finding a proper heir for George V
    C.   The Hohenzollerns' concerns about the stability of Wilhelm II
    D.   The Habsburgs' search for approval for the Pragmatic Sanction

Questions 27–31 refer to the following passage.

> In the confusion of wartime we ourselves are at a loss as to the significance of the impressions which bear down upon us and as to the value of the judgements which we form. We cannot but feel that no event has ever destroyed so much that is precious in the common possessions of humanity, confused so many of the clearest intelligences, or so thoroughly debased what is highest. Science herself has lost her passionless impartiality; her deeply embittered servants seek for weapons from her with which to contribute towards the struggle with the enemy. Anthropologists feel driven to declare that enemy inferior and degenerate, psychiatrists issue a diagnosis of his disease of mind or spirit.
>
> The individual who is not himself a combatant—and so is a cog in the gigantic machine of war—will welcome any indication, however slight, which will make it easier for him to find his bearings within himself at least. I propose to pick out two among the factors which are responsible for the mental distress felt by non-combatants and to treat them: the disillusionment which this war has evoked, and the altered attitude towards death which this—like every other war—forces upon us.
>
> —Source: Sigmund Freud, "Thoughts for the Times on War and Death," 1915.

27. Based on your knowledge of European history, which of the following most likely contributed to Freud's essay?

    A.   The efficiency of total war
    B.   The brutality of war
    C.   The mass destruction of private property during war
    D.   The exclusion of women as soldiers of war

28. Which of the following evidence best supports Freud's 20th-century ideas expressed in his essay?

    A. Mass casualty lists of the war
    B. Debt assumed by governments during the war
    C. The rise in the number of mentally ill during the war
    D. The destruction of several cities during the war

29. Based on your knowledge of European history, which of the following postwar phenomena is NOT suggested by the essay?

    A. Widespread disillusionment in society
    B. Questioning of scientific certainty
    C. Dismissal of traditional values
    D. Undermining of established sex taboos

30. Based on the passage, which of the following works best matches Freud's point of view?

    A. Erich Maria Remarque's *All Quiet on the Western Front*
    B. Pablo Picasso's *Guernica*
    C. Rene Magritte's *The Treachery of Images*
    D. F. Scott Fitzgerald's *The Great Gatsby*

31. Which of Freud's famous psychological concepts is most evident in the argument?

    A. The death drive
    B. The unconscious
    C. The irrational
    D. The id

Questions 32–35 refer to the following passage.

One is not born, but rather becomes, woman. No biological, psychic, or economic destiny defines the figure that the human female takes on in society; it is civilization on the whole that elaborates this intermediary product between the male and the eunuch that is called feminine. Only the mediation of another can constitute an individual as an Other. In as much as he exists for himself, the child would not grasp himself as sexually differentiated. For girls and boys, the body is first the radiation of a subjectivity, the instrument that brings about the comprehension of the world: they apprehend the universe through their eyes and hands, and not through their sexual parts. The drama of birth and weaning takes place in the same way for infants of both sexes; they have the same interests and pleasures; sucking is the first source of their most pleasurable sensations; they then go through an anal phase in which they get their greatest satisfactions from excretory functions common to both; their genital development is similar; they explore their bodies with the same curiosity and the same indifference . . . sometimes even starting from early childhood she already appears sexually specified, it is not because mysterious instincts immediately destined her to passivity, coquetry, or motherhood but because the intervention of others in the infant's life is almost ordinary, and her vocation is imperiously breathed into her from the first years of her life.

—Source: Simone de Beauvoir, *The Second Sex,* 1949.

32. The passage served as a starting point for which of the following movements?

    A.   The anti-nuclear movement
    B.   Second Wave Feminism
    C.   The civil rights movement
    D.   Women's suffrage movement

33. Which of the following 20th-century social groups would have been most receptive to de Beauvoir's argument?

    A.   Educated women
    B.   Upper-class men
    C.   Working-class socialists
    D.   Government bureaucrats

34. Which of the following social attitudes of the late-20th century is most likely connected to the main ideas of the passage?

    A.   A new focus on economic rights for women
    B.   The inclusion of lesbians in the feminist movement
    C.   A shift to seeing sex as anatomical, but gender as culturally constructed
    D.   The desire to view gender as interconnected with race and class

35. Which of the following best describes de Beauvoir's reasoning?

    A.   Women are superior to men in some respects.
    B.   Men teach women to be sexual objects.
    C.   One may be born an anatomical female, but being a woman must be taught.
    D.   Anyone can become a member of the female sex.

Questions 36–40 refer to the following passage.

  6. And not to leave any occasion of trouble and difference among our Subjects, we have permitted and do permit to those of the Reformed Religion, to live and dwell in all the Cities and places of this our Kingdom and Countries under our obedience, without being inquired after, vexed, molested, or compelled to do anything in Religion, contrary to their Conscience, nor by reason of the same be searched after in houses or places where they live, they comporting themselves in other things as is contained in this our present Edict or Statute.

  7. We also permit to all Lords, Gentlemen and other Persons, as well as inhabitants and others, making profession of the Reformed Religion, having in our Kingdom and Countries under our obedience, high Justice as chief Lord (as in Normandy) be it in proprietary or usage, in whole, moiety, or third party, to have in such of their houses of the said high Justice or Fiefs.

—Source: King Henry IV of France, Edict of Nantes, 1598.

36. The Edict of Nantes in 1598 protected rights of all French citizens. Which of the following monarchs later revoked the Edict of Nantes?

   A. Louis XVI
   B. Napoleon III
   C. Louis XIV
   D. Henry IV

37. Based on your knowledge of 16th-century European history, which of the following nations would have been most opposed to the Edict of Nantes?

   A. Spain
   B. England
   C. Holland
   D. Portugal

38. Which of the following best summarizes the significance of the Edict of Nantes?

   A. It ushered in the tolerance of Protestants in France for a century.
   B. It promoted religious freedom for all Christians in France.
   C. It helped to free France from Muslim attacks.
   D. It strengthened the power of the French aristocracy over the king.

39. Based on your knowledge of European history, which European foreign treaty was most comparable to the Edict of Nantes?

   A. Peace of Augsburg
   B. Treaty of Versailles
   C. Treaty of Utrecht
   D. Peace of Westphalia

40. King Henry IV, who created the Edict of Nantes, was associated with which of the following famous declarations?

   A. "The Bourbons learned nothing and forgot nothing."
   B. "Let them eat cake."
   C. "I am the state."
   D. "Paris is worth a Mass."

Questions 41–45 refer to the following passage.

Article 1. The National Assembly abolishes the feudal system entirely. They declare that among feudal and taxable rights and duties, the ones concerned with real or personal succession right and personal servitude and the ones that represent them are abolished without compensation. The rights that will not be suppressed by this decree will continue to be collected until they are entirely paid back. [. . .]

Article 3. The exclusive right of hunting is also abolished. Any landlord has the right to destroy or have someone destroy any kind of prey, but only on the land he owns. All administrative districts, even royal, that are hunting preserves, under any denomination, are also abolished. The preservation of the King's personal pleasures will be provided—as long as properties and freedom are respected. [. . .]

Article 5. Any kind of tithes and fees, under any denomination that they are known or collected. . . are abolished. . . .

Article 6. All perpetual loans . . . can be bought back. Any kind of harvest share can also be bought back.

Article 7. Venality of judicial fees and municipal offices is abolished. Justice will be dispensed at no cost. And nevertheless officers holding these offices shall fulfill their duties and be paid until the assembly finds a way to reimburse them.

Article 8. County priests' casual offerings are abolished and the priests will not be paid anymore.

Article 9. Financial, personal, or real privileges are abolished forever. Every citizen will pay the same taxes on everything.

Article 10. . . . Every specific privilege of provinces, principalities, regions, districts, cities and communities of inhabitants, either in the form of money or otherwise, are abolished.

Article 11. Every citizen, whatever their origins are, can hold any ecclesiastic, civilian, or military job.

—Source: French National Constituent Assembly, "August 4 Decrees," 1789.

41. The articles written by the French National Constituent Assembly in the 18th century established which of the following decrees?

    A. Meritocracy in offices
    B. Equality between men and women
    C. Nationalization of church lands
    D. Introduction of constitutional monarchy

42. Which of the following social classes was least likely to benefit from the decrees written by the French National Assembly?

    A. The aristocracy
    B. The bourgeoisie
    C. The peasantry
    D. The military

43. Which of the following historical events would most likely have been connected to the decrees?

    A. The Reign of Terror
    B. The Great Fear
    C. The Thermidor Reaction
    D. The 100 Days

44. Which aspect of the following French Revolutionary ideologies is NOT represented in the decrees?

    A. Separation of church and state
    B. Ending of aristocratic privilege
    C. Elevation of ability over station of birth
    D. Universal manhood suffrage

45. A historian might use the above passage to support which of the following claims?

    A. The French Revolution was guided by the sans-culottes.
    B. The clergy was universally opposed to the French Revolutionary government.
    C. The Revolution resulted in the bourgeoisie overturning the aristocracy.
    D. The Revolution was not primarily driven by Enlightenment philosophy.

Questions 46–50 refer to the following passage.

It is clear that things have changed. The Western States of our old continent have rebuilt their economies. They are rebuilding their military forces. One of them—France—is becoming a nuclear power. Above all they have become aware of their natural ties. In short, Western Europe appears likely to constitute a major entity full of merit and resources, capable of living its own life, indeed, not in opposition to the New World, but right alongside it. [. . .]

The result of all these new factors, complicated, and interrelated, is that the division of the world into two camps led by Washington and Moscow. With respect to the gradually splitting totalitarian world or the problems posed by China, the conduct to be adopted toward many countries of Asia, Africa and Latin America, or the remodeling of the United Nations Organization that necessarily ensues, or the adjustment of world exchanges of all kinds, etc., it appears that Europe, provided that it wishes it is henceforth called upon to play a role which is its own.

But which Europe? That is the question. According to us French, it is a question of Europe's being made in order for it to be European. A European Europe means that it exists by itself for itself, in other words in the midst of the world—it has its own policy. In reality, the fact that Europe, not having a policy, would be subject to the policy that came to it from the other side of the Atlantic appears to them, even today, normal and satisfactory. [. . .]

That is why France took the initiative of proposing to her five partners of the Rome Treaty a beginning for the organization of their cooperation. Thus, we would begin to live in common, pending the time when habit and evolution would gradually draw the ties closer together.

—Source: Charles de Gaulle, President of France, "Europe and Its Role in World Affairs," 1964.

46. A 20th-century historian might use the above passage by de Gaulle to support which of the following arguments?

    A. France was seeking to maintain a strong position relative to the two global superpowers.
    B. The French felt cornered by domestic communist protests.
    C. France was seeking to gain an advantage over the Italians.
    D. De Gaulle sought to make France more dependent upon NATO for protection.

47. Which of the following was NOT a goal of de Gaulle in the passage?

    A. To secure Europe as a strong counterweight to the U.S. and the Soviet Union

    B. To keep France as a great power to be reckoned with

    C. To maintain French colonies as much as possible

    D. To form a balance of power against a strong resurgent Germany

48. Which of the following events was NOT inspired by the same reasons as mentioned in de Gaulle's passage?

    A. The Algerian War

    B. The French-Indochina War

    C. The May 1968 protests

    D. The Suez Canal Crisis

49. Based on your knowledge of European history, which 20th-century European country would have been most concerned with the developments described in the passage?

    A. The USSR

    B. Britain

    C. Italy

    D. Spain

50. The Treaty of Rome was suggested in de Gaulle's passage. Which of the following organizations did the Treaty of Rome establish?

    A. The North Atlantic Treaty Organization

    B. The European Union

    C. The European Economic Community

    D. The United Nations

Questions 51–55 refer to the following passage.

We have ordered provision to be made that from henceforward the Indians in no way be made slaves, including those who until now have been enslaved against all reason and right and contrary to the provisions and instructions thereupon. [. . .] We command that the Audiencias appoint persons who may pursue this cause for the Indians and be paid out of the Exchequer fines, provided they be men of trust and diligence. Also, we command that with regard to the lading of the said Indians the Audiencias take especial care that they be not laden, or in case that in some parts this cannot be avoided that it be in such a manner that no risk of life, health and preservation of the said Indians may ensue from an immoderate burthen. [. . .]

So also, the said Audiencias are to inform themselves how the Indians have been treated by the persons who have held them in encomienda, and if it be clear that in justice they ought to be deprived of the said Indians for their excesses and the ill-usage to which they have subjected them, we ordain that they take away and place such Indians under our Royal Crown. [. . .]

Moreover, we ordain and command that from henceforward no Viceroy, Governor, Audiencia, discoverer, or any other person have power to allot Indians in encomienda by new provision, or by means of resignation, donation, sale, or any other form or manner, neither by vacancy nor inheritance, but that the person dying who held the said Indians, they revert to our Royal Crown.

        —Source: Emperor Charles V (Carlos II) of Spain, "The New Laws," 1542.

51. Which of the following significant historical events was most similar to the 16th-century events described in this passage?

    A. Russia's emancipation of the serfs in 1861
    B. Austria's emancipation of the Jews in 1867
    C. The Treaty of Tordesillas in 1494
    D. The Glorious Revolution of 1688

52. This passage most clearly reflects which of the following contemporary developments in Europe?

    A. The spread of religious tolerance
    B. The centralizing tendencies of the New Monarchs
    C. The early notions of representative democracy
    D. The ideas about a return to feudalism

53. Based on your knowledge of European history, which of the following Spanish monarchs made similar attempts to alleviate the exploitation of the colonized Indians?

    A. Philip II
    B. Isabella
    C. Ferdinand
    D. Philip V

54. Which of the following 16th-century groups was positioned to lose the most from Charles V's New Laws?

    A. The conquistadores
    B. The royal viceroys
    C. The royal family
    D. The clergy

55. A historian might use the New Laws passage to support which of the following arguments?

    A. Spain was reducing its mercantilist policies in this period.
    B. Spain had a vigorous debate about the humanity and rights of indigenous Indians.
    C. Spain wanted to claim the New World colonies for itself.
    D. Spain's monarchy was strengthening its power in an effort to weaken the nobles.

IF YOU FINISH BEFORE TIME IS CALLED, CHECK YOUR WORK ON THIS SECTION ONLY. DO NOT WORK ON ANY OTHER SECTION IN THE TEST.

This part of the exam contains free-response questions. Four short-answer questions, one document-based question, and one long-essay question. Answer questions within the recommended writing time frames using lined paper and a pen with black ink.

Part B: Short-Answer Questions

3 questions
40 minutes

Reading Time: 10 minutes (brainstorm your thoughts and organize your response)
Writing Time: 30 minutes

Directions: The short-answer questions will not require that you develop and support a thesis statement. Some short-answer questions include texts, images, graphs, or maps. Use complete sentences—bullet points or an outline are unacceptable. Write answers for Questions 1 and 2, and choose EITHER Question 3 or Question 4 (not both) to write an answer. Answer **all** parts of three questions to receive full credit.

> Note: The following short-answer questions are for instructional purposes and may not reflect the time period format of the actual exam.

Question 1: Use both sources below and your knowledge of European history to answer all parts of the question that follows.

Source 1: Malcolm Mafi, "The Decline of Spain," 2015.

The House of Austria ruled Spain from 1516 to 1700. The historical narrative constructed around those two centuries featured a swift rise and equally swift fall of the House of Austria. The fall of the House of Austria, beginning in 1588, and perhaps the oldest accounting, focused on the destruction of the Spanish Armada. By 1621 (or 1643, because some historians point to the Battle of Rocroi when Spain was defeated by France), it was essentially a straight downward fall.

This claim should be contested because the Spanish Armada was not the central reason for Spain's decline. While Spain had its share of humiliations during the reign of Philip III (1598–1621), Spain experienced a tremendous resurgence in the early years of his son, Philip IV's reign. In 1620, Spain had a time of revitalization: the Spanish economy boomed, expenditures diminished, armies won victory after victory in the Palatinate, Holland, and Bohemia. After that period, from 1620 to 1640, Spain experienced several disasters. Portugal and several Italian cities revolted, France defeated Spain on the field of battle, and the Dutch preyed on Spain. Despite the destruction of the Spanish Armada, this should have been a period of opportunity when Spain could have returned to her previous glory days, and perhaps even surpassed them. That the Spaniards failed to take advantage of the revitalization under Philip IV's reign, was due to a combination of bad luck and risky gambits from the Spanish crown.

Source 2: Francis X. Rocca, "The King who Sent the Armada," 1997.

The heretics were not to be stopped, however, Spain never recovered the breakaway provinces of Holland and Zealand, nucleus of the modern Dutch nation. The struggle against them proved a huge and constant drain on the taxpayers of Castile and gobbled up the output of the Peruvian silver mines—one of the major reasons that Philip declared bankruptcy more than once during his reign. Neighboring powers took advantage of the conflict to harm Spain and help the Protestant cause. The French Huguenots and the Lutheran princes of Germany aided the Dutch rebels, and in 1585 England sent 8,000 soldiers to free Antwerp from Spanish occupation. This last action—combined with Sir Francis Drake's raids on Spanish ships and ports in the Old and New Worlds—spurred Philip to send the "Invincible Armada" in 1588. The result was a legendary disaster that led Philip, normally so sure of divine favor, to wonder if God had abandoned him. It remains the biggest single reason that people in the English-speaking world tend to remember him as a failure, the initiator of his country's long, slow decline.

(a) Provide ONE piece of historical evidence (not mentioned in the passage) that would support Mafi's argument.

(b) Provide ONE piece of historical evidence (not mentioned in the passage) that would support Rocca's argument.

(c) Explain how the Spanish Armada's defeat to England led to different interpretations.

Question 2: Use the passage below and your knowledge of European history to answer all parts of the question that follows.

Source: Niccoló Machiavelli, *The Prince*, 1532.

This opportunity, therefore, ought not to be allowed to pass for letting Italy at last see her liberator appear. Nor can one express the love with which he would be received in all those provinces which have suffered so much from these foreign scourings, with what thirst for revenge, with what stubborn faith, with what devotion, with what tears. What door would be closed to him? Who would refuse obedience to him? What envy would hinder him? What Italian would refuse him homage? To all of us this barbarous dominion stinks. Let, therefore, your illustrious house take up this charge with that courage and hope with which all just enterprises are undertaken, so that under its standard our native country may be ennobled, and under its auspices may be verified that saying of Petrarch:

Virtu contro al Furore
Prendera l'arme, e fia il combatter corto:
Che l'antico valore
Negli italici cuor non e ancor morto.

[Virtue against fury shall advance the fight,
And it I' th' combat soon shall put to flight;
For the old Roman, valour is not dead,
Nor in th' Italians' breasts extinguished.]

(a) Briefly identify and describe ONE reason for Machiavelli's declaration in this passage.

(b) Briefly identify and describe ONE result of Machiavelli's declaration in this passage.

(c) Briefly explain how Machiavelli's declaration corresponded with Renaissance political debates during this time frame.

Choose EITHER Question 3 or Question 4:

Question 3: Use the argument below and your knowledge of European history to answer all parts of the question that follows.

Historians have argued that the European exploration of the New World in the 15th and 16th centuries directly led to the Scientific Revolution, an argument sometimes called the *Epistemological Shock*.

(a) Briefly identify and describe ONE example of evidence that supports this argument.
(b) Briefly identify and describe ONE example of evidence that undermines this argument.
(c) Briefly explain why historians have disagreed on this topic.

OR

Question 4: Use the argument below and your knowledge of European history to answer all parts of the question that follows.

Historians have argued that by the early-20th century a general European war appeared inevitable because there were long-term trends such as militarism, alliance systems, and imperialism.

(a) Briefly identify and explain ONE piece of evidence that supports this argument.
(b) Briefly identify and explain ONE piece of evidence that undermines this argument.
(c) Briefly explain why historians have disagreed on this topic.

IF YOU FINISH BEFORE TIME IS CALLED, CHECK YOUR WORK ON THIS
SECTION ONLY. DO NOT WORK ON ANY OTHER SECTION IN THE TEST.

Section II

Part A: Document-Based Question

1 question
60 minutes

Reading Time: 15 minutes (brainstorm your thoughts and organize your response)
Writing Time: 45 minutes

Directions: The document-based question is based on the seven accompanying documents. The documents are for instructional purposes only. Some of the documents have been edited for the purpose of this practice exercise. Write your response on lined paper and include the following:

- **Thesis**. Present a thesis that supports a historically defensible claim, establishes a line of reasoning, and responds to all parts of the question. The thesis must consist of one or more sentences located in one place—either the introduction or the conclusion.
- **Contextualization.** Situate the argument by explaining the broader historical events, developments, or processes that occurred before, during, or after the time frame of the question.
- **Evidence from the documents.** Use the content of at least three to six of the documents to develop and support a cohesive argument that responds to the topic question.
- **Evidence beyond the documents.** Support or qualify your argument by explaining at least one additional piece of specific historical evidence not found in the documents. (Note: The example must be different from the evidence used to earn the point for contextualization.)
- **Analysis.** Use at least three documents to explain the documents' point of view, purpose, historical situation, and/or audience relevant to the topic question.
- **Historical reasoning.** Use historical reasoning to show relationships among the documents, the topic question, and the thesis argument. Use evidence to corroborate, qualify, or modify the argument.

Based on the documents that follow, answer the question below.

Question 1: Evaluate the origins of totalitarianism and its perception among Europeans.

Document 1

> **Source: George Orwell, *1984*, 1949. A political fictional book about living in a world of tyranny ruled by a "Big Brothers" iron fist.**
>
> [The speaker of this quote, O'Brien, is an agent of a totalitarian government. He is addressing Winston Smith, a dissident whom he is torturing.]
>
> Obedience is not enough. Unless he is suffering, how can you be sure that he is obeying your will and not his own? Power is in inflicting pain and humiliation. Power is in tearing human minds to pieces and putting them together again in new shapes of your own choosing. Do you begin to see, then, what kind of world we are creating? A world of fear and treachery is torment, a world which will grow not less but more merciless as it refines itself. Progress in our world will be progress towards more pain. In our world there will be no emotions except fear, rage, triumph, and self-abasement. Everything else we shall destroy: everything. There will be no loyalty, except loyalty towards the Party. There will be no love, except the love of Big Brother. There will be no art, no literature, no science. When we are omnipotent we shall have no more need of science. There will be no distinction between beauty and ugliness. There will be no curiosity, no enjoyment of the process of life. All competing pleasures will be destroyed. But always—do not forget this, Winston—always there will be the intoxication of power, constantly increasing and constantly growing subtler. Always, at every moment, there will be the thrill of victory, the sensation of trampling on an enemy who is helpless. If you want a picture of the future, imagine a boot stamping on a human face—forever.

Document 2

> **Source: Adolf Hitler, "On National Socialism and World Relations," speech delivered in the German Reichstag on January 30, 1937.**
>
> I am speaking of a National Socialist Revolution.
>
> Throughout thousands of years the conviction grew up and prevailed, not so much in the German mind as in the minds of the contemporary world, that bloodshed and the extermination of those hitherto in power—together with the destruction of public and private institutions and property—were essential characteristics of every true revolution. Mankind in general has grown accustomed to accept revolutions with all these consequences somehow or other as if they were legal happenings. I do not mean that people endorse all this tumultuous destruction of life and property; but they certainly accept it as the necessary accompaniment of events which, because of this very reason, are called revolutions.
>
> Herein lies the difference between the National Socialist Revolution and other revolutions, with the exception of the Fascist Revolution in Italy. The National Socialist Revolution was almost entirely a bloodless proceeding. When the party took over power in Germany, after overthrowing the very formidable obstacles that had stood in its way, it did so without causing any damage whatsoever to property. I can say with a certain amount of pride that this was the first revolution in which not even a window-pane was broken.
>
> Don't misunderstand me however. If this revolution was bloodless that was not because we were not manly enough to look at blood.

Document 3

Source: Benito Mussolini, "Fascist Government and Values," 1935.

Fascism sees in the world not only those superficial, material aspects in which man appears as an individual, standing by himself, self-centered, subject to natural law, which instinctively urges him toward a life of selfish momentary pleasure; it sees not only the individual but the nation and the country; individuals and generations bound together by a moral law, with common traditions and a mission which suppressing the instinct for life closed in a brief circle of pleasure, builds up a higher life, founded on duty, a life free from the limitations of time and space, in which the individual, by self-sacrifice, the renunciation of self-interest, by death itself, can achieve that purely spiritual existence in which his value as a man consists.

Life, as conceived of by the Fascist, is serious, austere, and religious; all its manifestations are poised in a world sustained by moral forces and subject to spiritual responsibilities. The Fascist disdains an "easy" life.

The Fascist conception of life is a religious one, in which man is viewed in his immanent relation to a higher law, endowed with an objective will transcending the individual and raising him to conscious membership of a spiritual society. Those who perceive nothing beyond opportunistic considerations in the religious policy of the Fascist regime fail to realize that Fascism is not only a system of government but also and above all a system of thought.

Document 4

Source: Constitution of the Union of Soviet Socialist Republics, Chapter 1: The Organization of the Soviet Society, 1936.

Article 1. The Union of Soviet Socialist Republics is a socialist state of workers and peasants.

Article 2. The Soviets of Working People's Deputies, which grew and attained strength as a result of the overthrow of the landlords and capitalists and the achievement of the dictatorship of the proletariat, constitute the political foundation of the U.S.S.R.

Article 3. In the U.S.S.R. all power belongs to the working people of town and country as represented by the Soviets of Working People's Deputies.

Article 4. The socialist system of economy and the socialist ownership of the means and instruments of production firmly established as a result of the abolition of the capitalist system of economy, the abrogation of private ownership of the means and instruments of production and the abolition of the exploitation of man by man, constitute the economic foundation of the U.S.S.R.

Article 5. Socialist property in the U.S.S.R. exists either in the form of state property (the possession of the whole people), or in the form of cooperative and collective-farm property (property of a collective farm or property of a cooperative association).

Article 6. The land, its natural deposits, waters, forests, mills, factories, mines, rail, water and air transport, banks, post, telegraph and telephones, large state-organized agricultural enterprises (state farms, machine and tractor stations and the like) as well as municipal enterprises and the bulk of the dwelling houses in the cities and industrial localities, are state property, that is, belong to the whole people.
[. . .]

Article 12. In the U.S.S.R. work is a duty and a matter of honor for every able-bodied citizen, in accordance with the principle: "He who does not work, neither shall he eat."

The principle applied in the U.S.S.R. is that of socialism: "From each according to his ability, to each according to his work."

Document 5

Source: Arthur Koestler, *Darkness at Noon*, 1940. Koestler's fictional story was based on his disillusionment with Russia while witnessing the brutality of Stalin's communist reign of terror.

[This passage presents a conversation between Ivanov, a communist official, and Rubashov, an Old Bolshevik who is now imprisoned by the regime he helped to create.]

"For a man with your past," Ivanov went on, "this sudden revulsion against experimenting is rather naive. Every year several million people are killed quite pointlessly by epidemics and other natural catastrophes. And we should shrink from sacrificing a few hundred thousand for the most promising experiment in history? Not to mention the legions of those who die of under-nourishment and tuberculosis in coal and quicksilver; mines, rice-fields and cotton plantations. No one takes any notice of them; nobody asks why or what for; but if here we shoot a few thousand objectively harmful people, the humanitarians all over the world foam at the mouth. Yes, we liquidated the parasitic part of the peasantry and let it die of starvation. It was a surgical operation which had to be done once and for all; but in the good old days before the Revolution just as many died in any dry year—only senselessly and pointlessly.

He paused, Rubashov did not answer. He went on: "Have you ever read brochures of an anti-vivisectionist society? They are shattering and heartbreaking."

Document 6

Source: Hitler addressing the Reichstag, 1939.

Document 7

> **Source: Hannah Arendt, *The Origins of Totalitarianism*, 1951. Examines the use of terror to eliminate civil and political rights while creating isolationism and total domination.**
>
> Only the mob and the elite can be attracted by the momentum of totalitarianism itself; the masses have to be won by propaganda. It was recognized early and has frequently been asserted that in totalitarian countries propaganda and terror present two sides of the same coin. This, however, is only partly true. Wherever totalitarianism possesses absolute control, it replaces propaganda with indoctrination and uses violence not so much to frighten people (this is done only in the initial stages when political opposition still exists) as to realize constantly its ideological doctrines and its practical lies. He who does not work shall not eat. Or when, to take another instance, Stalin decided to rewrite of the Russian Revolution, the propaganda of his new version consisted in destroying, together with the older books and documents, their authors and readers: the publication in 1938 of a new official history of the Communist Party was the signal that the super purge which had decimated a whole generation of Soviet intellectuals had come to an end. Similarly, the Nazis in the Eastern occupied territories at first used chiefly anti-Semitic propaganda to win firmer control of the population. They neither needed nor used terror to support this propaganda. When they liquidated the greater part of the Polish intelligentsia, they did it not because of its opposition, but because according to their doctrine Poles had no intellect, and when they planned to kidnap blue-eyed and blond-haired children, they did not intend to frighten the population but to save "Germanic blood."

Part B: Long-Essay Question

1 question
40 minutes

Directions: Choose ONE question to answer—Question 2, Question 3, or Question 4—and write your response on lined paper.

You must demonstrate your ability to use specific historical evidence and write an effective essay to support your argument. Your essay is considered a first draft and may contain some grammatical errors that will not be counted against you. However, to receive full credit, your essay must demonstrate historically defensible content knowledge and the following:

- **Thesis**. Provides a thesis that is a historically defensible claim, establishes a line of reasoning, and responds to all parts of the question—rather than merely restating or rephrasing the question. The thesis must consist of one or more sentences and must be located in one place—in the introduction or the conclusion.
- **Contextualization.** Describes how the historical context is relevant to the question. Relates the topic to broader historical events, developments, or processes that occurred before, during, or after the time frame. (Note: Must include more than a phrase or reference.)
- **Evidence.** Supports and develops the argument by identifying specific and relevant historical examples of evidence related to the topic of the question.
- **Historical reasoning.** Uses historical reasoning (comparison, causation, or continuity/change over time) to structure the argument that addresses the question.
- **Analysis.** Demonstrates a complex understanding of the historical development that focuses on the question to corroborate, qualify, or modify the argument. (For example, analyze multiple variables, explain similarities/differences, explain cause/effect, explain multiple causes, explain both continuity and change, explain connections across periods of time, corroborate multiple perspectives across themes, or consider alternative views.)

Question 2: Compare the long-term and short-term causes of the Thirty Years' War (1618–1648). (*Reasoning skill: Comparison*).

OR

Question 3: Compare the long-term and short-term causes of the War of Spanish Succession (1701–1715). (*Reasoning skill: Comparison*).

OR

Question 4: Compare the long-term and short-term causes of World War I (1914–1918). (*Reasoning skill: Comparison*).

IF YOU FINISH BEFORE TIME IS CALLED, CHECK YOUR WORK ON THIS SECTION ONLY. DO NOT WORK ON ANY OTHER SECTION IN THE TEST.

Answer Key

Section I – Part A: Multiple-Choice Questions

1. D	12. A	23. B	34. C	45. C
2. C	13. A	24. C	35. C	46. A
3. C	14. A	25. A	36. C	47. D
4. D	15. B	26. A	37. A	48. C
5. A	16. C	27. B	38. A	49. B
6. B	17. A	28. A	39. A	50. B
7. B	18. C	29. D	40. D	51. A
8. C	19. D	30. A	41. A	52. B
9. A	20. D	31. A	42. A	53. B
10. A	21. C	32. B	43. B	54. A
11. D	22. A	33. A	44. D	55. D

Answer Explanations

Section I

Part A: Multiple-Choice Questions

1. **D.** The author's qualification rejects the purely structural explanation, eliminating choice A. Choices B and C are true statements, but they are not relevant to the argument in this passage. The best answer is choice D because that is what the author addresses in the second paragraph.

2. **C.** Choice C is the best answer because it would undermine the author's argument. The author is claiming that the particulars of the July crisis led to war, but if an analogous crisis in 1880 (a roughly comparable time period) failed to provoke war, that would seem to contradict the author's argument. Choices A, B, and D are true statements, and therefore, do not undermine the author's argument.

3. **C.** The author does not mention *class* or *gender* in this passage, therefore, choices A and D are incorrect. The author does mention counterfactual history (choice B), but specifically disregards this as "superficial" under normal circumstances. Rankean history (choice C) fits squarely with the traditional, high-diplomatic history of the Rankean school that is described in the passage. (German historian Leopold von Ranke wrote modern political-scientific history in the 19th century that focused on studying the "spectrum of history" as a force for historical change.)

4. **D.** Choice A is incorrect because the author has a negative attitude about counterfactual history. The author does not seem to believe in the *inexorability* (inevitability) of the war except in the most general terms, so you can eliminate choice B. Choice C is perhaps a bit too extreme, as the passage describes

counterfactual history as facile but not necessarily absurd. Choice D is the correct answer because the author examines all possibilities in which the postwar world could have been different to show just how important the war was in crafting the modern world as we know it today.

5. **A.** This 19th-century poem refers to the Corn Laws (Britain's tariff and price laws that inflated the price of bread and restricted imported grain in order to help domestic producers between 1815 and 1846). The imposed restrictions kept grain prices high. The laws were deeply unpopular among poor and working people, who had to pay exorbitant prices for bread and wheat products. Thus, choice A is correct. The Factory Act of 1833 (choice B) is incorrect because it was a labor bill that regulated the number of hours that young children could work. The Poor Laws (choice C) is incorrect because it was a welfare system for the poor that was passed in medieval Britain in 1587. The Cat and Mouse Act (choice D) is incorrect because it was a law enacted in 1913 to deal with the problem of women (suffragettes) going on hunger strikes. The law helped women get released from prison early to recover and return to good health.

6. **B.** You can eliminate choices A, C, and D because this poem has nothing to do with restoring the Jacobite movement (to restore the Stuart Roman Catholic James VII of Scotland to the throne), the Suffragist movement (women's movement), or the Abolitionist movement (to end slavery). The Chartist movement (choice B) was an attempt to build an independent political party which demanded an end to the Corn Laws among the working class. Choice B is the only possible answer.

7. **B.** You can eliminate choices A and C because communism and Keynesianism (an economic theory developed in the 1930s to increase government spending and lower taxes) did not exist in 1830. Choice D, classical economics (liberal economics such as Smithian), in this era promoted free trade with minimal government interference. Britain adopted classical economics after the Corn Laws were repealed. Mercantilism (choice B) was the economic system that was in vogue in the early-19th century, as wealthy landowners and aristocrats still held dominant sway in Parliament.

8. **C.** Choices A and B are incorrect because the peasants and the bourgeoisie (working class) were the very people most hurt by the Corn Laws. The clergy (choice D) were not prime beneficiaries of the laws. The landowners who produced wheat and bread benefited most, choice C.

9. **A.** The Penal Laws required Catholics to forgo allegiance to the papacy and instead submit to the civil and religious rule of the English monarch, Elizabeth I. The Church of England was the secular and religious authority in 1558. Choice A is correct.

10. **A.** The suppression of the Jesuits occurred in Catholic countries such as France, Spain, and Portugal. The Jesuits had fled from England by 1558, so choice B is incorrect. The War of the Roses and the Glorious Revolution took place more than a century from this date of 1558, so you can eliminate choices C and D. The best answer is choice A because the Gunpowder Plot (a plot to kill King James I of England in 1605) was sparked from the Catholic disappointment with James I (Mary Queen of Scots' son) and his failure to curb his mother's anti-Catholic laws.

11. **D.** Choice C may be an attractive choice because it deals with Ireland specifically, but the Home Rule Act was not passed until the 20th century. The Act of Union (choice A) brought Ireland under official English domination. The Navigation Acts (choice B) refer to an economic mercantilist measure passed over a century later. The best choice is choice D because the Catholic Emancipation Act of 1829 provided a blanket ban of anti-Catholic legislation.

12. **A.** The facial features of the "devil" in this image clearly portray communist Leon Trotsky (choice A), who led the Bolshevik Party (along with Vladimir Lenin) and engineered the Russian Revolution in 1917 during World War I. The red "devil" image symbolized the Bolsheviks, known as the "Reds."

13. **A.** The Trotsky "red devil" in this image serves as the color of the Evil One himself and the political color associated with communism. Thus, you can eliminate choice B because it was the Whites (monarchists and other anti-Bolsheviks) who illustrated this cartoon. This image is not relevant to the First World War (choice C) or to Stalin's purges (choice D), which began after Trotsky had been exiled from the USSR, but rather the mass murder of anti-Bolsheviks, choice A.

14. **A.** While the Whites hated anarchists as much as communists, because of the assassinations of Tsar Alexander II, Peter Stolypin, and others by anarchists, there is no anarchist connection in this image (choice B). Choice C is incorrect because Stalin is not referenced here explicitly or implicitly. Eliminate choice D because the Whites created this propaganda cartoon. Choice A is the best answer based on a close analysis of the Asiatic-looking soldiers working for the devilish Trotsky. Communists were consistently portrayed as the *other* (not only in political terms, but also in racial characterizations).

15. **B.** The Nazis exploited the Bolshevik tendency for mass murder in their propaganda; therefore, choice A may seem like a good choice. However, choice B is the correct answer because of the heavy-handed anti-Semitic imagery here, with the Star of David around Trotsky's neck.

16. **C.** With its nightmarish, terrifying imagery, this illustration demonstrates the brutality of the First World War (choice A). Notice the horrifying depiction of soldiers using gas masks to protect against exposure to poison gas (choice B), and the dehumanization of soldiers advancing as inhuman monsters (choice D). The illustration does not portray civilians, which makes choice C the correct answer.

17. **A.** The soldiers' protective equipment and apparent readiness to throw a grenade alludes to their expertise and discipline, choice B, but that is not clear in this image. Units of specially-trained German soldiers were known as "storm troops, shock troops, or assault troops" but the bravery of the soldiers is not depicted, choice C. The illustration portrays very little of the political nature of World War I, eliminating choice D. The monstrosity of the image makes choice A the best answer.

18. **C.** Dix's illustration is clearly anti-war propaganda, so he would have most likely supported treaties or pacts that ended or prevented wars such as the Brest-Litovsk Treaty (choice A), the Kellogg-Briand Pact (choice B), and the Locarno Pact (choice D). Choice C is correct. Dix would have likely opposed an action that would lead to further war, such as the remilitarization of Germany.

19. **D.** The date of the illustration (1924) and its portrayal of poison gas warfare should make it clear that this portrays World War I, choice D.

20. **D.** The visual images of this illustration clearly identify it as modernist anti-war art, which might have infuriated Hitler. Hitler believed the war experience to be overwhelmingly positive for Germany. Hitler viewed modern art as "degenerate art," choice D. He even created a museum to display this type of art.

21. **C.** This timeline covers 1478 to 1700. The New World was conquered in the 1490s and 1500s (choice A), the Thirty Years' War took place from 1618 to 1648 (choice B), and the Spanish Armada failed in 1588 (choice D). However, the French Revolution began in 1789, which is after this timeline. Therefore, choice C is the correct answer.

22. **A.** The War of the Spanish Succession emerged because Charles II was physically and mentally disabled, which made him an ineffectual leader of Spain and made him incapable of having children. Choice A is correct.

23. **B.** While Spain certainly boasted of skilled rulers in its past, Charles II was not one of them, eliminating choice A. Royal marriages had strengthened Spain's diplomatic position, helping to grant Spain a massive world empire from Charles V forward, but the royal family timeline shown here does

not establish that, eliminating choice C. Choice D is also incorrect, especially in regards to the tail end of the Habsburg reign in Spain. Charles II epitomized how years of endogamy (marrying within a specific social or ethnic group) and inbreeding had disastrous results for the Spanish monarchy. Therefore, choice B is correct.

24. **C.** The Trastamara family's rule ended in Spain in the early-16th century (choice A). Choice B is incorrect because the Bourbons came to power in Spain after the War of the Spanish Succession, a result of the French intervention. The Romanovs (choice D) ruled Russia, not Spain. The Habsburgs (choice C) is correct. Remember that the Habsburgs, the House of Austria, married into the Spanish royal family and ruled from 1516 to 1700.

25. **A.** The death of Charles II without heirs set off the War of the Spanish Succession (choice A), named for its *casus belli* (the cause of the war).

26. **A.** Choice B is incorrect because George V of Britain had sons, but the question was which one would be the next king. Choice C is incorrect because while Wilhelm II may have been unpredictable and neurotic, he was not as severely handicapped as was Charles II of Spain. Choice D references the Pragmatic Sanction, but this had nothing to do with the topic here because Charles II had no daughters. Choice A is correct; the Romanovs suffered from hemophilia due to family inbreeding with the other royal families of Europe.

27. **B.** There is a reason that this passage was written in 1915 and not 1905 or 1895. Freud was directly responding to the horrors of World War I, specifically the inhumanity of man in war, choice B.

28. **A.** Choice B is incorrect because Freud is unconcerned with the economics of the war in this passage. Choice C is an attractive distractor; Freud did specialize in psychiatry and treating the mentally ill, but his essay's focus was on attitudes toward death, and his death drive theory. Choice D focuses on the destruction of property, but Freud is focused on the destruction of human lives, not cities. Choice A is correct.

29. **D.** All four answer choices reference actual postwar developments, but choice D is the only answer choice that is not suggested in the passage. Unlike Freud's earlier works, this passage focuses on the death drive and not on sexual urges.

30. **A.** While Picasso's *Guernica* (choice B) does show the brutality of war, it is not linked to the First World War. Magritte's *The Treachery of Images* (choice C) is a modernist portrait; it has more to do with questioning artistic standards than with war or destruction. *The Great Gatsby* (choice D) does embody the disillusionment of the Lost Generation of which Fitzgerald was a part, but it is only tangentially connected to World War I. Choice A is correct; Remarque's *All Quiet on the Western Front* encapsulates Europeans' horror of brutality and mass deaths resulting from war.

31. **A.** While Freud wrote extensively elsewhere on the unconscious (choice B), the irrational (choice C), and the id (choice D), this passage deals with the death drive, choice A.

32. **B.** Simone de Beauvoir's writings led to Second Wave Feminism (1960s to 1980s), choice B. Second Wave Feminism included women of color, but the civil rights movement (choice C) was a separate movement of the 1960s. The anti-nuclear movement (choice A) is not mentioned anywhere in the passage. First Wave Feminism was in the 19th and early-20th centuries, and led to women's suffrage (choice D). The women's suffrage movement gained momentum in the 19th century when women campaigned for the right to vote; however, that is not the point of the passage.

33. **A.** While de Beauvoir had her own radical ideas about politics, she was not primarily speaking to socialists, so you can eliminate choice C. Choices B and D would be unlikely audiences for her message. Educated women (choice A) would have been the most receptive to de Beauvoir's argument.

34. **C.** Second Wave Feminism focused on economic rights (choice A) and began to include lesbians in their movement (choice B), but these attitudes are not connected to the main ideas of this passage. The desire to view gender as interconnected with race and class (choice D) is associated with the later Third Wave Feminism, not the Second Wave. Therefore, choice C is correct. The author's 20th-century views are reflected in the passage when she writes that "one is not born," but learns to become a woman because of culturally constructed norms and expectations.

35. **C.** The author does not believe women are superior to men, eliminating choice A. Choices B and D are technically true, but they are not the author's primary focus here. Instead, choice C best sums up the author's main idea in the passage: One may be born an anatomical female, but being a woman must be taught.

36. **C.** The Edict of Nantes was revoked in 1685 by Louis XIV (choice C). It is easy to confuse Louis XIV, the Sun King and greatest French monarch, with the less illustrious Louis XVI, who oversaw the collapse of the Old Regime in France.

37. **A.** The Edict of Nantes sanctioned religious tolerance and was opposed by rigid Catholic nations. England (choice B) and Holland (choice C) were Protestant during this time period. Although Portugal (choice D) was a Catholic state, it was not particularly secular and had little influence in France. In contrast, Spain (choice A) was deeply entrenched in French politics in the 1590s.

38. **A.** Choice A is correct; the Edict of Nantes protected religious tolerance. Protestants did not have complete equality with Catholics, but they were no longer persecuted by the government. Choice B is incorrect because many Christian churches, such as the Anabaptists, remained banned and did not receive protection from the Edict.

39. **A.** Choice D may seem like an attractive option since the Peace of Westphalia did accept the religious division in Germany, but it is not the best choice. The Peace of Augsburg (choice A) cemented religious toleration, whereas the Peace of Westphalia focused on the European nation-state (rather than churches) as the center of international politics and established a European balance of power. The Treaty of Versailles of 1918 (choice B) was not about religious toleration. The treaty was formed after World War I and changed territories within Europe. It caused resentment among Germans because they were punished for starting the war. The Treaty of Utrecht in 1713 (choice C) reorganized the powers in Europe after Spain's surrender in the War of the Spanish Succession. France became the dominant power in Europe.

40. **D.** Choice A was spoken by a French politician, Talleyrand, about the Bourbons after the French Revolution. Choice B is also connected to the French Revolution, as it was allegedly spoken by Queen Marie Antoinette. Choice C was spoken by Louis XIV. Choice D is correct because Henry IV allegedly said "Paris is worth a Mass" in cynical recognition of the necessity of converting to Catholicism in order to take the French throne.

41. **A.** Article 11 in the decrees justifies choice A as the correct answer because it establishes meritocracy (a political philosophy stating that power should be measured based on talent and ability) in offices throughout France. Gender equality (choice B) was not part of the French Revolution movement. While the French Revolution eventually saw nationalization of church lands (choice C) and the introduction of constitutional monarchy (choice D), these were introduced much later.

42. **A.** The bourgeoisie (working class) and the peasantry made large gains from these laws after the French Revolution; therefore, choices B and C are incorrect. The military (choice D) had to tolerate many changes, such as meritocratic promotions among officers, but they had far less to lose than the aristocracy. The aristocracy (choice A) stood to lose the privileges of the social upper class.

43. **B.** The Reign of Terror, the Thermidor Reaction, and the 100 Days were all events dated much later than 1789, eliminating choices A, C, and D. It stands to reason that the Great Fear, which gripped the French countryside and cities that same year because peasants attacked nobles, had the strongest connection to this passage, choice B.

44. **D.** Choice D is correct. Suffrage, or voting, is not mentioned anywhere in the passage.

45. **C.** The sans-culottes (choice A) were working-class radicals who did not collaborate to write these decrees. While most of the clergy opposed the Revolution (choice B), it is not accurate to say that they were universally opposed to the French Revolution. These decrees reflected Enlightenment beliefs, so choice D is also incorrect. Choice C is correct; the articles in the passage support the bourgeoisie interests at the expense of the aristocracy.

46. **A.** Choice A is correct; this passage makes an argument that France could retain its strength and independence even in a divided world of the Cold War.

47. **D.** De Gaulle sought to use Europe as a counterweight to the two superpowers, as evidenced by his support for the Treaty of Rome (choice A). De Gaulle also wanted to maintain French power (choice B) and its colonies (choice C). Choice D is correct; a unified and resurgent Germany seemed a very distant threat in the 1960s.

48. **C.** The desire to maintain France's great power status led to its conflicting colonial actions in Algeria (choice A), Indochina (choice B), and the Suez Canal Crisis (choice D). Choice C is correct; the May 1968 protests were socially inspired protests about internal French issues, and were not inspired for the same reasons as mentioned in the passage.

49. **B.** Britain had the most to fear by the spirit of the message in the passage because of the author's comments about the Treaty of Rome, choice B. De Gaulle expressed an interest in bringing Britain fully into economic cooperation with Europe, which Britain had long opposed.

50. **B.** The Treaty of Rome established the European Union, choice B.

51. **A.** This passage details the liberation of Indian slave labor and the ratification of new labor systems in Spanish America, "The Good Treatment and Preservation of the Indians." Russia's emancipation of the serfs in the 19th century is similar to the events described in the passage, choice A. Choice B is an attractive choice because the Jews were emancipated in 1867, but they were liberated from political repression, not from slavery or forced servitude. The Treaty of Tordesillas (choice C) divided newly discovered lands between Spain and Portugal. The Glorious Revolution (choice D) was when King James II of England was overthrown.

52. **B.** This passage represents the boasting of power over nobles and colonists by the Spanish monarchy, choice B. The New Laws replaced the feudalistic labor system that had come before the New Laws enactment. Although these reform laws were only partially successful, they helped to free thousands of indigenous Indian workers.

53. **B.** Philip II of Spain did little to improve the status of Indians in the Spanish colonies beyond what had already been in place, eliminating choice A. Choice D is incorrect because Philip V actually sought to further exploit Indian labor to advance the monarchy. Of the Catholic monarchs, Isabella (choice B) and Ferdinand (choice C), only Isabella campaigned for fair and humane treatment of the Indians of the New World. Therefore, choice B is correct.

54. **A.** Spain's royal family (choice C), servants, clergy (choice D), and viceroys (choice B) were greatly strengthened by the New Laws. However, the conquistadores (choice A), who had conquered the

colonies and created an *encomienda* (grant) labor system based on Indian labor, were greatly concerned about the New Laws of 1542. According to the new reform laws, if indigenous Indians worked, they should be paid wages. Choice A is correct.

55. **D.** This passage has little to do with mercantile policies (choice A) or foreign relations (choice C). These laws were the first example of humanitarian laws in the New World, but they were not analyzed by historians for intellectual debates about humanity (choice B). The reform laws were called for by Charles V after complaints about exploiting indigenous people of the Americas. The New Laws were enacted as a political move by Charles V to limit the power of landowners and nobles. Choice D is correct.

Part B: Short-Answer Questions

Question 1

(3 points possible)

Based on the two sources provided, you must identify and describe the TWO differing reasons for Spain's decline, and ONE explanation why there are different historical interpretations of Spain's decline. To receive full credit, your response might include some of the following.

Possible evidence of Spain's decline for reasons other than the destruction of the Spanish Armada:

- Spain was still the most powerful nation in Europe despite the Armada's defeat in 1588.
- Spain had internal political rebellions and an ineffective king.
- Spain made poor investments from its overseas treasures.
- Spain relied on a steady income from silver and spice imports.
- Spain lacked astute economists to plan long-term goals.
- Spain had a false sense of a robust economy.
- Spain's infrastructure was weakened over time and not restored.
- Spain's continuous religious wars depleted its resources.

Possible evidence that Spain's decline was due to the destruction of the Spanish Armada:

- The Armada was once an invincible fleet, but it began to show wear, like Spain.
- Philip II of Spain underestimated Britain's Queen Elizabeth I.
- The Armada was one of Spain's greatest achievements and showed its great strength.
- Spain's national and political spirit was broken by the defeat.
- The defeat caused Philip II to make political and economic mistakes.
- Spain's military leaders and soldiers were faltering from previous wars.

Question 1 Sample Response

Mafi's argument, Source 1, addresses alternative causes of the 17th-century decline of the most powerful empire in the world—Spain. Many historians have differing views about the Spanish Armada as the cause of Spain's decline. For example, Rocca, in Source 2, shows the importance of the defeat of this great armada and the crushing blow it sent to the pride and power of Spain. The Spanish Armada was known to be an invincible fleet with 130 powerful ships. The Armada's crushing defeat by the British started a downward spiral in Spain's power: economically, politically, and spiritually. Spain was brought to its knees.

However, according to Source 1, there were many other factors that led to Spain's decline in power and this explains why there are different historical viewpoints. Spain had suffered through other defeats, like the Battle of Rocroi with France, which caused their resources to be depleted. Although Spain had accumulated great wealth from the Americas, they did not have effective rulers or economists to invest and develop a varied infrastructure. By the 17th century, Philip IV had overstretched Spain's finances and manpower to fight several religious wars (e.g., the Thirty Years' War), and because of his dogmatic faith, he continued to spend money on wars without replenishing the economy. Spain's enormous wealth of gold and silver from its overseas imperialistic explorations was poorly managed. Hence, Spain's decline was not only due to the Armada's defeat, but also due to a lack of internal business logic to rebuild and reinvest, huge loans, political oversights, and growing internal difficulties.

Question 2

(3 points possible)

In this question, you must identify and describe ONE reason and ONE result of Machiavelli's declaration expressed in the passage. To receive full credit, your response must also explain how Machiavelli's declaration was relevant to political debates during this period.

Possible reasons for Machiavelli's exhortation:

- The Habsburg-Valois Wars
- The Italian Wars
- The Sacking of Rome
- The Italian Renaissance
- To give advice about the best methods to maintain power
- Machiavelli wanted to impress Lorenzo dé Medici
- Machiavelli wanted to regain political power with the Medici family
- The role of the pope and the Papal States

Possible results of Machiavelli's exhortation:

- Italian realpolitik in balancing Spain and France off of one another
- Rebellions against foreign rule, such as Sardinia in 1640
- Italian nationalism in the later centuries
- Eventual unity of Italy in the 1800s
- Don't trust anyone

Question 2 Sample Response

This passage by Niccoló Machiavelli shows that the longing for Italian unification went back over 300 years before it was realized in the 19th century. Machiavelli calls for the expulsion of the French and Spanish barbarians and the restoration of a greater Italian hero. This was a political debate during this time frame that led to Italian revolts to expel France and Spain. One reason of this exhortation was the Sacking of Rome in 1527. In that year, the eternal city was ransacked and degraded by the forces of Holy Roman Emperor Charles V, who had been at war with the papacy. Charles' multinational army epitomized Machiavelli's "barbarians." On the other hand, the exhortation resulted in numerous Italian rebellions against foreign domination, most notably against the Spanish. For example, in 1647, a year when a series of disasters had nearly brought Spain to its knees, the Sardinians and the Neapolitans rose up in military rebellion against Spanish rule. They were momentarily victorious and it took nearly two years to put these rebellions down.

Question 3

(3 points possible)

In this question, you must identify and describe ONE piece of evidence that supports the argument of Epistemological Shock and ONE piece of evidence that undermines the argument of Epistemological Shock expressed in the passage. Your response must also explain why historians have different interpretations about Epistemological Shock. To receive full credit, your response might include some of the following.

Possible evidence to support the contention:

- The Scientific Revolution's obsession with cataloging and understanding everything
- European fascination with new flora and fauna from the New World colonies
- The Enlightenment's obsessive empiricism

Possible evidence to undermine the contention:

- Scientific discoveries in the Renaissance period
- Scientific developments before 1492
- Medieval dissidents who supported scientific inquiry
- The time gap between 1492 and the Scientific Revolution

Question 3 Sample Response

Many historians have seen the European exploration of the Americas as the First Wave of Imperialism an Epistemological Shock. The idea is that Europeans were so stunned to see their Aristotelian view of the natural world upended that they turned to what would become the Scientific Revolution. One piece of evidence that would undermine this argument is the scientific developments during the Renaissance and even the late Medieval Period. For example, Nicholas Copernicus wrote his most influential works while virtually nothing of the New World was known to Europeans. More evidence to support the claim is illustrated by Europeans showing an impressive zeal for New World items such as tobacco, tomatoes, and potatoes. The Scientific Revolution demonstrated an obsessive zeal for cataloging and understanding every piece of information about the natural world, a passion that was later continued by the great thinkers of the Enlightenment.

The reason that historians have disagreed on this topic over the years is that some historians have pointed to the negative consequences that Europe suffered as a result of the discovery of the New World (i.e., wars, imperialism, slavery). Other historians have pointed to the important contributions of philosophers and scientists who brought modernization to Europe.

Question 4

(3 points possible)

In this question, you must identify and describe ONE piece of evidence that supports the argument that World War I was inevitable, and ONE piece of evidence that undermines the argument that World War I was inevitable. Your response must also explain why historians have disagreed on this topic. To receive full credit, your response might include some of the following.

Possible evidence to support the contention:

- The prevalence of militarism throughout Europe
- A new focus on nationalism throughout European countries
- Imperialism's increasing the number of diplomatic crises after 1880
- The role of modern technology such as the telegraph, railroads, and artillery
- The rigid alliance systems such as the Franco-Russian Alliance and the Triple Alliance

Possible evidence to undermine the contention:

- The importance of the July Crisis
- The prevalence of brinkmanship before 1914
- The many war scares of 1898–1914
- The importance of the assassination of Franz Ferdinand
- The role of the Schlieffen Plan
- The surprise of European leaders and the public at the outbreak of war in 1914

Question 4 Sample Response

There are many historians who believe that World War I was an inevitable war. Most famously, Sidney Bradshaw Fay points to for the importance of militarism, alliance system, imperialism, and nationalism. At first glance, it seems clear that this argument would be supported by the role of imperialism in increasing diplomatic crises several times over after 1880. Consider the views of Fashoda, Dogger Bank, Agadir, Liman von Sands, etc. The role of modern technology such as the telegraph, railroads, artillery, and poison gas has been referenced by historians such as A. J. P. Taylor. However, this long-term, structuralist thesis fails to account for one simple question, "Why did war break out in the July Crisis of 1914, and not in all of the other crises that preceded it?" That question can only be answered by showing the specifics of the July Crisis, including the requirements of the Schlieffen Plan and the carte blanche extended to Vienna by Berlin.

What has caused the debate is the paradox of the outbreak of war in July 1914. On one hand, European societies had fears of a general war, going back as far as the 1880s. On the other hand, the specific conflict over the assassination of the Archduke Franz Ferdinand and the resulting Austro-Hungarian ultimatum to Serbia seemed to come as a startling surprise to most Europeans. To this day, the origins of World War I are still a controversial issue.

Section II

Part A: Document-Based Question

DBQ Scoring Guide

To achieve the maximum score of 7, your response must address the scoring criteria components in the table below.

Scoring Criteria for a Good DBQ Essay	
Question 1: Evaluate the origins of totalitarianism and its perception among Europeans.	
Scoring Criteria	**Examples**
A. THESIS/CLAIM	
(1 point) Presents a historically defensible thesis that establishes a line of reasoning. (Note: The thesis must make a claim that responds to *all* parts of the question and must *not* just restate the question. The thesis must consist of *at least* one sentence, either in the introduction or the conclusion.)	The response provides a well-developed thesis and responds with a historically defensible argument. The sample response provides a line of reasoning that characterizes totalitarianism as a political ideology and develops a clear description of the causes of totalitarianism, contradictory perspectives, and examples.
B. CONTEXTUALIZATION	
(1 point) Explains the broader historical context of events, developments, or processes that occurred before, during, or after the time frame of the question. (Note: Must be more than a phrase or reference.)	A good response should always discuss the historical context relevant to the question prompt—the big picture. For example, the origins of totalitarianism in the context of World War I and the interwar period. The development of totalitarianism (and fascism) were not an accident in timing or in scope. It arose out of the carnage of World War I and it took root most strongly with the losing nations of the post–World War I settlement based on the punishment outlined in the Treaty of Versailles (1919).
C. EVIDENCE	
<u>**Evidence from the Documents**</u> **(2 points)** Uses at least six documents to support the argument in response to the prompt. OR **(1 point)** Uses the content of at least three documents to address the topic prompt. (Note: Examples must describe, rather than simply quote, the content of the documents.)	To earn 2 points, the essay response on this topic should reasonably be able to provide evidence from six or seven documents to support the main thesis. Make sure your evidence is valid and relevant to totalitarianism, and when possible, group your documents into themes and categories. For example, supporting references might include Documents 1 and 5 as cultural or literary representations of totalitarian governance in action and Documents 2, 3, and 4 as examples of totalitarian nations.

Continued

Scoring Criteria	Examples
C. EVIDENCE	
Evidence Beyond the Documents **(1 point)** Uses at least one additional piece of specific historical evidence beyond those found in the documents that is relevant to the argument. OR (Note: Evidence must be different from the evidence used in contextualization.)	Essays earning an acceptable response show an understanding of European history and evidence not included in the documents. In your conclusion, show at least one piece of outside evidence. For example, you may want to include the historical differences between totalitarian states across periods of time (for example, the far-left Soviet Union and the far-right German Third Reich) while finding a common thread that unites them.
D. ANALYSIS AND REASONING	
(1 point) Uses at least *three* documents to explain how each document's point of view, purpose, historical situation, and/or audience is relevant to the argument. (Note: References must explain how or why, rather than simply identifying.)	Cite at least three documents with the document's point of view, purpose, historical situation, and/or audience. Your references might include Document 7 (supporting the unifying theory of totalitarianism) and Documents 2, 3, and 4 (foundational documents for Nazi Germany, fascist Italy, and the communist Soviet Union). Other examples may include the cultural representation of totalitarianism (Arendt, Orwell, and Koestler), and the others that demonstrated how the regimes saw themselves.
(1 point) Uses historical reasoning and development that focuses on the question while using evidence to corroborate, qualify, or modify the argument. (Examples: Explain what is similar and different; explain the cause and effect; explain multiple causes; explain connections within and across periods of time; corroborate multiple perspectives across themes; or consider alternative views.)	The essay focuses on the historical skill of *causation* to corroborate the argument. When developing your essay on this topic, be sure to support your thesis by explaining what caused totalitarianism. Also, you may want to include different perspectives of totalitarian regimes. For example, the differences between totalitarianism and other political ideologies such as fascism (fascism was based on nationalism and racial superiority).

Sample Response

After the calamities of the First World War, a new political movement arose in Europe. The violence and brutality of the Western front had undermined the confidence of European nations in the last thousand years of Western culture and civilization, especially the political and social assumptions of the Enlightenment. What came forth from the carnage of the war was an ugly new reality, an ideology that went by many names but was called totalitarianism by twentieth-century political philosopher Hannah Arendt in Document 7. While it took many guises of right and left political views (and in various countries), totalitarianism was a quintessentially modern experience united by its insistence that every person and all of their wishes and efforts be subordinated to the state. Documents 2, 3, and 4 illustrate the state-controlled governments of Germany, Italy, and Russia.

Arendt illustrates this point and Orwell goes further to call attention to the inhumaneness of totalitarianism (Documents 1 and 7). Arendt points to the fact that totalitarianism was a modernizing ideology that focused on bringing (or forcing) all people into the arms of the state. First, through violence, terror, and propaganda and later through indoctrination and censorship. The overarching historical point here is that totalitarianism was never seen by its most prominent supporters as a temporary measure or necessary evil, which Hitler, Mussolini, or Stalin might have said early in their rule (Documents 2, 3, 4, 6). No, totalitarianism was meant to be a permanent fixture in countries where mobilization, militarization, and service to the state were perpetual and meant to foster and create a new class of society.

Documents 2 through 6 demonstrate totalitarianism in its dominance. Hitler's speech (Document 2) demonstrates the belief in a Nazism that will subordinate the wills and abilities of all Germans to the cause of a greater, more glorious Third Reich. This was a different type of revolution from Hitler's point of view. Mussolini's article (Document 3) exemplifies the belief that fascism in Italy was a form of totalitarian governance that had to be pursued with a religious type of zeal and ardor. Mussolini's ruminations also show the totalitarian hatred for the scientific rationalism, pluralism, and liberalism of the 19th century. The Soviet Constitution (Document 4) shows that all workers and peasants of the Soviet Union were in theory the owners and stakeholders. In reality, they were subjects and pawns of the Soviet state and the Communist Party of the Soviet Union. The communal ownership of land and the subordination of civilian economic interests to those of the military and the nation's defense highlight the totality of Soviet totalitarianism: the state is everything and nothing is outside of it.

Documents 1 and 5 are fictional literary works that show cultural portrayals of totalitarianism. In both cases, we see that totalitarianism is shown to be a dystopian, deceptive ideology that destroys the humanity of its followers and opponents. Both documents show the horror of educated Europeans who were immune to the lure of totalitarianism and viewed it as horrific and brutal. Essentially, it is a reign of the club and the jackboot. On the other hand, there are also key differences between the two texts. Both the Orwell passage (Document 1) and the Koestler passage (Document 5) portray totalitarianism in a dismally negative light, but they also have important historical distinctions that set each other apart. Koestler's Ivanov character seems to think that totalitarian leadership is actually beneficial to the human race, and the millions of corpses that come with it are a necessary price to pay for human progress; Orwell's O'Brien character is blatant in his distrust and cynical confession that totalitarian rule is not really for a better future, but is simply about holding power for power's sake.

Thanks to the sacrifices made by many during World War II (and the later collapse of the Soviet Union in 1991), today the fear of global totalitarianism is a distant memory for most of the western world's citizens. Despite this fact, a new, less Orwellian and more Aldous Huxley-inspired form of mass control threatens our nation today. Not one of censorship and mass terror, but of voluntary apathy and withdrawal from politics. Hopefully, citizens can avert a new form of totalitarianism from gaining ground in the world and becoming increasingly consumed by cynicism and intellectual laziness.

Part B: Long-Essay Question

Long-Essay Scoring Guide

Each point is earned independently. (For example, you can earn a point for developing a historically defensible thesis and earn a point for providing evidence.) To achieve the maximum score of 6, your response to ONE topic must address the scoring criteria components in the table below.

Note: The directions asked you choose one of the three LEQ topic options. The sample essay below is written for LEQ Question 4, but you can use some of the suggested ideas presented in the table below, "Scoring Criteria for a Good Essay," to formulate a written response for Question 2 or Question 3.

Scoring Criteria for a Good Essay	
Question 4: Compare the long-term and short-term causes of World War I (1914–1918).	
Scoring Criteria	**Examples**
A. THESIS/CLAIM	
(1 point) Presents a historically defensible thesis that establishes a line of reasoning. (Note: The thesis must make a claim that responds to *all* parts of the question and must *not* just restate the question. The thesis must consist of *at least* one sentence, either in the introduction or the conclusion.)	Whichever of these essay topics you choose to write on, many long-term and short-term causes are at stake. A good essay will provide a persuasive thesis that can be defended by historical facts and recognizes multiple long-term and short-term causes. Certainly World War I would be a more difficult question to answer, with much more to write about. For example, secret alliances, colonial conflicts, and nationalism.
B. CONTEXTUALIZATION	
(1 point) Describes the broader historical context of events, developments, or processes that occurred before, during, or after the time frame of the question. (Note: Must be more than a phrase or reference).	A good essay looks at the context of the big picture. To further support your claim, you might describe the broader impacts of World War I that have been arrived at by historians. For example, Marxist historians such as Arno J. Mayer have seen World War I much as the Soviet Union's Vladimir and Lenin did: an imperialist war between various capitalist powers letting loose their wanton aggression on the world. Other historians in the diplomatic school, such as Sidney Bradshaw Fay, have seen the war as a culmination of long-term political and diplomatic processes. Others, such as A. J. P. Taylor, have seen it more as a conflict spurred by technological advances, a theme picked up by postmodernists such as Stephen Kern.

C. EVIDENCE	
(2 points) Supports the argument in response to the prompt using specific and relevant examples of evidence. OR **(1 point)** Provides specific examples of evidence relevant to the topic of the question. (Note: To earn 2 points, the evidence must *support* your argument.)	To earn the highest point value in this category, your essay must not only provide multiple examples, but the examples must support the argument. A good essay will provide specific historical examples between long- and short-term causes of World War I. This evidence should be linked to the thesis statement and explain its relevance to the topic. For example, in a World War I essay, Sidney Bradshaw Fay's classic nationalism/imperialism/militarism/alliance systems argument would fit perfectly to link to the long-term causes of the war. When it comes to short-term causes, the July Crisis provides an enormous amount of material on which to write. From recent crises to carte blanches and ultimatums, there is much evidence to write about on this subject.
D. ANALYSIS AND REASONING	
(2 points) Demonstrates a complex understanding of historical development that addresses the question and uses evidence to corroborate, qualify, or modify the argument. (Examples: Explain what is similar and different; explain the cause and effect; explain multiple causes; explain connections across periods of time; corroborate multiple perspectives across themes; qualify or modify the argument by considering alternative views.) OR **(1 point)** Uses historical reasoning (comparison, causation, or continuity/change over time) to frame and develop the argument while focusing on the question. (Note: Must be more than a phrase or reference.)	A good essay on this topic must show more than the reasoning skills of comparison and causation. The essay must connect the reasoning skill(s) to develop the argument by corroborating the argument using the following examples: 1) compare and contrast long- and short-term causes of the war, 2) explain the significant differences in the causes of the war, 3) explain the patterns of change between short- and long-term causes, and 4) provide the historical context for what was happening during that particular time that may have led to the causes. For example, a response on World War I would provide multiple perspectives much in the way of short-term reasons for the causes of the war. The response should provide a great deal of specific reasons for the causes of war to dive into, such as nationalism and secret alliances.

Sample Response for Question 4

What were the causes of World War I? There were both long-term causes and short-term causes. The long-term causes were countries having alliances with other countries, many new technologies invented, countries wanting to look strong and tough, and expansive colonies, which led to a greater chance of war. By looking at the long-term causes, we might be tempted to think that World War I was inevitable, but the short-term causes explain why it was unpredictable. For example, the time tables forced countries to mobilize and didn't allow them any other choice. Also, countries threatening other countries to get something out of it without going into war.

From a historical context, there were four major long-term causes of the First World War: militarism, alliances, imperialism, and nationalism. This meant that these four reasons provided evidence why World War I happened in the long run. First, militarism made it more likely that conflict would turn into war because countries were ready for war. Countries developed new technologies like machine guns and poison gas, and wanted to appear powerful. Second, many countries had secret alliances, so if there was a small war between two countries, larger countries would back them up and a small regional conflict would lead to a massive world war. Germany, Austria-Hungary, and Italy had a secret pact called the Triple Alliance. These alliances were like a chain reaction, which was why the historian Sidney Bradshaw Fay thought that World War I was caused by several responsible countries, not just one country. European leaders had not intended to launch a big war against each other. There were also bigger chances of war because countries had colonies and if the colonies declared war then the country would back them up, which would have led to a larger fight. The fourth long-term cause was nationalism. Nationalism meant that there was more hatred between the countries because each country felt superior.

In War by Timetable, British historian A. J. P. Taylor talked about a short-term cause of World War I. He said that the "time-table took command," which meant countries slid into war because of the mobilization timetables. This means that nations were forced to mobilize and didn't have a choice. It was like a snowball effect: when there is a war between two nations the alliance systems lead to a bigger war. When Germany saw that Russia was mobilizing from the timetables, they thought Russia wanted to declare war, but actually Russia was scared that Germany was going to declare war. The Schlieffen Plan was created by the Germans because of the threat of the two-front war from Russia and France. It caused the Germans to invade Belgium to get to France, which got the British involved in the war. It was a misconception of countries thinking other countries wanted to fight so each country would be forced to mobilize because of the timetables. It was the mobilization schedules and timetables that were in charge, rather than the national leaders, like the tail wagging the dog.

Some historians, such as Christopher Clark, suggest that no one was responsible for the war because it was an accident. Clark argued that this tragedy created a tunnel vision; instead of failing to learn from the crises of their recent past, the European powers learned too well, to their own destruction. They thought they could flirt with disaster while avoiding war; this led to leaders of European nations to falsely think they were in control. Clark said that European leaders were "sleepwalkers, watchful but unseeing, blind to the reality of the horror they were about to bring into the world." The leaders of Europe were sleepwalkers because they thought they were in control when they weren't. Just like sleepwalkers, they thought they knew where they were going, but they were just dreaming and fell into catastrophe. They had false confidence that led to disaster.

World War I is significant not only because of all these causes mentioned above, like the alliance system and new technology, but the war also caused many terrible developments that followed. Fritz Stern said that World War I was "the calamity of the 20th century, the calamity from which all other calamities sprang." This means that World War I set off a chain of events that led to the Great Depression, the reign of Hitler, the Second World War, and even the Holocaust. The historical causes of World War I are so important to study because of all the results that the war left in its wake.